General editor

JOHN LABAND

KINGDOM and COLONY
at WAR

The Anglo-Zulu War of 1879 might seem familiar ground to many readers with an interest in the colonial wars of the nineteenth century. Yet there are many aspects of this conflict which historians have previously neglected. These sixteen studies, all based on extensive original research in Britain and South Africa, open up unexpected vistas by investigating entirely new aspects of the war, or by viewing those already known from a fresh perspective. Among the studies are investigations of the Zulu political and diplomatic responses to the British invasion. Also included are re-examinations of their strategy and tactics in the battles of Rorke's Drift and Khambula. Other studies throw the spotlight on the fascinating, but generally unknown low-intensity war along the borders of Zululand, and on the equally absorbing but sometimes amusing efforts in colonial Natal to prepare against a Zulu invasion. This collection is an addition of real significance to the literature on the Anglo-Zulu War.

John Laband and Paul Thompson, both of the Department of Historical Studies at the University of Natal, Pietermaritzburg, are leading authorities on the Anglo-Zulu War. They have previously collaborated in *Field Guide to the War in Zululand and the Defence of Natal 1879* (2nd rev. ed., 1987); *War Comes to Umvoti: The Natal–Zululand Border 1878–9* (1980); and *The Buffalo Border 1879: The Anglo-Zulu War in Northern Natal* (1983). Both have also independently published extensively on the history of Natal and Zululand.

John Laband is the general editor of the **Anglo-Zulu War Series**, and has edited and introduced *Moodie's Zulu War* and Ashe and Wyatt-Edgell's *The Story of the Zulu Campaign*.

The ruins of oNdini in the Mahlabathini Plain, depicted in August 1879. The British had burned King Cetshwayo's great place on 4 July 1879.

THE ANGLO-ZULU WAR SERIES

KINGDOM and COLONY at WAR

SIXTEEN STUDIES ON THE
ANGLO-ZULU WAR OF 1879

John Laband
and
Paul Thompson

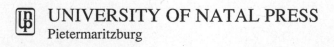 **UNIVERSITY OF NATAL PRESS**
Pietermaritzburg

N & S PRESS
Cape Town

Co-published by

University of Natal Press,
P.O. Box 375,
Pietermaritzburg 3200

and

N & S Press,
P.O. Box 186,
Constantia 7848

ISBN 0 86980 765 X (paperback edition)

ISBN 0 86980 766 8 (hardback edition)

The cover picture showing the surrender of Zulu
chiefs at Port Durnford is based on the original
picture by Colonel C.P. Cramer.

Printed by Kohler Carton and Print
Box 955,
Pinetown 3600
South Africa

Contents

Illustrations

The authors and publishers would like to thank the following individuals and institutions for their assistance and permission to reproduce illustrations.

Killie Campbell Africana Library, Durban, frontispiece, 21, 39, 52, 123, 147, 236; University of Natal Library, Pietermaritzburg, 287; Natal Archives Depot, 287 (top); Natal Museum Library, 254; The Local History Museum, Durban, 299; S.B. Bourquin, 173, 199; The Sherwood Foresters (Nottinghamshire and Derbyshire Regiment), 97, 153; Army Museums Ogilby Trust, Aldershot, 313.

The cover picture shows the surrender of Zulu chiefs to General Crealock at Port Durnford, 5 July 1879. This picture is adapted from the original by Colonel C.P. Cramer and, like the frontispiece and the drawings on pages 21, 39 and 52, comes from an album in the Killie Campbell Africana Library, Durban. They have never been previously published and are of particular interest as Cramer was an eye-witness to the important events in the eastern half of Zululand.

Captain Cramer, as he was then, arrived in Durban on 20 March 1879 with the 3rd Battalion, 60th Rifles. On 2 April he took part in the battle of Gingindlovu, and in the subsequent relief of the Eshowe garrison. His battalion spent the next two months building Fort Chelmsford, and as an element of the First Division advanced to Port Durnford, which it reached on 29 June. When the Division was broken up in early July, the battalion formed part of Clarke's Column, which was to hunt down the fugitive Zulu king. It encamped near the ruins of oNdini on 11 August, and on 22 August Cramer, now acting Major, advanced to the Black Mfolozi in command of two companies. On 30 August the captive Cetshwayo was handed over to him, and he escorted him back to the camp near oNdini. Clarke's Column left Zululand via Middle Drift on 18 September.

The original illustrations are done in dark blue ink with Chinese white.

Maps

Abbreviations

AGO	Attorney-General's Office, Natal, papers in Natal Archives Depot, Pietermaritzburg
AU	Argief Utrecht, papers in Transvaal Archives Depot, Pretoria
B.P.P.	*British Parliamentary Papers*
CE	Colonial Engineer, Natal, papers in Natal Archives Depot, Pietermaritzburg
CO	Colonial Office, London
CP	Chelmsford Papers, National Army Museum, Chelsea
CSO	Colonial Secretary's Office, Natal, papers in Natal Archives Depot, Pietermaritzburg
DCLB	Durban Corporation Letter Book, volumes in Natal Archives Depot, Pietermaritzburg
DTCM	Durban Town Council Minutes, Natal Archives Depot, Pietermaritzburg
FC	Fannin Collection, papers in Natal Archives Depot, Pietermaritzburg
GH	Government House, Natal, papers in Natal Archives Depot, Pietermaritzburg
II	Indian Immigration, papers in Natal Archives Depot, Pietermaritzburg
JSA	Webb, C. de B. & Wright, J.B. (eds. & trs.) *The James Stuart Archive of Recorded Oral Evidence Relating to the History of the Zulu and Neighbouring Peoples*, Pietermaritzburg & Durban, 1976, 1979, 1982, 1986, vols. 1–4.
KCAL	Killie Campbell Africana Library, Durban
NAD	Natal Archives Depot, Pietermaritzburg
NGG	*The Natal Government Gazette*

SNA	Secretary for Native Affairs, Natal, papers in Natal Archives Depot, Pietermaritzburg
SS	Staatsekretaris, Transvaal, papers in Transvaal Archives Depot, Pretoria
TS	Sir Theophilus Shepstone Papers, Natal Archives Depot, Pietermaritzburg
WC	Sir Evelyn Wood Collection, Natal Archives Depot, Pietermaritzburg
WO	War Office, papers in Public Record Office, Kew
ZA	Zululand Archives, papers in Natal Archives Depot, Pietermaritzburg

Booth Papers: Papers of Clr.-Sgt. A. Booth, William Cullen Library, University of the Witwatersrand, Johannesburg

MacLeod Letters: Norman MacLeod Letters and Documents, 1878–80, Africana Library, Johannesburg

Watson Letters: Capt. H.J. Watson's Letters from South Africa, 1879–80, Killie Campbell Africana Library, Durban

Wolseley's Journal: Wolseley Papers: Sir Garnet Wolseley's South African Journal, 1879–80, Public Record Office, Kew

Woodgate's Military Diary: Woodgate Papers: Capt. E. Woodgate's Military Diary, 1 January – 6 May 1879, Collection of Dr. G.K. Woodgate, Oxford

Woodgate's Private Diary: Woodgate Papers: Capt. E. Woodgate's Private Diary, 28 January – 30 December 1879, Collection of Dr. G.K. Woodgate, Oxford

Chronology of the War

7 August 1878	Lord Chelmsford arrives in Durban.
24 August	Chelmsford's memorandum on an invasion of Zululand.
28 September	Sir Bartle Frere arrives in Pietermaritzburg.
26 November	Proclamation of Colonial Defensive Districts in Natal.
26 November	Calling out of Natal Volunteer Corps.
11 December	Presentation of British ultimatum to Zulu king.
11 January 1879	British invasion of Zululand begins.
13 January	Colonial Defensive Districts along border with Zululand put under imperial officers.
22 January	British Right Column fights through Zulu ambush at Nyezane River.
22 January	Main Zulu army overwhelms camp of British Centre Column at Isandlwana.
22–23 January	British garrison at Rorke's Drift holds off attack by part of Zulu army.
23 January	Centre Column retires to Natal.

28 January	Right Column decides to hold fast at Fort Eshowe, where Zulu forces blockade it.
31 January	British Left Column entrenches at Khambula Hill, and successfully raids surrounding countryside.
24–27 February	Call up of additional Natal levies for duty along Zululand border.
6 March	Arrival of HMS *Shah* at Durban with first reinforcements of British troops.
10 March	Prince Hamu defects to British.
12 March	Zulu force destroys British convoy and escort at Ntombe River.
24 March – 14 April	British demonstrations and raids along the Zulu border.
28 March	Eshowe Relief Column advances into Zululand.
28 March	Zulu forces rout British patrol from Khambula on Hlobane Mountain.
29 March	Left Column repulses and routs main Zulu army at Khambula.
2 April	Eshowe Relief column repulses and routs Zulu army at Gingindlovu.
3 April	Eshowe garrison relieved and evacuated to Natal.
21 April	Renewed British offensive begins with building of supply depots along Zulu coast for First Division.
2–28 May	British demonstrations and raids along Zulu border.
1 June	Second Division advances across Blood River into Zululand.

17 June	Second Division and Flying Column (reorganized Left Column) join up for march on oNdini.
19 June	First Division advances across Thukela River into Zululand.
25 June	Zulu raid across Thukela at Middle Drift.
27 June	Second Division and Flying Column encamp on Mthonjaneni heights.
28 June	First Division encamps in Mlalazi plain.
4 July	Submission of coastal chiefs.
4 July	Zulu army repulsed and routed by Second Division and Flying Column at Battle of Ulundi and King Cetshwayo flees.
19 July	Formal surrender of coastal chiefs to Sir Garnet Wolseley.
15 August	Submission of influential chiefs to Wolseley near oNdini.
28 August	Capture of King Cetshwayo.
1 September	Qulusi submit.
1 September	Chiefs formally accept Wolseley's terms for a settlement and the division of Zululand into thirteen fragments.
2 September	British begin evacuation of Zululand.
22 September	Manyonyoba submits.

Preface

Interest in the Anglo-Zulu War of 1879 shows little sign of abating. Indeed, increasingly sophisticated treatment of the British invasion of the Zulu kingdom indicates that a steadily more informed readership is being addressed. *Kingdom and Colony at War* is intended for that specialist readership. The most recent popular works, such as Robert Edgerton's *Like Lions They Fought* (1988) and Ian Knight's *Brave Men's Blood* (1990), are essentially reworkings of material already published. This work, in contrast, is based on original research among private and official documents, as well as contemporary printed sources, in collections both in South Africa and in the United Kingdom. It consists of sixteen studies on various aspects of the Anglo-Zulu War. They appeared first between 1979 and 1988 (with the exception of the study of the Zulu at the battle of Rorke's Drift, which is published for the first time) in various academic journals and specialist military history publications, or as papers at meetings of professional historians. They are presented in this volume as originally published, except for some minor corrections, chiefly of earlier printing errors, while the spelling of Zulu names has been standardized to conform with the current orthography (unless the names appear in direct quotations). Also, the study of the defence of Durban has been abridged.

All sixteen studies focus on the war itself. They attempt to clarify and expand perspectives, either through illuminating less familiar events of the conflict, or treating better known ones from a revisionist standpoint. The themes covered fall naturally into three sections. *Part I: The War in Zululand*, is concerned primarily with Zulu responses – political, diplomatic and military – to the British invasion of their kingdom, and in connection with the invasion the nature and purpose of British fieldworks in Zululand are also investigated. *Part II: The War along the Borders*, deals with an extended theatre of operations, one that has been neglected in the past, possibly for want of the high drama associated with pitched battles. Yet the generally low-intensity fighting along the borders of Zululand (the battles of

Rorke's Drift and Ntombe being the spectacular exceptions) reveal much about the nature of the war itself, and of the Zulu and colonial societies involved in it. *Part III: The Defence of the Natal Interior*, is an examination of the hitherto ignored responses, essentially administrative and precautionary, within the colony to the apparent threat of a Zulu invasion.

We are most grateful to the following for permission to reprint those articles originally published elsewhere: the editors of the *Journal of Natal and Zulu History* for 'The Zulu Army in the War of 1879: Some Cautionary Notes', 'The Cohesion of the Zulu Polity under the Impact of the Anglo-Zulu War: A Reassessment', 'Captain Lucas and the Border Guard: The War on the Lower Tugela, 1879', and 'Mbilini, Manyonyoba and the Phongolo River Frontier: A Neglected Sector of the Anglo-Zulu War of 1879'; the editors of *Theoria* for 'Humbugging the General? King Cetshwayo's Peace Overtures during the Anglo-Zulu War', and 'Bulwer, Chelmsford and the Border Levies: The Dispute over the Defence of Natal, 1879'; the editor of the *Military History Journal* for 'British Fieldworks of the Zulu Campaign of 1879, with Special Reference to Fort Eshowe', and 'The Active Defence after Isandlwana: British Raids across the Buffalo, March-May 1879'; and Ian Knight, editor of *There will be an Awful Row at Home about This* (Zulu Study Group, Victorian Military Society, Shoreham-by-Sea, 1987) for 'The Battle of Khambula, 29 March 1879: A Re-examination from the Zulu Perspective', 'The Natal Native Contingent at Rorke's Drift, January 22nd, 1879', and 'The Griqua and Mpondo Marches: Natal's Southern Border during the Anglo-Zulu War, 1879'.

We would also like to thank Helena Margeot and Raymond Poonsamy of the Cartographic Unit, University of Natal, Pietermaritzburg, for preparing the finished maps to their habitually high standards under trying circumstances; S.B. Bourquin for so readily allowing us to use photographs from his collection; Adrian Koopman, senior lecturer in Zulu at the University of Natal, Pietermaritzburg, for his advice over the spelling of Zulu names; and the staff of University of Natal Press for their advice and help in guiding this book to completion.

John Laband
Paul Thompson
Department of Historical Studies
University of Natal, Pietermaritzburg

The Cohesion of the Zulu Polity under the Impact of the Anglo-Zulu War

A reassessment

J.P.C. LABAND

It has become an historical commonplace that Zulu resistance to the British invasion of 1879 was singularly united. Jeff Guy, for example, while recognizing existing tensions and divisions within King Cetshwayo's kingdom, has adduced from this supposedly concerted response the essential cohesion of the Zulu polity.[1] This approach should not blind us, however, to the reality that ambitions among some of the Zulu ruling élite for greater local autonomy, coupled with a pragmatic sense of self-preservation when threatened by the hostile British presence, often led to accommodation with the invaders at the expense of abiding loyalty to the king and the Zulu state.

The nature of the Zulu polity has of late been subject to considerable investigation.[2] It is not the intention here to retread this ground, though, for purposes of what follows, it is necessary briefly to consider certain salient features.

It seems increasingly clear that the Zulu kingdom was not as effectively centralized, nor the king's power as absolute, as was once supposed, and that there was considerable scope for independent action by members of the élite. Theoretically, all authority lay with the king, and through the institution of *amabutho* (age-grade regiments) he was able to exercise a real degree of social and economic control over his subjects, and to undermine the power-base of potential rivals.[3] Even so, on the eve of the Anglo-Zulu War, forces of decentralization, which had always to a degree neutralized the political integration of the Zulu state, were distinctly in evidence.

Most fundamental in this regard was the basic social unit of the kingdom, the homestead itself, which was also a self-sufficient productive unit. The state depended on the homestead for part of its labour potential through the *amabutho* system, as well as upon its surplus production. Cattle, so central to Zululand's political economy, though in theory belonging to the king, in reality were part of the homestead unit. Individual's control over ordinary cattle was almost complete, while even the king's own cattle, for reasons of pasture availability, were entrusted to *amakhanda* (military homesteads) or local homesteads. This reality was inevitably a force militating against political cohesion, for as the Zulu people were not dependent on centralized authority for the economic functioning of their homesteads, their way of life was secured as long as the homestead structure survived. And as the Anglo-Zulu War was to show, this consideration all too frequently came before a commitment to the political structure.

The patrilineal segmentary lineage system was the basis of Zulu social organization (as the homestead unit was the basis of the economy), and with similar consequences to state integration. Lineage segmentation gave rise to clans in which there was a concentration of wealth in the dominant lineage. The clan formed part of a chiefdom, where political power was vested in the dominant lineage of the strongest clan. Such chiefdoms, where they had survived the Shakan revolution, were a force for decentralization which the Zulu kings had been unable to overcome. Despite centralizing institutions such as the *amabutho*, there was always the danger that members of a chiefdom would give their first loyalty to their hereditary chief and kinsman, rather than to the king. And far from countering this check to his authority, it would seem that a king such as Cetshwayo often recognized such traditional leaders as district chiefs, or *izikhulu*, who also comprised with him the *ibandla*, or council of state. Consequently, subordinated pre-Shakan chiefdoms still maintained their essential political cohesion and, through the *izikhulu*, exerted their influence in the highest council of the land.[4]

In effect, this meant that the central state authority was in the habit of delegating authority to existing political hierarchies. This might have been unavoidable, considering problems of communication and the lack of means to support a developed bureaucracy, but it had its grave disadvantages. It placed in the hands of *izikhulu*, already enjoying the advantages of a personal following and a developed local power-base, additional authority, vested in them through royal recognition. This inevitably gave them considerable political power and the opportunity to amass wealth through tribute, fines and royal gifts. Similarly, *abantwana*, or princes of the royal clan, with whom the king could not avoid sharing power, and who possessed status that was a reflection of the king's own, were naturally permitted to function as *izikhulu*. They were consequently in a position to build up a regional following which, as with the *izikhulu* who were hereditary chiefs, could serve as the basis for a movement towards regional autonomy, especially in those parts remote from the focus of authority in the Mahlabathini plain.

The *izinduna*, whom the king appointed to perform administrative functions, such as commanding the *amabutho*, or ruling over a district where they had no strong claims of hereditary power, were more tightly under his control, for they owed that status to royal favour and not necessarily to illustrious lineage. They frequently augmented the *izikhulu* and *abantwana* on the *ibandla*, without whose corporate approval the king was unlikely to take vital decisions of policy. And, as shall be shown, the regional concerns of members of the *ibandla* were to have an increasing effect on the king's policy as the British columns penetrated Zululand.

By Cetshwayo's reign the temptation among some of this ruling élite towards local autonomy was accentuated by interaction with whites along Zululand's borders. Goods brought in by trade, especially firearms, were of considerable political value. The king was unable to retain a monopoly of this trade, and chiefs, through the status of possessing the desired articles, or through redistributing them as rewards to their adherents, were able to enhance their own prestige and power at the expense of the central authority.[5] Furthermore, it would seem that in some instances their political allegiance to the king was complicated by their connections with white traders. These men, once they had gained a chief's confidence, were inclined to use their influence and knowledge of the existing rivalries and tensions within the kingdom to their own advantage, and to promote a chief's ambitions towards autonomy and closer integration with the white economy to the detriment of the integrated state and royal control.[6]

When they invaded Zululand, the British put knowledge of such centrifugal tendencies in the Zulu state, and of the particular ambitions of certain chiefs, into conscious use. What is to be assessed is their degree of success in detaching chiefs and their adherents from the cause of national resistance and from loyalty to their king. In pursuing such an investigation, it must constantly be borne in mind that the evidence upon which it is based is, in a number of particulars, unsatisfactory. British reports on direct dealings with the Zulu might, through factors such as cultural differences, fail to extract the full significance of Zulu actions and words. Language, naturally, was the greatest barrier. It is the unfortunate reality that all the Zulu testimony of this period, even that of King Cetshwayo in captivity, has been filtered through the medium of white interpreters, whose own perceptions and preoccupations must inevitably have coloured what they recorded. Particularly problematical is the fact that a good deal of the testimony concerning developments in Zululand was relayed to Natal Border Agents, military intelligence officers and clergymen through Zulu emissaries, spies, refugees, border policemen, prisoners-of-war and Christian converts. Their unreliable and often conflicting evidence has naturally to be treated with the greatest caution. Even so, despite difficulties and short-comings such as these, a clear picture does emerge of how the Zulu polity responded to the disintegrative impact of the British invasion.

Sir Theophilus Shepstone, whose advice was so eagerly sought and accepted by the High Commissioner, Sir Bartle Frere, prognosticated with some accuracy on the eve of the war that the bulk of the Zulu people were opposed to the prospect of a conflict with Britain, but that a desperate resistance might be expected, especially from the younger *amabutho*, who had their honour to satisfy. He was quite wrong, though, in supposing that public opinion in Zululand might influence the king into accepting the ultimatum Frere was planning to issue.[7] The Lieutenant-Governor of Natal, Sir Henry Bulwer, was much nearer the mark when he suggested that the king could never accept the terms of the ultimatum, which effectively required the surrender of his sovereignty. He foresaw, nevertheless, a division in the *ibandla* between those wishing for accommodation with Britain, and those determined to resist, but with the latter prevailing.[8] And indeed, cleavages did open up in the *ibandla* that presaged the lines of future political fragmentation.

Despite some reports to the contrary,[9] it is clear that the king consulted his assembled council over the terms of the British ultimatum. It seems that the issue of turning over the sons of Sihayo, as demanded, to the Natal authorities for punishment for border violations was the one on which discussion focused, for it was generally felt if this single condition were complied with, all else would be well.[10] But Sihayo kaXongo was a great favourite of King Cetshwayo, who had confirmed him as *induna* of the Qungebe in south-western Zululand.[11] The king steadfastly refused to move against Sihayo's sons, despite the advice of his brothers and most of his councillors.[12] It appears, however, that Cetshwayo was fortified in his stand by public opinion, which did not endorse the *ibandla's* cautious and conciliatory approach,[13] and which allowed him to withstand pressure from his councillors. On the other hand, there was apparently general agreement that John Dunn, the king's powerful and influential white *induna* in south-eastern Zululand, and chief channel of communication with Natal, had misled Cetshwayo and the *ibandla* over Britain's hostile intent.[14] Some of the councillors demanded that Dunn be put to death in consequence. Perceiving this antagonism, and knowing that his economic and political future in Zululand depended upon abstracting himself from a war Britain was bound to win, Dunn crossed over into Natal on 31 December 1878 with 2 000 adherents and 3 000 cattle.[15] Thus he, who had been raised to his position of power in Zululand solely through the king's favour, was the first of the ruling élite to abandon Cetshwayo in order to seek his own interests. Intending initially to remain neutral, he was increasingly drawn into aiding the British as they advanced into what had been his chiefdom. With his intimate knowledge of Zulu affairs and personal acquaintance with so many of the kingdom's leaders, he was destined to be of inestimable value to the British, especially in negotiating these chiefs' submissions.

Though an alien, Dunn's defection can only have shaken the Zulu political establishment, and have caused concern that others might follow his example. It is significant that of those in the *ibandla* who had advocated a conciliatory approach and the surrender of Sihayo's sons, three were among the very most powerful men of the kingdom: Chief Mnyamana kaNgqenge-lele Buthelezi, Chief Zibhebhu kaMaphitha, and Prince Hamu kaNzibe.[16]

Since 1873 the realistic and cautious Mnyamana had been Cetshwayo's chief minister, and was consequently of immense influence in the kingdom. He was also powerful in his own right, having been since King Mpande's reign district chief of the area in north-western Zululand dominated by his large Buthelezi clan, and being very rich in cattle.[17] Zibhebhu was of royal blood, a cousin to the king. He was also chief of the Mandlakazi, a Zulu lineage, in the north-eastern corner of the kingdom, far from the centre of power. His elevated position was further buttressed by his position as *induna* of the uDloko *ibutho*. Although he had been a vital supporter of Cetshwayo in the civil war of 1856, his developed trading contacts with colonial Natal probably tempted him, like John Dunn, to put his own commercial interests before those of the kingdom as a whole. Coupled with his known yearning for greater political independence, this made his loyalty to the king a matter of some concern.[18]

Yet is was Hamu's opposition to the war which was the most immediately dangerous to the king. He was an *umntwana*, full and elder brother to Cetshwayo, though through *ukuvuza* custom heir not to Mpande, but to his deceased brother Nzibe. He was the *induna* of the prestigious uThulwana *ibutho*, of which the king himself was a member. Moreover, as an *isikhulu* since the 1850s, he had built up a strong personal following among the Ngenetsheni in north-western Zululand, just south across the Phongolo River from Swaziland. Like Zibhebhu, he was far from the focus of authority, and also had close trading connections with the colonial world. Through the influence of Herbert Nunn, a white trader who had resided in his district since the 1860s, and on whom he relied for advice and trading goods, the groundwork had been laid for future collaboration with the British.[19] Furthermore, although he had aided Cetshwayo in the civil war, he had differed increasingly with him over the years about the way in which the king was handling the long-standing border dispute with the Transvaal. Bordering the Transvaal, Hamu's territory was prey to Boer encroachments, and any concession made to them by Cetshwayo was at his expense.[20] His high lineage, power, wealth, and local interest combined to predispose Hamu to flout the king. This had perhaps been most spectacularly apparent at the *umkhosi* festival of 1878, when his uThulwana fell upon the iNgobamakhosi, the king's favourite *ibutho*.[21] Magema M. Fuze has gone so far as to suggest that Hamu fomented this fracas in order to advance his claim to the kingship.[22] Certainly, it can be regarded as nothing less than an assertion of power and independence by Hamu in his relationship with the king, while the king definitely suspected that Hamu had long intended to usurp his throne.[23]

This affair at the *umkhosi* decidedly strained the already uneasy relations between Hamu and the king. Hamu retired to his district, and persistently refused the king's summons to oNdini,[24] only appearing at the great council before the war, where he joined Mnyamana in leading opposition to the king's policy over the British ultimatum. He was, in any case, playing a double game. Clearly convinced by November 1878 that the British intended war against Zululand, he anticipated the consequences by initiating negotiations with them. On 6 November his emissary, Ngwegwana, delivered a message to G. M. Rudolph, the landdrost of Utrecht in what was now the British Transvaal. He requested that the British keep him informed of their intentions, as in the case of war he would 'run over with all his people to the Government, if Government, [would] receive and protect him.'[25] To reinforce this notice of his intentions, Hamu also sent several messengers to Colonel Evelyn Wood, commanding the British No. 4 Column at Utrecht, enquiring why 'the British did not trust him'?[26]

Lord Chelmsford, the British commander-in-chief of the planned invasion, was heartened by these overtures. He suggested to Wood that direct negotiations be opened up with Hamu through Nunn the trader, and that Hamu's mind be put at rest over his fear that his land might be forfeit. For Wood was to pass on Frere's assurances to chiefs who collaborated with the British that on surrender they would be placed in a location in Natal for the duration of the conflict, and that afterwards they would be reinstated in their territory and 'recognized as independent, owing allegiance to the Queen.'[27] Hamu was also in some anxiety that in case of war the Swazi would descend upon his district. Here Chelmsford tried to blackmail him, insisting that he could not help him, unless he openly aligned himself as an ally of the British.[28] Hamu was not yet willing to go this far but, taking an initiative seemingly unknown to the king, opened direct communication on his own account with the Swazi, assuring them of his pacific intentions.[29] Thus, while it was clear that Hamu was not yet prepared openly to abandon the Zulu cause, the British were left with every confidence that once they invaded Zululand, he would.

On 11 January 1879 the British Centre Column crossed into Zululand at Rorke's Drift, and the following day stormed Sihayo's homestead, Sokhexe. To prevent a similar attack, on 17 January Gamdana, a brother of Sihayo, with a number of elderly headmen, women, children and cattle, gave themselves up to Chelmsford, and were relocated in Weenen County in Natal. The rest of Gamdana's adherents, including all the young men, refused to follow him and continued to resist.[30] Their persistent resistance was ensured, and any further submissions in the region precluded, by the great Zulu victory at Isandlwana on 22 January, and the subsequent withdrawal of the remnants of the British Centre Column into Natal. Not until May were the British again in a position to make their presence effectively felt in the area.[31] Likewise, along the coast, the No. 1 Column, having brushed aside a Zulu attack on 22 January at Nyezane, found itself blockaded behind its defences at Eshowe, and consequently in no position to influence the loyalty of the surrounding Zulu. Indeed, it had immediately been demonstrated that if the British hoped to secure defections, they must prove successful in the field. Their debacle at Isandlwana, and the consequent raising of Zulu hopes for ultimate victory in the war, naturally only encouraged waverers to stick by the king.

In the north-west of the kingdom, where Wood's column was operating successfully, the obverse was proved true. On 10 December 1878, a month before Wood began his advance, Chelmsford had ordered him to make every effort to induce the Zulu along his line of march to come under his protection, and to relocate in his rear those who submitted.[32] In this spirit, on 9 January 1879, Wood had an interview with Bemba, an *induna* of the important Chief Sekethwayo kaNhlaka Mdlalose, an *isikhulu* in the north-western districts and the *induna* of the kwaNodwengu *ikhanda*.[33] Wood agreed to protect and feed Bemba, 80 of his adherents and over 800 heads of livestock who came in the next day. His people surrendered their arms, and were relocated in the Utrecht district.[34]

Bemba's submission was satisfactory, but it was Sekethwayo's that Wood sought. Because Sekethwayo was much embittered against the Transvaalers for their land claims in his territory, he was logically expected to be firmly

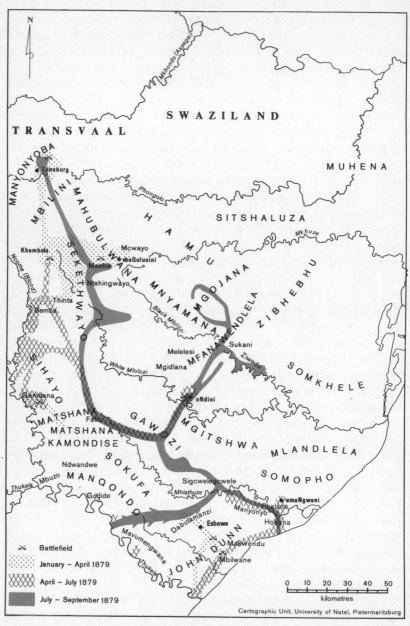

Main areas of British military activity in Zululand, Jan. – Sept. 1879.

against the British and of the war party.[35] But instead, old and infirm,[36] he was inclined to temporize. On 11 January he sent word to Wood of his desire to accept the British terms for surrender, and go with his disarmed people to the Transvaal for the duration of the war. Wood instructed him to surrender the next day, and his people by 14 January. In the interim, in order to encourage his surrender, Wood let Sekethwayo know that the cattle which had already been captured from him would be returned as soon as he did so.[37] These negotiations, so promising for Wood, were abruptly terminated on 15 January. An *impi*, despatched from oNdini by the king, had entered Sekethwayo's territory and brought him smartly back into line.[38] Even so, by 13 January some 50 of his adherents had availed themselves of the British terms, and more surrendered on 17 January, having been found by the British in some caves, where they had taken refuge.[39]

As the No. 4 Column continued its advance on the White Mfolozi, further Zulu – mainly old men, women and children – continued to surrender, much to the gratification of Wood, who naturally felt it 'cheaper and quicker' to accept Zulu as refugees, rather than to fight them.[40] On 20 January Thinta, Sekethwayo's uncle, surrendered to Wood, and he and his adherents were sent to Utrecht. They had also been taking refuge in caves, for they had expected to be attacked by the Qulusi,[41] a royal section attached to the ebaQulusini *ikhanda*, north of Sekethwayo's district, who, being without traditional local clan ties, were intensely loyal to the royal house.[42] Their adverse response to defections among Sekethwayo's adherents introduced a new element into the situation: potential conflict between those wishing to collaborate with the British, and those who were determined to stand by the king. When all the Zulu defections up to the end of January are taken into account, though, they must be seen to be of limited significance, and did not herald civil war or the break-up of the kingdom. Dunn's defection had been the most serious, though Sekethwayo's, had it not been foiled at the last moment, would have been nearly its equal. As it was, those who had surrendered (Dunn excepted) were primarily minor chiefs, and their adherents non-combatants.

The British still pinned much hope on Hamu's promised defection. Yet Hamu was not a free agent. At the outbreak of war he was at oNdini, held there by the king (as also was Mnyamana) in order to ensure his fidelity and as a hostage for his people's co-operation in the struggle.[43] Even so, Hamu contrived to pursue his negotiations with the British. Through his chief *izinduna*, Ngwegwana and Nymubana, who were still in his district, he exchanged secret messages with Wood, plaintively reaffirming his loyalty to the British and asking for advice on how to escape from oNdini.[44]

Simultaneously, he continued to treat with the Swazi king regarding his safe sanctuary should he flee Zululand.[45] The British at last decided to aid him openly by convincing the Swazi that if any of Hamu's cattle should be driven across their border for safety, they should be looked after, as Hamu was not to be considered a hostile belligerent.[46]

Throughout early February the king and Hamu were reported to be regularly quarrelling over responsibility for the war.[47] Then, at last, apparently at Mnyamana's urging,[48] Hamu managed to slip away from oNdini. The king sent after him with a gift of cattle in a vain attempt to appease him.[49] On 17 February two messengers from Hamu arrived at Wood's fortified camp at Khambula (whither he had retired on the news of Isandlwana), desiring military aid in bringing Hamu and his wives to safety.[50] For on hearing that Hamu was not simply returning home, but making for the British lines, the king had despatched an *impi* in pursuit (made up of district Mandlakazi and ukuBaza), which had succeeded in capturing some of Hamu's wagons and cattle, and was also apparently committing atrocities against Hamu's adherents.[51] Eventually, the harried Hamu took refuge across the Phongolo in Swaziland, whence he was escorted by a British patrol to Khambula, arriving there on 10 March. Over the next few days his adherents continued to trickle into camp, until they finally numbered about 1 300. The fighting men were drafted into an existing unit known as Wood's Irregulars, while the non-combatants, including Hamu and his many wives, were located near Utrecht.[52] Some of his adherents, trying to join him there, were massacred by the king's *impi*,[53] and as late as May, Ngwegwana, his chief *induna*, reported that the king had placed forces at the drifts across the Phongolo, and that these had prevented repeated attempts by some of Hamu's leading *izinduna* and adherents to escape.[54] Furthermore, to punish these would-be defectors, the king sent men during March and April to help themselves to their mealies and grain-stores. They succeeded — stripping the district bare.[55] The king's retaliation against Hamu, though adding to local bitterness, which would have its consequences in the later civil war, was nevertheless explicable. Hamu's defection was an alarming portent and a real blow to morale. It became a matter only to be mentioned in whispers, for it was generally perceived among the Zulu as the beginning of the break-up of the kingdom.[56]

The north-west of Zululand, where Wood continued effectively to harass the surrounding countryside from his Khambula camp, and so to demoralize the inhabitants, seemed the region most likely to be detached from its loyalty to Cetshwayo. Sekethwayo's allegiance had only been secured by threat of force, and to the king's concern was steadfastly refusing to attend him at oNdini.[57] Bemba, Thinta, and above all, Hamu had defected. Others too were wavering. As early as 9 February Manyonyoba, a renegade Swazi chief owing allegiance to Cetshwayo who, like the more famous Mbilini kaMswati, was operating in the region of the Phongolo, made his first tentative approaches to Wood.[58] Far more significant were the overtures made by Msebe kaMandaka, a second cousin of Cetshwayo's and an *induna* of the Qulusi.[59] On 22 February, while Hamu was attempting to make his escape, Msebe let him know that he too wished to defect but, being a cautious man, and in fear of retaliation by Qulusi who remained loyal, wanted to wait until Hamu had successfully led the way.[60] However, Mahubulwana kaDumisela, a senior *induna* of the Qulusi, foiled Msebe's plans. When he surrendered on 25 March, Mnkolisa kaMcwayo, a lesser Qulusi *induna*, reported that Mahubulwana had informed the king that Msebe, and Mnkolisa's own father, Mcwayo kaMangeda, were in contact with Hamu and in league with the British. The king had ordered their deaths, but they had been spared on the intercession of another Qulusi *induna*, Mhlahlo kaKhondlo. Both were now under surveillance.[61] The consequences of their intended treason were grave, both for them, and their adherents. The hostility of loyalist Qulusi forced them to quit their homesteads, and to take refuge in caves until their surrender to the British in August.[62]

In early March, Major H. Spalding of the Head-Quarters Staff pronounced that Zululand appeared 'to be breaking into fragments'.[63] Yet, despite the defections and incipient civil war in north-western Zululand, he was premature. Mnyamana's loyalty might be reported suspect,[64] but Eustace Fannin, the Umvoti Border Agent who was in constant communication with Zululand through his spies and informants, was sure that in reality there was 'no probability' of Mnyamana following Hamu's example.[65] Even Zibhebhu, though Hamu's adherents might suggest that he was contemplating defection,[66] seemed unlikely at that stage to change sides. Nevertheless, defections (especially Hamu's), disloyalty, and consciousness of the unacceptably high battle casualties, were undoubtedly creating consternation among the Zulu leadership.[67] In mid-March Cetshwayo summoned all the *izikhulu* of the land to reassemble at oNdini. With the obvious exception of Hamu, every one of them, including all the *abantwana*, obeyed. The purpose of the gathering was to reinforce loyalty and to discuss the best mode of prosecuting the war.[68] The upshot was the decision to contest the advance of Lord Chelmsford's Relief Column, which was moving to the aid of the beleaguered garrison at Eshowe, and to despatch the reassembled veterans of Isandlwana against Wood at Khambula. Both armies were routed, the one at Gingindlovu on 2 April, and the other at Khambula on 29 March. The latter defeat, especially, irrevocably broke Zulu fighting morale.[69] It was the turning-point of the war. The British regained the initiative which they had lost as a consequence of Isandlwana. The Zulu fell back on the defensive. The fighting men were demoralized and dispersed to their homes, while the Zulu leadership were forced at last to face the real possibility of ultimate defeat. It is not surprising, therefore, with the war entering its final phase, that the Zulu chiefs, and their people too, should begin to consider ever more seriously the prospect of accommodation with the invader.

In mid-April the heavily reinforced British advanced once more into Zululand, the First Division under Major-General Crealock up the coast, and the Second Division, accompanied by Lord Chelmsford, across the Ncome River in the north-west. Wood's column began an advance in early May to join the Second Division in its march on oNdini. The First Division was a formidable, if slow-moving column of 7 500 men, with an effective mounted force capable of telling raids against Zulu homesteads and livestock. On 21 April, near Gingindlovu, Makwendu kaMpande, with 130 men, women and children, gave himself up to the British.[70] Makwendu was a prince of little influence with only a small following, born of the same mother as Hamu and therefore expected to follow the lead of his elder brother.[71] All the same, the British were encouraged by his defection,[72] especially as there were persistent rumours that some of the major *izikhulu* of the southern coastal region were contemplating surrender. Prince Dabulamanzi kaMpande, a brother of Cetshwayo and a prominent general at Rorke's Drift and Gingindlovu, and Chief Mavumengwana kaNdlela Ntuli, one of the two commanders at Isandlwana,[73] were both reported to be arguing the case for submission,[74] and there were rumours that it was only by despatching loyal troops that the king had prevented their escaping into Natal with their followings.[75] Talk of their intended surrender persisted into May,[76] although Nkisimana and Mfunzi, two emissaries sent by the king to treat with Crealock, assured him that Dabulumanzi had never intended to desert the Zulu cause, and that, in any case, the Zulu nation would stand by their king to the last.[77] These sentiments contradicted what they had earlier confided to Fannin, namely that they were themselves anxious to submit and knew of thirty homesteads that would follow their lead, only that as they lived in the heart of Zululand they were unable to defect with safety.[78] A similar, hedging approach was made to Wood at much the same time, when a petty chief, Bagakama, let him know that he would submit once Wood's column had advanced sufficiently for him to do so with impunity.[79]

Zulu allegiance to the king was at last beginning to waver most seriously. In early May the king had again sent for all his principal chiefs, and it was reported that they had strongly urged peace.[80] Apparently unnerved by the disaffection of his *izikhulu*, not least on the part of Zibhebhu, the king had consented to negotiate.[81] On 14 May Crealock reported his discussions with a Zulu delegation under Ndwandwe, during which they had admitted that more chiefs would have given themselves up but for fear and jealousy of the others. Spurred on by this intelligence, John Dunn, who was serving with the First Division, immediately sent out messages to all the chiefs in the vicinity, inviting them to surrender, or to stay with their king and be destroyed.[82] Two of Dunn's scouts were Mfazi and Fanane, the latter being a half-brother of Sigcwelegcwele kaMhlekehleke, *induna* of the iNgobamakhosi *ibutho*, and a commander at Gingindlovu.[83] They were sent to him at Ngoye to persuade him to surrender. There, they found the king's messengers, sent to summon Sigcwelegcwele to oNdini. He refused to go, sending a brother in his stead. At the same time, he publicly assured Dunn's messengers that he could not be the first to desert the king (though by implication this did not rule out the possibility), yet he also told them that he considered the war a great mistake on the part of the king. Fanane, on the strength of a subsequent private interview with Sigcwelegcwele, reported that the chief and his people were in fact relieved that the king was negotiating peace, for they were apparently very tired of the war.[84]

This impression of war-weariness was confirmed for the British for another region by the prisoner Sibhalo kaHibana, who came from south-central Zululand. He told his interrogators that the people 'would gladly settle in their kraals again and live in peace', but added that the king, by detaining his chief men about him at oNdini, held the 'whole country in his hands' and so ensured that the people would continue to fight for him.[85] John Dunn disputed this conclusion for, on the strength of a conversation of 31 May with Sintwangu, another messenger of the king's, he was coming firmly to the opinion that Cetshwayo was beginning to find his influence 'passing away', and that in reality he was not obeyed as he was said to be.[86] An example of the king's weakening hold was the response of Muhena, regent of the Maputo people ('Tongas') to the north-east of Zululand. The Maputo were in a tributary relationship to the Zulu, and Muhena had become regent in 1876 for his nephew, Ngwanasi, only through Cetshwayo's support.[87] In May Cetshwayo ordered him, and other chiefs in the region, to join him with their forces. At this stage, H.E. O'Neill, the British Consul at Zanzibar, intervened, and persuaded Muhena not to comply with the king's demands. Instead, he ensured that Muhena pledge his support to the British.

O'Neill's threats concerning the future loss of independence if he should join Britain's enemies, coupled with promises of commercial advantages if he did not, were clearly considerations in Muhena's decision, but as weighty was the regent's belief that Cetshwayo must inevitably lose the war.[88]

It was along the coast, in the path of the First Division's advance, that a series of significant defections occurred, sufficient to deprive the king of his control of the south-east of his kingdom. In early June Dabulamanzi began at last to treat with the British, so confirming the earlier rumours concerning his intentions. On 8 June his messengers arrived at Crealock's camp, and stated that he was 'anxious to come in', but that he had been dissuaded to date by messages from the king, who had wished him to negotiate peace on his behalf.[89] Later in June, two of the king's messengers, Ntanjana and Sibungu, communicated to F. B. Fynney, the Border Agent along the lower Thukela, a private message entrusted to them by Dabulamanzi and Mavumengwana. They wished to assure the British that it was not out of deceit that they had failed to give themselves up, but that ever since Prince Makwendu's defection they had been closely watched (a fact which the British had already learned), and that they were awaiting a chance to slip away.[90]

While Dabulamanzi and Mavumengwana gingerly negotiated, two other major figures along the coast took more positive steps to come to terms with the British. Phalane kaMdinwa, *induna* of the Hlangezwa, and a commander at Gingindlovu,[91] and the even more prestigious Chief Somopho kaZikhala of the Mthembu, senior *induna* of the emaNgweni *ikhanda*, and commander-in-chief at Gingindlovu,[92] sent to Crealock on 5 June admitting they were beaten and asking for terms. Moreover, they took this step openly, for they also informed King Cetshwayo that their men would not reassemble at oNdini, as he had instructed.[93] These overtures, coupled with a number of defections by minor chiefs along the coast,[94] and the surrender of large numbers of women and children to the First Division,[95] persuaded Chelmsford to formulate definite terms for chiefs wishing to submit. He laid down that on surrender, a chief, with a small personal following, would be relocated to British territory. They would hand over their arms, and the chief would instruct the *izinduna* left in charge of his adherents to submit once troops entered his district.[96]

The situation shifted dramatically once more when, on 4 July, the Second Division, in conjunction with Wood's column, concluded their march on oNdini by utterly routing the warriors gathered in the Mahlabathini plain. The Zulu forces broke, never again to reassemble. The king fled north to seek sanctuary among Chief Mnyamana's adherents, telling his chiefs not to follow, but 'to look out for themselves'.[97]

Also on 4 July, a mounted force of the First Division crossed the Mhlatuze River and burned the emaNgweni *ikhanda*. That same day, before the news of the battle of Ulundi could have been known, a number of chiefs, with their families, adherents and cattle surrendered to Crealock. They included Mbilwane kaMhlanganiso, *induna* of the kwaGingindlovu *ikhanda*, and a commander at both Nyezane and Gingindlovu,[98] Manyonyo kaZongolo, an *induna* of John Dunn's and an officer in the iNgobamakhosi.[100] At the same time, Somopho, Phalane, the very influential *isikhulu*, Chief Somkhele kaMalanda of the Mphukunyoni, a first cousin of the king who dominated the northern coastal plain,[101] the *isikhulu* Chief Mlandlela kaMbiya of the Mthethwa, a cousin of the king and strongly under the influence of John Dunn,[102] and several other lesser *izinduna* sent word that they were 'coming in', and that the people, as far north as St Lucia Bay, wished to submit. On 5 July they tendered their formal submissions and, issued with passes, returned home.[103] General Crealock's lenient terms, which offered the Zulu their lives and property in return for surrendering their arms and royal cattle, [104] left the local economic and power structures intact, and persuaded the war-weary people that in submitting they were sacrificing nothing essential. Even Dabulamanzi surrendered himself on 12 July.[105] Thus, even before the consequences of the battle of Ulundi could be felt, and before much of the coastal plain had been penetrated by the British, the entire region had abandoned the royal cause and come to terms with the invaders.

Sir Garnet Wolseley, whom the British government had despatched to South Africa vested with full civil and military authority to end the war in Zululand with honour and economy, resolved to put these coastal submissions on a more formal basis. He consequently sent word to all the great men in the area to meet him at his camp at the emaNgweni *ikhanda*.[106] Almost all of them duly gathered, and on 19 July Wolseley addressed them. He announced the end of the Zulu kingdom and his intention to break it into a number of districts, to be ruled by chiefs whose names he would announce when he reached oNdini. Following Crealock's successful formula, he required of the chiefs only that they hand over their arms and royal cattle. The surrendered chiefs not unnaturally expressed their satisfaction with these easy terms, while some of the young men were heard to state that they never would have fought for Cetshwayo if they had known that this was all the British would have exacted from them.[107] Spokesmen for the chiefs were even reported to have declared that they never again wished for a black man as king, but wanted a white sovereign, namely John Dunn.[108] It is not improbable, though, that these last sentiments may have been inspired by Wolseley's known wishes, for it was already his intention that Dunn be made chief over the southern districts of Zululand bordering Natal, so that a buffer-zone under a reliable pro-British chief be created.[109]

Despite the very satisfactory coastal submissions, Wolseley was most concerned that more of the great northern chiefs had not as yet sued for peace.[110] He put this down to the fact that Cetshwayo was still at large, and the coastal chiefs had assured him that as long as the king was at liberty, fears of the possibility of his return to power could well impede further submissions, and would unsettle and discourage those who had already given up.[111] Furthermore, Wolseley was sure that Chelmsford's retiring from the vicinity of oNdini immediately after his victory had been a political blunder, for it had left the northern Zulu with a false impression of British intentions in Zululand.[112] For Wolseley, therefore, if the rest of Zululand besides the coastal region were finally to be pacified, it was necessary both to reoccupy oNdini and to recapture the king. With this in mind, he sent messages to the chiefs to meet him at oNdini on 10 August.[113]

Meanwhile, Wolseley caused instructions to be issued to all his officers concerning the procedure to be followed in inducing Zulu to give up the struggle and return home. This was to be achieved through the submission of chiefs and headmen, subject to Crealock's conditions, namely the surrender of arms and royal cattle. Conscious of what concerned them most, and doubtless having learned from the chiefs' reaction on 19 July, Wolseley required that not only should the chiefs be informed that both the military system and the monarchy were to be abolished, and the kingdom divided into independent chiefdoms, but that no land or cattle was to be transferred to the whites. It was again promised that Wolseley would announce at oNdini who the new independent chiefs were to be. Those chiefs who had not already submitted were invited to do so, bringing in their arms and cattle, and were reminded that if they neglected to surrender by 10 August that they would be treated as enemies.[114]

His Zululand policy thus defined, Wolseley made the practical arrangements necessary for its fulfilment. From the disbanded First Division he created a column under Lieutenant-Colonel C.M. Clarke, which was to reoccupy oNdini, and to send out patrols to attempt to capture the king. Wolseley himself was to accompany this column. A second column, made up from Wood's disbanded Flying Column, he put under the command of Lieutenant-Colonel Baker Russell. Russell's objective was the pacification of north-western Zululand, where Wolseley feared the Zulu, particularly the Qulusi, intended a last-ditch resistance.[115] Wolseley determined that Russell would be supported by a simultaneous invasion from the Transvaal by Lieutenant-Colonel the Hon. G. Villiers's troops stationed at Luneburg.

Swazi from across the Phongolo, and Hamu's warriors were to assist, mainly in covering the area to ensure that the king did not escape that way to Swaziland.[116] Wolseley, when he ordered Hamu to collect his warriors for this purpose, added greatly to his incentives to comply by promising him, if he were successful in bringing in the king, a reward of 5 000 cattle and an independent sovereignty over his own district.[117] Hamu's *izinduna* declared themselves willing on those terms to turn out their men and help capture the king.[118] Yet in the event, Hamu lost his nerve, and refused to lead his men beyond Luneburg, so ruining Wolseley's strategy.[119] It was only after Russell had effectively subdued the area alone that Hamu eventually entered it, his warriors looting at every opportunity as they advanced.[120]

Besides the north-west, where the royalist Qulusi were concentrated, there was another region where loyalty to the king persisted. This was southern Zululand, along the middle Thukela, a sector the British had never penetrated in force. There, the *isikhulu* Chief Godide kaNdlela of the Ntuli, Mavumengwana's brother, *induna* of the uDlambedlu *ibutho*, and commander at Nyezane; the old Chief Manqondo kaZwane of the Magwaza and his son, Qethuka, who was an *isikhulu*; and Chief Sokufa kaSotobe of the Cube, ancient and blind, whose son Sigananda ruled for him,[121] had waged a persistent local campaign of raid and counter-raid into Natal, and were loath to submit. During July and August they treated evasively with Natal officials, and stopped short of fulfilling the conditions set down by Wolseley for submission. It is clear, though, that their indecision was in part a reflection of divisions among their adherents. The married men were apparently content to accept the British terms, while the young warriors resented having to give up their arms, and were prepared to carry on the struggle.[122]

Upstream of them, it was different. Mbuzo, a Ntuli chief at the junction of the Thukela and Mzinyathi rivers, had put out peace feelers as early as June. After the battle of Ulundi, local officials exploited the favourable climate its impact had created to open negotiations with Chief Ndwandwe kaMhlala of the Langa, Chief Matshana kaSitshakuza of the Mchunu, an *isikhulu* with a long tradition of seeking for greater autonomy, and Chief Matshana kaMondisa of the Sithole who, like the other Matshana, officials had hoped before the war might throw in his lot with the British.[123] It took some time for the chiefs to conform with Wolseley's terms, for their people had taken refuge during the war in caves and forests, particularly as a result of extensive raids during May by the British,[124] and it was necessary that they return to their homesteads before the requisite guns and royal cattle could be collected. By mid-August it was done, and on 20 August the four chiefs and seven other lesser ones surrendered at Rorke's Drift to H.F. Fynn. There were no such formal surrenders among Sihayo's adherents. He and his son were prisoners-of-war, and the Qungebe were in their places of refuge, away from the border and the danger of British raids. Yet even with them, by the end of August many were drifting back to their homes, though it was not until October that they were all to return.[125]

By the time, then, when on 10 August Wolseley set up his camp at oNdini, the coastal region had submitted, the south-west was in the process of doing so, and it seemed likely that the south would follow suit. In central and even northern Zululand it appeared as if the chiefs were prepared to accept Wolseley's conditions and abandon the king's cause. Certainly, none of the important chiefs had assembled at oNdini by 10 August, but Wolseley was not perturbed, as he had word that they were coming in.[126] Zibhebhu was reported still to be in his district,[127] but Wolseley entertained high hopes of his co-operation. He had noted his 'time-serving disposition', and presumed (correctly, as it turned out) that the promise of an independent sovereignty under the British settlement would detach him from the king's cause.[128] By 13 August Zibhebhu had promised to come into Wolseley's camp, as had Mnyamana. It seems the latter had been delayed in doing so by his accession to the request of some of the other chiefs to wait until they could join him. To Wolseley, the submissions of Zibhebhu and Mnyamana were of the utmost significance. He was sure they would convince the remainder of the chiefs to follow their lead, and would have the effect of countering messages the king had apparently been sending out, requiring the chiefs not to give in.[129]

On 14 August Mnyamana, Chief Ntshingwayo kaMahole of the Khoza, an *isikhulu* in the north-west, *induna* of the kwaGqikazi *ikhanda*, joint commander at both Isandlwana and Khambula, a great friend of Mnyamana and after him probably the most influential man in Zululand; two uninfluential brothers of the king, Mgidlana and Sukani; Sitshaluza kaMamba, regent of the eMgazini in the north; chief Melelesi kaManyosi of the Mbatha in central Zululand;[130] and some 150 lesser chiefs presented themselves at Wolseley's camp.[131] They had with them 617 head of cattle, which had been collected by Mnyamana on the king's instructions.[132] These cattle indicated that Mnyamana and the other chiefs were overawed, and John Dunn and John Shepstone, who interviewed them, reported that they had declared that they had in fact come to surrender, and that they hoped for peace.[134] In which case, they had not met the required terms for submission, and Wolseley ordered that the five principal chiefs, including Mnyamana, be held hostage in camp until the necessary arms and royal cattle had been collected.[135] On 16 August Prince Ziwedu kaMpande came in, and was also detained.[136] Reportedly Cetshwayo's favourite brother, he was reputed second in status among the princes only to Hamu.[137] Then, on 26 August, Zibhebhu himself appeared. He had with him as tokens of submission a number of guns and cattle, and claimed that he had hesitated for so long in coming primarily for fear that he would be killed for the part he had played in the war.[138]

While these significant developments were occurring at oNdini, Baker Russell was also having success in the north-west. During the second week of August his patrols operating across the Black Mfolozi encountered some unfriendliness, but no outright resistance. Many Zulu, especially Seketh-wayo's Mdlalose, were clearly relieved that they did not have to fight, and surrendered both arms and cattle.[139] Then, on 25 August, Sekethwayo himself submitted at Fort Cambridge. Baker Russell ordered him to oNdini, but also promised him independence in his own district, and the restoration of his cattle.[140]

The Qulusi, on the other hand, were, as anticipated, proving more recalcitrant in their devotion to the royal cause. On 22 August Baker Russell's spies reported them to be mustering near the ebaQulisini *ikhanda* under the *induna* Mcwayo kaMangeda,[141] with the intention of fighting.[142] But on 28 August two sons of Msebe, the Qulusi *induna* who had opened negotiations in February and been subsequently victimized by the other Qulusi, informed Baker Russell that both he and Manyonyoba, the renegade Swazi who had also made contact during February, wished to surrender.[143] Msebe gave himself up on 29 August and, resentful at his treatment at the hands of the other Qulusi, indicated his desire to join the British in their operations against them. This proved unnecessary, however. On 28 August the king was captured by a British patrol in the Ngome forest, and this intelligence had an immediate effect on those Qulusi still resisting. At a council held on 30 August they decided to surrender, doubtless influenced by a secret message the captive king is reputed to have sent Mahubulwana kaDumisela, principal *induna* of the Qulusi and his commander in the field in the north-west,[144] ordering him to disband his men still under arms.[145] On 1 September Mahubulwana formally submitted on behalf of the Qulusi.[146] Only Manyonyoba, despite his declared intention to submit, continued a localized resistance until the end of September.[147]

The capture of the king was proving, as Wolseley had anticipated, a decisive event, as it took the meaning out of continued resistance. Initially, sheltered by the local population, Cetshwayo had succeeded in evading the patrols sent after him. Wolseley, though, by increasing the pressure on the chiefs in whose districts Cetshwayo was reported to be, succeeded in undercutting this aid. For long he remained frustrated by the general reluctance of the chiefs to come forward and help in the search, though he firmly believed that 'in their hearts' they were anxious for the king to be caught.[148] In the end he was rewarded. It is the argument of those chiefs who eventually betrayed their king that they had no choice. They claimed that the country was occupied by the British, and their people were threatened by starvation if they could not return to their homes in safety to plant their crops, the last harvest having been destroyed.[149] Certainly, the king's still remaining at large could only have hindered the inevitable settlement on terms dictated by the British. Yet by August much of the country directly affected by the war was already pacified, with the people returned to their fields, while vast areas had never seen so much as a British patrol. Moreover, British conditions for submission were not such as to disrupt the functioning of the ordinary Zulu's homestead. This was widely known. Therefore, the chiefs' position must be regarded as a realistic one, there being little point in persistent loyalty to an already fractured polity; or be viewed in terms of their personal ambitions, and their calculations on how best to enhance their power and independence in a Zululand where the centralized royal state was to be replaced by a number of independent sovereignties. Wolseley worked on these obvious perceptions.

On 23 August Colonel Clarke left with a strong patrol to pressure the neighbourhood where the king was reported to be in hiding. This was territory controlled by Somkhele, who had submitted on 4 July, of Mgojana kaSomaphunga, the Ndwandwe chief and husband of the king's sister, who came into camp on the same day Clarke left, and of Zibhebhu, who submitted three days later. It is particularly significant that Wolseley intended to make all three independent chiefs, but only 'if they behave[d] well'.[150] The chiefs could not have failed to understand this caveat. Wolseley used the same tactics with Mnyamana. In a crucial interview of 26 August between John Shepstone and Mnyamana, Shepstone was empowered to threaten the chief that if he did not co-operate he 'should have nothing'. Mnyamana hastily reassured Shepstone that both he and Mgojana were sending messages to their districts ordering their adherents to take the king captive. The former chief *induna* of the king added that since the battle of Ulundi the chiefs had 'lost all regard and interest' in the king, and that having done all that could be required of them for him, Cetshwayo could have 'no further claim' upon their loyalty. Mnyamana reportedly concluded:

> We were not afraid to kill Chaka and Dingaan, & Panda was saved because we feared the white men who were his friends, why should we therefore be afraid of Cetewayo?[151]

The captive King Cetshwayo under escort from the Black Mfolozi to the British camp near oNdini.

Mnyamana proved as good as his word, as the fugitive Cetshwayo was to discover. Mnyamana's adherents warned the king that their chief had promised Wolseley to assist in his capture, and that he had instructed them to deliver up the king if he should seek refuge in any of their homesteads. The king was aghast when he heard of what he considered to be Mnyamana's treachery, and was indeed almost immediately captured.[152]

Wolseley could now proceed to his final settlement of Zululand, which entailed the formal dismemberment of the Zulu polity into thirteen fragments. He signalled his intention to all the great chiefs of holding a meeting on 1 September at oNdini,[153] on which day he announced the thirteen chiefs favoured with independent sovereignties.[154] It is not at issue here that the boundaries of the chiefdoms were ill-conceived, or that the settlement paved the way for disastrous civil war..Rather, it is more relevant to understand the rationale behind Wolseley's division of the kingdom, and to see how the existing ambitions of the chiefs, so well known to him, coupled with their degree of collaboration during the war, affected his choice of the thirteen 'kinglets'.

Wolseley's settlement was dictated by strategic considerations, based on notions of defence in British India. As in India, where the North-West Frontier would be secured by fragmenting the Afghan state into a number of small principalities, ruled by petty chiefs under British supervision,[155] so too in South Africa, where Natal and the Transvaal would be made safe through the destruction of the unitary Zulu kingdom. The corollary was that the appointed Zulu chiefs must either be men of stature, who had already shown their willingness to work with the British, or more obscure chiefs who were unlikely to disturb the settlement. For, above all, the royalists must be prevented from reintegrating the kingdom and reasserting its military potential. It went without saying that in these calculations the reliability of the chiefdoms abutting the Transvaal and Natal borders were the most crucial, for they would act as buffer-zones against the conceivably more volatile chiefdoms created to the north of them. This is why Hlubi of the Tlokwa, whose men had fought for the British during the war, was given the strategic territory at the junction of the Thukela and Mzinyathi rivers.[156] He was put over Sihayo, concerning whose sons the Zulu thought the war had been fought, and over the two Matshanas. These two had at least shown themselves more amenable than Sihayo by eventually submitting, and Hlubi confirmed them in their chiefdoms.[157]

Hlubi was an alien, one who had never been a person of power and status in Cetshwayo's kingdom, and therefore owed his elevation entirely to the British. John Dunn's position was more ambiguous. He had been a chief and favourite of the Zulu king yet he had been the first of the leading men of Zululand to desert his cause. He had served the British well during the war, and had the fortune to have won Wolseley's confidence. So much so, in fact, that his advice was largely followed in choosing the other twelve chiefs.[158] He had no wish to see the king he had betrayed restored, and he possessed a firm power-base in south-eastern Zululand. So it was that Wolseley restored him to his chiefdom, and more besides. For Dunn was entrusted with a territory which, running along the Thukela frontier, was the most significant in Zululand in terms of Natal's security. It included those chiefs along the middle border whose submissions, even by early September, were still half-hearted and unsatisfactory. To bring them to heel, Wolseley ordered Clarke's Column to march out of Zululand by way of Middle Drift. Dunn joined the column on 4 September, and patrols were sent out as it advanced demanding arms and royal cattle, and exacting cattle-fines from those chiefs who had not complied in time. By 20 September all the chiefs had met the conditions for surrender, and Dunn's authority was established. Sensibly he confirmed Mavumengwana, Godide, Qethuka and Sigananda as principal chiefs, so perpetuating their existing local authority.[159]

The area where there was the greatest likelihood of a royalist resurgence was north of the Black Mfolozi, and there Wolseley ensured that he establish chiefs of great status and local power, who could be relied upon to suppress any such aspirations. Wolseley might assert in his typical style that Hamu was not a chief whom he himself would have selected, and that he had done so only to honour the pledges made him when he defected.[160] Yet, in reality, there was no one else with the status and hereditary authority capable of controlling the north-west where, after all, the Qulusi had been among the last to submit. Furthermore, Hamu's long-standing ambitions, which clearly were not satisfied even by the greatly enlarged chiefdom Wolseley awarded him,[161] ensured that he would keep the royalists down. Zibhebhu, thanks to his timely submission, was confirmed in his already quasi-autonomous chiefdom in the north-east, and had his sway extended considerably to take in the homesteads of some of the king's family and closest adherents, known as the uSuthu. Mgojana had not the record of ambition of these two members of the royal house, but he had co-operated in the hunt for the king, and was chief of the Ndwandwe, who, before their defeat, had been one of the great pre-Shakan clans.[162] Wolseley hoped that the chiefdom he had created for him would also serve to keep the royalists in check, as would Mlandela's, centred as it was on that other great pre-Shaka clan, the Mthethwa. Like Mlandlela, Somkhele had made an opportune submission and, thanks to the coherence of his existing power-base, was given the most northerly of the coastal chiefdoms. The only other chiefdom on the periphery of Zululand was that created for Sekethwayo. Wolseley might characterize him as 'a stupid and infirm old man',[163] but he had early attempted to throw in his lot with the British, and so merited his promised reward.

It is of note that all the chiefs appointed to territories along Zululand's borders or coasts had either materially aided the British during the war, or had abandoned the royal cause sufficiently early to have at least a degree of trust placed in them by Wolseley. They effectively neutralized the appointed chiefs in the interior of the country, who had not a similar record. Of these, Faku kaZiningo of the Ntombela was a nonentity, though Mfanawendlela kaThanga of the Zungu was an *isikhulu*.[164] Both were likely under the new arrangement to remain under the influence of their more dependable neighbours. Two of the others had been important chiefs, though their submissions had not been particularly sought or noticed. They were Gawozi kaSilwana, the Mpungose chief and an *isikhulu*, who had been a great favourite of the king's; and Mgitshwa kaMvundlana, a younger brother of Mkhosana, the Biyela chief, who had been killed at Isandlwana. Although both enjoyed a developed power-base, they were reputed to have been firmly of the peace party before the war, which was a distinct recommendation. Indeed, Mgitshwa was to prove a determined foe of the royal house.[165]

Only one of the great chiefs upon whose co-operation the British had relied, who was sufficiently powerful in his own right to maintain an independent sovereignty, and to whom Wolseley had promised one as a suitable reward, actually declined the offer. This was Mnyamana. The motives for his refusal were apparently mixed. Some of the Zulu ascribed it to his abiding loyalty to the king, while Wolseley supposed it was due to a sense of slight that his designated territory was not as large as he thought his due. Mnyamana himself insisted that it was because he did not wish to be split from the bulk of his adherents, who had been assigned to Hamu's territory.[166] Consequently, Wolseley awarded the chiefdom to Ntshingwayo who, although he had not had a large personal following in the time of the king, nevertheless had enjoyed a prestige and influence second only to Mnyamana's. Like his old friend, he had submitted in good time, and the chiefdom was the reward for his good sense.

In the final analysis, it would appear that the Zulu polity preserved its cohesion under the impact of the invasion of 1879 only so long as British arms seemed unlikely to prevail. Even so, it must not be forgotten that there were some chiefs, most notably Hamu and Sekethwayo, who, more perceptive than their fellows and anticipating the likely outcome of the looming conflict, accordingly entered into early negotiations with the

British, though their submissions were initially thwarted by the intervention of the king or local loyalists. In regions such as the west and south-east, where the British military presence was effective over a long period, the pattern was an accelerating one of negotiation and submission. (The exception was the far north-west, where some of the Qulusi and the quasi-independent Chief Manyonyoba maintained a die-hard resistance in the face of considerable British activity.) The southern border region, which the British had never penetrated in strength, maintained a desultory war of raid and counter-raid, and only ceased its half-hearted resistance when at last the British presence was firmly introduced. On the other hand, great districts in the east, centre and north, although never entered by the British, submitted as soon as the royal cause seemed lost.

This varying pattern of resistance must be explained in terms of the attitude of the Zulu ruling élite. Especially after the repeated defeats of the Zulu armies in the field, and the ever-more apparent inability of the Zulu state to continue the struggle at the national level, there was a concerted attempt by the majority of chiefs to preserve or even augment their positions by coming to an arrangement with the British. The British peace conditions facilitated this process for, by not disrupting the Zulu homestead economy, they made the fate of the Zulu state as such an irrelevancy to the bulk of the ordinary Zulu; while by generally recognizing the existing chiefs, and adding appreciably to the powers of a favoured few, they left the influence of the chiefly class undisturbed. Only the king's power was eliminated, and that of his family curtailed. The fact that almost without exception the chiefs accepted this situation cannot be attributed, as Sir Theophilus Shepstone was to maintain until the end of his life, to the yearnings of the incorporated tribes of the kingdom created by Shaka to throw off the Zulu monarchy and 're-enter upon their separate existence'.[167] Rather, it was because the chiefs (it seems) were pragmatic and ambitious men. The Zulu state had never been so monolithic that they, especially those on the periphery of the kingdom and in commercial contact with the whites, had not the ambition – and the relative scope – for greater local autonomy. The war gave these their opportunity, while the others stove to save at least their local positions from out of the débris of the kingdom's collapse. Both these objectives required a degree of co-operation with the British, which transcended any urge for self-defeating sacrifice in the ruined cause of a unified Zulu state under its king.

[Previously published in *Journal of Natal & Zulu History*, VIII, 1985.]

Notes

1. Jeff Guy, *The Destruction of the Zulu Kingdom*, London, 1979, pp. 39, 50.

2. Of the considerable literature in this field, the following are perhaps some of the best representative examples, and have been extensively consulted in writing this section: Peter Colenbrander, 'The Zulu Political Economy on the Eve of the War', in A. Duminy and C. Ballard (eds.), *The Anglo-Zulu War: New Perspectives*, Pietermaritzburg, 1981; Jeff Guy, 'Production and Exchange in the Zulu Kingdom', '*Mohlomi*': *Journal of Southern African Historical Studies*, II, 1978, and 'The Political Structure of the Zulu Kingdom during the Reign of Cetshwayo kaMpande', Chapter 2 in *The Destruction of the Zulu Kingdom*. Both of these have been reprinted in J.B. Peires (ed.), *Before and After Shaka: Papers in Nguni History*, Grahamstown, 1981. See also John Wright, '*Control of Women's Labour in the Zulu Kingdom*', in *Before and After Shaka*.

3. For a recent synthesis of literature on the *amabutho* system, see J.P.C. Laband and P.S. Thompson, *Field Guide to the War in Zululand and the Defence of Natal 1879*, Pietermaritzburg, 1983, pp. 3–4.

4. R. Mael, 'The Problem of Political Integration in the Zulu Empire', (unpublished Ph.D. thesis, University of California, Los Angeles, 1974), pp. 130–8.

5. Besides the works by Guy cited above, see also three pieces by Charles Ballard: 'John Dunn and Cetshwayo: the material foundations of political power in the Zulu kingdom 1857–1878', *Journal of African Studies*, 21, 1980; 'The role of trade and hunter-traders in the political economy of Natal and Zululand 1824–1880', paper presented at the Economic History Conference on southern Africa, University of Natal, Durban, July 1980; and 'Trade, Tribute and Migrant Labour: Zulu and Colonial exploitation of the Delagoa Bay hinterland 1818–1879', in *Before and After Shaka*.

6. See N.L.G. Cope, 'The Defection of Hamu', (unpublished B.A. Hons. thesis, University of Natal, Durban, 1980), p. 26.

7. *B.P.P.* (C. 2222), enc. 1 in no. 43: Shepstone to Frere, 30 November 1878; ibid., no. 45: Frere to Hicks Beach, 10 December 1878.

8. Ibid., enc. 1 in no. 46: Bulwer to Frere, 29 November 1878. For corroboration of the king's refusal even to consider terms such as the disbanding of his army, see C. de B. Webb and J.B. Wright (eds.), *A Zulu King Speaks*, Pietermaritzburg and Durban, 1978, pp. 28–9.

9. CSO 1925, no. 6/1879: Fannin to Colonial Secretary, 8 January 1879.

10. CSO 1925, no. 372/1879: Fannin to Colonial Secretary, 15 January 1879. See also, Webb and Wright, *Zulu King Speaks*, pp. 26–9, 53–4.

11. F.G. Fynney, *The Zulu Army and Zulu Headmen*, Pietermaritzburg, April 1879; and Elaine Unterhalter, 'Confronting Imperialism: the People of Nquthu and the Invasion of Zululand', in Duminy and Ballard, *The Anglo-Zulu War*, p. 99.

12. WC II/2/2: Chelmsford to Wood, 12 December 1878; CSO 1925, no. 4579/1879: Fannin to Colonial Secretary, 4 December 1878; SNA 1/1/34, no. 1171: Statement of Sihlahla, 3 June 1879; SNA 1/1/34, no. 73: Statement of Sibalo, 1 June 1879; *JSA* vol. I, p. 167: Statement of J. Hoye ka Soxalase; Webb and Wright, *Zulu King Speaks*, pp. 27–9.

13. Cornelius Vijn (J. W. Colenso, tr. and ed.), *Cetshwayo's Dutchman*, London, 1880, p. 17. The original MS is with the Anti-Slavery Papers, Rhodes House, Oxford, G12: Natal, Zululand, Bishop Colenso and Cetshwayo.

14. CSO 1925, no. 4579/1878: Fannin to Colonial Secretary, 4 December 1878.

15. SNA 1/1/33, no. R28: Fynney to Secretary for Native Affairs, 5 January 1879; C. C. Ballard, 'Sir Garnet Wolseley and John Dunn: The Architects and Agents of the Ulundi Settlement', in Duminy and Ballard, *The Anglo-Zulu War*, p. 133.

16. *JSA*, vol. III, p. 179: Statement of Mkando ka Dhlova.

17. Vijn, *Cetshwayo's Dutchman*, p. 162: Notes by the Bishop of Natal; Fynney, *Zulu Headmen*.

18. Fynney, *Zulu Headmen*; Guy, *Destruction of the Zulu Kingdom*, pp. 17, 37–8.

19. Cope, 'Defection of Hamu', pp. 43–4.

20. Ibid., 35–40.

21. Vijn, *Cetshwayo's Dutchman*, pp. 181–2: Notes by the Bishop of Natal; *JSA*, vol. I, pp. 31–2: Statement of Baleni ka Mlalaziko.

22. Magema M. Fuze (H. C. Lugg, tr. and A. T. Cope, ed.), *The Black People and Whence They Came*, Pietermaritzburg and Durban, 1979, p. 106.

23. Webb and Wright, *Zulu King Speaks*, p. 60.

24. SNA 1/4/2, no. 56/1878: Fynney to Acting Secretary for Native Affairs, 7 October 1878.

25. *B.P.P.* (C. 2222), enc. in no. 18: Hamu to Landdrost of Utrecht, recd. 6 November 1878.

26. CP 9, no. 71: Wood to Chelmsford, 3 November 1878.

27. WC II/2/2: Chelmsford to Wood, 11 December 1878.

28. WC II/2/2: Chelmsford to Wood, 23 December 1878.

29. CP 9, enc. in no. 5: Captain N. MacLeod (Political Agent in Swaziland) to Wood, 28 December 1878.

30. ZA 21, no. R920/1879: Minute, H. F. Fynn to British Resident, Zululand, 26 December 1879; CSO 1925, no. 409/1879: Fynn to Colonial Secretary, 16 January 1879; *B.P.P.* (C. 2260), enc. 2 in no. 4: Chelmsford to High Commissioner, 17 January 1879.

31. J. P. C. Laband and P. S. Thompson, with Sheila Henderson, *The Buffalo Border 1879: The Anglo-Zulu War in Northern Natal*, Durban, 1983, chaps. III and IV, passim.

32. WC II/2/2: Chelmsford to Wood, 16 December 1878.

33. Fynney, *Zulu Headmen*.

34. Woodgate's Military Diary: 10 January 1879; and *B.P.P.*(C. 2242), enc. 7 in no. 20: Wood to Chelmsford, 9 and 10 January 1879.

35. Fynney, *Zulu Headmen*.

36. GH 501: Wolseley to Lt.-Col. G. Villiers, Instructions for the Guidance of the Zululand Boundary Commission, 9 September 1879.

37. Woodgate's Military Diary: 11 and 12 January; *B.P.P.* (C.2242), enc.7 in no.20: Wood to High Commissioner, 13 January 1879; and ibid. (C.2252), no.20: Wood to Assistant Military Secretary, 13 January 1879.

38. Woodgate's Military Diary: 14 and 15 January 1879.

39. Ibid.: 17 January 1879; *B.P.P.* (C.2252), no.20: Wood to Assistant Military Secretary, 13 January 1879.

40. *B.P.P.* (C.2260), enc.3 in no.4: Wood to Frere, 20 January 1879.

41. Woodgate's Military Diary: 18 and 20 January; WO 32/7712: Journal of Operations of No.4 Column, 20 January 1879.

42. J.Y. Gibson, *The Story of the Zulus*, London, 1911, p.194; Guy, *Destruction of the Zulu Kingdom*, p.36.

43. CP 9, enc.f in no.4: L.H. Lloyd to Wood, 28 December 1878; CSO 1925, no.444/1879: Fannin to Colonial Secretary, 20 January 1879.

44. *B.P.P.* (C.2252), no.20: Wood to Assistant Military Secretary, 14 January 1879.

45. CP 9, no.9: MacLeod to Wood, 25 January 1879.

46. CP 9, no.18: Macleod to Wood, 8 February 1879.

47. CP 9, no.26: Memorandum by L. Lloyd, 16 February 1879.

48. CP 9, no.32: Wood to Major Crealock, 25 February 1879.

49. Woodgate's Military Diary: 16 February 1879. According to other accounts, Cetshwayo allowed Hamu to go home 'to cry and eat medicine' for the dead at Isandlwana, or possibly the death of a wife (CSO 1926, no.1346/1879: Fannin to Colonial Secretary, 3 March 1879), and gave him presents of rifles, oxen and horses, thinking he was now so mixed up in the war that he would never desert (*Times of Natal*, 24 March 1879).

50. *B.P.P.* (C.2367), enc.2 in no.3: James Rorke for Hamu to Wood, recd. 17 February 1879.

51. CP 7, no.32: Fynney to Col. Law, 8 March 1879; and Vijn, *Cetshwayo's Dutchman*, p.33.

52. Woodgate's Military Diary: 21–2, 27–8 February, 6, 10, 11, 13–16 March 1879; CP 9, no.32: Wood to Crealock, 25 February 1879; CP 9, no.34: J. Jackson to Col. Rowlands, 25 February 1879; CP 9, enc. in no.37: MacLeod to Wood, 28 February 1879; CP 9, enc. in no.39: MacLeod to Wood, 4 March 1879; CP 9, no.44: Wood to Military Secretary, 16 March 1879.

53. Woodgate's Military Diary: 25 March 1879.

54. *B.P.P.* (C.2374), enc.1 in no.40: Statement of Ugwegwana, 13 May 1879.

55. WO 32/7779: Journal of Col. Baker Russell's Column, 14 August 1879.

56. CSO 1926, no.1346/1879: Fannin to Colonial Secretary, 3 March 1879.

57. WO 32/7715: Diary of Operations, 10 March 1879.

58. Woodgate's Military Diary: 9 February 1879.

59. CP 9, no.12: Lloyd to Wood, 29 January 1879; Fynney, *Zulu Headmen*. For the demoralization of the Qulusi, see *B.P.P.* (C.2260), no.10: Statement of Ucadjana taken by H.C. Shepstone, 3 February 1879.

60. CP 9, no.26: Memorandum by Lloyd, 16 February 1879; Woodgate's Military Diary: 22 February 1879.

61. CP 14, no.9: Wood to Military Secretary, 27 February 1879; Woodgate's Military Diary: 25 March 1879.

62. WO 32/7782: Diary of Col. Baker Russell's Column, 29 August 1879.

63. WO 32/7715: Diary of Operations, 10 March 1879.

64. CSO 1926, no.1346/1879: Fannin to Colonial Secretary, 3 March 1879.

65. *B.P.P.* (C.2374), enc.1 in no.31: Fannin to Colonial Secretary, 30 May 1879.

66. CP 9, enc. in no.37: MacLeod to Wood, 1 March 1879.

67. CP 7, no.32: Fynney to Col. Law, 8 March 1879.

68. CSO 1926, no.1669/1879: Fannin to Colonial Secretary, 22 March 1879.

69. Laband and Thompson, *Field Guide*, p.22.

70. Sir F.T. Hamilton's Papers, National Maritime Museum, Greenwich, HTN/103: Journal, April–September 1879: 7–22 April 1879.

71. Fynncy, *Zulu Headmen*.

72. *B.P.P.* (C.2367), enc. in no.46: Bulwer to Frere, 26 April 1879.

73. Fynney, *Zulu Headmen*.

74. CSO 1926, no.1812/1879: Fannin to Colonial Secretary, 1 April 1879.

75. SNA 1/1/34, no.928: Fynney to Secretary for Native Affairs, 28 April 1879; SNA 1/1/34, no.1054: Fynney to Secretary for Native Affairs, 13 May 1879.

76. Colenso Papers 27, no.210: Bishop Colenso to Chesson, 4 May 1879.

77. CSO 1927, no.2515/1879: Fannin to Colonial Secretary, 15 May 1879.

78. CSO 1926, no.2051/1879: Fannin to Colonial Secretary, 17 April 1879.

79. Woodgate's Private Diary: 21 April 1879.

80. CP 35, no.3: Telegram, General Crealock to Chelmsford, 15 May 1879; WO 32/7750: Journal of Second Brigade, First Division, 16 May 1879.

81. CP 9, no.52: Wood to Military Secretary, 10 May 1879. Statement of Scouts from Zulu country.

82. CP 35, no.5: Telegram, General Crealock to Chelmsford, 14 May 1879.

83. Fynney, *Zulu Headmen*, and Bertram Mitford, *Through the Zulu Country*, London, 1883, pp.210–11.

84. CP 35, no.14: Telegram, General Crealock to Chelmsford, 29 May 1879; CP 35, no.16: Telegram, summary of information by Fanaene, 28 May 1879; *B.P.P.*(C.2374), enc.7 in no.37: Statement of Umfazi, 28 May 1879.

85. SNA 1/1/34, no.73: Statement of Sibalo, 1 June 1879.

86. WO 32/7747: Correspondence Regarding Peace. Summary of conversation between John Dunn and king's messenger, Usitwangu, 31 May 1879.

87. P. Harries, 'History, Ethnicity and the Ingwavuma Land Deal: The Zulu Northern Frontier in the Nineteenth Century', *JNZH*, VI, 1983, pp.12–14, 17.

88.   CO 179/131, no. Natal/12358: O'Neill to Lord Salisbury, 7 June 1879.

89.   CP 15, no. 4: Telegram, General Crealock to Military Secretary, recd. 8 June 1879.

90.   *B.P. P.* (C.2454), enc. 11 in no. 54: Message from Cetywayo to Fynney, 25 June 1879.

91.   Fynney, *Zulu Headmen*; Webb and Wright, *Zulu King Speaks*, p. 37. For Phalane's view in 1882 that Cetshwayo had been the cause of the fighting, and that his people had become tired of war, see Captain W. R. Ludlow, *Zululand and Cetewayo*, London, 1882, p. 72.

92.   Fynney, *Zulu Headmen*; Guy, *Destruction of the Zulu Kingdom*, p. 37; Laband and Thompson, *Field Guide*, p. 41.

93.   CP 16, no. 40: Drummond to Assistant Military Secretary, 10 June 1879. Statement of Zulu prisoner Umgaunsi; *B.P. P.* (C.2454), enc. in no. 33: Report of three messengers to W. Drummond, 5 June 1879.

94.   *B.P. P.* (C.2454), enc. 1 in no. 34: Bulwer to Frere, 10 June 1879. Surrender of Mbobo.

95.   Intelligence Branch of the War Office, *Narrative of the Field Operations Connected with the Zulu War of 1879*, London 1881, p. 107.

96.   *B.P. P.* (C.2454), enc. 7 in no. 51: Message from the Lieutenant-General . . . to the Zulu Chiefs, 16 June 1879.

97.   WO 32/7760: Wolseley to Secretary of State for War, 10 July 1879. See also Webb and Wright, *Zulu King Speaks*, p. 35.

98.   Fynney, *Zulu Headmen*; Laband and Thompson, *Field Guide*, pp. 39, 41.

99.   Ibid.; Webb and Wright, *Zulu King Speaks*, p. 59.

100.   Fynney, *Zulu Headmen*.

101.   Ibid.

102.   Ibid.; Guy, *Destruction of the Zulu Kingdom*, p. 34.

103.   WO 32/7772: Memorandum of Operations of First Division, General Crealock to Wolseley, 4 and 5 July 1879.

104.   Frere had given Crealock control over political affairs in Zululand. The terms Crealock devised were accompanied by the threat that homesteads would be burnt and cattle taken if they were not complied with. (WO 32/7772: Report of Operations of First Division, Crealock to Wolseley, 21 July 1879.)

105.   Woodgate's Private Diary: 14 July 1879; Colenso Papers 27, no. 223: Bishop Colenso to Chesson, 12 July 1879; *Natal Mercury*, 4 August 1879; Vijn, *Cetshwayo's Dutchman*, p. 157: Bishop Colenso's notes. See also Wolseley's Journal: 13 July 1879. Adrian Preston (ed.), *Sir Garnet Wolseley's South African Journal 1879–80*, Cape Town, 1873, is an edited transcription of the Journal, though not sufficient care has been taken, particularly with Zulu names.

106.   WO 32/7760: Wolseley to Secretary of State for War, 10 July 1879.

107.   Wolseley's Journal: 19 July; WO 32/7756: Wolseley to Secretary of State for War, 21 July 1879; *B.P. P.* (C.2482), no. 28: Wolseley to Secretary of State for Colonies, 19 July 1879.

108.   *The Graphic*, 9 August 1879.

109. Wolseley's Journal: 8 July 1879.
110. Ibid.: 23 July 1879.
111. *B.P.P.* (C.2482), no.28: Wolseley to Secretary of State for Colonies, 19 July 1879.
112. Wolseley Papers I: 163/v (1878–87), no.14 B: Wolseley to his Mother, 21 July 1879.
113. WO 32/7756: Wolseley to Secretary of State for War, 21 July 1879. See also, Wolseley papers I: 163/v (1878–87), no.15: Wolseley to his Mother, 4 August 1879: '. . . please God I shall there (oNdini) be able to make peace and catch or kill Cetewayo'.
114. WO 32/7768: Brig.-Gen. G. Pomeroy Colley: Minute for the guidance of all officers commanding posts and all political officers dealing with the Zulu people, 26 July 1879.
115. Wolseley's Journal: 18 July 1879; War Office, *Narrative of Field Operations*, pp.126–130.
116. Wolseley's Journal: 18 July 1879; WO 32/7756: Telegram, Wolseley to Secretary of State for War, 21 July 1879; *B.P.P.* (C.2482): Wolseley to Secretary of State for Colonies, 18 July 1879.
117. WO 32/7760: Wolseley to Secretary of State for War, 10 July 1879.
118. WO 32/7773: Wolseley to Secretary of State for War, 2 August 1879.
119. Wolseley's Journal: 10 August 1879; WO 32/7775: Wolseley to Secretary of State for War, 13 August 1879; *B.P.P.* (C.2482), no.69: Wolseley to Secretary of State for Colonies, 13 August 1879.
120. Wolseley's Journal: 8 September 1879; *B.P.P.* (C.2482), enc.2 in no.157: Lt.-Col. Villiers to Bulwer, 16 September 1879.
121. Fynney, *Zulu Headmen*; Laband and Thompson, *Buffalo Border*, pp.23–4.
122. J.P.C. Laband and P.S. Thompson, *War Comes to Umvoti: The Natal-Zululand Border 1878–9*, Durban, 1980, pp.79–82.
123. Unterhalter, 'Nquthu and the Invasion of Zululand', pp.100–1.
124. Laband and Thompson, *Buffalo Border*, chap.IV, passim.
125. Ibid., pp.78–81.
126. *B.P.P.* (C.2482), no.69: Wolseley to Secretary of State for Colonies, 13 August 1879.
127. Wolseley's Journal: 8 August 18799.
128. *B.P.P.* (C.2482), no.27: Wolseley to Secretary of State for Colonies, 18 July 1879.
129. WO 32/7775: Wolseley to Secretary of State for War, 13 August 1879.
130. Fynney, *Zulu Headmen*; Guy, *Destruction of the Zulu Kingdom*, p.32.
131. Wolseley's Journal: 14 August 1879; *The Graphic*, 4 October 1879; C.L. Norris-Newman, *In Zululand with the British Throughout the War of 1879*, London, 1880, pp.237–8.
132. Webb and Wright, *Zulu King Speaks*, p.35.

133. Colenso Papers 27, no. 230: Bishop Colenso to Chesson, 13 September 1879; Vijn, *Cetshwayo's Dutchman*, pp. 159–60: Bishop Colenso's notes (information given by Ntshingwayo to Magema Fuze).

134. *The Graphic*, 4 October.

135. Wolseley's Journal: 14 August 1879.

136. Ibid.: 16 August 1979.

137. Fynney, *Zulu Headmen*.

138. Wolseley's Journal: 26 August 1879; *B.P. P.*(C. 2482), enc. 1 in no. 78: Gen. Clifford to Frere, 28 August 1879.

139. Woodgate's Private Diary: 7–9, 12, 13, 17, 22 August; WO 32/7779: Journal of Baker Russell's Column, 11–14 August.

140. WO 32/7782: Diary of Baker Russell's Column, 25 August 1879.

141. Fynney, *Zulu Headmen*.

142. Woodgate's Private Diary: 22 August 1879; WO 32/7782: Diary of Baker Russell's Column, 28 August 1879.

143. Woodgate's Private Diary: 28 August 1879.

144. Fynney, *Zulu Headmen*; Webb and Wright, *Zulu King Speaks*, p. 30.

145. WO 32/7782: Diary of Baker Russell's Column, 29, 30 August 1879; Guy, *Destruction of the Zulu Kingdom*, p. 63.

146. WO 32/7782: Journal of Baker Russell's Column, 1, 3 September 1879.

147. Woodgate's Private Diary: 5, 6, 8 September 1879; WO 32/7781: Wolseley to Secretary of State for War, 11 September 1879; ZA 21, enc. in no. G728/79: Report on relocation of Manyonyoba, 15 October 1879.

148. Wolseley Papers 2: Wolseley to his Wife, 26 August 1879.

149. Colenso Papers 27, no. 230: Bishop Colenso to Chesson, 13 September 1879; Fuze, *Black People*, p. 115.

150. Wolseley's Journal: 23 August 1879.

151. Ibid.: 26 August 1879; *B.P. P.* (C. 2482), no. 82: Wolseley to Secretary of State for Colonies, 27 August 1879.

152. Webb and Wright, *Zulu King Speaks*, p. 36; Fuze, *Black People*, p. 115.

153. *B.P. P.* (C. 2482), enc. 6 in no. 78: Wolseley to Secretary of State for War, 29 August 1879.

154. Ibid., no. 87: Wolseley to Secretary of State for Colonies, 3 September 1879.

155. Preston, *Wolseley's South African Journal*, pp. 2–3, 318 (note 53–22); Ballard, 'Wolseley and John Dunn', pp. 130–1.

156. For the thirteen appointed chiefs, see Guy, *Destruction of the Zulu Kingdom*, pp. 72–5; and Fynney, *Zulu Headmen*. For the boundaries of the chiefdoms, see ZA 19, enc. in St. L. A. Herbert to Melmoth Osborn, 24 February 1880: Report of the Zululand Boundary Commission by Lt.-Col. G. Villiers, Capt. J. Alleyne and Capt. H. Moore, 5 December 1879.

157. Unterhalter, 'Nquthu and the Invasion of Zululand', pp. 107–9; Laband and Thompson, *Buffalo Border*, p. 82.

158. Ballard, 'Wolseley and John Dunn', pp. 137–9.

159. WO 32/7785: Journal of Clarke's Column, 4, 5, 8, 11–20 September 1879. All the chiefs who submitted are listed. See also Laband and Thompson, *War Comes to Umvoti*, pp. 84–6, 89.

160. *B.P. P.* (C. 2482), no. 179: Wolseley to Secretary of State for Colonies, 11 November 1879.

161. Ibid., enc. in no. 179: Villiers to Bulwer, 7 October 1879.

162. Fuze, *Black People*, pp. 49–50.

163. *B.P. P.* (C. 2482), enc. 2 in no. 93: Wolseley to Villiers, 9 September 1879.

164. Fynney, *Zulu Headmen*; Guy, *Destruction of the Zulu Kingdom*, p. 32; Fuze, *Black People*, p. 22.

165. Fynney, *Zulu Headmen*; Guy, *Destruction of the Zulu Kingdom*, p. 171; Fuze, *Black People*, p. 129.

166. Wolseley's Journal: 1 September 1879.

167. Sir Theophilus Shepstone, *The Native Question. Answer to Resident Reitz*, reprinted from the *Natal Mercury*, 29 January 1892, p. 6.

The Zulu Army in the War of 1879

Some cautionary notes

J.P.C. LABAND

In January 1879 British troops and colonial forces invaded the Zulu Kingdom, and during the course of the next six months engaged Zulu units in a series of pitched battles and severe skirmishes.[1] Information on these engagements, as perceived by the British, is extensively available not only in contemporary sources such as official civil and military correspondence, letters, newspapers and memoirs, but also in the host of secondary works, which although originally basing themselves on the primary material, have tended increasingly to feed off each other.[2] Most modern accounts inherit a failing which was blatantly apparent in the primary sources: they still relegate the Zulu role in the war to one of providing the savage backcloth against which the feats of imperial arms can be highlighted. Scant attention is paid to Zulu strategy, let alone to identifying which Zulu units were involved in a particular engagement, their numbers, precise order of battle, commanders or casualties. While it is true that such a study is hampered by fragmentary evidence, it is also the case that even the evidence which is available in published form has not been seriously or critically examined by the vast majority of those who have written on the campaigns of the Anglo-Zulu War.

When the quality of the surviving evidence is assessed, it must be accepted that, while the observations by contemporary British soldiers and officials on the Zulu are often important and sometimes unique, these are unfortunately of restricted value on account of their authors' lack of discerning familiarity with the subject.[3] Those best equipped to provide information about the Zulu army and its conduct were the Zulu themselves, and it is on their testimony that the most reliance ought to be placed. Nevertheless, Zulu testimony must be handled with circumspection. It never comes to us directly, but is always filtered through the medium of white interpreters, recorders or translators[4] who tended, when conducting interrogations or transcribing statements, to direct Zulu testimony or so colour it that it mirrored their own particular preconceptions or concerns about the war, rather than those of the witnesses. The consequence is reflected in the number of detailed accounts that proliferate on the battle of Isandlwana (of such morbid and recurring fascination to the whites), but which are clearly less in demand concerning battles where the British were more content with their own victorious interpretation of events.[5]

In addition to these reservations, the fact that Zulu testimony does not derive directly from Zulu informants, and its uneven quality should also be taken into account. The surviving statements of individual Zulu prisoners-of-war and deserters interrogated in 1879 are of fundamental importance, but while some of them were eye-witnesses to the events they described, others merely based their testimony on hearsay, albeit Zulu.[6] Of less value are the conflated statements of numbers of Zulu prisoners which British staff officers prepared for their reports.[7] The detailed information which Natal Border Agents gleaned through their spies, border police, and Christian converts from the Zulu living in the border zones, and which they passed on to the military authorities, is suspect, if not demonstrably inaccurate.[8] Captured Zulu commanders were naturally able to give more complete impressions of a battle than could ordinary warriors,[9] while King Cetshwayo, though not present in person at any battle, was able to provide a unique survey of the Zulu strategy of the war based on his own orders and on the reports of his commanders.[10] The anecdotes of Zulu, interviewed very soon after the war in relaxed circumstances and on their own ground by sympathetic tourists, have a ring of spontaneity and verisimilitude.[11] Over the next fifty years Zulu veterans continued to reminisce over their part in the war, and although confusions and elisions increasingly marred such testimony, there seem to be no significant differences in quality and detail between statements made in the 1880s and the 1920s.[12] To complicate matters, some of the more informative Zulu accounts were reprinted in contemporary British and Colonial newspapers and journals, and also in memoirs and early histories; in the process they were variously shortened or otherwise tampered with, and require careful comparison before something near the fullness of the original statement can be adduced.[13]

Numbers of problems are encountered when this often unsatisfactory Zulu evidence is used to illuminate Zulu military activity in 1879. A contemporary Zulu statement, for example, might mention a number of *amabutho* (singular – *ibutho*), or 'regiments' as they are conventionally termed, as having taken part in a battle. Vagaries in Zulu orthography over a hundred years, however, can obstruct their positive identification with *amabutho* whose names are known to us. Yet even these very names pose difficulties. Individual *amabutho* were normally known to contemporary Zulu by a variety of titles: either by that which the king gave it when it was formed; or by the name of the 'military kraal' (*ikhanda*, plural – *amakhanda*) where it was stationed, which in a few exceptional cases might not receive the same name as the *ibutho*; or by a local nickname. Furthermore, a number of *amabutho* might be attached to a large *ikhanda* and for convenience be called collectively by the *ikhanda's* name.[14] The British in 1879 were not unnaturally confused by this nomenclature and found their uncertainties compounded, when, in order to establish against which Zulu units they had fought, they relied upon a list of 'regiments' prepared for them on the eve of war by a Natal Border Agent, F.G. Fynney. Besides inaccuracies, Fynney's list misled them by giving only one (and that not necessarily the most widely known) of an *ibutho's* names, and by occasionally confusing this with the name of an *ikhanda*, all in an attempt to make Zulu military organization more comprehensible to the British by the imposition of familiar labels such as 'corps' and 'regiment'.[15] Since then, A.T. Bryant and R.C. Samuelson, both of them relying upon Zulu oral evidence, have attempted to compile more accurate and comprehensive lists of *amabutho*.[16] Their conclusions not only sometimes differ from Fynney's, but fail to tally fully with each other. A convincing synthesis was then made by Professor E.J. Krige which, despite a number of unresolved obscurities, remains the best guide in the field.[17]

Once those *amabutho* mentioned in Zulu sources as having taken part in a battle have been identified with reasonable certainty, it still remains to be proved that these particular units were actually involved. A reasonable method of achieving some certainty on this point would be to compare all available Zulu statements, and if a unit were consistently mentioned, to accept its likely presence. It often happens, however, that a unit might be referred to in only one or two sources, so that its participation is left in doubt. Fortunately, an understanding of the *ibutho* system helps resolve this problem. This system was based on the practice of bringing together men of the same age-group from every part of Zululand to form an *ibutho*, which then performed many important functions within Zulu society, including a military one. After an initial period of unbroken service, the members of an *ibutho* split up and returned home, but they continued to perform their annual service at the regional *amakhanda* which they shared with local members of other *amabutho*. In time of war, the scattered local elements of an *ibutho* would be mobilized at their district *amakhanda* and would then proceed to the king's 'great place', where they formed up as a unit, as did the other *amabutho*, preparatory to proceeding on campaign.[18] Not all elements of an *ibutho* were necessarily called up by the king to join the main army. They might be ordered to remain in the vicinity of their district *amakhanda*, where they would combine with the local elements of other *amabutho* to operate in their own part of the country, possibly in conjunction with the main army, if it entered their area.[19] Thus, certain *amabutho* would have been present in strength and be mentioned in all accounts of a battle, while small local contingents of others, though present, might easily be overlooked by a number of sources.

That no single *ibutho* was ever complete in any one battle would also explain why in the Anglo-Zulu War *amabutho* seem to have performed the impossible by fighting in different engagements the breadth of Zululand apart within the space of a few days. In fact, as a typical case would show, while the coastal elements of the iNgobamakhosi, uThulwana, uMcijo and uMbonambi (who had remained in their own locality) were engaged at Gingindlovu on 2 April, their main elements (who had been summoned to the king) fought at Khambula, 160 kilometres (100 miles) away on 29 March.[20] Failure to realize that *amabutho* could be split up in this way led the British – and many subsequent writers on the war – to misinterpret Zulu testimony by assuming that all the *amabutho* mentioned in connection with a battle were fully represented there.

It is consequently very difficult to estimate the strength of any *ibutho* involved in an engagement. Some idea of numbers may be gained from Fynney's list,[21] though if it is remembered that the figures that he gives for Zulu 'regiments' are only approximations, referring to complete units in peacetime, they can bear little relation to a unit's active strength on campaign, especially as its full complement was most unlikely to be present. With the confidence of ignorance, the British always managed to arrive at estimates of numbers of Zulu facing them; but these were normally calculated according to Fynney's unreliable figures, and tended in any case to be exaggerated in order that more glory might redound to British arms.[22] Unfortunately, Zulu computations of their own numbers are not of much greater value. They reckoned the strength of an army in 'companies' (*amaviyo*, singular – *iviyo*), no standard number of which made up an *ibutho*, and which could also vary in size between 50 and 200.[23] It would seem that the age of an *ibutho* and the degree of favour in which it was held by the king determined the number and size of its component *amaviyo*,[24] but this diversity only adds to the general uncertainty. Consequently, even if Zulu testimony were to agree on the number of *amaviyo* present at a battle (which it does not),[25] this would hardly assure arrival at an accurate figure for the Zulu forces there, especially as the large but uncertain number of irregulars and auxiliaries – who were present at most battles of the war[26] – would not have been taken into account. The Zulu, therefore, were themselves reduced to making broad estimates of numbers as unreliable as those hazarded by the British;[27] today we can take little more than an informed guess, discarding what are obviously inflated figures.

The battlefield dispositions of Zulu units pose particular problems, and in this area modern writers have done more violence to the fragmentary and unsatisfactory evidence than in any other. Historians have always been tempted to provide clear-cut battle maps in which they have delineated Zulu dispositions and movements as confidently as the considerably better documented ones of the British.[28] However, although sufficient information exists to identify tentatively the units involved, as well as the general shape of the battle at Nyezane, Rorke's Drift, Hlobane and Gingindlovu, lack of detailed evidence hampers any attempt at precision over Zulu dispositions. Fortunately, it is possible to be more exact with three other battles. Ulundi poses special difficulties, for that day many Zulu hung back as uncommitted reserves. Nevertheless, it is evident that elements of all *amabutho* were present, and enough Zulu testimony survives to allow us to plot the lines of attack of the more prominent ones. Khambula is perhaps the engagement on which there is the greatest agreement between the Zulu sources, so that their tactical intentions, dispositions and movements can be reconstructed with some accuracy. Yet Isandlwana, on which battle more testimony has survived than on any other, still remains full of obscurities. The very volume of conflicting and often vague statements makes it impossible to reach firm conclusions on the Zulu dispositions.[29] Sources are divided, for example on whether the uMbonambi or iNgobamakhosi fought on the extreme left wing, and it is now unrealistic to assert definitively which did, especially when a further number of considerations are borne in mind.

The *amabutho* which fought in the front line – and sometimes irregulars and auxiliaries did as well – were supported and reinforced by others as the army deployed in combat. As a result, an *ibutho* could quite accurately be reported to have been engaged in different parts of the field by witnesses whose testimony does not conflict, but merely reflects their limited awareness of a unit's further movements. Moreover, as an attack was pressed home, the *amabutho* generally lost all formation and became intermingled,[30] making positive identification of their positions very difficult. One general rule, however, helps guide us in reconstructing Zulu battle stations (though even then, this does not apply to the battle of Ulundi or to instances where, as at Hlobane and Ntombe, only irregulars were

The Zulu army deploying before the British laager at Gingindlovu, 2 April 1879.

engaged): the fleeter though less battle-hardened young *amabutho* formed the 'horns' which attempted to outflank and surround the enemy, while the slower veteran *amabutho* fought in the centre and bore the brunt of the battle.[31] The ages of these *amabutho* can be deduced with some certainty, for in her authoritative synthesis Professor Krige seems to have settled the year in which each *ibutho* was born and formed up.[32]

Zulu commanders are as difficult to identify accurately as the forces they led. Witnesses tended to mention only those officers with whom they were familiar, or who distinguished themselves in battle, but who were not necessarily one of the high command; an understandable lapse considering that the overall command of an army seems never to have been clearly defined. At Khambula, for example, Mnyamana kaNgqengelele was present as commander-in-chief and devised the general strategy in accordance with the king's instructions, yet direction of the battle would appear to have been in the hands of Ntshingwayo kaMahole, who in turn seems to have been disregarded at a critical moment by the commanders of the uMcijo and iNgobamakhosi *amabutho*.[33] Furthermore, these high-ranking officers and their staffs always stationed themselves at some remove from the field of battle and, when need arose, despatched subordinate officers to spur on the men,[34] personalities better remembered by the mass than many of the distant commanders. And ultimately, much of the testimony elicited from prisoners-of-war about their commanders is suspect, because the British became obsessed with a few familiar figures such as Dabulamanzi kaMpande, and were more concerned with establishing the presence of such *bêtes noires* than trying to ascertain the Zulu chain of command. Incomplete and unreliable evidence, therefore, and the loose nature of the Zulu system of command, make it impossible to establish much more than the identity of the major Zulu commanders (though not their order of precedence) and the names of some of their more prominent subordinates.

The number of casualties which the Zulu suffered in an engagement can likewise be only approximately computed. It is true that the Zulu thrice remained in possession of the field and were thus in a position to take stock of their dead. Nevertheless, no account survives of their losses at Ntombe or Hlobane, while at Isandlwana, though it is known that the Zulu were shocked at the extent of their losses, they disposed of the dead with all haste and attempted nothing more than a broad estimate of their casualties.[35] The British drove the Zulu from the field in all the other battles of the war and always made a close tally of the Zulu dead within a few hundred metres of their position. This they followed by a more cursory count of the bodies of those dispersed and cut down in the course of a rout that could extend over

10 kilometres (6 miles).[36] Consequently, even if they are more accurate than the Zulu figures, British estimates of Zulu losses are only rough-and-ready, especially as they cannot take into account the wounded, who, even if they regained their homes, apparently seldom survived.[36]

While it is generally possible, therefore, to grasp basic Zulu strategy from the available evidence to reconstruct the broad pattern of a battle as it concerned the Zulu, many of the finer points must remain unclear or unknown. Once the surviving evidence has been carefully weighed, no more than necessarily approximate or tentative conclusions can be reached on the details of units' names, strengths, dispositions, commanders or casualties. To pretend to anything more definitive would be to fall into the same error as have so many commentators on the Anglo-Zulu War over the past hundred years.

[Previously published in *Journal of Natal & Zulu History*, II, 1979.]

Notes

1. The British suffered a major disaster at Isandlwana (22 January), but repulsed the Zulu at Rorke's Drift on the night of 22 January and at the Nyezane River on the same day. In skirmishes at the Ntombe River (12 March) and on Hlobane Mountain (28 March) they experienced severe reverses. They routed the Zulu at Khambula Hill (29 March), Gingindlovu (2 April) and finally at Ulundi on 4 July.

2. Only a full-scale bibliography could do justice to the available material. However, the correspondence and reports in the *British Parliamentary Papers* of 1878–1882 should be noted, as should the Intelligence Branch of the War Office's *Narrative of Field Operations Connected with the Zulu War of 1879*, London, 1881. Unofficial published material can be found in newspapers of the period such as the *Natal Witness*, the *Natal Mercury*, the *Times of Natal* and the *Natal Advertizer*. Soldiers' letters are collected and reprinted in Frank Emery, *The Red Soldier*, London, 1977. A good example of a published memoir is Sir E. Wood's *From Midshipman to Field Marshal*, London, 1906, vol. 2, and of contemporary history Major Ashe's and Captain the Hon. E. V. Wyatt Edgell's *The Story of the Zulu Campaign*, London, 1880. Donald Morris, *The Washing of the Spears*, London, 1966, still remains the standard authority, while works such as D. Clammer's *The Zulu War*, London, 1973, are very derivative.

3. In a class of their own are the comments of Cornelius Vijn (Bishop Colenso, tr. and ed.) in *Cetshwayo's Dutchman*, London, 1880, pp. 29, 31, 35–40, 52–3. Vijn, a white trader detained in Zululand by Cetshwayo during the war, was the only white man in a position to hear firsthand general Zulu comment on the conduct of the war, and to witness Cetshwayo's reaction to the performance of his commanders.

4. Prominent among these were W. H. Longcast, interpreter to Lord Chelmsford; Captain J. Ruscombe Poole and R. C. A. Samuelson, custodian and interpreter respectively to Cetshwayo at the Cape; J. W. Shepstone, Acting Secretary of Native Affairs for Natal, and his brother Captain T. Shepstone; the Hon. W. Drummond; J. E. Fannin, Special Border Agent for Umvoti; and H. J. Fynn, Resident Magistrate of Umsinga.

5. Of the 45 printed Zulu statements examined (21 in the *British Parliamentary Papers*, and 24 in contemporary newspapers, books and journals), 13 deal exclusively with Isandlwana and another 12 cover it extensively along with an assortment of other engagements.

6. See, for example, *B.P.P.* (C.2454), enc. 1 in no. 34: Statement by Sihlahla to J. W. Shepstone, 3 June 1879. Sihlahla was a member of the uMxhapho *ibutho* and fought at Nyezane; nevertheless, he provided many explicit details on Isandlwana.

7. See, for example, *B.P.P.* (C.2318), enc. 3 in no. 7: Epitome of Statements of Four Zulus of Ohamu's Tribe, 17 March 1879.

8. Typical of such reports are *B.P.P.* (C.2374), enc. in no. 9: H. J. Fynn to Colonial Secretary, 5 February 1879. Information supplied to Mrilwa, Segt. Frontier Border Police; ibid.: J. E. Fannin to Colonial Secretary, 31 January 1879. Information from policeman from Umpisi River; ibid.: J. E. Fannin to Colonial Secretary, 20 January 1879. Information from Entumeni Mission.

9. Mehlokazulu kaSihayo, a commander at Isandlwana, for example, gave one of the most important accounts of that battle. See *Royal Engineers Journal*, 2 February 1880.

10. C. de B. Webb & J. B. Wright, (eds.) *A Zulu King Speaks*, Pietermaritzburg & Durban, 1978, pp. 31–4, 36–7, 58–9.

11. Bertram Mitford, *Through the Zulu Country*, London, 1883, pp. 89–95, 159–61, 220, 262–3, 277–9. In a special category is the information gathered by Magema (M. M. Fuze), who was sent into Zululand in October 1879 by Bishop Colenso for that purpose. His comments are to be found in Vijn, *Cetshwayo's Dutchman*, pp. 116–17, 126–7, 143.

12. See especially the Supplement to the *Natal Mercury*, 22 January 1929: Zulu War Commemoration: 50th Anniversary. Eight Zulu survivors are interviewed.

13. A good example of this process concerns Mehlokazulu's statement. It is to be found in the fullest form in the *Royal Engineers Journal*, and only slightly changed in C. L. Norris-Newman, *In Zululand with the British Throughout the War of 1879*, London, 1880, pp. 79–86. An incomplete version appears in the *Natal Witness*, 2 October 1879, and an epitome in F. E. Colenso, assisted by Lt.-Col. E. Durnford, *History of the Zulu War and its Origins*, London, 1880, pp. 413–14.

14. A.T. Bryant, *Olden Times in Zululand and Natal*, London, 1929, pp.644–5; F.G. Fynney, *The Zulu Army and Zulu Headmen*, 2nd edn., Pietermaritzburg, 1879, p.3.

15. Fynney, *Zulu Army*, Tables of Regiments, passim. Most writers on the war since the British have accepted these tables uncritically, though they should be employed cautiously and with reservation. The British also came adrift when they tried to identify Zulu units in battle by using Fynney's detailed descriptions of their ceremonial dress, because on campaign the Zulu laid aside most of their finery. Thanks to Fynney, the British entertained another fallacy which this time concerned the different shields carried by the various *amabutho*. In Shaka's time these were originally distinctive to each *ibutho* and acted as a means of identification; but by 1879 this 'regimental' uniformity was falling away, and it was impossible to differentiate *amabutho* on the basis of their shields.

16. Bryant, *Olden Times*, pp.645–64; R.C.A. Samuelson, *Long, Long Ago*, Durban, 1929, pp.235–7.

17. E.J. Krige, *The Social System of the Zulus*, 2nd edn., Pietermaritzburg, 1974, pp.404–7.

18. J.P.C. Laband & P.S. Thompson, *A Field Guide to the War in Zululand 1879*, Pietermaritzburg, 1979, pp.3–5.

19. Webb & Wright, *A Zulu King Speaks*, p33; *B.P.P.* (C.2454), enc. in no.33: Statement of Faenane, 12 May 1879.

20. Laband & Thompson, *Field Guide*, pp.29, 77.

21. Fynney, *Zulu Army*, Tables of Numbers in Regiments and Corps, passim.

22. For official British estimates of Zulu numbers, see War Office, *Narrative*, pp.48, 65, 71, 75, 117.

23. J. Stuart, *A History of the Zulu Rebellion, 1906*, London, 1913, pp.71–2; Norris-Newman, *In Zululand with the British*, p.254.

24. *JSA*, vol.I, p.214: Evidence of Johannes Kumalo.

25. Compare Mehlokazulu's figures in *Royal Engineers Journal* with Sihlahla's in *B.P.P.*, (C.2454), enc. 1 in no.34.

26. *JSA*, vol.1, p.63: Evidence of Bikwayo ka Noziwawa; D.C.F. Moodie, *The History of the Battles and Adventures of the British, the Boers and the Zulus in Southern Africa*, Adelaide, 1879, p.364: Longcast's interview with prisoners at Ulundi.

27. For an exaggerated Zulu estimation of numbers see *B.P.P.* (C.2269), enc. 6 in no.14: Statement of Ulankana, son of Undikile, 10 February 1879.

28. An especially flagrant example of this practice concerns the battle of Khambula, where Sir Evelyn Wood was British commander. His excellent map of the engagement in *Midshipman to Field Marshal*, vol.2, opp. p.68, was bungled by his printers, so that the correct Zulu dispositions were shown *reversed* in relation to the British position. Instead of going to the Zulu evidence, which would immediately have shown up this printer's error, subsequent historians of the calibre of Donald Morris and Frank Emery, for example, have (with so many others) slavishly followed this misleading map. See Morris, *Washing of the Spears*, pp.493–4, and Emery, *Red Soldier*, p.165 (Map 6).

29. Tentative conclusions concerning the Zulu side in the battles and major skirmishes of the war are to be found in Laband & Thompson, *Field Guide*, pp. 22–9, 40–5, 60–1, 66–7, 74–7.

30. The *Natal Mercury*, 22 January 1929, Zulu War Supplement: Corroborative evidence of Dubane Mzimana, Mhlahlama, and Malumbela Ungune.

31. Fynney, *Zulu Army*, p. 6; Stuart, *Zulu Rebellion*, p. 86; H. H. Parr, *A Sketch of the Kafir and Zulu Wars*, London, 1880, pp. 112–13, 201.

32. Krige, *Social System*, pp. 404–7.

33. Webb & Wright, *A Zulu King Speaks*, pp. 33–4; Vijn, *Cetshwayo's Dutchman*, pp. 35–9; *B.P.P.* (C. 2454), sub-enc. 1 of no. 32: Statement of Sibalo to J. W. Shepstone, 1 June 1879.

34. Fynney, *Zulu Army*, p. 6; Mitford, *Zulu Country*, pp. 91, 312–13.

35. Webb & Wright, *A Zulu King Speaks*, pp. 36–7; *B.P.P.* (C. 2318), sub-enc. 4 in enc. 2 in no. 10: J. E. Fannin to Colonial Secretary, 22 March 1879. Information from Klaas, alias Barnabas, a Christian.

36. For official British estimate of Zulu casualties, see War Office, *Narrative*, pp. 24, 49, 65, 81, 117.

37. *B.P.P.* (C. 2374), enc. in no. 9: Fannin to Colonial Secretary, 23 February 1879. Information from two Christians from Entumeni.

Humbugging the General?

King Cetshwayo's peace overtures during the Anglo-Zulu War

J.P.C. LABAND

'You are humbug, the talk of peace is nonsense, you know the king don't want peace'.[1] So declared John Dunn, once King Cetshwayo's white chief, now working for the British invaders of Zululand, when brushing aside the protestations of Sintwangu, the king's messenger. This attitude, so common in 1879 in the British camp, has been perpetuated by Gerald French, the biographer of Lord Chelmsford, the British commander in Zululand. He praised the general's 'forbearance' in the face of the king's 'irresolute and humbugging attitude' towards peace negotiations, which he cynically attributed to Cetshwayo's attempts 'to wriggle out of an awkward situation'; while the majority of the king's 'purported' messengers he dismissed as no more than 'spies'.[2]

In contrast, Bishop Colenso, the king's indefatigable apologist, steadfastly insisted on Cetshwayo's sincere attempts to negotiate a settlement with the invading British. In his *Digest of Zulu Affairs*, which painstakingly notes every one of the king's peace-feelers, Colenso calculated that six times before the invasion began, and eighteen times during its course, royal emissaries made their way to the British authorities. In addition, on three occasions Cetshwayo sent to the Bishop himself in order to enlist his aid in his attempt to negotiate. All these messengers, Colenso indignantly recorded,

> when not detained or put in irons, were either delayed by being sent from one post to another, or were sent back with mocking and impossible demands, or deluded in some way or other, by their civilized and Christian adversaries.[3]

The issue, then, is not whether Cetshwayo attempted to negotiate, nor even, after Colenso's painstaking research, how often, when and with whom.

Rather, it is to assess the sincerity of the king's efforts, and the degree to which they were related to the fortunes of war and the political situation within the Zulu kingdom. At the same time, it is necessary to comprehend the minimum British requirements for a negotiated peace, and the extent to which the relevant civil and military authorities were seriously prepared to entertain Zulu approaches. For if either one of the two sides were not genuine, then it would be a matter of discovering who was humbugging whom. Or were they humbugging each other?

It seems logical in such an enquiry first to establish the aggressor's demands. There is no longer any doubt that Britain initiated the war in the interests of the confederation of the white states of southern Africa under the crown. For Sir Bartle Frere, to whom, as High Commissioner, this task had been entrusted, the 'native question' was the crux of the region's interrelated problems, and it was around the Zulu kingdom that it was centred. Militarily the most potent black state in south-eastern Africa, it was perceived as posing a threat to the Colony of Natal, and the Cape was known to be reluctant to join a confederation that might embroil it in fresh wars. Moreover, the Transvaal, annexed in 1877, would remain unreconciled (so it was thought) until its festering border dispute with Zululand was decided in its favour. And to top these issues, Frere had come to the conclusion that the Zulu king was the 'head and moving spirit' of a 'native combination'[4] forming to throw off white domination in southern Africa. It seemed obvious, therefore, that the Zulu 'menace' must be eliminated. Yet it did not seem possible that this could be done without resorting to violence. For Frere was deeply convinced that the nature of the Zulu state as he understood it, and its 'military system' in particular, meant that it was incapable of remaining within its own borders and living at peace with its neighbours. It would persist as a danger and a stumbling block to confederation until the 'military system' was dismantled and the king's power broken.[5] Yet Frere did not envisage absorbing a defeated Zululand. Rather, he favoured a system of indirect rule by compliant chiefs under a British agent on the Indian model.[6]

The ultimatum which was presented on 11 December 1878 to the Zulu envoys naturally reflected these concerns and objectives. While four demands concerned compensation for minor border incidents, the remaining six were aimed at taming Zulu military power and independence. The most significant of these insisted on the dismantling of the military system, thus subverting the social, economic and political structure of the Zulu kingdom; while another required the stationing of a British Resident in Zululand, which would have meant the effective end of Zulu independence.[7] Of course, if the Zulu king were tamely to accept these conditions, then Frere's objectives would have been achieved. But the king was not expected to give up his sovereignty without a fight, and Chelmsford was under orders, once the period of grace stipulated in the ultimatum had expired, to 'take the matter in hand' and ensure Cetshwayo's compliance through force of arms.[8]

Frere was of opinion that when, as seemed inevitable, it came to war, there would remain little room for 'pacific negotiations', at least not until Cetshwayo had 'proved the strength of his young Regiments.'[9] In other words, Zulu military defeat was to be the precondition to any useful negotiations whose basis would remain the conditions set out in the ultimatum. Until then, any Zulu peace-feelers were to be regarded with suspicion, and any emissaries to be treated with the greatest caution as potential spies. Consequently, it was taken as aximiomatic that they were not to be admitted into the camps or fortifications of the military.[10] Thus the British marched into Zululand fundamentally determined not to treat with the Zulu king until he capitulated unconditionally.

If British objectives were clear enough to their leadership at least, then the Zulu were at a considerable loss to explain just what it was that the invaders of their country required. In September 1878, conscious of the military preparations along his borders, Cetshwayo sent to Sir Henry Bulwer, Lieutenant-Governor of Natal, challenging him to 'tell him plainly what wrong he has done to the English.'[11] During November the king's protestations, carried by his messengers into Natal, grew in proportion to the extent of the military build-up:

> . . . the King wishes to sit down, rest and be peaceful;[12]

> What have I done to the Great White Chief? I hear from all parts that soldiers are around me;[13]

> Cetywayo hereby swears, in presence of . . . all his Chiefs, that he has no intention or wish to quarrel with the English.[14]

The delivery of the ultimatum on 11 December was consequently something of a relief, for at last the king was given an inkling of what is was that the British wanted of him. The sense of that document of some 4 000 words was conveyed to him verbally by his emissaries, not an unusual feat among a people whose memories were suitably trained to do so.[15] Nevertheless, the British demands were sufficiently obscure, or astonishing, for the king to have to send six separate embassies to the British between the delivery of the ultimatum and the eventual invasion on 11 January 1879,[16] both to require clarification of the terms and to beg time to collect the cattle demanded in reparation for the border incidents. Furthermore, he needed space to put the matter before his council and gain their consent to his decisions.[17]

The British refused to take these messages seriously. Reports from Christian refugees convinced them that the Zulu army would 'stand by their king, and fight for the old institutions of their country';[18] while even Bishop Colenso's agent heard that Cetshwayo had no intention of complying with the British demands, and that he was saying 'there is now nothing for it but war.'[19] Thus the king's message of 11 January 1879 entreating more time for his councillors to consider the terms[20] Frere dismissed as a ruse,[21] for as his biographer explained, it was felt Cetshwayo was only temporizing in an attempt to defer hostilities for a few months until the harvest was safely in.[22] There was most likely some foundation to this suspicion, which also contributed to the dubious treatment of the king's emissaries on that occasion. Bishop Colenso charged that they were sent as prisoners to Stanger (doubtless because of the military suspicion that they were spies),[23] though the official version was that they had been 'located' there as they had refused to return to Zululand on account of the imminent hostilities.[24] In any event, their mission which had been to the forces stationed along the lower Thukela provoked a strict order from Chelmsford on 17 January laying down that any future emissaries must communicate only with him, and no other commander. Even more significantly for future Zulu overtures, he stressed that none would even be considered which was not 'preceded by . . . the unconditional acceptance of all demands (in the ultimatum) as before notified.'[25] Chelmsford was doing no more than affirm his and Frere's earlier opinions in this matter, but by issuing this general order he was making it a matter of policy, and slamming the door on any compromise settlement which the Zulu king might attempt to negotiate.

At the same time, the British were aware of existing rivalries and tensions among the élite of the Zulu kingdom, and knew that some of the king's leading councillors and chiefs were opposed to the war and hoped for accommodation with the British. They put such knowledge to good use, and from the very outset attempted to detach likely chiefs and their adherents from their loyalty to the king by appealing to their ambition or fear of British occupation.[26] Thus, by using every blandishment to win over the chiefs along their line of advance, and so creating a pool of collaborators from whom to select suitably compliant chieflings through whom Zululand was to be ruled, the British clearly hoped to isolate the king and his supporters, whose unconditional surrender and destruction were alone acceptable.

King Cetshwayo was long in grasping this hard truth. Despite all the rebuffs he had already suffered, he persisted in attempting to open negotiations with the invaders – indeed, right until the very end, when he was a fugitive in the Ngome forest.

The first phase in this essentially futile endeavour occurred before the fateful battle of Isandlwana on 22 January. Cetshwayo would seem to have instructed the commander of the main Zulu army, Chief Ntshingwayo kaMahole, not to move straight into the attack against the invading British Centre Column, but first to send a delegation of chiefs with an offering of 400 cattle to have 'a palaver'. The king subsequently claimed that the officers of the army were still engaged in deciding which among them should go on this mission, when a chance encounter with the British unintentionally triggered the battle.[27]

Though it cannot be certain that the king did indeed instruct Ntshingwayo as he said, there is no doubt that Isandlwana changed the whole nature of the war. Unlikely as it had been, a negotiated settlement was now quite impossible. Frere's plans for a quick successful war might lie in ruins, and his reputation with them, but it was now absolutely essential for the very presence of the British in southern Africa that the might of British arms be speedily vindicated. And to achieve this, nothing less than complete victory in the field was acceptable, and with it the overthrow of the existing Zulu state. No amount of talking on the Zulu part would ever shake the British resolve.

Yet this was not at all immediately clear to the Zulu. They had brought the British invasion to a halt, and it was the king's declared policy to use such an opportunity to menace the frontiers of Natal and so bring the British to the conference table. He knew, moreover, that he would have to move before the British were able to bring up reinforcements. Yet his plan was frustrated because his army, disheartened by heavy casualties, and obedient to post-combat purification rituals, had refused to stay in the field.[28] Unable, therefore, to exploit the temporary initiative he had gained, he nevertheless decided to use the opportunity to reopen negotiations.

There were other considerations, too, besides these. By early March the king was apparently in a state of alarm concerning the continuing loyalty of some of his more important chiefs. His brother Hamu kaNzibe, who long had entertained designs on the crown, and who had been in communication with the British since November 1878, finally had defected and, after various vicissitudes, was to reach the British lines on 10 March, there to await the defeat of his brother and his reward at British hands. This betrayal was seen by many Zulu as prefiguring the breakup of the kingdom, especially as there had already been other minor defections.[29]

It was to this background, therefore, that on 1 March two messengers crossed the Thukela at Middle Drift and made their way to Bishop Hans Schreuder's mission nearby at kwaNtunjambili. Despite having withdrawn from Zululand in 1877, Schreuder had maintained his longstanding friendship with Cetshwayo,[30] and it seems that this is why he had been singled out as the recipient of the king's message.[31] In substance, the king begged the British through his messengers to withdraw their forces from Zululand (Colonel Pearson was blockaded at Eshowe and Colonel Wood was mounting raids from his camp at Khambula) and to resume talks on a peaceful settlement. Once more, he used the opportunity to declare that he did not 'clearly understand' the demands of the British government, but professed himself willing to give his attention to any proposals.[32]

The British response to the feeler was both harsh and cynical. Frere, his resolve hardened by the promptings of J.E. Fannin, the Border Agent along the middle Thukela, showed himself as unprepared as ever to accept anything less than the king's unconditional surrender and the general disarmament of the Zulu people. Nor was he ready even to consider any message from the king that did not come 'in a form to bind him'.[33] It is Fannin, though, in his diary, who reveals what also lay behind Frere's curt and uncompromising response. The British, it is quite clear, welcomed the Zulu initiative, but not because it brought with it a hope of peace. Rather, they planned to take advantage of renewed negotiations to keep Zulu 'attention occupied', and by spinning out the process so give time for sufficient reinforcements to build up preparatory to a renewed offensive.[34]

Chelmsford's reaction was most straightforward. He stood convinced that no message from the king was anything but humbug, and that he would be 'doing the most foolish thing to accept this Zulu's protestations.'[35] 'I hope', he wrote to Wood, 'to be able to give him his answer next week by sending a column forward to Eshowe.'[36] As for the messengers, they were sent back with 'long faces' across the Thukela to tell the king of Frere's conditions.[37] Cetshwayo, it seems was to be duped.

Negotiations continued. One the evening of 21 March two further messengers contacted the Border Police at Middle Drift, and the following day delivered their message to Bishop Schreuder and Fannin. The Principal messenger was Klaas, alias Barnabas, a Christian convert, who had left the king's presence some week before. It had been his intention that he arrive at the same time as the first set of messengers, but he had been delayed by illness – or so he claimed. His mission was of a historic nature. He bore with him the book, 'beautifully bound in red morocco and gilt',[38] of the 'Coronation Laws' promulgated by Theophilus Shepstone at the time of the king's coronation in 1873, and later presented to him by Bishop Schreuder.[39] The king rhetorically demanded to know in what ways he had 'transgressed its provisions'. Fannin was not impressed. He handed back the book with the cold reply that the government ultimatum explained everything, and sent the messengers back.[40]

Fannin felt justified in his curt rejoinder by additional information he had gained from the messengers. Ten days previously, he was told, the king had summoned a meeting of his council to discuss the 'best mode of prosecuting the war.'[41] Doubtless Chelmsford's obvious preparations for a renewed attack had forced such a development, and the king had no choice but to be prepared for it. Yet if the British were stringing the Zulu along over negotiations, it seemed equally clear to the British that the Zulu were doing the same to them. This conviction only strengthened their existing suspicion that all Zulu messengers were no more than spies. Thus when on 23 March two messengers from the king attempted to approach the beleaguered entrenchment at Eshowe under the cover of a white flag, they were treated as such. The messengers' offer of a free passage to the Thukela if the garrison went peacefully was treated as a transparent ruse, and despite the traditional sanctity the Zulu messengers expected to enjoy, they were unceremoniously clapped into irons.[42]

By this stage the war was in any case regaining momentum after the lull produced by the British need to regroup. At the same time as Chelmsford's column was advancing up the coast to the relief of Eshowe, the king and his council determined to throw their main army against Wood at Khambula. Yet the king chose this very moment to despatch fresh messengers to the middle border. It seems the consistently uncompromising British response to his approaches had failed to daunt him, or perhaps he was simply keeping his options open. Yet the simultaneous despatch of armies and emissaries could only reinforce the British conviction that all messengers must be spies.[43]

On the very day of the battle of Hlobane (28 March), three messengers approached the ferry at Middle Drift. They were fired upon, but under an improvised white flag they were allowed to cross and were sent under guard to Fort Cherry. There they spent the night with their hands tied painfully behind their backs, before being interviewed by Fannin the next day.[44] The messengers handled as spies and subjected to such indignity were Johannes, a Christian convert, and Mfunzi and Nkisimana. The first was from Schreuder's eNtumeni Mission, while the latter two were of advanced age, respectable and thoroughly well-known messengers of Cetshwayo, who over the preceding six years had repeatedly been sent on important missions to the Natal government.[45] Their message was dignified. Cetshwayo wished them to declare yet again that he saw 'no reason for the war waged against him', and asked the government 'to appoint a place at which a conference could be held with a view to the conclusion of peace.'[46]

While Fannin was passing on what he clearly considered this spurious message to the military authorities for their consideration, the outcome of the war was decided. On 29 March Wood broke the main Zulu army at Khambula, and on 2 April Chelmsford brushed aside the Zulu forces at Gingindlovu and relieved Eshowe. The war had entered a new and final phase with the initiative now firmly in the hands of the British. Yet there was another lull while they prepared for the final blow, for which Chelmsford and Wood were to advance on oNdini from the north-west, and General Crealock from along the coast.

Meanwhile, what was to be done with the latest messengers, languishing now in Fort Buckingham? Fannin supposed that as likely spies they should be detained at least until the relief of Eshowe.[47] Chelmsford agreed, and at the same time reiterated his strict condition of 17 January concerning any future negotiations with Zulu emissaries: all communications from the Zulu king would have to be sent directly to him at his headquarters camp, wherever it might be.[48] Sir Henry Bulwer rightly feared that this order would cause unnecessary 'difficulties and delays' and hamper the cessation of hostilities he desired.[49] But Chelmsford's insistence that he alone should communicate with Cetshwayo reflected not only his determination that the

Zulu envoys with nose bags over their heads to prevent them 'spying'.

king must accede in full to the onerous British terms, but was also part of his campaign to keep anything pertaining to the conduct of the war out of Bulwer's civilian hands.[50]

Accordingly, on 15 April the Hon. W. Drummond of Chelmsford's Headquarters Staff appeared at Fort Buckingham to inform the incarcerated Mfunzi and Nkisimana that if they wished to make any peace proposals they must do so at Wood's camp in Zululand, whither Chelmsford was moving.[51] However, on account of a degree of confusion over who had the authority actually to give them permission to proceed (or perhaps it was part of a ploy deliberately to delay them), the two messengers remained where they were until an enquiry prompted by Bishop Colenso resulted in their leaving for Zululand on 9 May.[52] Yet their vicissitudes were not over. On 12 June they appeared under flag of truce in Pietermaritzburg, sent on by H.F. Fynn, the Resident Magistrate at Rorke's Drift. It would appear from their conversation with General Clifford in the capital that after leaving Fort Buckingham they had gone not to Chelmsford, but to consult with the king and his councillors, who had essentially confirmed their previous message, and had sent them back with an injunction to hurry. But the messengers were old and the rains heavy, and Chelmsford's precise whereabouts unknown to them. This is why they had fetched up at Rorke's Drift. Yet Clifford had not much better an idea than Fynn of the General's precise whereabouts, and sent the exhausted messengers off in the direction of Babanango.[53] Before they could locate him, they and the message they bore were quite outstripped by events.

In any case, in the course of their interrogation by Clifford, the messengers had let slip an observation which pinpointed the fundamental limitation of all Zulu peace initiatives thus far: they admitted they had no authority to talk about the actual terms of peace, only the king's desire to negotiate. This was in accordance with Zulu custom. Messengers were only sent out to make arrangements for a meeting of chiefs who alone had the power to discuss terms.[54] Yet as early as March Frere had made it clear that he was not prepared to consider any message that did not bind the king to the British terms.[55] With the king attempting to set the scene for negotiations, and the British insisting on total surrender in accordance with the demands of their ultimatum, the situation had plainly reached an impasse.

Moreover, the British were wedded to the concept of victory in the field. On 4 April Frere directed that 'no overtures of any kind must be allowed to delay military operations', at least until 'complete military command' of Zululand was secured. Then they could dictate any terms they wished. In this same minute Frere also gave attention to a complementary policy, pursued by the British since the beginning of the war, when he authorized that 'overtures for peace' would be acceptable from any other chief but the king.[56] For as the war turned decisively against the king, so the opportunity increased to detach his chiefs from his cause. This strategy gelled in the post-Khambula period. Every-increasing numbers of chiefs submitted to the advancing British on easy terms and accepted their suzerainty, abandoning the king whose power the British were determined to crush utterly.

Indeed, it was clear from early May that allegiance to the king was beginning to waver seriously, and it was reported that the king had sent again for his principal chiefs. They had strongly urged him to make every effort to negotiate peace, and to this he had consented.[57]

The consequence of the king's new peace initiative was that General Crealock, advancing laboriously up the coast, was soon complaining that he was 'in a state of chronic messengers from the King and his indunas.'[58] Not that he did any more than direct them to Chelmsford via Wood,[59] as insisted upon by Frere.[60]

Chief Ndwandwe, the first of this series of messengers, came into Fort Chelmsford on 15 May with Cetshwayo's plaintive message: 'What have I done? I want peace – I ask for peace.'[61] Chelmsford responded to word of this message by evolving additional terms for surrender over and above those contained in the ultimatum. All captured weapons and prisoners were to be surrendered, 10 000 stands of firearms should be handed over, as well as at least 10 000 cattle or 20 000 sheep.[62] Crushing and impossible terms surely designed to elicit resistance until the desired ultimate Zulu military disaster. Frere capped this with his harsh directive to Chelmsford that the king's messengers were to be told that unless acts were substituted for 'idle words' and the Zulu made genuine efforts to comply with the terms, their land would be devastated.[63]

On 27 May Crealock learned that the king was sending him further messengers,[64] and that he had ordered that whites were not to be fired upon during the period of negotiations.[65] There could no longer be any doubt that the king was under pressure to treat, and that he was in earnest. But could he possibly accept the inflexible British terms?

The messenger who arrived on 28 May[66] was Sintwangu, and *inceku* (or high official in the king's household), a well-known emissary who had attended the ultimatum ceremony as the king's eyes and ears.[67] In conversation with John Dunn on 31 May he reiterated Ndwandwe's message, and begged Dunn to use his influence to achieve peace. It was also clear from what Sintwangu said that he feared the king's influence was 'passing away'.[68] Patently, the time was at hand for the British to press submissions from the local chiefs. As for Sintwangu, he was sent off like the other messengers to negotiate directly with Chelmsford, if he could find him.[69] This was the fate of Ndwandwe, who appeared again on 7 June with another relay of messengers,[70] purveying what Crealock called his 'peaceful lies from the king.'[71] Simultaneously, the British were pursuing the local option with determination, and all the major coastal chiefs were in the process of suing for terms. This reality made a mockery of the efforts of the king's messengers, and even before the battle of Ulundi was fought the entire coastal region would have abandoned the royal cause and come to terms with the invaders.[72]

It was against this background of widespread betrayal in the eastern reaches of his kingdom, and Chelmsford's reiterated conviction that there could be no permanent peace until the king were deposed,[73] that Cetshwayo attempted to negotiate with the Second Division which was advancing on oNdini with considerably more expedition that the sluggish coastal column.

Three messengers, Mgcwelo, Mtshibela and Mphokothwayo, reached Wood's camp at the Nondwini River on 4 June. They had left the king at his kwaMayizekanye homestead on 30 May and had first, mistakenly, made for Khambula. It would seem that they had set out at the same time as Sintwangu had been despatched to Crealock, and Mfunzi and Nkisimana to Rorke's Drift. The three messengers carried a message which Cetshwayo had personally given them before his chief councillors.[74] Genuine emissaries though they might be, they made a bad impression on the British, who found them 'villainous-looking scoundrels'.[75] In turn, they were so strongly impressed at the spectacle of British armed might that they assured Drummond in their preparatory interview that they would 'strongly recommend' on their return that the king come to terms. They also let it be known that Cetshwayo was finally of intention to send his chief minister, Mnyamana, and other 'officers of state' to treat,[76] as Frere had always insisted they should.

However, in their formal interview on 5 June with Chelmsford, the General laid down conditions which were a refinement of those additional ones evolved in May, and which Bishop Colenso could only categorize as 'preposterous'.[77] Firstly, Chelmsford made it plain that on grounds of developments along the coast he no longer believed that the king was being obeyed, and that unless he could provide proof of his authority and desire for peace, the General would rather continue negotiating with his chiefs. Therefore, Chelmsford warned that he would continue his advance unless, in earnest of his power and genuine intentions, the king sent in the oxen at his royal homestead, and the two seven-pounder guns captured at Isandlwana, as well as promising that all the other firearms in Zululand would be collected and given up. In addition, an age-grade regiment, to be named by Chelmsford, must come into the British lines and lay down its arms. Then, and only then, would Chelmsford even entertain peace discussions, to be conducted, naturally, in terms of the demands of the ultimatum.[78]

Their mission thereby rendered absolutely futile, the disconsolate messengers left the British camp on 6 June,[79] bearing with them Chelmsford's written statement of his impossible terms. This punctilious sop to correct diplomatic form (for who in the Zulu camp would be able to read his words?) does not disguise Chelmsford's transparent cynicism. The king had already made it plain that although willing to negotiate, he could not accede to the demands of the ultimatum. How then could he accede to these outrageous preliminary conditions? How could Chelmsford expect him to? Clearly he did not. His conditions (in writing too!) were for the record. His intentions were to fight and win his battle and destroy the king whose warriors had ruined his reputation at Isandlwana. It was he who was humbugging Cetshwayo. It made not a jot of difference that there were reports of the king calling on his people to send him cattle to help buy off the British and make peace;[80] nor that he did not intend the British should be attacked unless they resumed their advance on oNdini.[81] By way of contrast, Chelmsford's instructions of 16 June laid down that chiefs, on submitting to designated authorities, be only required to give up their arms and the royal cattle in their keeping. In return, their people were to be spared and protected.[82] Only the king could expect no mercy, unless he totally surrendered his sovereignty.

Though being pushed into a situation where he must fight to the last, Cetshwayo nevertheless attempted even more urgently than before to negotiate, spurred on doubtless in these desperate endeavours by the realization that the invader could never be stopped by force of arms. Two new messengers, Ntanjana and Sibungu arrived at Fort Pearson on the lower Thukela on 25 June, begging that the British stay their advance until negotiations could take place. For if they continued to march on oNdini the king, they explained, 'cannot help fighting, as there will be nothing left but to try and push aside a tree that is falling upon him.'[83] Disregarded, the messengers left on 29 June.[84]

Sintwangu appeared on a new mission the following day, when he came into Crealock's camp at Fort Napoleon on the Mlalazi River bearing an enormous elephant tusk – the symbol of peace and friendship – in earnest of the authenticity of his mission.[85] He made the unfortunate impression messengers seemed now automatically to create in the minds of the prejudiced British, one of whom described him as manifesting 'a curious mixture of dogged determination, savage cunning and treachery.'[86] His interview with Crealock did not last twenty minutes, and when directed to address himself rather to Chelmsford, he took the rebuff as if he had expected it,[86] as well he might have.

Chelmsford's written conditions, meanwhile, which the two messengers had taken off on 6 June, still required an answer. It had been the General's condition that this be returned within eight days. Yet as Gibson reminds us, even in this emergency Zulu dignity did not 'permit of hurry'.[88] And, as the king could not read the message when it arrived, it was necessary to bring Cornelius Vijn, a trader whom the war had detained in Zululand, to the king to do so for him. Vijn was living at a distance, so it was not until about 17 June that he had arrived at the kwaMbonambi homestead, translated the note, and penned Cetshwayo's response.[89] Doubtless affronted by Chelmsford's impossible demands Cetshwayo, despite his perilous situation, dictated a proud and dignified reply, deprecating negotiations while the British army was advancing and plundering as it went.[90] Yet this letter never reached Chelmsford. The four messengers to whom it was entrusted were denied entry when they arrived before Fort Marshall on 22 June and fearing they should be shot, returned with the note undelivered.[91]

Vijn consequently wrote again. The three messengers, Mgcwelo, Mtshibela and Mphokothwayo (who had carried Chelmsford's written terms to Cetshwayo) were sent with Vijn's letter in a cleft stick,[92] carrying two great tusks of ivory and driving a herd of 150 of the cattle captured at Isandlwana. They were intercepted by a British patrol and on 27 June were brought into Chelmsford's camp on the Mthonjaneni heights overlooking oNdini and the Mahlabathini plain.[93] The tone of this second letter was much more placatory than that of the undelivered one, and probably reflected Cetshwayo's cooler second thoughts. It did not come to grips with Chelmsford's conditions. Consequently, the General declared that he would continue his advance, and so would not accept the symbolic tusks. However, in order to give the king a last chance to comply, he undertook not to cross the White Mfolozi to oNdini immediately and condescended to keep the cattle as a sign that he was still willing to have peace, if only entirely on his terms.[94]

With this the messengers had to be content, and left the next day telling the interpreter as they went that they 'would have to fight now' as it was impossible for the king to comply with Chelmsford's terms.[95] And indeed, Chelmsford remained prepared to 'stop hostilities' only on condition that his conditions were complied with in full.[96] For although he credited Cetshwayo and his councillors with a genuine desire to end the war — their desperate situation demanded nothing less — he was sure that it was still only on their terms, and not on his.[97]

Then, at midday on 30 June, the by now extraordinarily well-travelled and footsore Mfunzi and Nkisimana finally ran their quarry to ground. They carried yet a third letter penned by Vijn, as well as the sword of the ill-fated Prince Imperial in earnest of their mission, and promised the speedy arrival of the two captured seven-pounders and more cattle.[98] Yet unbeknown to them Vijn had done the king an evil turn, for the letter carried a postscript in which the trader informed Chelmsford that it was his opinion that the king and people, if not the princes and chiefs, really intended to fight.[99] Not unlikely either, considering that the British were showing themselves eager to treat leniently with the chiefs, while the king saw he had no hope left but through battle.

Chelmsford responded to this latest embassy by modifying his earlier terms somewhat. He was now prepared to accept a thousand rifles captured at Isandlwana in lieu of the surrender of an age-grade regiment. Furthermore, he announced that Cetshwayo had until noon on 3 July to comply with his conditions, and that his troops would remain on his side of the White Mfolozi up to that moment.[100] Lest we should be tempted to applaud what Major French would have as Chelmsford's magnanimity and readiness to avoid further bloodshed,[101] we should note two things. Chelmsford's small concession in his demands of the Zulu king was only a gesture calculated to appeal to the British sense of fair play, for it made no difference to Cetshwayo. More significantly, we should take note of Major C.W. Robinson's comment: 'Cetywayo was given time because we could not well make our preparations complete till the 4th [July].'[102] It was Chelmsford who intended well and truly to humbug Cetshwayo, and to prepare for the battle necessary to salve his reputation.

Yet as it turned out, Chelmsford's disingenuous new offer never reached Cetshwayo. On Mfunzi's testimony it seems that the chiefs were 'hopeless and desperate' and had no desire to prolong negotiations which were patently pointless. They would not allow him access to the king, and falsely informed him that Vijn had gone and that Chelmsford's letter could therefore not be translated. Nor were they prepared to take any heed of Mfunzi's oral version of its contents.[103] It seems that for the Zulu, too, battle was the only remaining possibility. The king did make one last effort to treat, and was again thwarted by his people. Chelmsford's force had moved down from Mthonjaneni, and by 1 July was encamped on the White Mfolozi. The next day a herd of at least 100 of the king's own special white oxen were seen being driven as a peace offering towards the British camp. But the young men of the uMcijo age-regiment turned them back, insisting they would fight rather than give up the cattle.[104] Events were now completely out of the king's hands. Having received no answer to his ultimatum, Chelmsford advanced across the river on 4 July and routed the Zulu army. Cetshwayo did not wait to witness the debacle, but struck off for the north to seek refuge.[105]

With the dispersal of his army and his own flight, the king found himself in an entirely new situation. Only a few shreds of authority still clung to him, while his chiefs were necessarily concerned with how best to come to terms with the British in such a way as to preserve at least their own local power and influence. The lenient policy which the British had adopted so far towards the chiefs showed them the way, and turned any lingering loyalty to the king's cause into an embarrassment. While the king was still at large it remained difficult for the chiefs to tender their final submission to the British and become part of their new dispensation for Zululand. Thus for Sir Garnet Wolseley, who had superseded Chelmsford, it was essential that the king be captured,[106] and that the chiefs should know where they stood. The second was the easier to achieve, and on 26 July he made known that the chiefs must surrender their arms and royal cattle, that the monarchy and military system were abolished, and that the names of the new independent chiefs would soon be announced.[107] Such favourable terms rapidly convinced more and more chiefs to comply,[108] and stripped the king of any remaining influence, so that his messages exhorting them to stand firm were largely ignored.[109]

What was left for the king to do? The British had achieved their objectives: Zulu military capability was destroyed and the royal power irrevocably shattered. If Cetshwayo were to continue his negotiations with the conquerors it could only be to ensure his personal safety and future liberty. For even these were no longer to be taken for granted. Had not Wolseley written to his wife that he 'should be quite happy if some kind friend would but run an Assegai through him [Cetshwayo]'?[110]

Wolseley noted on 20 July that reports were coming in indicating that the king saw his position as hopeless and was prepared to accept any terms which might be offered.[111] A suppliant royal messenger duly approached Colonel Clarke at kwaMagwaza on 26 July. Clarke replied that the king's life would be spared if he surrendered, and directed the envoy to Wolseley.[112] A spate of similar messages and replies were rapidly exchanged,[113] until on 7 August Wolseley interviewed an important delegation sent on by Colonel Clarke. It was led by the important chief Mavumengwana kaNdlela Ntuli.[114] He had with him yet another letter from the king taken down by Vijn, in which Cetshwayo pathetically declared that he was still collecting cattle which he would send in with his chief minister Mnyamana (in whose homestead he had taken refuge), and that he would follow in their wake. Meanwhile, 'the English should take pity on him and leave him the country of his fathers.'[115] But they had determined on his exile, and Wolseley demanded his immediate surrender.

Mavumengwana and his returning delegation fell in with Mnyamana and the cattle and decided to go back with them to Wolseley instead of reporting to the king. Cetshwayo, meanwhile, hearing that British patrols were out seeking him, took fright and fled from Mnyamana's ekuShumayeleni homestead to the fastnesses of the Ngome forest.[116] He was now being abandoned by all. Vijn, who had come into camp on 10 August with a last message from the king begging to be allowed to stay in Zululand, agreed, on the promise of a reward, to persuade Cetshwayo to surrender. But he could not overcome the king's dread of being sent into exile, and returned empty-handed to Wolseley on 13 August, while the king pushed on further into the forest.[117]

On 14 August, driving 617 cattle before them, which had been collected on the king's orders, Mnyamana, Chief Ntshingwayo kaMahole, two of Cetshwayo's brothers, and 150 other chiefs of varying degrees of importance presented themselves at Wolseley's camp.[118] The offering of royal cattle indicated that Mnyamana's intention was not to submit personally, but to sue for terms on the king's behalf.[119] At last, as the British had so long insisted, a major chief was to negotiate directly for the king. Negotiate, or simply beg? Ntshingwayo later told Magema Fuze:

> We had been sent by the king; we had not run away to the Whites. We had gone simply to ask for his head, that he might live and not perish.[120]

Yet, when obviously assured that the British would not execute Cetshwayo, their duty was done; and their thoughts turned to their own futures. They rapidly declared they had themselves come to surrender.[121] Wolseley detained them in his camp and sent out further patrols to apprehend Cetshwayo, aided by information from the chiefs who wanted to see an end to the king's hopeless plight.[122] He was captured on 28 August, and the chiefs were freed to accept the terms of Wolseley's settlement on 1 September.

When King Cetshwayo was brought a prisoner into Wolseley's camp near the burned oNdini royal homestead, he begged John Shepstone, who interrogated him, to be allowed to remain in Zululand, even if no longer as king. Shepstone told him that there was no possibility, and that he was to leave the country. On hearing these words the defeated king abandoned all hope, and 'the tears ran down his cheeks.'[123] Never once had his words swayed the adamantine British from their purpose. This, perhaps, was the truth behind the course of the king's overtures to the British throughout the war. Essentially, British terms were not negotiable. They always made that very clear, and in that sense they were not guilty of humbugging Cetshwayo. Yet Chelmsford was not above using negotiations on occasion to string the Zulu king along in the interests of his military preparations. In that sense there was an element of duplicity in the General's relations with Cetshwayo. It seems too that there was a disingenuousness in his framing preconditions for full negotiations that were patently beyond the king's power to fulfil.

If the British record is not absolutely clear of a degree of deliberate humbug, what about Cetshwayo's? For one thing, he did not apparently exhibit the consistency of the British, though this can be attributed to his role of victim, parrying the 'falling tree' of the British invasion. Thus his overtures ran the gamut from half-hearted fencing, to an attempt to impose a settlement from a position of some strength, to increasingly desperate efforts to stem the British advance as his chiefs abandoned him, to the final, broken pleas for clemency. There is a form of logic in this progression that underpins his sincerity. The real problem was that he wished for peace on terms acceptable to him and his councillors, and was never willing seriously to consider those of the British. In a sense, therefore, his overtures consistently bypassed the issue and thus antagonized the British. An additional problem was that in terms of Zulu custom the king's messengers were merely despatched in order to set up a meeting of the leaders, and did not have plenipotentiary powers of their own. This too frustrated the British. All contributed to a general sense of their being deliberately humbugged by the king.

While not denying that there was most likely an element of humbug in the king's diplomacy (as there was in the British), it seems that the real difficulty was not so much that the two sides were humbugging each other, as that they were passing one another by. Lack of mutual comprehension was, as it so often is, the root of the problem.

[Previously published in *Theoria*, 67, October 1986.]

Notes

1. WO 32/7747: Summary of the conversation between John Dunn and the King's messenger, Usitwangu, at Fort Chelmsford, 31 May 1979.

2. Major the Hon. G. French, *Lord Chelmsford and the Zulu War*, London, 1939, pp. 246, 251, 253.

3. Bishop J. W. Colenso and H. E. Colenso, *Digest of Zulu Affairs Compiled by Bishop Colenso and Continued after his Death by his Daughter, Harriette Emily Colenso*, Bishopstowe, 1878–1888, series no. 1, part 2, p. 605.

4. *B. P. P.* (C. 2222), no. 45: Frere to Sir Michael Hicks Beach, 10 December 1878.

5. Ibid., no. 6: Frere to Hicks Beach, 5 November 1878. See also CO 879/14, *African Confidential Print*, no. 164: Memorandum on the Zulu Question, compiled by Edward Fairfield, 19 March 1879.

6. G. A. Dominy, 'Routine of Empire. The Use of Force to Maintain Authority and Impose Peace as a Principle of Imperial Administration: the Cases of Waikato in 1863 and Zululand in 1879' (unpublished M.A. thesis, University College of Cork, 1983), p. 116.

7. SNA 1/6/3, n.n.: Original draft of the ultimatum, signed by Sir Henry Bulwer, 4 December 1878.

8. TS 35, n.n.: Chelmsford to Theophilus Shepstone, 13 December 1878; and Frere to Theophilus Shepstone, 19 December 1878.

9. TS 35, n.n.: Frere to Theophilus Shepstone, 4 December 1878.

10. TS 35, n.n.: Chelmsford to Theophilus Shepstone, 21 November 1878; F. E. Colenso, assisted by Lt.-Col. E. Durnford, *History of the Zulu War and its Origin*, London, 1880, p. 364.

11. *B. P. P.* (C. 2222), sub-enc. 19 in enc. 1 in no. 6: Message to the Lieutenant-Governor from Cetywayo, 20 September 1878.

12. *B. P. P.* (C. 2308), enc. 1 in no. 7: Message from Cetywayo by Umfunzi, Umkisimana and Somfino, Indunas of the King, 5 November 1878.

13. SNA 1/4/2, no. 31: Message from Cetywayo to Border Agent, Lower Tugela, conveyed by Ruqu, Umlamula and Ungumbane, 7 November 1878.

14. *B. P. P.* (C. 2308), enc. 1 in no. 7: Message from Cetywayo to the Lieutenant-Governor, 10 November 1878.

15. J. Y. Gibson, *The Story of the Zulus*, London, 1911, p. 164.

16. Colenso, *Digest of Zulu Affairs*, series no. 1, part 2, p. 540.

17. See especially SNA 1/1/31, no. 69: Message from Cetywayo to Border Agent, Lower Tugela, conveyed by Umgedi and Undlamini, 26 December 1878; and SNA 1/1/33, no. 2: Message from Cetywayo to the Border Agent, Lower Tugela, conveyed by Umsitwangu and Umpepa, 29 December 1878.

18. CSO 1925, no. C187/1878: J. E. Fannin to Colonial Secretary, 22 December 1878.

19. Colenso Papers 28, no. 2294: Statement by Magema Magwaza, 9 January 1879.

20. *B.P.P.* (C.2242), enc. 1 in no. 9: Message brought by Soignafasi, Mayolor and Uzizwayo, 11 January 1879.

21. Ibid., no. 9: Frere to Hicks Beach, 13 January 1879.

22. John Martineau, *The Life and Correspondence of the Right Hon. Sir Bartle Frere, Bart.*, London, 1895, vol. II, p. 271.

23. Colenso, *Digest of Zulu Affairs*, series no. 1, part 2, p. 537.

24. GH 1400, n.n.: F.B. Fynney to Colonial Secretary, 10 March 1879.

25. *B.P.P.* (C.2252), no. 20: Lord Chelmsford's Order of 17 January 1879.

26. J. Laband, *Fight Us in the Open: The Anglo-Zulu War through Zulu Eyes*, Pietermaritzburg and Ulundi, 1985, pp. 3–4; and J.P.C. Laband, 'The Cohesion of the Zulu Polity under the Impact of the Anglo-Zulu War: A Reassessment', *JNZH*, VIII (1985), pp. 36–40.

27. C. de B. Webb and J.B. Wright (eds.), *A Zulu King Speaks*, Pietermaritzburg and Durban, 1978, pp. 29, 56–7.

28. Ibid., pp. 31, 57.

29. CSO 1926, no. 1346/1879: Fannin to Colonial Secretary, 3 March 1879; WO 32/7715: Diary of Operations, 10 February–7 March 1879: Report by Major Spalding to the Quarter-Master-General, 10 March 1879; FC 2/4: Fannin to his wife, 5 March 1879.

30. J.P.C. Laband and P.S. Thompson, *War Comes to Umvoti: The Natal Zululand Border, 1878–9*, Durban, 1980, pp. 11, 29–30.

31. WO 32/7717: Report on the General Situation. Fannin to Colonial Secretary, 1 March 1879.

32. *B.P.P.* (C.2318), enc. 2 in no. 9: Fannin to Colonial Secretary, 2 March 1879.

33. Ibid.: Frere to Chelmsford, 3 March 1879.

34. FC 2/4: Fannin to his wife, 3 March 1879.

35. Sonia Clarke (ed.), *Zululand at War 1879: The Conduct of the Anglo-Zulu War*, Johannesburg, 1984, p. 155: Lt.-Col. Crealock to General Alison, 2 March 1879.

36. WC II/2/2: Chelmsford to Wood, 3 March 1879.

37. FC 2/5: Fannin to his wife, 10 March 1879.

38. FC 2/5: Fannin to his wife, 23 March 1879.

39. J. Laband and J. Wright, *King Cetshwayo kaMpande*, Pietermaritzburg and Ulundi, 1983, pp. 9–10.

40. CSO 1926, no. 1669/1879: Fannin to Colonial Secretary, 22 March 1879.

41. Ibid.

42. *Times of Natal*, 14 April 1879; *Natal Witness*, 26 April 1879. Still in irons, they were brought into Natal after the relief of Eshowe, and only released in early April after interrogation by Lord Chelmsford (Colenso, *Digest of Zulu Affairs*, series no. 1, part 2, p. 556).

43. CSO 1926, no. 1812/1879: Fannin to Colonial Secretary, 1 April 1879; CSO 1927, no. 2336/1879: Fannin to Colonial Secretary, 6 May 1879.

44. CSO 1926, no.1761/1879: Fannin to Colonial Secretary, 28 March 1879; Cornelius Vijn (translated from the Dutch and edited with a preface and notes by Bishop Colenso), *Cetshwayo's Dutchman*, London, 1880, p.136: Colenso's notes.

45. Bishop Colenso, 'Cetywayo's Overtures of Peace', *The Aborigine's Friend*, V, June 1879, p.150; Colenso, *Digest of Zulu Affairs*, serics no.1, part 1, pp.552–3.

46. CSO 1926, no.1761/1879: Fannin to Colonial Secretary, 28 March 1879.

47. *B.P.P.* (C.2318), sub-enc.1 in enc.2 in no.16: Fannin to Colonial Secretary, 29 March 1879.

48. Ibid., enc.1 in no.10: Telegram, Col. Horston to F.S. Haden, n.d.

49. Ibid., Bulwer to Frere, 3 April 1879.

50. J.P.C. Laband, 'Bulwer, Chelmsford and the Border Levies: The Dispute over the Defence of Natal, 1879', *Theoria*, 57, October 1981, pp.5–8.

51. CSO 1926, no.2051/1879: Fannin to Colonial Secretary, 17 April 1879.

52. GH 1054, minute 2262/1879: Bishop Colenso to Bulwer, 5 May; Fannin to Colonial Secretary, 6 May; Bulwer to Colenso, 8 May; Bulwer to Colonial Secretary, 8 May; Fannin to Colonial Secretary, 8 May 1879.

53. CP 13, no.50: General Clifford to Chelmsford, 13 June 1879.

54. Ibid.

55. See above.

56. CP 13, no.5: Minute by Frere, 4 April 1879.

57. CP 9, no.52: Wood to Military Secretary, 10 May 1879; CP 35, no.3: Telegram, General Crealock to Chelmsford, 15 May 1879; WO 32/7750: Journal of the 2nd Brigade, 1st Division, 16 May 1879; Webb and Wright, *Zulu King Speaks*, p.34.

58. Clarke, *Zululand at War*, p.220: General Crealock to Alison, 31 May 1879.

59. Ibid., 17 May 1879; WC II/2/2: Chelmsford to Wood, 16 May 1879.

60. *B.P.P.* (C.2374), enc.5 in no.32: Frere to Chelmsford, 19 May 1879.

61. WO 32/7750: Diary of the 1st Division, 15 May 1879; WO 32/7740: Telegram, General Crealock to Chelmsford, 16 May 1879.

62. CP 13, no.18: Colonel Crealock to Colonial Secretary, 21 May 1879.

63. *B.P.P.* (C.2374), enc.10 in no.32: Telegram, Frere to Chelmsford, recd. 30 May 1879.

64. Ibid., enc.3 in no.34: Telegram, General Crealock to Chelmsford, 27 May 1879.

65. CP 13, no.22: Statement by Umfazi, 28 May 1879.

66. *Natal Mercury*, 29 May 1879.

67. Colenso Papers 27, no.216: Colenso to Chesson, 31 May 1879; Colenso, *Digest of Zulu Affairs*, series no.1, part 2, p.576.

68. WO 32/7747: Correspondence regarding peace. Summary of the conversation between John Dunn and the king's messenger, Usitwangu, 31 May 1879.

69. Colenso, *Digest of Zulu Affairs*, series no. 1, part 2, p. 561.

70. *B.P.P.* (C. 2374), enc. 13 in no. 32: Telegram, General Crealock to Frere, n.d.

71. Clarke, *Zululand at War*, p. 222: General Crealock to Alison, 7 June 1879.

72. Laband, 'Cohesion of the Zulu Polity', pp. 13–15.

73. WO 32/7745: Chelmsford to Secretary of State for War, 2 June 1879.

74. *B.P.P.* (C. 2454), D in enc. in no. 33: Report by W. Drummond, 6 June 1879.

75. Sonia Clarke (ed.), *Invasion of Zululand 1879*, Johannesburg, 1979, p. 133: Arthur Harness to his sister Co, 4 June 1879.

76. CP 13, no. 40: Notes by W. Drummond on report of king's peace messengers, 5 June 1879.

77. Colenso, *Digest of Zulu Affairs*, series no. 1, part 2, p. 571.

78. CP 13, no. 37: Chelmsford's message to the Zulu king, 4 June 1879, with the amendment of 5 June 1879; CP 13, no. 39: Notes by Lt.-Col. Crealock on the conversation between Chelmsford and the Zulu messengers, 5 June 1879.

79. *B.P.P.* (C. 2454), no. 51: Chelmsford to Secretary of State for War, 6 June 1879.

80. CP 15, no. 44: General Crealock to Chelmsford, 11 June 1879.

81. CP 16, no. 40: Drummond to Assistant Military Secretary, 16 June 1879. Statement of the prisoner Umgaunsi.

82. *B.P.P.* (C. 2454), C in enc. 7 in no. 51: Message from Chelmsford to the Zulu Chiefs, 16 June 1879.

83. SNA 1/1/34, no. 117: Translation of message from Cetywayo by J. B. Fynney, 25 June 1879.

84. *B.P.P.* (C. 2482), no. 47: Sir Garnet Wolseley to Col. Walker, 29 June 1879.

85. Intelligence Branch of the War Office, *Narrative of the Field Operations Connected with the Zulu War of 1879*, London, 1881, p. 105. The tusk was 7 feet in length and half a yard in circumference (*Illustrated London News*, 20 September 1879). It was subsequently forwarded to Queen Victoria (*B.P.P.* (C. 2482), no. 79: Hicks Beach to Wolseley, 29 September 1879).

86. Major Ashe and Capt. the Hon. E. V. Wyatt Edgell, *The Story of the Zulu Campaign*, London, 1880, p. 317.

87. Ibid., p. 319.

88. Gibson, *Story of the Zulus*, p. 209.

89. Vijn, *Cetshwayo's Dutchman*, pp. 42–9; Colenso, *Digest of Zulu Affairs*, series no. 1, part 2, pp. 584–5.

90. Vijn, *Cetshwayo's Dutchman*, pp. 134–5: Colenso's notes.

91. Ibid., pp. 49–50; Colenso, *Digest of Zulu Affairs*, series no. 1, part 2, pp. 585–6.

92. *Illustrated London News*, 23 August 1879.

93. War Office, *Narrative of Field Operations*, p. 110.

94. CP 13, no. 54: Message from Cetywayo to Chelmsford, 26 June 1879; and message to Ketchwayo from Chelmsford, 27 June 1879. *B.P.P.* (C.2482), no. 47: Chelmsford to Secretary of State for War, 28 June 1879. In a curious incident, the king's messengers of 30 June refused Chelmsford's request to take back the cattle. The British believed at the time this was because the cattle had been doctored to ensure their defeat, and that the Zulu feared that if they accepted them the magic would be turned on them instead (*The Graphic*, 30 August 1879).

95. WO 32/7761: General Newdigate's Diary for the week ending 29 June 1879, 28 June 1879.

96. WO 32/7751: Telegram, Clifford to Secretary of State for War, 3 July 1879.

97. Clarke, *Zululand at War*, p. 229: Lt.-Col. Crealock to Alison, 28 June 1879.

98. *B.P.P.* (C. 2482), enc. in no. 32: Chelmsford to Secretary of State for War, 6 July 1879.

99. Ibid., Aa in enc. in no. 32: Message from the Zulu king to Chelmsford, 30 June 1879.

100. Ibid., A in enc. in no. 32: Message from Chelmsford to Ketshwayo, 30 June 1879.

101. French, *Lord Chelmsford*, p. 250.

102. Clarke, *Zululand at War*, p. 235: Major C. W. Robinson to Maude Lefroy, 6 July 1879.

103. Colenso, *Digest of Zulu Affairs*, series no. 1, part 2, pp. 595a–593b. Magema interviewed Mfunzi in October 1879 and was shown the still unopened letter.

104. Vijn, *Cetshwayo's Dutchman*, pp. 50–1; p. 144: Colenso's notes. War Office, *Narrative of Field Operations*, p. 113; Webb and Wright, *Zulu King Speaks*, p. 58; Magema M. Fuze (tr. H.C. Lugg and ed. A.T. Cope), *The Black People and Whence they Came*, Pietermaritzburg and Durban, 1979, p. 114.

105. Webb and Wright, *Zulu King Speaks*, pp. 34–5.

106. *B.P.P.* (C. 2454), no. 62: Wolseley to Hicks Beach, 10 July 1879.

107. WO 32/7768: Brig.-Gen. G. Pomeroy Colley, Minute for the guidance of all officers commanding posts and all political officers dealing with the Zulu people, 26 July 1879.

108. Laband, 'Cohesion of the Zulu Polity', pp. 16–18.

109. WO 32/7775: Wolseley to Secretary of State for War, 13 August 1879.

110. Wolseley Papers 2: Wolseley to his wife, 10 July 1879.

111. Wolseley's Journal: 20 July 1879.

112. Ibid.: 26 and 27 July 1879; WO 32/7769: Telegram, Wolseley to Secretary of State for War, 28 July 1879; Clark, *Zululand at War*, p. 259: Lt. Col. C. East to Alison, 26 July 1879.

113. See Wolseley's Journal: 6 and 7 August 1879; and Clark, *Zululand at War*, p. 261: W. H. James to Alison, 31 July 1879.

114. Wolseley's Journal: 7 August 1879; *Natal Witness*, 11 August 1879; *Natal Mercury*, 18 August 1879; Webb and Wright, *Zulu King Speaks*, p. 59.

115. Vijn, *Cetshwayo's Dutchman*, p. 54.

116. Webb and Wright, *Zulu King Speaks*, p. 35.

117. Wolseley's Journal: 10, 11 and 13 August 1879; Vijn, *Cethswayo's Dutchman*, pp. 58–62; Webb and Wright, *Zulu King Speaks*, p. 35.

118. Wolseley's Journal: 14 August 1879; C. L. Norris-Newman, *In Zululand with the British throughout the War of 1879*, London, 1880, pp. 237–8.

119. Colenso Papers 27, no. 230: Colenso to Chesson, 13 September 1879.

120. Vijn, *Cetshwayo's Dutchman*, p. 160: Colenso's Notes.

121. *The Graphic*, 4 October 1879.

122. Laband, 'Cohesion of the Zulu Polity', pp. 20–1.

123. J. W. Shepstone Papers 10: 'Reminiscences of the Past', part II, p. 104.

British Fieldworks of the Zulu Campaign of 1879

With special reference to Fort Eshowe

J.P.C. LABAND

The art of fortification, as taught to officers of the Royal Engineers during the course of their training at the Royal Military Academy, Woolwich, had, by the 1870s, reached a level of high – if unimaginative – competence. The lessons of the recent American Civil War and the Franco-Prussian War had been absorbed, and updated designs and methods of construction were specified for all situations, both military and topographical. Thus the Royal Engineer emerged from Woolwich technically competent to reproduce copybook fortifications whenever called upon to do so during the course of a campaign. This ability was exemplified throughout the Anglo-Zulu War of 1879. For, as will be shown, the British works constructed in Zululand[1] during that campaign conformed to a remarkable degree with the standard forms recognized at Woolwich.

In technical language, all the British fortifications in Zululand were fieldworks, 'constructed for purposes of temporary entrenchment only',[2] as a tourist commented on seeing the ruinous state of Fort Crealock only three years after the end of the war. For unlike the stone laagers erected by the colonial government in some of Natal's towns, and by the white settlers themselves in rural areas near the frontiers, they were not intended as permanent fortifications. The Natal laagers were constructed as abiding places of refuge from possible attack – especially by the neighbouring Zulu kingdom – for local settlers, their families, wagons, and servants. They were generally rectangular in shape, their perimeter varying between about 127,5 m (425 ft) and 226,5 m (755 ft), with loopholed masonry walls some 3 m (10 ft) high, flanked by two towers at opposite corners and surrounded by a ditch.[3] Many are still in use today – though suitably modified – for purposes ranging from gaols to cattle-laagers. Not so with the British fieldworks, the functions of which were purely temporary. Sometimes, as at Colonel E. Wood's camp at Khambula, or Lord Chelmsford's camp on the banks of the White Mfolozi, they were designed to command the entrenched wagon-laager of an army encamped in the field. More often, they served to protect depots of stores along a British force's line of communication and supply. Sometimes, they would fulfil both these roles in turn, as was the case with Fort Crealock. That fort was built 'within the outer line of the entrenchment of the 1st Division . . . in view of the subsequent demolition of the entrenchments and the retention of the fort as a depot station for a garrison not exceeding 300 men.'[4]

This last point concerning the size of a garrison opens up an important issue. A problem facing a British column advancing into Zululand was how to defend a large amount of stores in its rear with the least possible number of men. Army standing orders laid down that companies were never to be broken up into detachments, so the least garrison in any one case had to be one company.[5] At the same time, experience in the field had shown that for a garrison's defensive rifle-fire to be effective, the men should be ranged quite densely along the parapet of a fort, with about one rifle every 0.9 m (1 yard) and a fifth of the garrison in reserve.[6] In practical terms, these considerations resulted in an average-sized garrison of two companies per fort in Zululand and determined the size of the work, though its perimeter usually allowed for an increase to three companies, and was not so large that at a pinch it could not be held by one company.[7]

What shape then did these works take? As temporary fieldworks, they were mainly built of earth, though stone was used when it was available. This meant that they have not stood up well to the ravages of the elements and of neglect and, especially in the coastal region, have been ploughed under by sugar-cane farmers. Often thrown up in remote parts of the countryside, their very sites have frequently been forgotten by all save those living in close proximity. It has therefore often proved difficult to establish details about their design and construction.

Fortunately, it has been possible through consultation of contemporary descriptions and maps, and with the aid of aerial photographs and local lore to locate the sites of all the more substantial British fieldworks in Zululand.[8] Of the twenty forts which originally existed, only two have totally disappeared, and four have been partially obliterated.[9] This leaves enough for generalizations about their design to be made from an examination of the remains in the field, slight as these vestiges often might be. But it is one thing to discern the basic trace of a work; it is another to ascertain details of design and construction. Here it is necessary to fall back on contemporary descriptions which, unhappily, mainly deal more with generalities than with the peculiarities of particular works. Only with the forts of the coastal plain are we reasonably fortunate. For there survive not only detailed diagrams and cross-sections of a number of them, but a close description of the construction of Fort Eshowe, and a justification for its particular design. It is because of the fullness of this report on Fort Eshowe, and because of the fort's relatively good state of preservation, that that particular fieldwork, typical in so many of its features, has been selected as the most suitable model in the ensuing discussion on design and construction of the Zululand fieldworks.

The actual siting of a fieldwork was not much of a problem, mainly because of the Zulus' relative lack of military sophistication. Lieutenant-Colonel A. Harness, who served throughout the campaign from Isandlwana to Ulundi, commented on that score:

> . . . opposed to an enemy without artillery, and with the worst description of firearms . . . the advantages of a site, well drained, and possessing the somewhat rare recommendations of good water and grass, may justly be taken into consideration in favour of a somewhat indifferent military position.[10]

When it came to the selection of a site, therefore, even such prime 'qualifications' as 'good command of ground all round', which Lord Chelmsford himself considered absolutely essential,[11] could be sacrificed with relative impunity in the interests, say, of the availability of fuel. Nor was it even necessary that there be a supply of water within the fort itself. Because the Zulu, on account of their normal tactics and problems of supply, were incapable of completely investing a fort or maintaining an assault beyond a few hours, it was quite sufficient if water were within easy distance of the fort, with the only proviso that it be within range of covering rifle-fire.[12]

Considerations such as these explain the choice of position for Fort Eshowe, which was in fact considered 'weak and subject to great disadvantages in a military point of view' by the Royal Engineers responsible for its construction, Captains Wynne and Courtney.[13] But to serve its primary and typical function in Zululand, that of protecting stores, it had to be built around the existing church and other buildings of the Norwegian Mission on the site, which had been selected to contain No. 1 Column's supplies. This essential fact, coupled with the healthiness of the position and an ample supply of water from a nearby stream,[14] outweighed the disadvantage of the fort being commanded by hills on the northern and

FORT ESHOWE

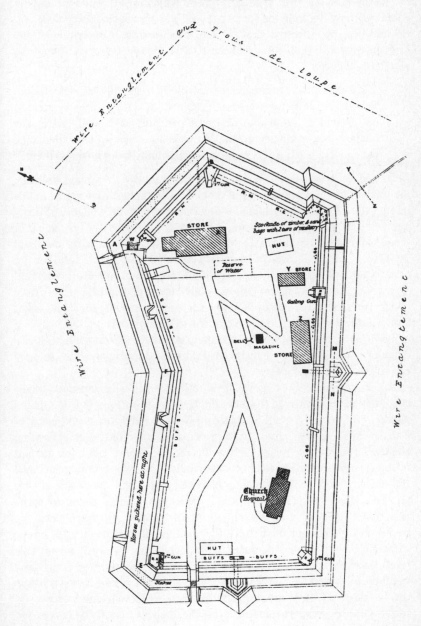

southern sides, and the problem posed by a wooded kloof and the valley of a stream on the western and northern flanks which could not be thoroughly commanded by fire from the fort's parapet. Yet even such drawbacks could be nullified by effective design and construction. Concerning these, Captain Bindon Blood, R.E., had these basic comments to make about the works in Zululand:

> The fortification works carried out were all of the simplest description. The various forts . . . were all designed on simple traces suitable to the ground . . . with musket-proof parapets and usually triangular ditches. The ordinary military obstacles – abatis, entanglements, &c. – were used, where time and opportunity recommended them.[15]

Obviously, as with Fort Eshowe, the configuration of the ground would be the final arbiter in determining the shape of a work, but whatever form this might take, every fort in Zululand fell within the technical category of being a redoubt, or 'closed work of square or polygonal figure'.[16] The parapet of the redoubt can be defined as a bank of earth (though on occasion this could be stone, or earth reinforced with stone) moulded into suitable form for fire over its summit, yet providing protection for soldiers firing from behind it. When high enough, as at Fort Eshowe where it was generally six feet (a little under 2 m, though at some of the angles it was increased to eight and a half feet (a little over 2,5 m),[17] to allow soldiers to load with ease and security and to move in safety from place to place along it, it was necessary to introduce a banquette or step (accessible by an easy slope) standing upon which soldiers could fire over the parapet.

A parapet, such as at Eshowe, was formed artificially, the earth for its construction being derived from the ditch, dug immediately in front of, and parallel to it, which formed by its depth (it was seven foot deep (just over 2 m) at Fort Eshowe)[18] one of the principal obstructions to an advancing enemy.[19] The construction of such works required heavy labour on the part of the soldiers, not made easier in the Anglo-Zulu War by the inadequate 'intrenching tools' with which they had been issued. All were made of very poor material, the picks and shovels being considered too small to be effective except for shelter-trenches in soft ground.[20] Nevertheless, the troops clearly persevered and once they had dug the ditch and piled up the parapet, they faced the parapets with revetments of hurdles (portable rectangular wooden frames) to prevent their crumbling in the often rainy weather. But when the hurdles decayed, as they did at Fort Eshowe within two months,[21] or when time allowed, they were replaced by more permanent sod revetments. Access to the fort across the ditch was usually by bridge, and at Fort Eshowe there were three of them: a rolling bridge with a 'wagon roadway' that was run in every night; and two drawbridges for 'foot passengers'.[22]

Normally, all redoubts whether square (the most simple shape) or polygonal, suffered from the same disadvantage: 'dead' salient angles, not covered by musketry fire from the straight faces of the parapets.[23] Usually, though, it was considered sufficient to place guns in the angles to command the ground in front of them.[24] Once again, this generalization is borne out by what occurred at Fort Eshowe: 7-pounder guns were mounted at the four salient angles. They were not placed in embrasures (openings in the parapet for guns) as these had the grave disadvantages of weakening the parapet and were difficult to construct and maintain. Rather, as was the British custom with redoubts, barbettes (platforms within the fort from which guns fired over the parapet) were constructed, the terreplein on which they were mounted being the standard three and a half feet (just over 1 m) below the crest of the parapet.[25] Blindages, or screens of sandbags resting on frames of timber, were provided for the protection of the gunners.[26]

A further problem with the square or polygonal design of redoubts was the lack of opportunity it provided for flanking fire. Only in one case in Zululand, that of Fort Crealock, was a proper bastion (a pentagonal projection with its base at the angle of the main works) constructed. In a few cases, notably again at Fort Crealock, a ravelin (an outwork of two faces forming a salient angle outside the ditch of the main work, its open gorge covered by fire from the higher parapet to its rear) gave additional flanking fire, as well as providing a laager for horses or cattle.[27] Another expedient was suggested by the small size of the garrisons the British preferred to leave to guard their depots of stores. At Fort Eshowe, the existing buildings of the Mission dictated that the redoubt be built around them, even if the perimeter of 450 yards (411 m) were thought to be strictly too large for the garrison of 1 300 men to hold.[28] But with most others, where a mere company or two was supposed to guard great quantities of stores dumped in the open veld, it was impossible to man a continuous perimeter thrown up around them. The solution adopted was to construct a pair of mutually supporting small redoubts (generally half the size of single redoubts) which not only covered the stores placed between them, but provided each other with flanking fire. Well-preserved examples of this procedure survive at Fort Cambridge, Fort George, and Conference Hill. At the last two sites, the pentagonal redoubts are connected by breastworks, enclosing a diamond-shaped area between them.[29]

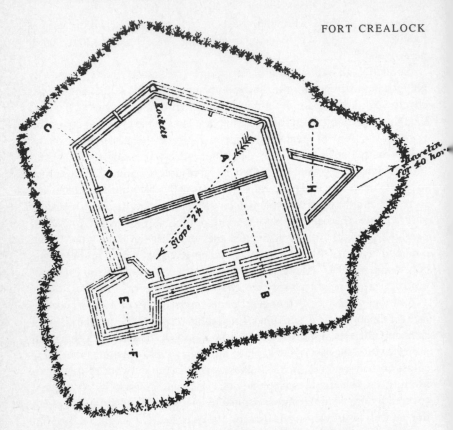

With a single redoubt, like Fort Eshowe, without bastions or ravelins, other means of creating opportunities for flanking fire had to be adopted. Fortunately, there were a number of standard methods in a Royal Engineer's repertoire. An indented angle was formed in the long north face of Fort Eshowe, and a demi-bastion (as at Fort Tenedos) at the south-east corner to provide oblique fire. Caponiers (covered passages across the ditch) were thrown out on the southern and western faces to give some flanking fire, and a Gatling gun was mounted on a barbette on the long and exposed south face between the caponier and the south-eastern corner in order to strengthen it further. At the south-eastern angle a seventeen foot high (just over 5 m) stockade was constructed, with two levels of loopholes, to flank the ditch and command the valley to the south.[30] Stockades, of course, had the great advantage over parapets in that the men behind them had a more effective command of the ground before them when firing through loopholes, than they could possibly have when firing over a parapet.[31]

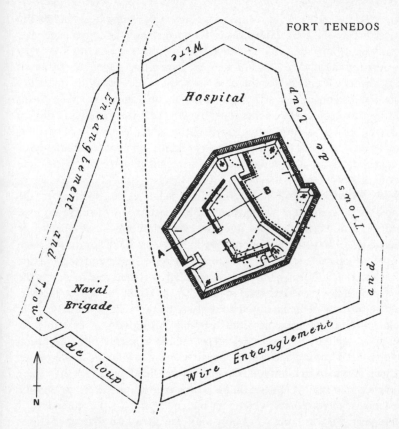

FORT TENEDOS

Related to problems of providing flanking fire were arrangements for security within the redoubt itself. The entrance to a redoubt, for example, would be made on its least exposed side, and be protected by a traverse placed behind it, which could in turn be connected to the main parapet by a stockade. (It was normal practice for gaps of about three inches (7,5 cm) to be left between the strong, pointed palisades of a stockade, the intervals being filled by shorter, square-cut palisades, the open spaces being employed as loopholes).[32] The entrance itself could be closed by gates or barriers.[33] Whenever, as at Fort Eshowe, or any of the other larger forts in Zululand like Forts Crealock and Tenedos, there was a very large area within the perimeter, traverses and parados were constructed to protect the garrison from reverse or enfilading fire. At Fort Eshowe these were originally made of sacks and wagons, but were gradually replaced by proper sod works.[34] Traverses, as at Fort Tenedos, could also serve to divide up the interior space of a redoubt to create a more secure and comfortable camping-ground for the garrison in part of the area. It was usual for magazines to be constructed in or against such traverses, which shielded them from the parapet.[35] At Fort Newdigate, where there was a pair of supporting redoubts, different arrangements were made for the convenience and security of the garrison. Normally, if a convoy had arrived at the depot, the wagons would be drawn up in a square laager between the forts. But when they moved off to bring up fresh supplies, it was the practice to arrange the stores (e.g. sacks of mealies, biscuit boxes, boxes of tinned meat and vegetables, and bottles of lime-juice in crates) to form a covered way between the two redoubts for safe communication between the two halves of the garrison.[36]

It was a general feature of temporary redoubts, as opposed to the complexes of permanent works that might be erected to fortify, say, the French city of Paris, that the ditch was too close to the parapet to be commanded from it.[37] This was obviously a serious drawback, as the ditch was the last obstacle an enemy had to surmount before attempting to scale the parapet itself. Effective defence of the ditch was therefore related to the whole problem of providing flanking fire. The difficulty, as at Fort Eshowe, could be partially overcome by the fire from the caponiers, banquettes, and stockade. But portions of the ditch, especially that along the eastern face, were not covered by fire from the parapet.[38] Other remedies, the application of which had become standardized, had to be resorted to in order to break up an attack by the enemy, for it was axiomatic that 'in all works the efficiency of defence must mainly depend on the power of arresting the progress of the assailants at those points which are under the fire of the defenders.'[39] Consequently, it was normal not only to fill the ditch with sharpened stakes and other obstacles (at Fort Eshowe the unflanked parts of the ditches were staked to make it more difficult for an enemy to rush the parapet),[40] but to raise a glacis. This was a mound of earth on the counterscarp (outer side) of the ditch, sloping gently upwards to the edge of the ditch. An assailant negotiating it would have the length of time he was fully exposed to fire from the parapet prolonged, as well as having his drop into the ditch increased.[41]

In addition to the staked ditch and exposed glacis, other obstacles were commonly employed to delay the enemy under direct fire from the parapet. Very commonly used in Zululand, though not as it happened at Fort Eshowe, were abattis. These were formed of felled trees, their sharpened branches interlaced outwards, their trunks fastened both to the ground and each other by pickets and iron wire. Arranged in rows on the glacis around the fort, and thus easily swept with fire from the parapet, abattis greatly hindered assailants, and made it very difficult to surprise a garrison. Employed at Eshowe, as they were elsewhere, were wire entanglements and *trous-de-loup* ('wolfpits'). The former were officially considered the best form of accessory defences. They could be applied everywhere, were easily transported, and did not interfere, as could abattis, with fire from the parapet. The normal method of setting them up was to drive stout stakes into the ground five feet (1,5 m) apart, 'disposed in rows chequer-wise', and to wind strong wire around them one and a half feet (0,45 m) from the ground. It was practice for such entanglements never to be less than 36 feet (a little under 11 m) in depth. *Trous-de-loup* were holes in the ground in the form of inverted cones six to eight feet (1,8 m – 2,4 m) in diameter and six feet deep, the depth being to prevent an enemy from using them as shelters from which to fire. At the bottom was fixed a sharp stake three feet (0,9 m) long, sharpened branches of a tree, or other sharp obstacles like "Crows' Feet".[42] It was normal to use special obstacles like wire-entanglements and *trous-de-loup* only where the terrain and relatively weaker sections of the other defences made them necessary, and at Fort Eshowe entanglements were set up only on the northern and southern faces of the glacis, and *trous-de-loup* on the eastern face.[43]

In sum, one cannot but agree with the French observer, James Plé, that the usual traces of British fieldworks in Zululand were very ordinary, as was also their execution.[44] Yet the Royal Engineers responsible for their design and construction were but implementing what they had learnt as cadets at Woolwich, and in the circumstances they made the sort of fieldworks deemed most suitable for the requirements of the Zululand campaign.

[Previously published in *Military History Journal*, 6, 1, June 1983.]

Notes

1. By 'Zululand' is meant the historic kingdom in 1879, an area bounded to the south by the Thukela River, by the Blood and Buffalo rivers to the west, and the Phongolo River to the north.

·2. Bertram Mitford, *Through the Zulu Country*, London, 1883, p. 193.

3. J. P. C. Laband and P. S. Thompson, *A Field Guide to the War in Zululand and the Defence of Natal 1839*, Pietermaritzburg, 1983, p. 25–6.

4. *B.P. P.* (C. 2505), sub-enc. G in sec. 2 of Appendix: Lt.-Col. C. M. Clarke's Report to Maj.-Gen. Crealock, 16 July 1879.

5. CP 26: Major W. C. F. Molyneux, *Notes on Hasty Defences as Practised in South Africa* (For private circulation only), p. 2.

6. James Plé, *Les Laagers dans la Guerre des Zoulous*, Paris, 1882, p. 7.

7. Perimeters could be as large as 350 m (1 167 ft), as with Fort Crealock, or as small as 50 m (167 ft) for the redoubt at the Khambula camp. But generally, the average was between 70 and 140 m (233 ft – 466 ft), paired redoubts being half the size of single ones.

8. This category excludes march laagers, the perimeters of which were surrounded by shelter-trenches.

9. Laband & Thompson, *Field Guide*, pp. 30, 37, 51, 93 and 101.

10. Lt.-Col. Arthur Harness, R.A., 'The Zulu War from a Military Point of View', *Fraser's Magazine*, 101, April 1880, pp. 479–80.

11. *B.P. P.* (C. 2505), sub-enc. B in enc. 2 of Appendix: Memorandum for Guidance of Maj.-Gen. Crealock by Lt.-Gen. Chelmsford, 12 April 1879.

12. Plé, *Les Laagers*, p. 7.

13. *B.P. P.* (C. 2367), enc. B in no. 19: Report on Fort Ekowe, 9 April 1879. (Henceforth referred to as Report on Fort Ekowe).

14. Ibid.

15. *B.P. P.* (C. 2505), sub-enc. C in enc. 2 of Appendix: Report on Work Performed by Corps of Royal Engineers Attached to the 1st Division, Zulu Field Force, by Capt. B. Blood, R.E., 18 July 1879.

16. Maj.-Gen. J. E. Portlock and Col. Sir Charles Nugent, 'Fortification', in *The Encyclopaedia Britannica*, 9th edition, Edinburgh, 1879, vol. 9, p. 434. (Maj.-Gen. J. E. Portlock, R.E., was Inspector of Studies at the Royal Military Academy Woolwich, and Member of the Council of Military Education. Col. Sir Charles Nugent, K.C.B., R.E., was on the Royal Engineers Ordnance Committee.)

17. Report on Fort Ekowe.

18. Ibid.

19. Portlock & Nugent, 'Fortification', pp. 421–2.

20. Reports by Maj.-Gen. Newdigate and Col. Clarke, 'Abstract of Information on Operations in Zululand', in Intelligence Division of War Office, *Précis of Information Concerning Zululand*, London, 1895, pp. 131–2.

21. Report on Fort Ekowe.

22. Ibid.
23. Portlock & Nugent, 'Fortification', p. 438.
24. Ibid.
25. Ibid., p. 432.
26. Report on Fort Ekowe.
27. Fort Marshall provides an interesting variant. There, the main work is a pentagon, on one side of which another, but considerably lower pentagon, commanded by the parapet of the main fort, was constructed for the livestock.
28. Report on Fort Ekowe.
29. Laband & Thompson, *Field Guide*, p. 109, 112–113.
30. Report on Fort Ekowe.
31. Portlock & Nugent, 'Fortification', p. 424.
32. Ibid.
33. Ibid. p. 438.
34. Report on Fort Ekowe.
35. Portlock & Nugent, 'Fortification', p. 438.
36. Molyneux, *Hasty Defences*, p. 2.
37. Portlock & Nugent, 'Fortification', p. 434.
38. Report on Fort Ekowe.
39. Portlock & Nugent, 'Fortification', p. 438.
40. Report on Fort Ekowe.
41. At Fort Eshowe, the elevation of the ridge of the glacis was two feet (0.61 m).
42. Portlock & Nugent, 'Fortification', pp. 422–4.
43. Report on Fort Ekowe.
44. 'Leur tracé était ordinairement trop simple, leur exécution trop ordinaire.' (Plé, *Les Laagers*, p. 1.)

The Battle of Khambula, 29 March 1879

A re-examination from the Zulu perspective

J.P.C. LABAND

'We are the Boys from Isandhlwana!' shouted the Zulu forces as they advanced against the fortified camp of Colonel Evelyn Wood's Left Column at Khambula, known to them as inqaba kaHawana (or Hawana's stronghold).[1] They were then still buoyed up with their spectacular success earlier in the Anglo-Zulu War when on 22 January 1879 they had overrun the camp of the British Centre Column. Yet their rout on 29 March at Wood's hands was, as historians increasingly accept, the 'turning-point' of the Anglo-Zulu War.[2] The Zulu defeat had the effect of raising British spirits by demonstrating that the Zulu warriors were not, after all, invincible;[3] while the high morale of the Zulu army was irreparably broken in the four hours of desperate fighting. Word of its defeat and heavy casualties 'shook the country',[4] and King Cetshwayo instantly grasped the implication that from that moment there could be no doubt as to the inevitable outcome of the war.[5]

Yet despite the fact that Khambula, as Commandant Schermbrucker who fought there that day was to rejoice, was the British victory 'which really broke the neck of the Zulu power',[6] it remains a neglected battle. Any battle, Michael Howard would remind us, presents great problems for the military historian attempting to sort order out of the chaos of the battlefield and the confused and usually contradictory evidence.[7] Khambula is obscurer than it need be because the Zulu involvement is particularly under-researched, even for a campaign which traditionally has put all the emphasis on the British. Indeed, the British perspective of the battle is clear enough. For unlike the case of Isandlwana, where the picture has had to be pieced together from meagre scraps of information from the few survivors, with Khambula there are full accounts of dispositions, strategy and tactics from many different perspectives within the British camp that day, ranging from official reports to soldiers' letters home, all combining to make a detailed, if one-sided, reconstruction possible.

It is otherwise when attempting to understand the battle from the Zulu point of view, for the evidence is more fractured and problematical than in the case of the British. True, it is possible to plot the general movements of the Zulu from British eye-witness accounts of the battle, but problems begin to arise when, for example, the historian attempts to fathom Zulu strategy or to pin-point the precise dispositions of Zulu units during the engagement. The misleading map of the battle which Sir Evelyn Wood included in his memoirs of 1906 is a case in point.[8] Wood based his representation of the Zulu dispositions on his interrogation after the battle of between fifteen and twenty prisoners.[9] This circumstance has persuaded several influential twentieth-century historians of the Anglo-Zulu War to adopt Wood's map without any question or further investigation.[10] In fact, as the unanimous weight of surviving Zulu evidence from other sources would show, Wood's conception of the Zulu dispositions was precisely back-to-front. The historian can only surmise that this mirror-image was derived from confusion over the prisoners referring, say, to their right, and Wood taking it to mean his own. What this demonstrates, of course, is that evidence from British sources must be augmented and tested against as wide a range as possible of Zulu testimony. The difficulty here, is that what survives of it just over a century after the battle is scanty, and has in any case come down filtered through the pens of white interpreters. Nevertheless, it is essential to use it despite its shortcomings, and enough is extant to allow the historian to gain insights into what the Zulu themselves were hoping to achieve on the day, and into how they perceived the events and consequences. Only thus can a fuller and more balanced understanding of the battle be achieved.

The battle of Khambula was the crucial moment in what historians identify as the second phase of the Anglo-Zulu War. In the first, the main Zulu army had shattered the British Centre Column at Isandlwana, thus quite disrupting the British invasion strategy. The Right Column had been forced to entrench itself at Eshowe, where the Zulu were engaged in blockading it; while Wood's Left Column, although operating successfully against Qulusi irregulars in north-western Zululand, and those of Mbilini kaMswati (a renegade Swazi prince owing allegiance to Cetshwayo), had felt it prudent to retire on the fortified camp at Khambula. Wood's patrols, however, continued very effectively to dominate the vicinity. Lord Chelmsford, the British commander, was meanwhile regrouping his forces and building them up with reinforcements from overseas. Before embarking on a major new offensive, he wished first to march to the relief of the Eshowe garrison, thus initiating the second phase of the war. By the end of March his preparations were complete, and he was poised at the lower Thukela River to advance into Zululand.

To coincide with his advance, Chelmsford instructed all other available forces to create diversions in his favour. Small garrisons along the Thukela and Buffalo rivers mounted raids into Zululand, while Wood led a major expedition east from Khambula against Hlobane Mountain, the stronghold and cattle depot of the Qulusi. Wood hoped thereby to prevent the local warriors from reinforcing the forces the Zulu king was bound to despatch to dispute Chelmsford's advance, and at the same time to draw off a portion of the regular Zulu forces blockading Eshowe. In this, Wood succeeded more completely than he could have wished. For while at the battle of Gingindlovu on 2 April the victorious Chelmsford was confronted only by the forces investing Eshowe, reinforced by local irregulars and elements of the age-grade regiments (*amabutho*) stationed in the military homesteads of the region, Wood had to bear the full might of the Zulu army. King Cetshwayo sent it against him because Wood's previous string of successes marked him out in the king's mind as a more dangerous adversary than Chelmsford (who had, after all, been out-manoeuvred and defeated in the Isandlwana campaign),[11] while in any case the Qulusi and Mbilini had long been begging him for assistance in containing Wood's continuous raiding.[12]

Yet in making this decision, it would seem that the king's hand had been forced by the British preparations for the relief of Eshowe. Once the battle of Isandlwana had brought the British invasion to a halt, Cetshwayo had attempted to use the opportunity to negotiate from his temporary military advantage to bring the war to an end. But the moment had been frittered away because his army, disheartened by heavy casualties, and obedient to post-combat purification rituals, had refused to stay in the field, and the king lost his diplomatic leverage.[13] The British had meanwhile been allowed to recover their nerve and were filled with determination to avenge Isandlwana. Thus the king's attempts throughout March to open negotiations with the British had been rebuffed, as nothing short of unconditional surrender was now acceptable.[14] Cetshwayo's *bona fides* had in any case been impugned by the intelligence which had reached the British that on about 12 March he had called a meeting of his chief councillors in order to discuss the 'best mode of prosecuting the war'.[15] Yet the king had to be prepared for the British to renew hostilities, especially as the arrival of reinforcements indicated that this was imminent.

Thus during the course of March – at the same time as he was sending emissaries to the British[16] – Cetshwayo summoned his army to reassemble at oNdini, his 'great place'.[17] Men of all *amabutho* were called up, except those living in the coastal strip, who were to face Chelmsford.[18] It seems there was no difficulty in calling up the army, dispelling British speculations that the warriors would be loath to fight again after their heavy losses.[19] By the third week of March the full army was present at oNdini,[20] though it was not expected to move off for another week on account of the need for some units still to be ritually prepared for war.[21] As commander of his army, the king appointed Chief Mnyamana kaNgqengelele Buthelezi, his chief minister.[22] The veterans of Isandlwana made up the bulk of what was a formidable force. A spy reported its composition to the British, as well as its strength. The difficulty for the historian, however, is that, as was normal for the Zulu, numbers were computed in terms of *amaviyo* (or companies), which could vary in size between 50 and up to 200 in favoured *amabutho*.[23] A reasonable average could be taken to be about 80 an *iviyo*, though this still means it is impossible to arrive at an accurate figure. According to the spy, the army was made up as follows: 30 *amaviyo* of the uMcijo *ibutho*; 40 of the iNgobamakhosi; 20 of the uMbonambi; 40 of the uNdi corps[24] (uThulwana, iNdlondlo and iNdluyengwe *amabutho*); 20 of the uNokhenke; 30 of the uDloko; and 30 of the uNodwengu corps (uDududu, iMbube and iSangqu *amabutho*). That is, a total of 210 *amaviyo* or about 17 000 warriors. On the march they were to be reinforced by local units, especially the Qulusi irregulars, in whose district the battle would take place. Their strength was estimated by the spy to stand at between 35 and 40 *amaviyo*, thus making a combined force of about 20 000.[25] This total is reasonably corroborated by other sources. After interrogating his prisoners, Wood estimated the number who had attacked him to be 'over 23,000 men';[26] while the *Natal Mercury's* 'Kambula Correspondent' came to the conclusion after his turn with the prisoners that 23 000 had marched from oNdini, and that after being joined by others on the road, finally totalled 25 000.[27]

It is not possible to be more precise with the Zulu numbers, though one suspects that Wood and the newspaper correspondent probably inflated them somewhat in order to enhance the scope of the British victory. As for the Zulu units involved, a degree of uncertainty also persists, despite the apparent precision in this regard by the spy. This is attributable to the fact that while most *amabutho* were present in almost their full strength for the Khambula campaign, varying elements were absent operating against Chelmsford.[28] Consequently, the official *Narrative of Field Operations* confines itself to mentioning only the larger units present,[29] leaving out some of those on the spy's list; while in other accounts by individual Zulu insignificant units are listed which do not otherwise appear.[30] What is certain is that this army was at least as large as the one sent against Isandlwana, and that all the crack *amabutho* were present, with the warriors in their prime of life.[31]

More than any other engagement of the Anglo-Zulu War, Khambula was King Cetshwayo's own. No other battle, he told the *Natal Mercury* correspondent while prisoner of the British, was so under his immediate supervision. He himself gave the most minute instructions to his commanders on how to attack, on what ground to occupy, and on what dispositions they were to make.[32] Having so carefully planned the battle, he later admitted to the correspondent of the *Cape Times*, he had never dreamed that it could have resulted in defeat.[33]

The king's instructions conformed with British expectations that the Zulu army would never directly assault the fortified camp at Khambula, but would seek to outflank it.[34] Indeed, according to the testimony of Sihlahla, who had fought in the battle, the king had issued orders that no entrenchments were to be attacked, but that 'the force would . . . seize the camp cattle and so draw the white men away from their waggons and tents.'[35] This precisely echoes the king's own words, taken down while held captive in Cape Town.[35] Mehlokazulu kaSihayo revealed while in captivity that if encamping close by Wood and harassing his camp and livestock failed to draw him into the open, then the Zulu army was to pass on into Transvaal territory, and by threatening white farms, Utrecht and his line of supply, force Wood out in their defence.[37] This was the Zulu strategic object, for as Bishop Schreuder had earlier grasped from his informants in Zululand, the Zulu had the 'inflating conviction' after Isandlwana that any numerically overwhelming force of theirs must crush the British in the open field.[38] It is a matter for some puzzlement, then, that when their spy reported to the British on the eve of the battle, he insisted that he had been informed by the warriors of the advancing army that the king's instructions had been to attack and sack Wood's camp, as at Isandlwana.[39] Perhaps this reflects the potentially disastrous gap between Cetshwayo's and his generals' perception of British power and preparedness and the expectations of the ordinary warriors, which was to lead on the day of the battle to their fatal disregard of their commanders' orders. Certainly, this seems to be borne out by the comments of Cornelius Vijn, a trader detained by the war in Zululand, who recorded that the warriors were dismayed when they realized that, contrary to their expectations, Wood's position at Khambula was fortified.[40]

The Zulu army set off from oNdini on 24 March.[41] It advanced north-west by forced marches of about 20 miles (32 km) a day,[42] covering the ground at about the same rate as in the Isandlwana campaign.[43] From the fact that the corpses of several of the Zulu who had managed to penetrate Wood's laager during the course of the battle were found with their hands and mouths full of food taken from the British cooking-pots,[44] it has been deduced that the Zulu marched without provisions,[45] with the expectation that they would eat when the British camp fell into their hands.[46] However, it was normal for a Zulu army to live off the land after the first day or so as it advanced,[47] and it has been pointed out that in the case of the Khambula campaign the supply of food had become more plentiful with the advance of the season than it had been at the time of the Isandlwana campaign, and that the warriors were probably better fed and in better condition than on the earlier campaign.[48] These conflicting conclusions are most satisfactorily resolved by Trooper Hewitt who, in a letter to his sister, mentioned that on the day of the battle itself, the Zulu army, which had been on the move since early morning, had not stopped again to eat, intending to do so once they had taken the camp.[49]

On the afternoon of 27 March Wood's Irregulars (black auxiliaries), scouting beyond Hlobane Mountain, saw smoke and fires to the east, which they correctly assumed to be the camp-fires of a Zulu army. They refrained, however, from commenting on them to the white mounted troops with them (to whom the camp-fires were equally visible) as they had long learned that their words were never heeded.[50]

Unaware, therefore, of the near presence of the Zulu army, Wood proceeded with his plans to raid Hlobane. At 3.30 a.m. on the misty morning of 28 March Lieutenant-Colonel Redvers Buller and 675 men started to scale the eastern slopes of Hlobane, while the 640 men of Lieutenant-Colonel John Russell's men moved onto the adjoining Ntendeka Mountain from the west. Buller moved his men west across the flat crown of Hlobane, brushing aside Qulusi snipers and rounding up their cattle. By 9 a.m. he was ready to descend with his booty, especially as resistance was stiffening on the plateau.[51] It was only then that Buller experienced the horrifying sight of a Zulu army advancing across the plain on Hlobane from the south-east, its horns thrown out either side of the chest in traditional order of battle.[52] Initially moving on Khambula past the southern flank of Hlobane, realization of the skirmish on its summit had caused the Zulu army to change direction. Yet in the event it did not itself move up the mountain, but was content to detach an *ibutho* (either the uMcijo or the iNgobamakhosi)[53] to cut off many of Buller's force whom the Qulusi harried down the mountain in

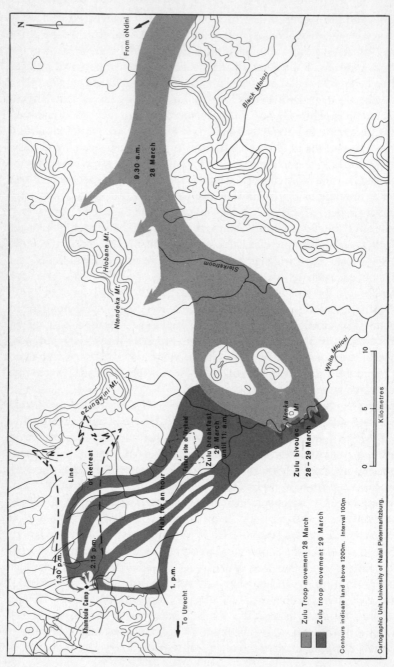

Advance of the Zulu army on Khambula, 28–29 March 1879.

their precipitate retreat.[54] Wood's force fell back in disorder on Khambula, leaving 15 officers and 79 men dead behind them, as well as over 100 of their black levies.[55] The Zulu army did not pursue them far, but decided to encamp for the night on the banks of the White Mfolozi River, near Nseka Mountain (Tinta's Kop).[56]

Despite their debacle on Hlobane, the British remained in a strong position. It was axiomatic that in the 'small wars' of the colonial period the advantage always lay with the European armies of regulars, especially if they were able to maximise their superior armaments and discipline by selecting and fortifying their own ground, and inducing their opponents to forgo their one advantage of superior mobility by mounting a frontal attack on their prepared position.[57] In this particular case, the outcome of the campaign would most likely depend on whether the Zulu were successful in drawing the British into the open, as the king had intended, or whether, by a combination of circumstances, they decided to take the unfavourable gamble of directly assaulting the camp. The latter alternative was indeed foolhardy, for Khambula camp was strong and well-prepared, manned by a force armed with breech-loading rifles, supported by artillery, and with an almost unlimited supply of ammunition.[58]

According to the official accounts, Wood had under his command 2 086 officers and men. The infantry consisted of 8 companies of the 90th Light Infantry (711) men, and 7 companies of the 1/13th Light Infantry (527) men. The mounted force under the command of Lieutenant-Colonel Buller, was made up of 1 squadron of Mounted Infantry (99 men), 4 troops of the Frontier Light Horse (165 men), 2 troops of Raaff's Transvaal Rangers (135 men), and troopers of Baker's Horse (99 men), the Kaffrarian Rifles (40 men), the Border Horse (16 men), the Mounted Basutos (74 men), and a local commando of Dutch Burghers (41 men). There were also 58 of Wood's black Irregulars remaining, the rest, as with many of the Boers, having decamped after Hlobane. In addition there were 11 Royal Engineers and the 110 men of No. 11 Battery, 7th Brigade, Royal Artillery, with their six seven-pounder guns.[59]

This garrison had few preparations still to make, for every man had long been allotted his duties and place behind the defences.[60] The key of the position was the elongated earthwork redoubt on a narrow ridge of table-land. In it were placed two of the guns. The redoubt was connected to the main wagon-laager 20 yards (18 m) below and 280 yards (256 m) behind it by the four remaining guns. The wheels of the wagons of the laager were chained together, each wagon-pole was lashed to the wagon in front, and sods were thrown up under the wagons to form a rampart. Bags of provisions were placed along the outside buckrails of the wagons with regular interstices for firing through.[61] Below the redoubt and to its right was a smaller wagon-laager, connected by a palisade, into which the force's 2 000 cattle were crammed. Its right outer edge, and that of the main laager, stood on the edge of a rocky ravine, affording any assailant a considerable amount of cover. To the left of the position the ground sloped gently away, giving a much better field of fire. The main force was stationed in the laager, with small garrisons in the redoubt and the cattle-laager.[62] All points around the camp had been carefully measured and range markers set up to aid the accuracy of the defenders' fire.[63]

Such preparations minimized the ability of the Zulu ever to come close enough to the British defences to employ their traditional methods of hand-to-hand fighting with the assegai. Sheer courage and weight of numbers might prevail, but at the cost of fearful casualties. Yet once they had determined to attack a fortified position, the Zulu seem not to have contemplated any form of attack other than variations of the mass charge. This is not to say that other methods were impossible, especially as they did possess considerable numbers of firearms, which traders brought in, primarily through Delagoa Bay. Schermbrucker commented that a large portion of the Zulu coming against Khambula was armed with some sort of firearm.[64] Most of these were of very inferior quality, being muzzle-loaders of some variety, mainly Tower muskets and Enfield rifles, as is confirmed by an analysis of the firearms captured by the British at Khambula. Of the 325 taken, only 15 were breach-loaders. One of these was a Snider carbine marked as belonging to the Royal Artillery, and the other 14 had belonged either to the 24th or 80th Regiments, showing that they had been captured either at Isandlwana or Ntombe Drift on 12 March. These prized breach-loaders appear to have been distributed among the *amabutho*.[65] The likely reason why more were not recaptured at Khambula is that whenever the possessor of one was disabled, it was immediately taken over by one of his comrades.[66]

It was most fortunate for the British that on the whole the possession of these firearms did not substantially change Zulu tactics. The likely reason was that the Zulu had little reason to put particular store in them, as their wild and ill-aimed fire had little apparent effect. Thus while at Khambula they subjected the British to a heavy fire, their poor marksmanship (they generally aimed too high) meant that their own men on the far side of the laager – rather than the British within – were often the victims.[67] But what British casualties there were, suffered mainly from high scalp wounds,[68] all except two being from Martini-Henry fire.[69] It is possible to speculate what the cumulative effect might have been if the Zulu had been content to harass the camp with long-range fire, but as it was, firearms were only allowed to play a subordinate harassing role to the mass charge.

When the morning of the 29 March dawned, therefore, it was clear that much depended on the ability of the Zulu commanders to ensure that they conformed with the king's strategy, and to resist pressure from their warriors to adopt the traditional tactic of storming the enemy's position.

Chief Mnyamana, the commander of the army, had the direction of the campaign as a whole. About 65 years of age, tall and thin, with a slight peaked beard and moustache, going grey, and suffering from rheumatism, he was chief of the Buthelezi clan in northern Zululand, and had been the king's chief *induna* since 1873. Expressing himself in a deep, resonant voice, he was known not to be easily swayed from his stand-point, though he was reputed to have a gentle heart. The king had depended on his advice even before his accession,[70] and it was as a statesman, rather than as a general, that he had made his mark. His presence at the head of the army was thus an indication of the king's personal concern with the conduct of the campaign. Rather than Mnyamana, it would be Chief Ntshingwayo kaMahole Khoza who would lead them into actual battle. He was a general of considerable personal renown, and had been the senior commander at Isandlwana. He and Mnyamana had always been as close as brothers, and Ntshingwayo was second only to him in prestige in the kingdom. Physically they provided a real contrast, Ntshingwayo being shorter, fatter and greyer, with a sharp intelligent face and greater powers of speech.[71]

Nevertheless, despite his reputably lesser oratorical powers, it was Mnyamana as commander-in-chief who formed his men into the traditional circle at their bivouack on the White Mfolozi in order to harangue them.[72] According to the testimony of Mpatshana kaSodondo, who was a member of the iNgobamakhosi *ibutho*, Mnyamana's eloquence had an unsettling effect. Doubtless only too conscious of the consequences to the kingdom of the outcome of the campaign, he allowed it to become apparent that he was 'unduly apprehensive and fearful of the results'. So while stirring up the *impi* to 'burn like a fire', he also left it in a state of alarm.[73] It is no longer known what he actually said, though the historian must presume that while ordering an advance on the British camp, it was to carry out the king's strategy, and not to mount a direct assault. Though whether once in sight of it it would be possible to hold back his inflamed warriors was another matter.

The British had the distinct advantage of knowing of the Zulu advance on Khambula, which allowed Wood to concentrate his forces and complete his preparations. Information came from one of Hamu's men who had been fighting with Wood's column since his chief's defection in March. To save himself at the battle of Hlobane he had divested himself of his British insignia and had attached himself to his old *ibutho*. He had marched with them as far as the White Mfolozi, where in the early morning he gave his unsuspecting comrades the slip. He fell in with a patrol of Raaff's Transvaal Rangers, who sent him back with his intelligence to the camp. He told Wood that the *impi* was already on the march, and that he thought it would attack the camp at 'dinner time'.[74] Naturally, Wood had also had information from other sources, and had received a particularly detailed statement of the Zulu forces the evening before.[75] That informant has been identified by J.Y. Gibson as Mbangulana, a petty chief of Hamu's.[76] However, it is difficult to agree with oral tradition that this intelligence lost the Zulu the battle.[77] Wood obviously knew the Zulu army was in the close vicinity, and that he must be prepared to be attacked. Nor was it yet certain that the Zulu intended storming the camp rather than by-passing it – despite the spy's tale – and this uncertainty was borne out by the movements of the Zulu army later that day.

Commandant Raaff's reconnaisance brought him to the edge of the eZungwini plateau, and when the morning mist lifted at about 10 a.m. he saw the Zulu army cooking its meal on the banks of the White Mfolozi and a tributary stream (where Vryheid now stands), apparently a few miles north of their overnight bivouack near Nseka Mountain. At 11 o'clock Raaff reported that the Zulu army was advancing north-west against the British camp some twelve miles (19 km) away. Wood immediately called in all outlying units and prepared to meet an attack.[78] The Zulu army made its approach in five principal columns at considerable intervals.[79] As their line of advance tended to the west, Wood feared that his intelligence had indeed been faulty, and that the Zulu intended to march on Utrecht, whose citizens had begged him in vain to garrison their town.[80] It seems as if the Zulu were going to follow the strategy laid down by the king. But when the Zulu army reached the hills some four miles (6 km) south-east of the camp, it halted. There it stayed in its dense masses for over an hour, in full sight of the anxious British garrison, who could only wait for the Zulu council of war to decide on its next move.[81] The British became aware that a decision to attack the camp had finally been reached when the Zulu army began to deploy, moving slowly and deliberately so as to conserve the warriors' energy for the struggle ahead.[82]

The Zulu centre stayed where it was, while the left horn resumed the march in column in the direction of Utrecht, until at about 1 p.m. it wheeled to the right and began a rapid advance on the camp, halting about 3 miles

(5 km) away. The right horn, meanwhile, which had further to go, spread out to the north of the camp, where it halted about a mile and a half (2 km) away, just out of range of the guns.[83] A portion of the force was detached to secure about 200 of the camp cattle which had not been rounded up in time and had strayed.[83] Wood estimated that when fully deployed the Zulu front stretched for over 10 miles (16 km),[85] and a nervous young officer confided to his diary that 'the whole country round was black with the enemy & it seemed as if these legions would swamp us completely.'[86] The Zulu warriors, poised to charge, had discarded all their ceremonial and distinctive regalia for the battle, and wore nothing besides their loin-covers and necklaces of charms and medicine wood.[87]

Why had the Zulu commanders decided to launch an attack on the camp, despite the king's instructions to the contrary? Mpatshana later claimed that when it came to the point Mnyamana lost control of his army and that it took up position by itself.[88] There are indications that the commanders were overruled by their young men when they came in sight of the camp. For as the king himself complained, their success of the previous day at Hlobane had greatly elated the warriors, and the prospect of the small and apparently vulnerable British position convinced them that they had another easy victory in their grasp.[89] Moreover, they were greatly encouraged when at 12.45 p.m., dinner being over, Wood ordered that the tents be struck and the men take up their battle-posts.[90] The Zulu took the sudden striking of the tents as a sign that the British were preparing for immediate flight, and abandoned whatever remaining hesitations they had about attacking the camp.[91]

Expecting to be attacked by the Zulu left, which had been the most active in its deployment, the British were surprised when the Zulu right horn suddenly broke from its stationary line into column, and began to advance at a tremendous pace. This movement persuaded some of the British onlookers that it must be the Zulu strategy to refuse their left, and by feinting with their right to draw some of the British defenders into the broken and difficult ground of that salient, so weakening the camp for a subsequent blow from the Zulu left.[92] A far more likely reason for this premature movement by the right horn, which was in closer striking distance of the camp than was the left, lay in the intense rivalry between the crack *amabutho* of the two wings. Hamu's adherents explained to the British that there was a dispute as to whom belonged the honour at Isandlwana of being the first among the British tents: the iNgobamakhosi or the uMcijo. It had thus apparently been agreed that when the army came upon Khambula the other *amabutho* would look on while the iNgobamakhosi of the right horn, and the uMcijo of the left, settled the issue by vying to be first into the camp.[93]

Most likely this was a rationalization by the Zulu for what actually occurred – and Mehlokazulu made the suggestion that the iNgobamakhosi only advanced as they thought, erroneously, that the rest of the army was in position to attack[94] – but whatever the cause, it was a godsend for the British. It was a standard manoeuvre in 'small wars' against troops whose discipline was not as tight as the British to attempt to draw part of the opposing force into a premature and uncoordinated attack, thus weakening the remainder and throwing them off balance. This was best achieved through a feint attack or simulated retreat.[95] When Wood saw the forward movement of the Zulu right horn at 1.30 p.m., he immediately sent out Buller and two squadrons of his mounted men to egg it on into a fully committed but unsupported attack on the camp.[96]

Buller's force rode out of the main laager when the Zulu were something under a mile (1,6 km) away.[97] Clouds of Zulu skirmishers, fed by supports and reserves, preceded the main body of the right horn. Buller led his force to within good rifle range, and ordered it to dismount and open fire. The sight of this puny body of some hundred men was too much for the mettle of the over 2 000 iNgobamakhosi, who swept forward determined to overrun it, their skirmishers falling back to reveal the more solid line of the dense column.[98] Buller's men remounted, fell back, dismounted and fired again, repeating the operation with great precision and coolness, drawing on the enemy with complete success.[99] That the Zulu did not comprehend the purpose of the manoeuvre is borne out by the comments they later made, denigrating the 'mounted redcoats' who were 'very much afraid, and quickly cried and ran away.'[100] As it was, they taunted Buller's men, calling out: 'Don't run away Johnnie; we want to speak to you!'[101]

Buller's action rapidly drew the iNgobamakhosi to within the previously marked distances for artillery practice, and the guns opened fire at 1.45 p.m.[102] The artillery did not do the damage it was anticipated it would because the Zulu were able to take advantage of the cover afforded by some broken terrain between the flats and the camp.[103] But when the right horn came to within 300 yards (274 m) of the camp, they were checked by the accurate rifle fire of the 90th Light Infantry and the enfilading fire from the redoubt. Finding the open ground quite untenable under this withering fire, the iNgobamakhosi were eventually forced to fall back to the cover of some rocky outcrops to the north-east of the camp.[104]

The luring on and subsequent repulse of the Zulu right horn, all within the space of three-quarters of an hour, was a brilliant success for the British. It helped disrupt Zulu strategy, for the intention of the right horn must surely originally have been to complete a flanking movement along the left of the

KEY

British positions taken from sketch in
Narrative of Field Operations, p. 80.

A   1st positions of guns
B   2nd positions of guns
----   British sorties
◆   Zulu General

|_____|_____|_____|_____|
100   0   100   200   300
metres

Battle of Khambula, 29 March 1879.

Contour Interval : 5 metres

Cartographic Unit, University of Natal, Pietermaritzburg

iNgobamakhosi 1st Attack 1.45 p.m.

iNgobamakhosi 2nd Attack 4.30 p.m.

4.30 p.m.

site of old camp

uDloko

iMbube   Ntshingwayo ◆

iSangqu

uDududu

uThulwana

iNdlondlo

iNdluyengwe

huts

uNokhenke

uMbonambi

uMcijo

3.00 p.m.

3.00 p.m.

Fort

cattle kraal

rocks

rubbish heaps

1412.3 △

N

British position, eventually to join up with the left horn, and so completely surround the camp. Such at least were classic Zulu battle tactics, where the flanking horns were sent out in advance of the more slowly advancing chest, one horn generally more extended than the other.[105] Buller's sortie deflected the right horn from its purpose, while its repulse before the camp and the devastating blow to its morale[106] ensured that it made no further effort to outflank the camp, but was content to keep up a fire on the British from the rocky ledges where it had retired. The result was that for the remainder of the engagement the left and rear of the British position remained unsurrounded and unthreatened, freeing the garrison the better to face the unsupported Zulu onslaught from the opposite quarter.[107]

As the attack from the Zulu right dwindled away, the heavy masses of the left and centre began at about 2.15 p.m. to develop their own belated assault. The centre moved against the south-eastern side of the redoubt, while the left, taking advantage of the cover provided by the steep ridge on the south side of the laager, assembled in the dead ground to attack the position from that direction.[108] Mnyamana, as was the usual custom with high-ranking Zulu officers, did not come under fire, but watched the battle (which was occurring despite his instructions or intentions) from a hill about three miles (5 km) away. The actual direction of the day's operations devolved upon Ntshingwayo,[109] who was seen to take up position at about 2.30 p.m. about 700 yards (640 m) from the camp, and to remain there under cover of a low hill until his men retreated.[110] This unusual action by a senior commander – which could only have encouraged his troops – is an indication of the vital importance the Zulu put on this battle.

The British who witnessed the waves of the Zulu assault could not but admire their striking courage under fire, their 'dash, élan and fearless-ness'.[111] Despite the effects of the artillery in particular, 'which scattered them like chaff before the wind' and drove great 'roads' through their ranks, they closed up and came on, keeping to a steady trot.[112] This is not to say that the Zulu were utterly foolhardy, and did not make use of whatever cover was offered. But they had to cross the numerous small streams which form the headwaters of the White Mfolozi, and to traverse at least 800 yards (731 m) of open ground commanded by the defenders' fire. The left horn could at least make for the ravine on the right flank of the camp and take cover there, though when they charged out of it they faced the concentrated fire from the laager at a distance of only 100 yards (91 m).[113] The chest and right horn had to take what little cover they could in the open ground, the centre being able to utilize the partially obliterated remains of Wood's previous camp (he had been forced to relocate it on sanitary grounds).[114] Sihlahla, a member of the uMxhapho *ibutho*, admitted that he took cover behind a large white marker stone placed by the British,[115] and others were reported to have carried large stones on their head, which they threw down to shelter behind.[116]

Yet there was inevitably a limit to what even the Zulu could stand. The destructive effect of artillery shells to whole groups was particularly disheartening, especially as they could not be easily dodged, despite every effort.[117] There were certainly moments when heavy and accurate fire paralysed Zulu movements and sowed panic.[118] As has been seen, the iNgobamakhosi was eventually demoralized by such fire. It was pinned down in its most advanced position as 'it could not face the bullets',[119] and had eventually to fall back to the shelter of the rocky outcrops. The other horn and the chest who came on after them were 'literally mowed down'[120] until they too had to retire. This is not to denigrate the extraordinarily courageous endeavour of the Zulu army. As Trooper Mossop put it, assaulting a prepared position defended by modern artillery and rifles with assegais and inadequate firearms amounted to attacking it with bare hands.[121] And the point is that there was even a moment when it looked as if the left horn might carry the laager. Yet the nightmare quality of this desperate effort was expressed in the shocked comment of some Zulu after the battle who, doubtless having seen the pets kept by the British garrison, swore that among the defenders were dogs and apes 'clothed and carrying firearms on their shoulders.'[122]

The sustained attack of the Zulu centre and left, although ultimately unsuccessful, was extremely determined. It went through several phases. To the British onlookers, the as yet unengaged units of the Zulu army seemed to be resting and taking food while the right wing was being repulsed. Then, with a great rattle of shields and assegais, they swarmed down the slopes opposite the centre and right of the camp in a series of great waves, kept as much as they could to the shelter of the bed of the little stream in the dead ground along the right flank of the camp, and finally charged up in successive lines to assault the British position. The main body remained concentrated in the dead ground, evidently waiting to make a decisive rush once the first waves had gained a foothold on the defences.[123] The uNdi corps, and notably the uNokhenke *ibutho*, succeeded in getting into the cattle kraal,[124] and eventually drove out the garrison of one company of the 1/13th. From the vantage of captured wagons they opened fire on the main laager. Encouraged by this success, a column of about 1 000 to 1 500 Zulu (evidently the uMbonambi *ibutho*) formed up west of the cattle kraal for an assault on the main laager.[125] Wood saw some thirty *izinduna* exhorting their men, while their commander waved them on with a red flag.[126] To meet this crisis, Wood ordered two companies of the 90th under Major Hackett to counter-attack with the bayonet.[127] This force marched out as if on parade, and took the Zulu greatly by surprise.[128] Their unexpected and determined advance down the slope between the two laagers broke up the Zulu concentration, forced the warriors to abandon the advantage they had previously gained, and to retire sullenly to the cover of the stream-bed and to sheltered positions to the right and left of Hackett's force.[129] Once sufficiently down the slope, Hackett's men opened fire, supported by case-shot from the artillery.[120] Fire from the redoubt and the guns also swept the cattle-laager, making it untenable for the Zulu.[131]

The two companies of the 90th were then in their own turn forced to retire on the main laager, for the Zulu caught them in a most telling cross-fire, kept up by marksmen armed with Martini-Henry rifles positioned in the vacated huts of Wood's Irregulars and behind the camp's refuse dump 350 yards (320 m) away. At much the same time, Wood was obliged temporarily to withdraw a company of the 1/13th posted at the right rear of the main laager because of the Zulu enfilading fire.[132] The fact that this fire inflicted almost all the most serious casualties of the day on the British,[133] shows what the Zulu might have achieved with proper use of their weapons, and with tactics other than the frontal assault. In the end, the British cleared the huts of the Zulu posted there with artillery fire,[134] while they flattened the rubbish-dumps with volleys of rifle-fire. Sixty-two dead Zulu were found behind them the next day.[135]

Almost simultaneously with Hackett's sortie at about 3 p.m., a company of the 1/13th was also constrained to advance out of the south-west corner of the main laager to drive off a dense mass of the Zulu left horn with the bayonet. This was the uMcijo *ibutho*, whose impetuous rush came near enough for them to grasp the rifles of the defenders.[136] Altogether, it was a most critical moment for the main laager, for a wagon had to be removed for the sortie, and when the company retired, fresh Zulu who had been in support rushed forward to try and seize the gap.[137]

The temporarily successful Zulu attack on the cattle-laager, followed by the two effective British sorties, marked both the limit of Zulu success that day and the turning-point of the battle. The British sensed that this was the decisive moment, and that the advantage lay henceforth with the defenders.[138]

There followed, nevertheless, some two further hours of fierce Zulu attacks at different points of the camp. At one time the Zulu came almost within grasp of the Artillery horses, which were kept outside the redoubt in the open between it and the laager; while at another they came right up to the very trenches along the right flank of the redoubt.[139] At 4.30 p.m. the Zulu switched the focus of their attack away from the south of the British position, and made a second attempt at the north and north-east faces. Simultaneously, the iNgobamakhosi from the position among the rocks where they had retired earlier, and elements of the uNdi corps from the shelter of the remains of Wood's previous camp, charged the British position. But they came again under a heavy cross-fire at about 300 yards (274 m) from the laager and redoubt, and enfiladed by the guns, had to retire.[140]

By about 5.00 p.m. it was obvious to the British that the Zulu attack was at last beginning to slacken. Within half-an-hour, as the sun began to go behind the ridge to the west of Khambula camp, it became evident that the Zulu had finally accepted that they could not take the position, and that they were preparing to retire.[141] Noting this, Wood at 5.30 p.m. ordered a company of the 1/13th to clear the cattle-kraal, where some Zulu still crept among the oxen they had been unable to remove; while on its right he advanced a company of the 90th to the edge of the krantz in front of the cattle-laager, where it first pushed the Zulu back with the bayonet, and then poured a heavy fire into the Zulu in the stream-bed below.[142] Everywhere the Zulu were now falling back, at this stage 'in the most orderly and leisurely style', while a great cheer from the defenders rang in their ears.[143]

The Zulu army attacking the British position at Khambula,
29 March 1879.

The Zulu, however, were not to be allowed to retire with impunity in their own time. As the garrison poured its fire into the retreating masses, and the guns discharged cannister-shot,[144] the bugles sounded to horse, and every mounted man in the laager started in hot pursuit.[145] One of the chief functions of cavalry is to complete a victory by turning an orderly retreat into a rout leading to the dispersal of the enemy.[146] This the mounted men at Khambula achieved with complete success. Three columns under Buller's command dashed upon the demoralized Zulu, and with nearly ten miles (16 km) of open country before them, with a couple of hours before darkness remaining, with fresh horses and a quarry already on the point of exhaustion, the slaughter was awful. The carnage lasted for more than two hours. It was after 9.00 p.m. before the last of the mounted men returned to camp, having followed the Zulu up to the foot of eZungwini Mountain, when night saved the fugitives.[147]

Once their flight began in earnest the Zulu seemed to lose their capacity to resist, and in their own words the British horsemen 'turned them about as if they were cattle.'[148] It seems Mnyamana made some attempt to rally his men and to persuade them to take advantage of the fact that the British were at last in the open. But Chief Zibhebhu kaMaphitha, one of his senior commanders and a man of enormous influence in the kingdom, dissuaded him, pointing out that the rout, once begun, was irreversible.[149] Indeed, the exhausted Zulu soon were unable to move faster than a walk, and were too dazed even to fire in their own defence.[150] That the Zulu were 'completely done up'[151] was only to be expected, considering the prodigious physical and emotional effort they had been called on to make since early morning. It is not to be wondered at, therefore, that in their flight they were 'falling down in every direction',[152] and that some tried to simulate death or to creep into hiding places such as ant-bear holes, reeds or long grass.[153] But the British infantry and their black auxiliaries scoured the immediate neighbourhood of the camp and killed as many of those hidden away as they could find.[154] There are reports of some of the fugitives begging on their knees for their lives,[155] but most met their deaths with silence and valiant stoicism,[156] some turning to expose their chests to their pursuers, others just standing waiting to be shot.[157] It was reported that some, sooner than die at British hands, stabbed themselves.[158]

It is well that most of the flying Zulu expected no quarter (they usually gave none themselves), for they received none. Their pursuers were out to avenge Isandlwana and Hlobane only the day before,[159] and as Major D'Arcy of the Frontier Light Horse exhorted his men: 'No quarter, boys, and remember yesterday!' He reported that they heeded his words, 'butchering the brutes all over the place.'[160] They shot them down at only 10 to 15 yards' (9 to 13 m) range,[161] and lamented the lack of sabres for more efficient killing,[162] as shooting Zulu when they became exhausted took 'too much time'.[163] Many therefore made do with captured assegais, using them as if 'giving point' with the sabre,[164] and thereby also economized on ammunition.[165] Schermbrucker saw Buller 'like a tiger drunk with blood',[166] a condition he doubtless shared with many of his men.

Harried mercilessly, it was inevitable that the Zulu army should fall into great disorder and begin to break apart in various directions.[167] The general line of flight was eastwards towards eZungwini Mountain, and the main body continued on in the direction of Hlobane, though smaller groups broke off to the north and east.[168] Strong elements remained on Hlobane for the next few days, not fully evacuating it until 3 April,[169] but the main force withdrew towards the south-east.[170] Most did not return to oNdini to report to the king as was customary, but considering themselves thoroughly beaten, mainly dispersed to their own homes, despite the efforts of the *izinduna* to keep them together.[171] To Mnyamana's entreaties they replied quite simply that they had had enough. The unhappy Mnyamana had to be content to go on with only the fraction of his defeated army which consented to stay by him to inform Cetshwayo of the disaster which had befallen the forces under his command.[172]

The extent of the losses which the Zulu army had suffered is a matter for some debate. Certainly, the British did not take over-many prisoners. They were not inclined to spare many in the heat of the pursuit, while their black auxiliaries were in the habit of killing all the wounded they found as a matter of course. The survival of any of the wounded at all was the consequence of Wood promising the auxiliaries the reward of a 'stick' of tobacco for each prisoner they brought into the camp. Those prisoners whom Wood himself interrogated he released in the direction of eZungwini Mountain. The badly wounded received medical attention and were put in the care of the auxiliaries, who were rewarded with an ox to slaughter at the end of the week.[173]

These prisoners were the lucky few. The alternative of death or flight was the option for the great majority. Yet how many Zulu did die in the battle or as a consequence of the wounds they had received? Their losses were undoubtedly out of proportion with those suffered by the British. For, considering the length and intensity of the engagement, these were light: 18 NCOs and men killed, 8 officers and 57 NCOs and men wounded. It is true though that 3 officers and 7 men subsequently died of their wounds, and that a considerable number of unrecorded casualties occurred among the black non-combatants in the camp.[174] Compared with these figures, the official British estimation put the Zulu losses at 'nearly 2,000',[175] and a triumphant soldier might boast in a letter home of 6 000 dead.[176] More soberly, Captain Woodgate reported 785 dead Zulu (some horribly mutilated by shell-fire)[177] collected in the two days following the battle,[178] though the work continued for some days more, and further bodies were brought in.[179] The Zulu corpses were buried three-quarters of a mile (1,2 km) outside the British lines in large pits, described as being 200 feet (60 m) long, 20 feet (6 m) broad, and 10 feet (3 m) deep. Wagon-load after wagon-load of bodies were deposited in them.[180] Yet the Zulu dead were collected only within a one-mile (1,6 km) radius around the camp,[181] and because they had done their best to keep cover when assaulting the camp, fewer were found in its proximity than the British had anticipated.[182] The ground in the direction of their rout, on the other hand, was thickly strewn with bodies.[183] On the line of pursuit which he had followed, Captain D'Arcy the next day counted 157 bodies. It was also his significant reflection that there were 'hundreds and hundreds of them some miles off, that are being eaten by dogs and vultures.'[184] For as Mossop commented, the Zulu would travel for many miles with a wound which would prevent a white man from taking a step and, indeed, for months afterwards patrols were coming across Zulu corpses at great distances from the battlefield.[185]

This surely is the crucial point when estimating the number of Zulu casualties. As Gibson pointed out, great numbers of the wounded doubtless never regained their homes. The battle had taken place in one of the more sparsely inhabited parts of the Zulu kingdom, so the wounded had to press on to find succour, and had no means of travelling the often great distances to their homes except by foot.[186] British scouts near Hlobane reported that in the retreating *impi* nearly every two men carried a wounded comrade between them,[187] but there was a limit to how long they were prepared to do so, or how long the wounded man could survive. A month after the battle patrols along the line of the *impi's* retreat found various bodies buried head-first in ant-bear holes, each covered with a shield.[188] In the end, it seems that only the walking wounded ever reached their homes.[189]

Not knowing how many Zulu were mortally wounded or died on the road, it is therefore impossible to arrive at an accurate casualty figure based on the number of bodies found near the British camp. This is why the British had to estimate, and why the Zulu had to as well. Zulu consensus was the 3 000 men were missing after Khambula.[190] Yet as Gibson would remind us, the Zulu counted their casualties in 'an imperfect way', for the commanders were content to make up estimates from information they were able to obtain from subordinate officers,[191] and this must surely have been most imperfect after Khambula because of the rapid break-up of the army. What is clear, though, is that the Zulu felt the casualties they sustained at Khambula were at least comparable, if not greater, than those suffered at Isandlwana.[192] A problem here, as King Cetshwayo himself pointed out, is that at Isandlwana the Zulu were left masters of the battlefield and could realize the extent of their losses, which they could not at Khambula. He thus did not consider a comparison really valid.[193]

No one could quibble, though, over the devastating impact of the Zulu losses on the kingdom as a whole. Natal Border Police were awed to hear the terrible sounds of lamentation coming from the Zulu homesteads near the junction of the Mzinyathi and Thukela rivers, a region where almost the whole male population had been called up for the Khambula campaign, and in which they had suffered badly. The two most important chiefs of the region, Godide kaNdlela Ntuli and Manqondo of the Magwaza, both were reported to have lost a number of sons.[194] What made it worse was that it was the flower of the army which had died, the young men of the crack *amabutho*. Those burying them in the pits near Khambula noted their fine physiques and the fact that few wore the head-ring of the married man.[195] It seems those *amabutho* which suffered the greatest casualties in the attack on the camp were, in order of their loss, the uMbonambi, uNokhenke and iNgobamakhosi.[196] The Qulusi irregulars, who were less disciplined, lost most heavily in the rout.[197] Among the dead were a great many *izinduna*, more than at any other battle of the war, for as the king commented, they 'exposed themselves a great deal, attempting to lead on their men'[198] – a fact Wood had noted. Among the dead were also men of the highest status, including the king's own cousin, Madlangampisi kaThondolozi,[199] two sons of Mnyamana, and the sons of various other important chiefs and royal councillors,[200] such as Godide and Manqondo, mentioned above.

King Cetshwayo was understandably furious with his army for its defeat and dispersal, and attached particular blame to its commander, Mnyamana, for not following his instructions and allowing a frontal attack on Wood's prepared position.[201] The extent of the king's displeasure was not sufficient, however, to decide Mnyamana to take refuge with the British;[202] nor for the king to carry out his original intention of executing the commander of the iNgobamakhosi for permitting the fatal and unsupported attack of his men.[203] As for the warriors themselves, although they had finally learned the basic lesson that it was hopeless to attack laagers or otherwise fortified posts, they were still prepared to fight the British if they could be brought into the open, and were apparently still determined to continue the war in the hope that they would be able to do so.[204] The king laboured under no such hopes or illusions. Although his warriors would not confess themselves beaten, the battle of Khambula had taught him that he could no longer hope to win the war in the field, and that his only hope now lay in negotiations with the British – if they were prepared to enter into them after their decisive victory.[205]

[Previously published in Ian J. Knight (ed.), *There will be an Awful Row at Home about This*, Victorian Military Society, 1987.]

Notes

1. D.C.F. Moodie (ed.), *The History of the Battles and Adventures of the British, the Boers and the Zulus in Southern Africa*, Sidney, Melbourne and Adelaide, 1879, p.290: 'anonymous soldier's account'; H.C. Lugg, *Historic Natal and Zululand*, Pietermaritzburg, 1949, p.147.

2. Frank Emery, *Marching over Africa*, London, 1986, p.64.

3. C.L. Norris-Newman, *In Zululand with the British throughout the War of 1879*, London, 1880, p.162.

4. SNA 1/1/34, no.73: Statement of Sibalo taken by J.W. Shepstone, 1 June 1879.

5. *Natal Colonist*, 25 September 1879: The king's comments, taken from the *Cape Times*; Norris-Newman, *In Zululand*, p.255; Bertram Mitford, *Through the Zulu Country*, London, 1883, p.279: Statement of Warrior of the Tulwana.

6. F. Schermbrucker, 'Zhlobane and Kambula', *The South African Catholic Maga-zine*, III, 30 and 31, 1893, p.337.

7. Michael Howard, *The Causes of Wars*, London, 1983, pp.212–3.

8. Sir Evelyn Wood, *From Midshipman to Field Marshal*, London, 1906, vol.II, p.68.

9. Ibid., p.67.

10. See, for example, D.R. Morris, *The Washing of the Spears*, London, 1966, pp.493–4; Frank Emery, *The Red Soldier*, London, 1977, p.165; and G.A. Chadwick, *The Zulu War in Northern Natal* (Natal Educational Activities Association Pamphlet, n.d.), p.11.

11. *B.P.P.* (C.2374), enc. in no.9: Minute, J.E. Fannin to the Colonial Secretary, 12 February 1879.

12. CP 8, no.49: Bishop Schreuder to Chelmsford, 10 February 1879.

13. C. de B. Webb and J. B. Wright (eds.), *A Zulu King Speaks*, Pietermaritzburg and Durban, 1978, pp. 31, 57.

14. See J. P. C. Laband, 'Humbugging the General? King Cetshwayo's Peace Overtures during the Anglo-Zulu War', *Theoria*, 67, December 1986, passim.

15. CSO 1926, no. 1669/79: Fannin to the Colonial Secretary, 22 March 1879.

16. On 1 March, 21 March, 23 March and 28 March 1879.

17. CP 9, no. 37, enc. in Wood to Military Secretary, 3 March 1879: MacLeod to Wood, 1 March 1879; *B.P.P.* (C. 2318), sub-enc. 6 in enc. 3 in no. 16: Fannin to Colonial Secretary, 9 April 1879.

18. Webb and Wright, *Zulu King Speaks*, p. 33.

19. *The London Times*, 23 May 1879, quoted in W. C. Holden, *British Rule in South Africa*, London, 1879, p. 159.

20. CSO 1926, no. 1669: Fannin to Colonial Secretary, 22 March 1879.

21. CP 14, no. 9: Report by L. H. Lloyd, submitted by Wood to Military Secretary, 27 March 1879.

22. Webb and Wright, *Zulu King Speaks*, p. 33.

23. J. P. C. Laband, 'The Zulu Army in the War of 1879: Some Cautionary Notes', *JNZH* II, 1979, p. 32.

24. This was the British term for a number of *amabutho* all attached to the same military homestead (*ikhanda*) and known collectively by its name (ibid., p. 30).

25. TS 39: Henrique Shepstone to Theophilus Shepstone, 30 March 1879.

26. Wood, *Midshipman to Field Marshal*, vol. II, p. 68.

27. *Natal Mercury*, 9 April 1879: Kambula correspondent, 1 April 1879.

28. Laband, 'Zulu Army', p. 31.

29. Intelligence Branch of the War Office, *Narrative of the Field Operations Connected with the Zulu War of 1879*, London, 1881, p. 81.

30. The 'Warrior of the Tulwana' also mentions the 'Umpunga' or uMxhapo *ibutho* (Mitford, *Zulu Country*, p. 278).

31. *Natal Colonist*, 10 April 1879: Kambula correspondent, 31 March 1879.

32. Ibid., 20 September 1879: *Natal Mercury* correspondent on the march with the king to the coast.

33. Ibid., 25 September 1879: the king's comments, taken from the *Cape Times*.

34. *The London Times*, 23 May 1879, quoted in Holden, *British Rule*, p. 157.

35. SNA 1/1/34, no. 85: Statement of Sihlahla, made to J. W. Shepstone, 3 June 1879.

36. Webb and Wright, *Zulu King Speaks*, p. 33.

37. Cornelius Vijn (Bishop J. W. Colenso, tr. and ed.), *Cetshwayo's Dutchman*, London, 1880, p. 115: Mehlokazulu's statement.

38. CP 8, no. 49: Bishop Schreuder to Chelmsford, 10 February 1879.

39. Woodgate's Military Diary: 29 March 1879.

40. Vijn, *Cetshwayo's Dutchman*, p. 36.

41. Wood's official report to the Deputy Adjutant-General, 30 March 1879, quoted in Norris-Newman, *In Zululand*, p. 160.

42. Schermbrucker, 'Zhlobane and Kambula', p. 348; Major Ashe and Captain the Hon. E. V. Wyatt Edgell, *The Story of the Zulu Campaign*, London, 1880, p. 134.

43. *Natal Witness*, 24 February 1879: Statement of Zulu deserter from the uNokhenke.

44. George Mossop, *Running the Gauntlet*, London, 1937, p. 74; *Natal Mercury*, 22 January 1929: F.A.R. Scoble (Ferreira's Light Horse), 'How Piet Uys met his Death'.

45. Ashe and Wyatt Edgell, *Zulu Campaign*, p. 134.

46. E. D. McToy, *A Brief History of the 13th Regiment (P.A.L.I.) in South Africa during the Transvaal and Zulu Difficulties*, Devonport, 1880, p. 53.

47. J. P. C. Laband and P. S. Thompson, *Field Guide to the War in Zululand and the Defence of Natal 1879*, Pietermaritzburg, 1983, p. 6.

48. J. Y. Gibson, *The Story of the Zulus*, London, 1911, p. 197.

49. KCM 53791, Zulu War File no. 3: Trooper C. Hewitt of Frontier Light Horse to his sister Annie, 3 January 1920.

50. TS 39: Henrique Shepstone to Theophilus Shepstone, 30 March 1879.

51. War Office, *Narrative*, pp. 73–5; Laband and Thompson, *Field Guide*, p. 105.

52. Buller Papers, WO 132/1: Buller to A.G., 30 March 1879.

53. Woodgate's Military Diary: 29 March 1879; Laband and Thompson, *Field Guide*, p. 105.

54. Norris-Newman, *In Zululand*, pp. 84–5: Mehlokazulu's account.

55. Laband and Thomspon, *Field Guide*, p. 105.

56. Wood, *Midshipman to Field Marshal*, vol. II, p. 53.

57. Col. C. E. Callwell, *Small Wars*, London, 3rd edn., 1906, pp. 90–1, 279–81.

58. Schermbrucker, 'Zhlobane and Kambula', p. 375.

59. War Office, *Narrative*, p. 161; Laband and Thompson, *Field Guide*, p. 107.

60. Ashe and Wyatt Edgell, *Zulu Campaign*, p. 135.

61. Schermbrucker, 'Zhlobane and Kambula', p. 376.

62. Wood, *Midshipman to Field Marshal*, vol. II, p. 59; War Office, *Narrative*, p. 79.

63. Norris-Newman, *In Zululand*, p. 163.

64. Schermbrucker, 'Zhlobane and Kambula', p. 376.

65. Woodgate's Military Diary: 30 and 31 March 1879.

66. *The London Times*, 23 May 1879, quoted in Holden, *British Rule*, p. 159.

67. E. Clairmonte, *The Afrikander*, London, 1896, p.106.

68. McToy, *The 13th Regiment*, p.53.

69. Moodie, *British, Boers and Zulus*, p.278: Captain Cecil d'Arcy's letter.

70. *Times of Natal*, 27 August 1879: Correspondent near Ulundi, 15 August 1879; Vijn, *Cetshwayo's Dutchman*, p.162: Bishop Colenso's notes; Private information from Dr Mangosuthu Buthelezi.

71. *Times of Natal*, 27 August 1879: Correspondent near Ulundi, 15 August 1879; F. Fynney, *The Zulu Army and Zulu Headmen*, Pietermaritzburg, April 1879.

72. Woodgate's Military Diary: 29 March 1879.

73. *JSA*, vol.3, p.314: Mpatshana kaSodondo's testimony.

74. Schermbrucker, 'Zhlobane and Kambula', p.376; McToy, *The 13th Regiment*, p.48; Norris-Newman, *In Zululand*, p.160; Ashe and Wyatt Edgell, *The Zulu Campaign*, pp.133–4; *The London Times*, 23 May 1879, quoted in Holden, *British Rule*, pp.156–7.

75. War Office, *Narrative*, p.79.

76. Gibson, *Story of the Zulus*, p.197.

77. Private information from Dr Buthelezi.

78. Wood, *Midshipman to Field Marshal*, vol.II, pp.57–8.

79. Woodgate's Military Diary: 29 March 1879.

80. War Office, *Narrative*, pp.79–80.

81. Ashe and Wyatt Edgell, *The Zulu Campaign*, p.136; *The London Times*, 23 May 1879, quoted in Holden, *British Rule*, p.157.

82. *Natal Colonist*, 10 April 1879: Kambula correspondent, 31 March 1879.

83. *Natal Colonist*, 10 April 1879: Kambula correspondent, 31 March 1879; War Office, *Narrative*, p.80; Ashe and Wyatt Edgell, *The Zulu Campaign*, pp.136–7; Major D.D. Hall, 'Artillery in the Zulu War – 1879', *Military History Journal*, 4, 4, January 1979, p.160. The maximum range of the 7-pounder was 3 100 yards (2 834 m).

84. Ashe and Wyatt Edgell, *The Zulu Campaign*, p.136.

85. Wood to Sir A. Horsford, 6 April 1879, quoted in Emery, *Red Soldier*, p.176.

86. Slade Papers: Captain Frederick Slade, R.A. to his mother, 29 March 1879.

87. *The London Times*, 23 May 1879, quoted in Holden, *British Rule*, p.159.

88. *JSA*, vol.3, p.314: Mpatshana's testimony.

89. Webb and Wright, *Zulu King Speaks*, p.33.

90. War Office, *Narrative*, p.79.

91. Wood, *Midshipman to Field Marshal*, vol.II, p.64; Mossop, *Running the Gauntlet*, p.67.

92. *Natal Colonist*, 10 April 1879: Kambula correspondent, 31 March 1879; Ashe and Wyatt Edgell, *The Zulu Campaign*, pp.136–7.

93. TS 39: Henrique Shepstone to Theophilus Shepstone, 30 March 1879; Mitford, *Zulu Country*, p.278: Testimony of Warrior of the Tulwana.

94. Vijn, *Cetshwayo's Dutchman*, p.114: Mehlokazulu's statement.

95. Callwell, *Small Wars*, pp.228–30.

96. War Office, *Narrative*, p.80.

97. Vijn, *Cetshwayo's Dutchman*, p.114: Mehlokazulu's statement; Letter by Private Edmund Fowler in *The Wigan Observer and District Advertiser* 28 April 1879, quoted in Emery, *Marching over Africa*, p.78. Not all the mounted men were stationed in the main laager during the battle. Wood had permitted the Basuto Horse under Major Cochrane to fight in their own fashion outside the camp, hovering on the extremes of the Zulu horns, harassing them whenever possible (Schermbrucker, 'Zhlobane and Kambula', p.380).

98. Ashe and Wyatt Edgell, *The Zulu Campaign*, pp.137–8.

99. Correspondent in the *Cape Argus*, quoted by Moodie, *British, Boers and Zulus*, p.286; Wood, *Midshipman to Field Marshal*, vol.II, p.60.

100. Vijn, *Cetshwayo's Dutchman*, p.38.

101. Captain W.E. Montague, *Campaigning in South Africa*, Edinburgh and London, 1880, p.263. The Zulu had picked up this term for the Redcoats from the Basutho.

102. Schermbrucker, 'Zhlobane and Kambula', pp.377–8.

103. McToy, *The 13th Regiment*, p.49. Shrapnel fired by 7-pounders had in any case little effect because of the low muzzle velocity of the guns and the small bursting charge of the common shell, (Hall, 'Artillery in the Zulu War', pp.157–8).

104. Wood, *Midshipman to Field Marshal*, vol.II, p.60.

105. Laband and Thompson, *Field Guide*, p.8.

106. Vijn, *Cetshwayo's Dutchman*, p.114: Mehlokazulu's statement.

107. Buller Papers, W.O. 132/1: Buller to A.G., 30 March 1879.

108. War Office, *Narrative*, p.80; Wood, *Midshipman to Field Marshal*, vol.II, p.60.

109. Wood to D.A.G., 30 March 1879, quoted in Norris-Newman, *In Zululand*, p.159; Mitford, *Zulu Country*, p.278: Statement of Warrior of Tulwana; *The London Times*, 23 May 1879, quoted in Holden, *British Rule*, p.157; Laband, 'Zulu Army', p.34.

110. CP 14, no.21: Wood to D.A.G., 3 April 1879.

111. Schermbrucker, 'Zhlobane and Kambula', p.378.

112. KCM 53791: Trooper Hewitt to Annie, 3 January 1920; Moodie, *British, Boers and Zulus*, p.289: Soldier's account; Mossop, *Running the Gauntlet*, p.72.

113. *The Times of London*, 23 May 1879, quoted in Holden, *British Rule*, p.158. The edge of the ravine was 200 yards (182 m) from the wagons, but owing to the rapidly falling ground there was only 100 yards (91 m) of clear fire (Wood, *Midshipman to Field Marshal*, vol.II, p.63).

114. TS 39: Henrique Shepstone to Theophilus Shepstone, 30 March 1879; McToy, *The 13th Regiment*, p.50.

115. SNA 1/1/34, no.85: Statement of Sihlahla to J.W. Shepstone, 3 June 1879.

116. McToy, *The 13th Regiment*, p.50.

117. Mitford, *Zulu Country*, p.160: Testimony of two warriors of the Undi and one of the Tulwana.

118. *Natal Colonist*, 10 April 1879: Kambula correspondent, 31 March 1879.

119. SNA 1/1/34, no.85: Statement of Sihlahla, 3 June 1879.

120. McToy, *The 13th Regiment*, p.51.

121. Mossop, *Running the Gauntlet*, p.75.

122. Vijn, *Cetshwayo's Dutchman*, p.38.

123. Norris-Newman, *In Zululand*, pp.163–4.

124. Vijn, *Cetshwayo's Dutchman*, p.114: Mehlokazulu's statement; Mitford, *Zulu Country*, p.278: Testimony of warrior of Tulwana.

125. War Office, *Narrative*, p.80; Moodie, *British, Boers and Zulus*, p.274: Correspondent to a Natal newspaper.

126. Wood, *Midshipman to Field Marshal*, vol.II, p.61.

127. Wood to D.A.G., 30 March 1879, quoted in Norris-Newman, *In Zululand*, p.160. For the propriety of such a sortie, see Callwell, *Small Wars*, p.400.

128. Ashe and Wyatt Edgell, *Zulu Campaign*, p.139.

129. Wood to D.A.G., 30 March 1879, quoted in Norris-Newman, *In Zululand*, pp.60–1; Wood, *Midshipman to Field Marshal*, vol.II, p.62; Schermbrucker, 'Zhlobane and Kambula', p.379.

130. Sergeant E. Jervis to his brother, 31 March 1879, quoted in Emery, *Red Soldier*, p.172.

131. Norris-Newman, *In Zululand*, p.164.

132. War Office, *Narrative*, p.81; Wood, *Midshipman to Field Marshal*, vol.II, p.62.

133. Norris-Newman, *In Zululand*, p.164.

134. McToy, *The 13th Regiment*, p.51.

135. KCM 53791: Trooper Hewitt to Annie, 3 January 1920.

136. Moodie, *British, Boers and Zulus*, p.286: Correspondent to *Cape Argus*; Schermbrucker, 'Zhlobane and Kambula', p.379.

137. Mossop, *Running the Gauntlet*, p.73.

138. Wood, *Midshipman to Field Marshal*, vol.II, p.62; Schermbrucker, 'Zhlobane and Kambula', p.379.

139. Ibid.

140. Ashe and Wyatt Edgell, *Zululand Campaign*, p.142.

141. Schermbrucker, 'Zhlobane and Kambula', p.379.

142. Wood to D.A.G., 30 March 1879, quoted in Norris-Newman, *In Zululand*, p.161; War Office, *Narrative*, p.81; Wood, *Midshipman to Field Marshal*, vol.II, p.63.

143. Norris-Newman, *In Zululand*, p.164.
144. Moodie, *British, Boers and Zulus*, p.275: Correspondent to a Natal newspaper.
145. Norris-Newman, *In Zululand*, p.165.
146. Callwell, *Small Wars*, pp.172, 211.
147. Buller Papers, W.O. 132/1: Buller to A.G., 30 March 1879; *Natal Colonist*, 10 April 1879: Kambula correspondent, 31 March 1879; Vijn, *Cetshwayo's Dutchman*, p.114: Mehlokazulu's statement; Schermbrucker, 'Zhlobane and Kambula', pp.379–80.
148. SNA 1/1/34, no.73: Statement of Sibalo to J.W. Shepstone, 1 June 1879.
149. Vijn, *Cetshwayo's Dutchman*, p.37.
150. Wood to D.A.G., 30 March 1879, quoted in Norris-Newman, *In Zululand*, p.161; Letter by an officer in Wood's Swazi Irregulars to *The Friend of the Free State and Bloemfontein Gazette*, 1 May 1879, quoted in Emery, *Marching over Africa*, p.65.
151. Moodie, *British, Boers and Zulus*, p.275: Correspondent to a Natal newspaper.
152. *Natal Colonist*, 10 April 1879: Kambula correspondent, 31 March 1879.
153. *Natal Mercury*, 16 April 1879: Young Natalian's account; Norris-Newman, *In Zululand*, p.165.
154. Moodie, *British, Boers and Zulus*, p.287: Correspondent in *Cape Argus*.
155. *Natal Colonist*, 10 April 1879: Kambula correspondent, 31 March 1879.
156. Norris-Newman, *In Zululand*, p.165.
157. Mossop, *Running the Gauntlet*, p.74; Letter by Private E. Fowler in the *Wigan Observer and District Advertiser*, 28 April 1879, quoted in Emery, *Marching over Africa*, p.79.
158. McToy, *The 13th Regiment*, p.52.
159. Letter by Sergeant Edward Jervis in *The Dover Express*, 5 September 1879, quoted in Emery, *Red Soldier*, p.172.
160. Captain C. D'Arcy to his parents, quoted in Moodie, *British, Boers and Zulus*, p.279.
161. *Natal Mercury*, 16 April 1879: Young Natalian's account.
162. McToy, *The 13th Regiment*, p.52.
163. Letter by F. Schermbrucker in *The Friend of the Free State and Bloemfontein Gazette*, 1 May 1879, quoted in Emery, *Marching over Africa*, p.65.
164. Norris-Newman, *In Zululand*, p.165.
165. Moodie, *British, Boers and Zulus*, p.275: Correspondent in a Natal newspaper.
166. Letter by F. Schermbrucker in *The Friend of the Free State and Bloemfontein Gazette*, 1 May 1879, quoted in Emery, *Marching over Africa*, p.65.
167. *Natal Colonist*, 10 April 1879: Kambula correspondent, 31 March 1879.
168. Woodgate's Military Diary: 30, 31 March 1879; McToy, *The 13th Regiment*, p.53.

169. Woodgate's Military Diary: 30, 31 March, 1, 3 April 1879.

170. *Natal Mercury*, 19 April 1879: Utrecht correspondent, 11 April 1879.

171. John Wesley Shepstone Papers, vol. 10: 'Reminiscences of the Past', p. 108; *Natal Colonist*, 26 April 1879.

172. Woodgate's Military Diary: 21 April 1879; SNA 1/1/34, no. 73: Statement of Sibalo, 1 June 1879; SNA 1/1/34, no. 85: Statement of Sihlahla, 3 June 1879; Vijn, *Cetshwayo's Dutchman*, pp. 36–7.

173. Wood, *Midshipman to Field Marshal*, vol. II, pp. 67–8; McToy, *The 13th Regiment*, p. 52; Emery, *Red Soldier*, p. 22.

174. War Office, *Narrative*, pp. 81, 161.

175. Ibid., p. 81.

176. Letter by Private E. Fowler in *The Wigan Observer and District Advertiser*, 28 April 1879, quoted by Emery, *Marching over Africa*, p. 79.

177. Letter by Sergeant E. Jervis in *The Dover Express*, 5 September 1879, quoted in Emery, *Red Soldier*, p. 173.

178. Woodgate's Military Diary: 30, 31 March 1879.

179. Ashe and Wyatt Edgell, *Zululand Campaign*, p. 144.

180. Schermbrucker, 'Zhlobane and Kambula', p. 380.

181. McToy, *The 13th Regiment*, p. 52.

182. TS 39: Henrique Shepstone to Theophilus Shepstone, 30 March 1879.

183. Schermbrucker, 'Zhlobane and Kambula', p. 380.

184. Captain C. D'Arcy to his parents, quoted in Moodie, *British, Boers and Zulus*, p. 278.

185. Mossop, *Running the Gauntlet*, pp. 74–5.

186. Gibson, *Story of the Zulus*, p. 199.

187. *Natal Colonist*, 24 April 1979: Kambula correspondent, 10 April 1879.

188. *Times of Natal*, 9 May 1879: Kambula correspondent, 2 May 1879.

189. CSO 1926, no. 2076: Fannin to Colonial Secretary, 19 April 1879.

190. *Natal Mercury*, 9 April 1879: Kambula correspondent, 1 April 1879; *Natal Colonist*, 14 June 1879.

191. Gibson, *Story of the Zulus*, p. 198.

192. J. W. Shepstone Papers, vol. 10: 'Reminiscences of the Past', pp. 107–8; Mitford, *Zulu Country*, p. 279: Testimony of Warrior of the Tulwana; Webb and Wright, *Zulu King Speaks*, p. 36.

193. Webb and Wright, *Zulu King Speaks*, p. 37.

194. CSO 1926, no. 1939/79: Fannin to Colonial Secretary, 9 April 1879; J. P. C. Laband and P. S. Thompson, *War Comes to Umvoti: The Natal-Zululand Border 1878–9*, Durban, 1980, p. 51.

195. *Natal Colonist*, 10 April 1879: Kambula correspondent, 31 March 1879.

196. SNA 1/1/34, no. 73: Statement of Sibalo, 1 June 1879; SNA 1/1/34, no. 85: Statement of Sihlahla, 3 June 1879.

197. Wood, *Midshipman to Field Marshal*, vol. II, p. 63.

198. Webb and Wright, *Zulu King Speaks*, p. 37.

199. Ibid.

200. Woodgate's Military Diary: 30, 31 March 1879; CP 14, no. 21: Wood to D.A.G., 3 April 1879.

201. SNA 1/1/34, no. 85: Statement of Sihlahla, 3 June 1879.

202. *B.P. P.*(C. 2374), enc. in no. 31: Special Border Agent, Umvoti, to Colonial Secretary, n.d. [April 1879?]

203. Vijn, *Cetshwayo's Dutchman*, p. 115: Mehlokazulu's statement.

204. FC 2/5: Fannin to his wife, 21 April 1879; CSO 1926, no. 2169: Fannin to Colonial Secretary, 26 April 1879.

205. *Natal Colonist*, 25 September 1879: King Cetshwayo's comments taken from the *Cape Times*.

'O! Let's go and have a fight at Jim's!'

The Zulu at the battle of Rorke's Drift

J.P.C. LABAND

During the late afternoon and night of 22–23 January 1879, a strong Zulu force which had crossed the Buffalo River into the Colony of Natal, was repulsed with heavy losses at kwaJim, or Rorke's Drift. The British regarded their defence of Rorke's Drift as an epic action which secured Natal from the horrors of a Zulu invasion. It also provided them with suitable propaganda with which to counter their disaster at Isandlwana earlier that day, and to tarnish the Zulu success in that battle.

In reality, the defence of Rorke's Drift merely diverted a large Zulu raiding party from going about its short-term business of ravaging the Buffalo River valley in the vicinity, and not from marching on Pietermaritzburg. Yet it did have the important consequence of serving the Zulu notice that their tactics of envelopment and hand-to-hand fighting – which had only prevailed at very high cost at Isandlwana against an over-extended and poorly positioned foe – were ineffective against prepared positions defended with modern rifles, no matter how outnumbered the garrison. This lesson, which the Zulu were reluctant to absorb, was to be the key to future British success in battle against them.

When the British Centre Column advanced across the Buffalo River into Zululand on 11 January, it left behind a small garrison, consisting of a company of the 2/24th Regiment, a company of the 2/3rd NNC and various detached personnel, to secure its depot at Rorke's Drift. Not anticipating a Zulu attack, the British had neglected to fortify the Swedish mission church and house at the place, which had been converted respectively into a commissariat store and hospital. Shortly after 3 p.m. on 22 January some fugitive horsemen from Isandlwana arrived at the drift below the post with the alarming intelligence that the Zulu army had overrun the British camp, and that a large Zulu force was making for Rorke's Drift.

Lieutenant J.R.M. Chard, R.E., the senior officer present, resolved that the garrison must stand and defend itself until it could be relieved. The post was hastily fortified by erecting a breast-high barricade of large 200 lb. (90,7 kg) mealie-bags, which, incorporated with two wagons, connected the barricaded and loopholed store with the similarly prepared hospital, and then ran back along the top of a rocky terrace to a stone-walled cattle-kraal next to the store. Since the Zulu had no artillery, and were inadequately equipped with firearms, it was hoped that these improvised fortifications would be sufficient, especially since the Zulu would have to face the concentrated Martini-Henry rifle fire of the garrison. Moreover, their usual tactics of enveloping the enemy's flanks would lose their effectiveness against an all-round defensive position. While this work was in progress, about 100 men of the Natal Native Horse, who had formed part of Durnford's ill-fated No. 2 Column, arrived at the drift from Isandlwana. Chard positioned them at the river to give warning of and to retard the Zulu advance.[1]

The approaching Zulu force consisted of the uThulwana, iNdlondlo, iNdluyengwe and uDloko *amabutho*.[2] They were the reserve that had not been engaged with the rest of the army in the battle at Isandlwana, but had passed north of the British camp to form up on the high ground above it. Their combined strength, inevitably, is difficult to compute, but it is reasonable to suggest that it was somewhere between 3 000 and 4 000. They did not advance in one unit from Isandlwana towards the vicinity of Rorke's Drift, but in three separate contingents. The younger men of the iNdluyeng-we moved in open order in advance of the others around the rear of Isandlwana, following the path of the British fugitives and searching out and killing those making for Sotondose's (or Fugitives') Drift across the flooded Buffalo. The other two contingents first went through various disciplinary exercises – dividing, wheeling and reforming – before also moving off at some distance from each in open order, sweeping the country in the direction of the drifts upstream of Sotondose's.[3]

Their leader was Prince Dabulamanzi kaMpande, the king's over-confident and aggressive half-brother. He was not actually one of the generals of the army appointed by the king, but his royal status and domineering personality gave him natural precedence over the other officers of the reserve. His undoubted intelligence, as well as his notorious unscrupulousness, showed in his handsome face, which was adorned with well-cared moustache and pointed beard. Indeed, he was a sophisticated man, at ease socially with whites. He consequently liked to wear European clothes, had developed a distinct taste for gin, and was a magnificent shot with the rifle. A vigorous 40 years of age, he was finely muscled, though he was fat about the legs, which was typical of all King Mpande's sons. He was not, however, a general of proven ability.[4] Unfortunately for the Zulu, the courageous Chief Zibhebhu kaMaphitha Mandlakazi, *induna* of the uDloko and unquestionably the most imaginative Zulu commander in the field, seems to have sustained a wound and turned back when the reserve reached the Buffalo.[5]

The iNdluyengwe forded the Buffalo just up from Sotondose's Drift where the water was calmer, and sat down to rest and take snuff on a small hill on the Natal side. The uThulwana, iNdlondlo and uDloko (the latter apparently undeterred by their commander's absence) crossed further upstream where the Batshe runs into the Buffalo. They spent a long time in the river, cooling down and forming long human chains to assist each other through the water, which only reached up to their waists. When they gained the opposite bank, having brushed aside the foolhardy attempt of some of the Natal Native Horse posted along the river to oppose their crossing, they too sat down on reaching the higher ground and took snuff. (It is known that before battle the Zulu often took narcotics, such as *Cannabis sativa*, so perhaps the snuff-taking should be viewed in this light.)[6]

There is the distinct possibility that the politic Zibhebhu, who in any case questioned the wisdom of going to war against the British,[7] had baulked at crossing the river into Natal and so extending the conflict. Besides, the king had made it very clear to his army that as the victim of unprovoked British aggression, it was his policy to fight only in defence of Zulu soil. No wonder, then, that Cetshwayo was subsequently to be extremely angry that his explicit wishes had been disobeyed, and his policy compromised.[8] Not that Zibhebhu was alone among the Zulu commanders in his scruples about invading Natal. The dignified and influential Vumandaba kaNtati (who was second-in-command of the uMcijo, a personal friend of the king's, one of his most trusted *izinduna*[9] and consequently privy to his intentions), reportedly shouted to the iNgobamakhosi, who were beginning to cross the river in pursuit of the fugitives at Sotondose's Drift, to come back as the king had not given them permission to invade Natal. The exhausted iNgobamakhosi were probably relieved to obey him.[10] The uMbonambi were also disinclined to prolong their day's fighting, and so declined to obey the aggressive exhortations of Prince Ndabuko kaMpande, the king's younger full brother,[11] who urged them to join the reserve in invading Natal. Not unreasonably, they insisted that they should rather return to Isandlwana to tend their wounded.[12]

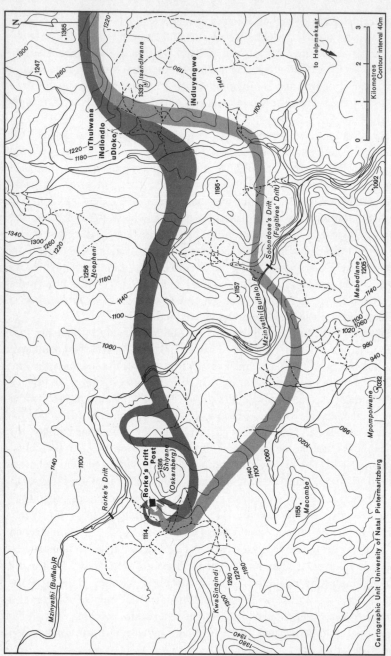

Advance of the Zulu forces on Rorke's Drift, 22 January 1879.

Cartographic Unit   University of Natal   Pietermaritzburg

It is perhaps typical of the arrogance and pretensions of some of the king's brothers that both Ndabuko and Dabulamanzi should have so blatantly disregarded his orders. Yet what considerations motivated this disobedience?

The contrasting acceptance and rejection by the iNgobamakhosi and uMbonambi of Vumandaba's and Ndabuko's orders underlined what had already been made apparent in the opening moments of the battle of Isandlwana: Zulu warriors were only going to obey their commanders if their orders coincided with the inclinations of their men. Dabulamanzi, as he was later freely to admit, was chagrined at having missed the fighting at Isandlwana, and 'wanted to wash the spears of his boys.'[13] His 'boys' felt similarly, and feared that should they return without fighting, they would be the laughing-stocks of all Zululand. It seems clear, though, that tired and hungry as they were after their already long march, they had no plans for a serious incursion into Natal. Their intention was simply to scour the countryside as far as the foot of the Helpmekaar heights, burn farms and *imizi*, lift what cattle they could find, and then retire to Zululand with honour salvaged. In other words, what they had in mind was something akin to the limited but destructive raid across the middle Thukela River to the foot of Kranskop, which about 1 000 Zulu were later to make on 25 June 1879.[14] Dabulamanzi's men, however, were diverted from this traditional course of a punitive raid into enemy territory when they came up to the little post at Rorke's Drift, garrisoned by a handful of British soldiers. It seemed a tempting and prestigious prize, to be snatched up lightly on the way. Never did they suppose that its determined defence would compel them to commit all their strength to attempt its capture, and force them to curtail their intended ravaging of the plain.[15]

It would appear then, that the more sophisticated strategic motives ascribed the Zulu by the British – namely, either to prevent any help reaching Isandlwana from Rorke's Drift;[16] or, conversely, to cut off Chelmsford's retreat to Rorke's Drift[17] – were unfounded. To people in Zululand, Dabulamanzi's attack on Rorke's Drift seemed afterwards to have been both unpremeditated and absurd. As they said: 'You marched off. You went to dig little bits with your assegais out of the house of Jim, that had never done you any harm!'[18]

While the two contingents of older *amabutho* were taking their snuff near the confluence of the Buffalo and Batshe, an advance guard of about ten men of the iNdluyengwe scouted up the valley between Rorke's Drift and the Macembe and kwaSingindi hills to its rear. The main body of iNdluyengwe duly followed them at an easy pace. Meanwhile, some detached sections went about their primary objective of ravaging the plain in the direction of Helpmekaar, and set fire to the farmhouse and *imizi* on a white farm neighbouring Rorke's Drift. Having rested for about half an hour, the first of the two contingents of older men set off in their turn. They bore to their left behind Shiyane Mountain (Oskarsberg), apparently to support the iNdluyengwe in their advance. The remaining contingent sent out a number of scouts, who ran hard up the river bank towards the main drift below the post. It then proceeded in their wake, led by two stout chiefs on horseback, one of whom must have been Dabulamanzi, who was a practiced horseman.[19] The advancing Zulu forces started rietbuck and duiker, driving them along before them. But none of the Zulu took any notice of the game,[20] for a far greater prize had come in sight.

At about 4.20 p.m. the British garrison heard the sound of firing coming from behind Shiyane Mountain, which overlooked Rorke's Drift from the south-east. It seems that the Natal Native Horse, who were deployed along the river, were skirmishing with the Zulu as they advanced. An officer of the NNH appeared to report the proximity of the Zulu force, and then galloped off with his men to the safety of the heights at Helpmekaar, where there was a strong British post. The company of NNC followed their craven example, so depriving the post in all of about 200 of its defenders. The perimeter of the fortified position was now too long for the remaining garrison of 8 officers and 131 men (35 of whom were sick) to hold.[21] Chard ordered it to be halved by building a four-foot (1,3 m) high barricade of heavy, wooden biscuit boxes across the position from a corner of the storehouse to the mealie-bags along the stony ledge. But as it was still incomplete when the Zulu attacked, and since all the sick had not yet been evacuated from the hospital which would have been left outside the reduced defensive position, the depleted garrison was forced to try and hold the original perimeter.[22]

Nevertheless, the Zulu had lost the advantage of surprise, and the British were waiting for them behind prepared defences. It did not matter that these were incomplete and rather inadequate, for they were sufficient to prevent the Zulu from employing their usual tactics. All-round defence meant that extend as they might, the Zulu could not turn the British flank. Nor did it help them to envelope the position, for the garrison's concentrated and effective cordon of rifle-fire meant that Zulu could not charge through it in the open to engage in their preferred hand-to-hand fighting with the assegai. They had therefore to seek out suitable cover to concentrate, and could mount attacks only where it was available.

At about 4.30 p.m. the Zulu came in sight of Rorke's Drift around the southern side of Shiyane.[23] Considering the direction of their advance, they must have been of the iNdluyengwe. Only about 20 appeared at first, formed in a line in skirmishing order, just as the British had been trained to do in similar circumstances.[24] They were rapidly reinforced until they were between 500 and 600 in number, so that their fighting line, formed silently in the classic crescent shape,[25] extended from Shiyane towards kwaSingindi to its south-east. Keeping up a heavy if ineffective fire, the Zulu in this formation then wheeled to their right and advanced at a run against the south wall. Stooping with their faces near the ground, they took the fullest advantage of the cover afforded by the many anthills, dongas and steeply banked streams on their line of approach. The British opened fire at between 500 and 600 yards (450–540 m), dropping many of them. Undeterred, some of the Zulu rushed on to within 50 yards (45 m) of the south wall. There they were caught in such a heavy cross-fire from the hospital and storehouse that they could proceed no further in that direction.[26] Without stopping, the majority then swerved to their left in search of a less well-defended sector. Those pinned down before the south wall occupied the cook-house ovens and took advantage of the cover provided by numerous banks and ditches on that side of the post. It was perhaps fortunate for the British that the Zulu there did not perceive the opportunity presented by a large hay rick which had been left standing nearby, for if they had set it alight the smoke could have severely discomforted the defenders and provided cover for an attack.[27]

Those Zulu continuing to manoeuvre surged around the western end and back of the hospital, and made a rush at the building and the north-western line of mealie-bags. This was a much better sector to attack than the southern perimeter, for there was less chance of being caught in a cross-fire, and plenty of cover was available because the defenders had not had time to cut down the bush or trees. The Zulu consequently succeeded in advancing right up to the walls in what was to be one of the three most determined onslaughts of the day. There were a few moments of desperate hand-to-hand fighting before they were repulsed and took cover among the bushes and behind the stone wall below the terrace, and in the garden of mealies and peach trees.[28] A feature of that brief struggle, which was to have important implications for the further course of the battle, was the Zulu disregard of bullets, but reluctance to face cold steel. It was an inexplicable though oft-repeated feature of Britain's colonial wars that the warriors people they encountered, although trained from childhood in the use of spear or sword, nevertheless dreaded the infantryman's sword-bayonet.[29]

A frequent habit with the Zulu was to abandon an engagement after an initial repulse.[30] In this case they persisted. Perhaps this was because their

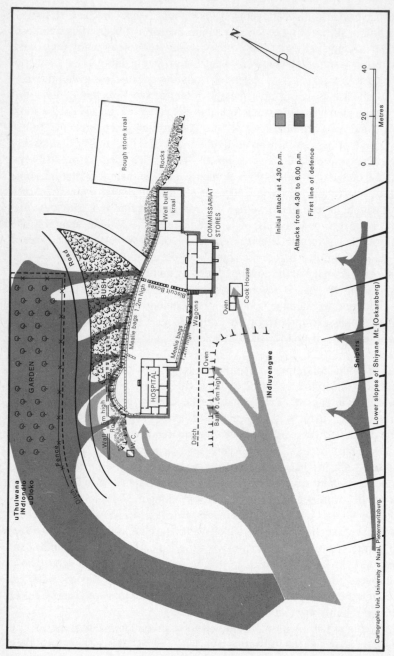

Zulu assault on Rorke's Drift, from 16h30 to 18h00 on 22 January 1879.

Cartographic Unit. University of Natal, Pietermaritzburg.

first attack had been unsupported, and reinforcements were at hand who could hardly march on and leave them to their fate. Indeed, the other two contingents of older *amabutho*, who had apparently joined up in the meantime to the east of Shiyane, now came up around the southern shoulder of the mountain. Their options were limited, for they found the iNdluyengwe fully committed to their attack on the post, and the lineaments of the battle already formed. So while some lined the ledges of rocks and caves on the mountainside, and from this position overlooking the British kept up a constant harassing fire in support of those already firing from the ovens below, the majority moved on to the north-west of the post. They kept further to their left than the iNdluyengwe had done – and so more out of range of the British fire – and occupied the garden, sunken road and bush on that side.

This considerable reinforcement encouraged the iNdluyengwe already there. Because of the heavy cover, they and the new arrivals were able to advance with relative impunity right up to the British defences. They then launched a series of desperate assaults on the hospital and along the wall of mealie-bags as far as the bush reached, which was about up to where the cross-wall of biscuit-boxes began. The Zulu seem not to have thrown their assegais at all, but to have kept them for stabbing the defenders once they reached them.[31] Once the garrison had repulsed each charge in intense hand-to-hand fighting, the Zulu took cover in the bush, kept up their fire on the defenders while regrouping, and then tried again with great determination. If it had not been for the dead ground to the north-west of the post, the wall and heavy bush, it is difficult to see how they could have maintained their position in dangerous proximity to the post for so many hours. From the dead left upon the ground, the British were able to establish that it was the uThulwana, with whom the iNdluyengwe were incorporated, who must have borne the brunt in this violent second stage of the fighting.[32] Meanwhile, the snipers on Shiyane were taking the British completely in reverse, and though on account of their bad marksmanship the damage was not as great as it should have been, it was serious enough.

At length, at about 6 p.m. as the shadows gathered, the Zulu began to extend their attack further to their left beyond the bush along the more exposed parts of the north-west perimeter. In doing so, they were embarking on what was to be their only night battle of the war. The Zulu did not usually fight at night, but in this case they had unfinished business to complete, and perhaps they hoped that the gathering darkness would compensate for the lack of other cover. In any event, they began to develop their formidable and prolonged third assault. Chard, fearing that in their determination the Zulu would get over the wall behind the line of biscuit-boxes and breach his position, and anxious at the mounting casualties from the snipers on Shiyane, decided to withdraw to the shorter position he had prepared behind the biscuit-boxes. The Zulu immediately occupied the wall the defenders had abandoned and, in emulation of the British, used it as a breastwork to fire over.

At first, a heavy fire from the biscuit-boxes prevented the Zulu from getting over the mealie-bags and into the hospital which its occupants were attempting to evacuate, but at length they succeeded in setting the thatched roof alight at its western end and burst into the building. The hospital garrison retired room by room, bringing out all the sick they could.[33] As to be anticipated, the Zulu ritually slit open the bellies of those whom they succeeded in killing.[34]

The capture of the hospital and the retreat of the British behind the line of biscuit-boxes greatly increased the Zulus' confidence. While some looted the camp of the company of the 24th outside the defences, the majority pressed their attack with renewed vigour.[35] Whenever repulsed, they retired for ten or fifteen minutes to have a war-dance and work themselves up for a renewed assault.[36] While some attempted (without ultimate success) to fire the roof of the storehouse, others began an assault on the stone cattle-kraal which formed the defenders' eastern perimeter. Faced with the real possibility that the storehouse might have to be abandoned and that the line of defences would be breached there and elsewhere, the British set about converting two great heaps of mealie-bags into a sort of redoubt. This redoubt provided a second and elevated line of fire all round, and could serve as a final defence should it come to that, which for a time seemed quite likely.

Ironically, the glare from the burning hospital, whose flames only died out towards midnight, probably saved the British. When setting it alight, the Zulu had not reckoned on the advantage the light would give defenders with superior firearms whose attackers were thrown up into silhouette. Moreover, by illuminating the whole battlefield, the Zulu lost the advantage of night and the possibility of launching surprise attacks from unexpected quarters.[37] Despite this inadvertent loss of advantage, the Zulu nevertheless managed after several repulses to clear half the cattle-kraal of its defenders and to take possession of the wall across its middle. However, the wall was too high for them to fire over effectively, and they were shot down by the British holding the inner wall as soon as they showed themselves.

The capture of half the kraal and subsequent stalemate there marked the turning of the Zulu tide. For as darkness finally fell, the Zulu seemed to pause, and some of the British swore they had just seen redcoats advancing

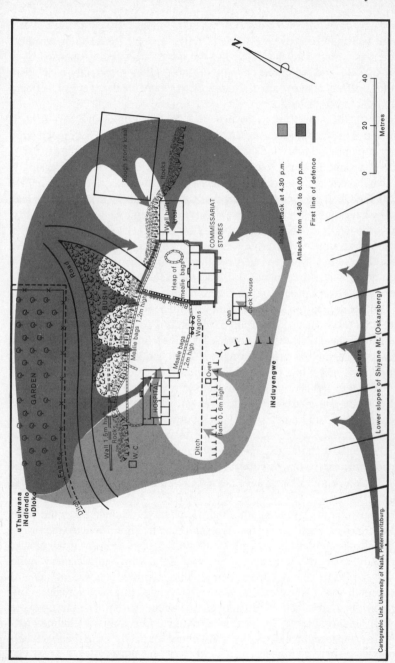

Cartographic Unit, University of Natal, Pietermaritzburg.

Zulu assault on Rorke's Drift, from 18h00 on 22 January to 04h30 on 23 January 1879.

in support down the road from Helpmekaar. Indeed, two companies of the 1/24th had marched towards Rorke's Drift, and by sunset their advance guard was within 3 miles (4,8 km) of the post. But on being opposed by a body of Zulu, and seeing the hospital in flames, they incorrectly concluded that the post had already fallen, and retired to secure the depot at Helpmekaar from anticipated attack.[38]

Nevertheless, the Zulu were unsettled by the knowledge that further British troops were moving unpredictably in the vicinity. This, coupled with the uncertainties of night and the awareness of their persistent failure to carry the post despite repeated efforts and heavy losses, made them increasingly reluctant to attempt a fourth full-scale assault. Consequently, although they maintained their positions along the walls the defenders had abandoned, and kept up a heavy fire from all sides until about midnight, they did not actually charge up again in a body after about 9 or 10 p.m. Even so, they kept the garrison in a state of alarm by every now and again setting up a confused shout of 'uSuthu!' from one side and then another, leaving the defenders in doubt as to where they intended to attack. They kept this up into the early hours, as well as a desultory fire from Shiyane and the garden and bush on the other side. But as the Zulu later admitted, it was no longer fighting, merely an 'exchange of salutations'.[39] Even this ceased at about 4 a.m. The British remained on the alert, however, for they feared that the Zulu would renew their assault at dawn. If only the Zulu had known, the garrison was down to one-and-a-half boxes of ammunition, and could not have defended themselves for much longer against a determined attack.[40]

Yet when day broke, the Zulu were out of sight, having retired in the direction they had come, around the southern shoulder of Shiyane. The majority moved back across the Buffalo towards Isandlwana. It was these exhausted and demoralized warriors who encountered Chelmsford's returning column near the Batshe valley. Fortunately for them, the British were in a similar state, and the two forces passed each other by without a shot being fired.[41]

Meanwhile, the garrison, who had no means of knowing that the main Zulu force had retired across the river, and who had no idea when they were to be relieved, feverishly strengthened their defences against further attack. And duly, at about 7 a.m. a large body of Zulu, who had remained in the vicinity of Rorke's Drift, appeared in growing numbers on kwaSingindi Hill to the south-west of the post. The garrison presumed that they were intending to renew the attack,[42] but Chard later came to believe they had gone up to the high ground to observe Chelmsford's advance. Certainly, as Chelmsford's column came in sight of Rorke's Drift at about 8 a.m., the Zulu finally melted away.

The relief of the British post at Rorke's Drift, 23 January 1879.

Chard had been fairly certain that the Zulu were in no condition to attack again on the morning of 23 January because of the unacceptably heavy casualties they had sustained.[43] What gives force to this conclusion is the fact that the majority of Zulu began their withdrawal from Rorke's Drift while Chelmsford was still encamped at Isandlwana, and posed them no immediate threat. Independent of considerations about being caught by the arrival of a relieving British force, or being terribly short of food and sleep, must have been the stark awareness among the surviving Zulu that their companions had vainly died, literally in heaps, before the British defences. The great truth must have dawned that prepared defences, manned by determined men armed with modern rifles, were almost impregnable to frontal attack. Certainly, after their experience before Rorke's Drift, the Zulu flinched at even the suggestion of ever pressing on to Pietermaritzburg. It was sufficient to say: 'There are strongholds there.'[44]

Zulu casualties had indeed been insupportable at Rorke's Drift, perhaps around 15 per cent of those engaged. In future battles of the war, considerably less severe losses sustained in attack were to prove quite sufficient cause for the Zulu to retire. In those situations, moreover, British mounted pursuit was inevitably to transform an ordered withdrawal into rout, and was to be responsible for a large proportion of the total Zulu losses. At the battle of Ulundi, for example, where the Zulu casualty rate was about 10 per cent, nearly half the losses occurred during the rout.[45] That at Rorke's Drift the Zulu were able to withdraw without hindrance or loss, underscores the atypical extent of their casualties sustained in frontal attack, and draws attention to their extraordinary bravery and persistence.

When the British inspected the abandoned field that morning, they found the Zulu dead piled in heaps, sometimes three deep. They lay especially thickly in front of the verandah outside the hospital, and round the walls on the north-western and north-eastern sides of the post, their heaped bodies sloping off from the top of the barricades.[46] Most were grotesquely disfigured, mutilated by Martini-Henry bullets (often fired at point-blank range) and frozen by death in extraordinary attitudes.[47] About 100 guns and rifles and some 400 assegais were also found upon the field, where the Zulu had abandoned them.[48]

If only for hygienic reasons, the British immediately set about burying the rapidly putrefying Zulu dead. The men of the 3rd NNC and 24th Regiment of Chelmsford's relieving column provided the fatigue parties. Since the NNC had a great repugnance to touching the dead, it was arranged that they should dig the necessary pits, to which the 24th dragged the bodies with the aid of leather reims, there being few carts or draught animals available for the gruesome task. The corpses were then burnt with wood cut from thorn trees before being finally covered over with earth. The operation took two days.[49]

Chard reported that they buried 351 Zulu,[50] though Commeline put the figure at 367,[51] and Holt at 375.[52] In reality, the number of Zulu dead must greatly have exceeded any of these figures based on body-counts, though reported Zulu estimates of 2 000 are clearly exaggerated.[53] What makes any accurate computation especially difficult to achieve is the fact that the Zulu were not forced to retire in haste. This meant that relatives were enabled to dispose of unknown numbers of their dead in dongas and the river, and were allowed to carry off many of their wounded with them.[54] Some of these drowned while trying to cross the Buffalo,[55] and a large (but unknowable) percentage of the remainder would inevitably have died of their wounds on their way home, or soon afterwards. Many other wounded were too seriously injured even to attempt to withdraw into Zululand. For months afterwards the garrison at Rorke's Drift were coming across bodies where the wounded had crept away to die in the long grass, in caves and among the rocks a great distance away. But the British no longer bothered to keep an accurate tally of the dead.[56]

There is an even darker side to the fate of the Zulu wounded, one which the British would rather have suppressed, and certainly attempted to rational-ize.[57] Fannin reported on the very morning after the battle that a further 200 Zulu dead had been found a way off from those killed and buried near the post.[58] Unfortunately, there can be but little doubt that a great many of these 'dead' had actually been wounded or exhausted Zulu lying hidden in the orchard, mealie garden and on Shiyane. They were systematically finished off with bayonet, rifle butt and assegai by British patrols who were trying to conserve their ammunition.[59] Of course, it must not be forgotten that the British troops had been worked up to an implacable fury by the sight of their disemboweled dead, both at Isandlwana and Rorke's Drift; and it should be accepted that it was the custom of the NNC (as it was that of the Zulu) to kill any wounded they encountered. Consequently, as they expected no quarter, the Zulu wounded instinctively fought back when located by the British, usefully justifying their inevitable despatch through their 'treachery'.[60] In the end, only three wounded Zulu were taken alive, and these were ostentatiously cared for by the surgeons with the British.[61] This publicized concern could not disguise, however, how merciless and thorough the British mopping-up operation had been.

How many Zulu did die then in the battle of Rorke's Drift? It is impossible to know exactly, but when to the bodies counted by the British are added the numbers of wounded they killed and those who subsequently died of their wounds, the estimate of 600 (which Henrique Shepstone had from Marulumba kaThinta of the Mdlalose), is a reasonable figure.[62]

In comparison, the British casualties of 15 men killed and 1 officer and 9 men wounded (2 mortally) were relatively light.[63] Because they had fought behind walls and barricades their wounds were all in the upper parts of the body, and those who died had been hit in the head.[64] If Zulu fire had been more effective, there is no doubt that the British casualty rate would have been much higher. But even in subsequent battles, when they had the Martini-Henry rifles captured at Isandlwana, the Zulu failed to make proper use of this arm. They persisted in mass frontal attacks with the objective of engaging in hand-to-hand fighting. In doing so, they disregarded the lesson of Rorke's Drift, which proved that as long as the British could hold an all-round defensive perimeter with a reasonable field of concentrated fire, they were secure from a conventional Zulu assault.

The battle of Rorke's Drift thus provided the model for all successful British engagements throughout the remainder of the war, and vividly demonstrated the inadequacy of traditional Zulu tactics. No wonder King Cetshwayo learned of the repulse of Dabulamanzi's forces before Rorke's Drift with foreboding, and did his best in the future to dissuade his generals from fruitless repetitions against fortified positions. Ordinary Zulu, however, did not always see the implications of the failure to take Rorke's Drift, and jeered at the 'shocking cowards' whom they considered to have been so ignominiously repulsed: 'You! You're no men! You're just women, seeing that you ran away for no reason at all, like the wind!'[65] How unfortunate for Dabulamanzi's men, that they should have marched into Natal to avoid becoming laughing-stocks for missing the battle of Isandlwana, only to become objects of derision for failing to take so apparently weak a position as kwaJim.

Notes

1. WO 32/7737: Lt. Chard's report on the defence of Rorke's Drift, 25 January 1879 (henceforth Chard's report); G. Paton, F. Glennie and W. Penn Symons, *Historical Records of the 24th Regiment from its Formation, in 1689*, London, 1892, p. 247: Revd G. Smith's account, 3 February 1879 (henceforth Smith's account); N. Holme, *The Silver Wreath. Being the 24th Regiment at Isandhlwana and Rorke's Drift*, London, 1979, p. 63: Pte. A. H. Hook's account (henceforth Hook's account); J. P. C. Laband and P. S. Thompson, *The Buffalo Border 1879: The Anglo-Zulu War in Northern Natal*, Durban, 1983, p. 107; J. P. C. Laband and P. S. Thompson, *Field Guide to the War in Zululand and the Defence of Natal 1879*, Pietermaritzburg, 1983, pp. 25, 59.

2. The men of the uThulwana were 45 years old in 1879, those of the iNdlondlo 42, and of the uDloko 41. The men of the iNdluyengwe, who were incorporated with the uThulwana, were only 33 years old. (E. J. Krige, *The Social System of the Zulus*, Pietermaritzburg, 1974, p. 406.)

3. Holme, *Silver Wreath*, p. 50: Maj. J. R. M. Chard's account of the Battle of Rorke's Drift, January 1880 (henceforth Chard's account of 1880); *Natal Mercury*, 7 April 1879: The Defence of Rorke's Drift by an Eye-Witness; *B. P. P.* (C. 2318), no. 3: Epitome of statements by four Zulus of Hamu's tribe, 17 March 1879; SNA 1/1/34, no. 73: Statement of Sibalo, 1 June 1879; SNA 1/1/34, no. 85: Statement of Sihlahla, 3 June 1879; C. L. Norris-Newman, *In Zululand with the British throughout the War of 1879*, London, 1880, p. 65; Ibid., p. 86: Mehlokazulu's account.

4. F. Fynney, *The Zulu Army and Zulu Headmen*, Pietermaritzburg, April 1879: Zulu Headmen; *Natal Witness*, 19 July 1879: Correspondent with General Crealock, 13 July 1879; *The Graphic*, 11 October 1879, p. 350; W. C. Holden, *British Rule in South Africa*, London, 1879, p. 186; Fleet-Surgeon H. F. Norbury, *The Naval Brigade in South Africa during the Years 1877–78–79*, London, 1880, pp. 298–9; Major Ashe and Capt. the Hon. E. V. Wyatt Edgell, *The Story of the Zulu Campaign*, London, 1880, p. 365; B. Mitford, *Through the Zulu Country*, London, 1883, pp. 179–81; *JSA*, vol. IV, p. 373: testimony of Ndukwana.

5. Fynney, *Zulu Army*: Zulu Headmen; H. Rider Haggard, *Cetywayo and his White Neighbours*, London, 1888, p. xviii; H. C. Lugg, *Historic Natal and Zululand*, Pietermaritzburg, 1949, pp. 95, 147–9.

6. *Natal Mercury*, 7 April 1879: The Defence of Rorke's Drift by an Eye-Witness; *Illustrated London News*, 8 March 1879, p. 218: Narrative of the Revd Mr Witt; Cato Papers I, MS 1602a: Cato to Richards, 2 February 1879; Laband and Thomspon, *Field Guide*, p. 6.

7. Haggard, *Cetywayo*, p. xviii.

8. J. W. Shepstone Papers, vol. 10: J. W. Shepstone, 'Reminiscences of the Past', p. 110; SNA 1/1/34, no. 73: Statement of Sibalo, 1 June 1879; SNA 1/1/34, no. 85: Statement of Sihlahla, 3 June 1879; C. de B. Webb and J. B. Wright (eds.), *A Zulu King Speaks*, Pietermaritzburg and Durban, 1978, p. 31; M. M. Fuze (tr. H. C. Lugg and ed. A. T. Cope), *The Black People and Whence They Came*, Pietermaritzburg and Durban, 1979, p. 113.

9. Fynney, *Zulu Army*: Zulu Headmen; Mitford, *Zulu Country*, p. 217; J. Guy, *The Destruction of the Zulu Kingdom*, London, 1979, p. 251.

10. *Natal Colonist*, 11 February 1879; C. Vijn (tr. and ed. J.W. Colenso), *Cetshwayo's Dutchman*, London, 1880, p.97: Colenso's notes.

11. Guy, *Zulu Kingdom*, p.250.

12. J.Y. Gibson, *The Story of the Zulus*, London, 1911, p.182: testimony of Ndabuko.

13. W.R. Ludlow, *Zululand and Cetewayo*, London and Birmingham, 1882, p.61.

14. J.P.C. Laband and P.S. Thomspon, *War Comes to Umvoti: The Natal-Zululand Border 1878–9*, Durban, 1980, pp.67–70.

15. TS 37: H.C. Shepstone to T. Shepstone, 9 September 1879; J.W. Shepstone Papers, vol.10: J.W. Shepstone, 'Reminiscences of the Past', pp.109–10; H.C. Lugg, 'Short Account of the Battle of Rorke's Drift' (1 September 1944, ts. in Natal Archives); Mitford, *Zulu Country*, p.161: Account of Warrior of the Undi. See the comments of Gunner A. Howard in the *Daily Telegraph*, 25 March 1879, quoted in S. Clarke, *Invasion of Zululand 1879*, Johannesburg, 1979, p.82: 'When the Zulu arrived . . . they did not find it quite as comfortable as they thought, for they expected they would have nothing to do but assegai us at their pleasure and possess the place'.

16. Cato Papers I, MS 1602a: Cato to Richards, 2 February 1879.

17. Commeline Letters, D 1233/45: Commeline to his father, 31 January 1879.

18. C. de B. Webb (ed.), 'A Zulu Boy's Recollections of the Zulu War', *Natalia*, December 1978, pp.12–13.

19. *Natal Mercury*, 7 April 1879: The Defence of Rorke's Drift by an Eye-Witness; *Illustrated London News*, 8 March 1879, p.218: Narrative of the Revd Mr Witt; Chard's account of 1880, p.50.

20. Carl Faye Papers 8: Statement of Lugubu Mbata kaMangaliso (who had fought with the NNC) taken by Faye on 4 November 1938.

21. Laband and Thompson, *Field Guide*, p.59.

22. Chard's report; Chard's account of 1880, p.50; Holme, *Silver Wreath*, p.60: Lt.-Col. F. Bourne's account, 30 December 1936; Hook's account, p.63; P.S. Thomspon, 'The Natal Native Contingent at Rorke's Drift, 22 January, 1879', in I. Knight (ed.), *There will be an Awful Row at Home about This*, Shoreham-by-Sea, 1987, p.12.

23. The basis of the following account of the battle is drawn from Chard's report; Chard's account of 1880, pp.50–3; and Smith's account, pp.251–4.

24. Holme, *Silver Wreath*, p.59: Pte J. Water's account, 13 June 1879.

25. Ibid., p.61: Cpl. J. Lyons's account, 13 June 1879; Ibid., Pte. F. Hitch's account, p.62 (henceforth Hitch's account).

26. Hook's account, p.63.

27. Col. H. Harford (ed. D. Child), *The Zulu War Journal*, Pietermaritzburg, 1978, p.41.

28. Zulu War file 2, KCM 42358: Letter from R.J. Hall to the editor of the *Natal Witness*, 25 October [?].

29. Col. C.E. Callwell, *Small Wars: Their Principles and Practice*, London, 1906, p.399; Hitch's account, p.62.

30. Gibson, *Story of the Zulus*, p. 183.

31. *Natal Mercury*, 7 April 1879: Defence of Rorke's Drift by an Eye-Witness.

32. H.F. Fynn, Jnr. Papers, file no. 26031: 'My Recollections of a Famous Campaign and a Great Disaster', p. 16.

33. For details of the defence of the hospital, see Hook's account: pp. 64–5.

34. Holme, *Silver Wreath*, p. 61: Sgt. G. Smith's account, 24 January 1879.

35. Hitch's account, p. 62.

36. Hook's account, p. 64.

37. F. Emery, *The Red Soldier*, London, 1977, p. 134: Gunner A. Howard's account; Hook's account, p. 64; Callwell, *Small Wars*, p. 495.

38. Intelligence Branch of the War Office, *Narrative of the Field Operations Connected with the Zulu War of 1879*, London, 1881, p. 47; Chard's account of 1880, p. 52.

39. Webb, 'Zulu Boy's Recollections', p. 12: comment of Munyu, who fought at Rorke's Drift.

40. WC II/1/6: A.F. Pickard to Wood, 14 October 1879; D.C.F. Moodie, *The Battles and Adventures of the British, the Boers, and the Zulus*, Adelaide, 1879, p. 221.

41. Norris-Newman, *In Zululand*, p. 64; F.E. Colenso with E. Durnford, *History of the Zulu War*, London, 1880, p. 406: Dabulamanzi's testimony; Harford, *Journal*, p. 35; J. Maxwell (ed. L. T. Jones), *Reminiscences of the Zulu War*, Cape Town, 1979, pp. 6–7; A.F. Hattersley, *Later Annals of Natal*, London, 1983, pp. 148–9: Trooper F. Symon's account.

42. H. Hallam Parr, *A Sketch of the Kafir and Zulu Wars*, London, 1880, p. 245; Hitch's account, p. 65.

43. Chard's account of 1880, p. 52.

44. Webb, 'Zulu Boy's Recollections', p. 13.

45. J. Laband, *The Battle of Ulundi*, Pietermaritzburg, 1988, p. 45.

46. H.F. Fynn, Jnr. Papers, file no. 26031: 'Recollections', p. 17; H.G. Mainwaring, 'Isandhlwana January 22nd, 1879' (1895, ts. in Natal Museum), p. 17; *Natal Mercury*, 7 April 1879: The Defence of Rorke's Drift by an Eye-a4 Witness.

47. Chard's account of 1880, p. 52; Hallam Parr, *Kafir and Zulu Wars*, p. 243; G. Hamilton-Browne, *A Lost Legionary in South Africa*, London, 19[?], p. 151.

48. *Natal Mercury*, 7 April 1879: The Defence of Rorke's Drift by an Eye-Witness.

49. Maxwell, *Reminiscences*, pp. 7, 9; Hallam Parr, *Kaffir and Zulu Wars*, p. 261; Laband and Thompson, *Buffalo Border*, p. 44.

50. Chard's account of 1880, p. 53.

51. Commeline Letters, D1233/45: Commeline to his father, 31 January 1879.

52. H.P. Holt, *The Mounted Police of Natal*, London, 1913, p. 68.

53. AC, p. 123: Wood to Crealock, 25 February 1879.

54.   Hallam Parr, *Zulu and Kaffir Wars*, pp.246, 265; Emery, *Red Soldier*, pp.130–1: Hook's account; Maxwell, *Reminiscences*, p.9.

55.   H.C. Lugg, 'Short Account of the Battle of Rorke's Drift' (1 September 1944, ts. in Natal Archives).

56.   Maxwell, *Reminiscences*, p.9; Chard's account of 1880, p.53; Hallam Parr, *Kaffir and Zulu Wars*, p.262.

57.   See the arguments in Hallam Parr, *Kafir and Zulu Wars*, pp.263–7.

58.   FC/2/4: Fannin to his wife, 23 January 1879.

59.   Hamilton-Browne, *Lost Legionary*, p.152; Hattersley, *Later Annals of Natal*, p.150; Symons's account.

60.   KC MS 31185: W.J. Clarke, 'My Career in South Africa', part I, p.27; Hallam Parr, *Kaffir and Zulu Wars*, p.263–4; Hook's account, p.65.

61.   Hallam Parr, *Zulu and Kafir Wars*, pp.263, 265–6.

62.   TS 37: Henrique Shepstone to T. Shepstone, 9 February 1879.

63.   War Office, *Narrative*, p.158.

64.   D. Blair Brown, 'Surgical Notes on the Zulu War', *The Lancet*, 5 July 1879, p.6.

65.   Webb, 'Zulu Boy's Recollections', p.12.

The Natal Native Contingent at Rorke's Drift, 22 January 1879

P.S. THOMPSON

The battle of Rorke's Drift, 22 January 1879, is so familiar to students of the Anglo-Zulu War, and to others as well, that still another account of it may seem tiresome. In this instance it is not intended to re-tell the story of the battle, but to develop an aspect of it which probably has *seemed* uninteresting and unimportant – what happened in relation to the units of the Natal Native Contingent in the lead-up to the battle. This *is* interesting, because of the paucity and fragmentary nature of the evidence, which challenge collation; and important because what the NNC units did or did not do affected the defence of the mission station. With regard to the latter, the very presence of the infantry company influenced the extent of the fortified position, and then its sudden absence made it untenable as such. The cavalry troop that paused near by in its retreat from the Isandlwana battlefield was probably too used up to fight effectively, but it does seem to have provided some sort of skirmish line, out of sight of the station, which would account for the firing that warned the little garrison that the Zulu *impi* was indeed upon them and thus deprived the attackers at the last minute of the advantage of surprise.

In his official report of the action, as it is reproduced in the *Historical Records of the 24th Regiment* (edited by Colonels Paton, Glennie and Symons and published in 1892), pp. 247–48, Lieutenant Chard has written in connection with the Natal Native Contingent:

> About 3.15 p.m. on that day I was at the ponts, when two men came riding from Zululand at a gallop, and shouted to be taken across the river. I was informed by one of them, Lieutenant Adendorff of Londsdale's regiment (who remained to assist in the defence), of the disaster at Isandlwana camp, and that the Zulus were advancing on Rorke's Drift. The other carabineer rode off to take the news to Helpmakaar.

Almost immediately I received the message from Lieutenant Bromhead, commanding the company of 24th Regiment at the camp near the commissariat stores, asking me to come at once.

I gave the order to inspan, strike tents, put all stores, etc., into the waggon, and at once rode up to the commissariat store, and found that a note had been received from the third column to state that the enemy were advancing in force against our post, which we were to strengthen and hold at all cost.

Lieutenant Bromhead was most actively engaged in loopholing and barricading the store building and hospital, and connecting the defence of the two buildings by walls of mealie-bags and two waggons that were on the ground.

I held a hurried consultation with him and Mr Dalton, of the commissariat, who was actively superintending the work of defence (and whom I cannot sufficiently thank for his most valuable services), entirely approving of the arrangements made. I went round the position, and then rode down to the pont and brought up the guard of one sergeant and six men, waggon, etc.

I desire here to mention the offer of the pont man, Daniells, and Sergeant Milne, 3rd Buffs, to moor the ponts in the middle of the stream and defend them from their decks with a few men. We arrived at the post at 3.30 p.m. Shortly after, an officer of Durnford's Horse arrived and asked for orders. I requested him to send a detachment to observe the drifts and ponts, to throw out outposts in the direction of the enemy, and check his advance as much as possible, falling back upon the post when forced to retire and assisting in its defence.

I requested Lieutenant Bromhead to post his men, and having seen his and every man at his post, the work once more went on.

About 4.15 the sound of firing was heard behind the hill to our south. The officer of Durnford's returned, reporting the enemy close upon us, and that his men would not obey his orders, but were going off to Helpmakaar, and I saw them, apparently about one hundred in number, going off in that direction.

About the same time, Captain Stephenson's detachment of Natal Native Contingent left us, as did that officer himself.

In his account for the Queen, written a little over a year later, which is given in *The Silver Wreath* (compiled by Norman Holme and published in 1979), pp.49–50, he elaborates on the official report. Taking it up at his return from the Isandlwana camp:

. . . on arrival I found the following order had been issued. The copy below was given me, and preserved from the fact of its being in my pocket during the fight:

Camp Rorke's Drift.
22nd January 1879.

Camp Morning Orders.

1. The force under Lt. Col. Durnford, R.E., having departed a Guard of 6 Privates and 1 NCO will be furnished by the detachment 2/24th Regiment on the ponts.

A Guard of 50 armed natives will likewise be furnished by Capt. Stevenson's detachment at the same spot – The ponts will be invariably drawn over to the Natal side at night. This duty will cease on the arrival of Capt. Rainforth's Company 1/24th Regiment.

2. In accordance with para. 19 Regulations for Field Forces in South Africa, Capt. Rainforth's Company, 1/24th Regiment, will entrench itself on the spot assigned to it by Column Orders para. – dated – .

H. Spalding, Major,
Commanding.

The Guard as detailed was over the ponts – Captain Rainforth's Company had not arrived . . .

After Spalding's departure for Helpmekaar the crisis was revealed:

I then went down to my tent by the river, had some lunch comfortably, and was writing a letter home when my attention was called to two horsemen galloping towards us from the direction of Isandlwana. From their gesticulation and their shouts, when they were near enough to be heard, we saw that something was the matter, and on taking them over the river, one of them, Lieut. Adendorff of Lonsdale's Regiment, Natal Native Contingent, asking if I was an officer, jumped off his horse, took me on one side, and told me that the camp was in the hands of the Zulus and the army destroyed; that scarcely a man had got away to tell the tale, and that probably Lord Chelmsford and the rest of the column had shared the same fate. His companion, a Carbineer, confirmed his story – He was naturally very excited and I am afraid I did not, at first, quite believe him, and intimated that he probably had not remained to see what *did* occur. I had the saddle put on my horse, and while I was talking to Lieut. Adendorff, a messenger arrived from Lieut. Bromhead, who was with his Company at his little camp near the Commissariat Stores, to ask me to come up at once.

I gave the order to inspan the wagon and put all the stores, tents, etc., they could into it. I posted the sergeant and six men on the high ground over the pont, behind a natural wall of rocks, forming a strong position from which there was a good view over the river and ground in front, with orders to wait until I came or sent for them. The guard of natives had left some time before and had not been relieved. I galloped up at once to the Commissariat Stores and found that a pencil note had been sent from the 3rd Column by Capt. Allan Gardner to state that the enemy were advancing in force against our post – Lieut. Bromhead had, with the assistance of Mr Dalton, Dr Reynolds and the other officers present, commenced barricading and loopholing the store building and the Missionary's house, which was used as a Hospital, and connecting the defence of the two buildings by walls of mealie bags, and two wagons that were on the ground. The Native Contingent, under their officer, Capt. Stephenson, were working hard at this with our own men, and the walls were rapidly progressing.

Further information of the disaster arrived. The ponts were secured and abandoned:

We arrived at the Commissariat Store about 3.30 p.m. Shortly afterwards an officer of Durnford's Horse reported his arrival from Isandhlwana, and I requested him to observe the movements, and check the advance, of the enemy as much as possible until forced to fall back. I saw each man at his post, and then the work went on again.

Several fugitives from the Camp arrived, and tried to impress upon us the madness of an attempt to defend the place. Who they were I do not know, but it is scarcely necessary for me to say that there were no officers of H.M. Army among them. They stopped the work very much – it being impossible to prevent the men getting around them in little groups to hear their story. They proved the truth of their belief in what they said by leaving us to our fate, and in the state of mind they were in, I think our little garrison was as well without them. As far as I know, but one of the fugitives remained with us – Lieut. Adendorff, whom I have before mentioned. He remained to assist in the defence, and from a loophole in the store building, flanking the wall and Hospital, his rifle did good service.

And as the first shots were fired, the NNC fled:

About 4.20 p.m. the sound of firing was heard behind the Oscarberg. The officer of Durnford's returned, reporting the enemy close upon us, that his men would not obey his orders but were going off to Helpmakaar, and I saw them, about 100 in number, going off in that direction. I have seen these same men behave so well since that I have spoken with several of their conduct – and they all said, as their excuse, that Durnford was killed, and it was no use. About the same time Capt. Stephenson's detachment of Natal Native Contingent left us – probably most fortunately for us. I am sorry to say that their officer, who had been doing good service in getting his men to work, also deserted us. We seemed very few, now all these people had gone, and I saw that our line of defence was too extended, and at once commenced a retrenchment of biscuit boxes, so as to get a place we could fall back upon if we could not hold the whole.

Also in *The Silver Wreath* are the accounts of Colour Sergeant Bourne and Private Hook, which contain some information on the NNC. Both apparently were written much later, being published in 1936 and 1905, respectively. Bourne recollects (p. 60):

I was instructed to post men as look-out, in the hospital, at the most vulnerable points, and to take out and command a line of skirmishers. Shortly after 3.30 an officer commanding a troop of Natal Light Horse arrived, having got away from Isandlwana, and asked Lieutenant Chard for instructions. He was ordered to send detachments to observe the drift and pontoons, and to place outposts in the direction of the enemy to check his advance.

About 4.15 the sound of firing was heard behind the hill on our front; the officer returned and reported the enemy close upon us. He also reported that his 100 men would not obey his orders and had ridden off. About the same time another detachment of 100 men belonging to the Natal native contingent bolted, including their officer himself. I am glad to say he was brought back some days later, court-marshalled and dismissed from the service. The desertion of these detachments of 200 men appeared at first sight to be a great loss, with only a hundred of us left, but the feeling afterwards was that we could not have trusted them, and also our defences were too small to accommodate them anyhow.

Hook recalls (p. 63) how the news of disaster was received:

Suddenly there was a commotion in the camp, and we saw two men galloping towards us from the other side of the river, which was Zululand. Lieutenant Chard of the Engineers was protecting the ponts over the river and, as senior officer, was in command at the drift. The ponts were very simple affairs, one of them being supported on big barrels, and the other on boats. Lieutenant Bromhead was in the camp itself. The horsemen shouted and were brought across the river, and then we knew what had happened to our comrades. They had been butchered to a man. That was awful enough news, but worse was to follow, for we were told that the Zulus were coming straight on from Isandhlwana to attack us. At the same time, a note was received by Lieutenant Bromhead from the Column to say that the enemy was coming on and that the post was to be held at all costs.

For some little time we were all stunned, then everything changed from perfect quietness to intense excitement and energy. There was a general feeling that the only safe thing was to retire and try to join the troops at Helpmekaar. The horsemen had said that the Zulus would be up in two or three minutes; but luckily for us they did not show themselves for more than an hour . . .

And the approach of the Zulu:

. . . just before half past four we heard firing behind the conical hill at the back of the drift, called Oskarsberg Hill, and suddenly about five or six hundred Zulus swept around, coming for us at a run. Instantly the natives — Kaffirs who had been very useful in making the barricade of wagons, mealie-bags and biscuit boxes around the camp — bolted towards Helpmakaar, and what was worse their officer and a European sergeant went with them. To see them deserting like that was too much for some of us, and we fired after them. The sergeant was struck and killed.

The Reverend G. Smith, another participant, whose account is reproduced also in the *Historical Records of the 24th*, adds (p. 252) something more about the flight of the contingent:

The garden must have soon been occupied, for one unfortunate Contingent Corporal, whose heart must have failed him when he saw the enemy and heard the firing, got over the parapet and tried to make his escape on foot, but a bullet from the garden struck him, and he fell dead within a hundred and fifty yards of our front wall. An officer of the same corps who had charge of the three hundred and fifty natives before referred to, was more fortunate, for being mounted he made good his escape and 'lives to fight another day.'

These would seem to be the only participants' accounts which mention the NNC in any detail, and from them one may piece together the actions of its units at Rorke's Drift on the 22nd. There are, however, a few questions to be answered, and other, ostensibly primary accounts to be considered.

First, let us ask *who* were the men and *which* were the units of the Natal Native Contingent at Rorke's Drift. The foot were under Captain Stevenson or Stephenson — the correct spelling remains in doubt. William Stephenson came with a great many others from the Eastern Cape to the 3rd Regiment; the *Natal Mercury* of 26 November 1878, lists them, including Stephenson as a captain in the 2nd 'Regiment' (though Battalion is meant), and General Orders No. 213 (3 December 1878) state that W. Stephenson is a captain in the 2nd Battalion of the 3rd Regiment. No report has been found of his being court-martialled; however, General Orders No. 37 (19 February 1879) state the services of Captain Stevenson, 2/3 NNC are dispensed with, being no longer required! Presumably his was the company stationed at Rorke's Drift. The size of the company probably cannot be precisely determined. In theory it should have had nine white leaders — the captain, two lieutenants, and six non-commissioned officers — and 101 blacks — the native officer, ten non-commissioned officers, and ninety privates. The above-quoted accounts might suggest that there were fewer whites and more blacks on the eve of the battle. Obviously Lieutenant Adendorff did not belong to the company — the same *Mercury* puts 'T'. Adendorff in the 2nd Battalion, but General Orders No. 213 place 'J'. Adendorff in the 1st Battalion, as does the journalist Charles Norris-Newman in his *In Zululand with the British* (1880), p. 65. How Adendorff came to be separated from his unit is a question that has not been satisfactorily explained.

The roll of those present at the defence of Rorke's Drift, dated 3 February 1879, which is reproduced (p. 71) and discussed at some length by Holme in *The Silver Wreath*, names eight members of the NNC. One is Adendorff. Then there are six corporals: William Doughty, J. H. Mayer, C. Scammell, W. Anderson, F. Schiess, and J. Wilson. No record has been found of the battalion or company of Doughty or Wilson. The surgeon D. Blair Brown, in his *Surgical Experiences in the Zulu and Transvaal War, 1879–1881* (published in 1883), describes in detail (pp. 13–15) an assegai wound in a thigh, which he treated and which belonged to 'Private J. H. M.', of the 1st Battalion, who received it on 12 January at Sihayo's kraal and was then taken to hospital at Rorke's Drift; the man is Corporal Mayer, which the Reverend Smith confirms (p. 254). Brown also describes briefly (pp. 35–6) the gunshot wound in a shoulder of 'Corporal C. S.', of the 2nd Company of the 1st Battalion, who got it in the battle at Rorke's Drift; this must be Scammell, whom the roll mentions being wounded there. Finally, Brown describes (p. 73), again briefly, the gunshot wound in a foot, also received in the battle (and so the roll records and Smith attests) of 'Mr F.S., a non-commissioned officer in the Native Contingent, a native of Switzerland', who doubtless is Corporal Schiess, recipient also of a V.C. Corporal Anderson is ascribed in a different report – that of the Isandlwana dead in the *British Parliamentary Papers* (C.2260, p.98) – to the 1st Battalion, but the Rorke's Drift roll states that he was killed in that battle. Stevenson and Schiess belonged to the same battalion (if secondary sources are correct respecting the latter), and possibly could have belonged to the same company; in the absence of any information to the contrary, Doughty and Wilson *may* be considered for similar assignment. It is difficult then to account for Anderson's presence – could he be the unfortunate who was killed trying to escape, mentioned by Hook and Smith? The black soldier who was killed is not named; the roll tells only that he was one of 'Umkungu's tribe'. Mkhungu's Xhosa, of Weenen County, contributed 273 to the Contingent and suffered 54 dead and missing, most presumably at Isandlwana.

The infantry proved a liability to the defence, but the same cannot be said so easily for the cavalry. The question is, who were they? Durnford had gone over the river with five troops of the Natal Native Mounted Contingent; Lieutenant Richard Wyatt Vause, one of their leaders, later recounted the order of march: the Hlubi troop (fifty-five BaSotho) under Lieutenant Henderson; the Edendale troop (fifty Kholwa), under Lieutenant Davies; then the three troops of Sikali's men (fifty Ngwane in each), under Lieutenants Raw, Roberts, and himself. Vause does not state whether there was an overall commander of the cavalry, and there does not appear to have been any *per se*. Which officer returned then from Isandlwana by way of Rorke's Drift? It was not Vause; he tells of a harrowing ride down to an unfamiliar drift, presumably Sotondose's ('Fugitives'), and then up to Helpmekaar. It was not Roberts: he was killed in battle. It was not Raw: he stated officially that he crossed five miles (8 km) below Rorke's Drift. Nor was it Davies, who similarly stated that he crossed downstream, but mentions: 'Lieutenant Henderson I believe escaped by the road to Rorke's Drift; some of my men and his own accompanying him.' Henderson made no report, but there is an interesting letter in typescript in the Killie Campbell Africana Library (in the Zulu War File No.2, KCM 42358). It is worth quoting in full:

> To the Editor of the Natal Witness.
> Sir,
>   I notice in your issue of today an account of the defence of Rorke's Drift, and wondered whether another account, written by one who was

there, would be of interest to your readers. Lieut. Chard is mentioned in your article as having fortified the place etc. but the man who really saved Rorke's Drift was Mr Dalton of the A.S.C.

When Mr Alfred Henderson and myself arrived at Rorke's Drift from Isnadhlwana [sic] about 1 or 2 p.m. on that fatal day, Mr Dalton asked us if we couldn't get the native contingent back to build a laager. These natives were empoyed [sic] by the A.S.C. with their waggons etc. but had just bolted. We got on to our horses, fetched them back and stood over them while the laager was built under the direction of Mr Dalton. Chard and Bromhead were not there. The former was down by the river near the punt and the latter was smoking his pipe above the house. When the laager was completed, Mr Dalton asked Mr Henderson and myself if we [would] go and reconnoitre over the hill, and we saddles [sic] up and went off. At that time all the native contingent had again disappeared, also some natives Mr Henderson had brought with him, mounted boys from Edendale.

We went over the hill and as we were returning we saw some Zulus making a rush for Rorke's Drift House. I remarked, 'The Zulus are upon us', and we galloped towards the house.

My horse was the faster of the two, and I got to the house first above the fence, and as I passed within a few yards of the Zulus, the first shots were fired from the hospital and whizzed about my ears.

Mr Henderson went round below the fence and we met outside the wall of the Commissariat shed and the cattle kraal. Here we took shelter and there we stayed and fired away at the Zulus as they came down the hill and squatted themselves in the garden under the peach trees and among the mealies.

I must now tell you that when the Zulus first attacked Rorke's Drift, there were not more than twenty five of them and they kept coming on in batches of twenty five to fifty and so they continued rolling up, until they set the hospital on fire. At this time Mr Henderson and I had exhausted all our ammunition and had to move further away to a thorn tree about 500 yards below the house. It was getting dusk, and as we saw no chance of returning to the laager, as the whole place would soon be on fire, we decided to leave, and started to ride to Helpmakaar.

On the way we fell in with a convoy taking ammunition to Rorke's Drift and quietly trekking along in complete ignorance of what had happened there. Mr Henderson stayed with them the night, and I went off after my cattle at Helpmakaar.

Now, I am not saying anything against the bravery of Lieuts. Chard and Bromhead after the Zulus attacked Rorke's Drift. But I know they did nothing before the attack. Mr Dalton was the man who saved the place. Captain Dunne was also there, and well I remember his words to Dalton, 'Do whatever you think best.' Carbineers, Mounted Police, Edendale Mounted Natives, many who had escaped from Isnadhlwana [sic] before us, had been there but would not stay, and no laager would have been built had Mr Henderson and myself not turned up as we did, to make the native contingent return and work at the laager. These natives numbered about 100, and only a few soldiers and A.S.C. men were there, not sufficient to do the work required.

Reading over yoyr [sic] account in the 'Witness' today, I could not help comparing to myself the ghastly failure of that campaign with the list of unbroken successes achieved by our men in this last native rebellion. All honour to Colonel McKenzie.

As an eye witness I know what happened at Isandlwana and Rorke's Drift, up to the time the hospital was fired, and well can I see the whole thing as it commenced and ended. This I can safely say with fear of contradiction. I was the last white man to leave Isandlwana camp alive. Mr Henderson, some Natal Police, and Edendale Mounted Natives, were also eye witnesses and we fired several shots at the Zulus who were blocking the way.

When we left the hill where I caught up Mr. Henderson and the Police, the whole of Isnadhlwana [sic] Nek and hills were covered with the Zulu army. One or two gun carriages were caught just over the Nek, and we watched these being taken back and then we rode on to Rorke's Drift, to end our day working at the laager and eventually being shut out after all.

So ended that day of tragedy, January 22nd 1879. Some other day I will tell you about Isandlwana.

Yours etc.

R.J. HALL

Boschfontein, Brakwal.
October 25th.

It is hardly necessary to add that this document is *extremely* suspect. The first problem is to date the year of the letter. The invidious comparison of Chelmsford and McKenzie suggests 1906 or shortly afterwards; indeed the *Natal Witness* of 25 October 1906 has a column article headlined 'Rorke's Drift Hero – Late Sergeant Hook – Memorial Unveiled – A Chapter of History.' The second problem is to verify it in the *Witness*. Every issue till the end of December has been examined, but Hall's letter has not been found. The third problem is to identify Hall. A brief report in the *Witness* of 30 January 1879, mentions that R.J. Hall, reported missing, has turned up; since he was not with Carbineers, he *may* have been with the NNC, but more likely he was, as an undated cutting from an unidentified newspaper at the Johannesburg Public Library states, one of 'The Civilian Conductors Who Escaped from Isandhlwana'.

There is a tantalizing mention of Hall in a letter by Harry Lugg, of the Natal Mounted Police. The account, which is somewhat broken and rather too dramatic, appears in Frank Emery's *The Red Soldier* (pp. 131–133):

> . . . It must have been about two forty p.m. when a carbineer rode into the little yard, without boots, tunic, or arms and leading a spare horse. All we could glean from his excited remarks was 'Everyone killed in camp, and 4,000 Kaffirs on their way to take the mission station' (or rather hospital) – not pleasant tidings for a hundred men you may be sure. When he came to himself a bit he said, 'You will all be murdered and cut to pieces,' and the only answer he received was, 'We will fight for it, and if we have to die we will die like Britishers.'
>
> All those who were able began to throw up sacks and knock loop-holes out with pickaxes, and otherwise make preparation to receive them. We had some 2,000 Native Contingent there on a mountain, and occupying the krantzes and caves. Noble savages! As soon as they heard the Zulus were to attack us they made a great noise, had a big dance, clashing their assegais against their shields, and otherwise showed their war-like spirit . . .
>
> In the meantime a mounted infantryman and two of our men, Shannon and Doig, came in excited and breathless. Upon my asking, 'What is it, is it true?' Doig replied, 'You will all be murdered,' and rode off with his comrade. Consolatory, certainly, but nothing remains but to fight, and that we will do to the bitter end. A man named Hall, of [the] Natal Mounted Police, rode out to see if he could see anything of them, and on going about 1,000 yards out he could see them just a mile off, as he described it, 'as black as hell and as thick as grass'. 'Stay operations and fall in!' . . . At about three thirty they came on, first in sections of fours, then opened out in skirmishing order. Up came their reserve, and then they were on us . . .

Lugg may have forgotten to add a sentence to round off the NNC performance. He does not add anything more about Hall.

After reading a draft of this article, the chairman of the Dundee (Natal) museum committee, who has collected a great deal of information on the local history, wrote:

> Now to Mr Hall. He sounds delightful. 'Bob' Hall was an enormous landowner and cattle dealer and butcher in the Klip River area, when my Father-in[-]law first came into the district with the N.M[.]P. i.e. about 1885. He was also a mighty high liver, well known for ordering whisky by the wagonload! . . . Brakwal is under the Berg escarpment. They seem to have been quite [a] bunch, the Overberg farmers, building smugglers' passes, riding off to war . . ., raiding and rustling cattle, living from the look of it prettywell [sic] out of reach of the law.

This oblique reference amounts to hearsay evidence, but whatever its value it does not enhance the credibility of Hall's account.

Interesting, too, are two letters from Henderson, dated Helpmekaar, 25 and 28 January 1879, reproduced in the family's *Henderson Heritage* (published privately in Pietermaritzburg in 1972), pp. 228 and 230, respectively. The first reads –

> My dear Father,
>   You will have heard before this reaches you of the fight and massacre in Zululand. I would have written you yesterday only I wanted to try and hear something about George [Shepstone]. I am afraid there is no hope for him. Colonel Durnford we think was killed as he has not turned up. The kaffirs surrounded us in thousands. We were fighting from about 9.30 a.m. until about 2 p.m. when the Zulus drove us into the camp. Our kaffirs fought well and stood their ground until we were surrounded. I never saw George all through the fight as he was with another part of our mounted men. There must have been about five hundred of our men killed. Twenty-two of the Natal Carbineers are killed. I don't know what they are going to do with us just now. We have lost everything belonging to us. We may have to go down to town to fit out again then I will be able to give you more particulars.
>   With best love to you all, I remain your affectionate son,
>   A.F.H.
> I am afraid that old Bootlegs and Adam are killed.

And the second –

My dear Father,

I wrote you the other day to say that I had got out of the fight the other day. I have not as yet heard anything about George. If I had known what sort of a man Durnford was (when he got into action) I don't think I would have gone with him. He was close to me during most of the fight and he lost his head altogether in fact he did not know what to do. The General was (I think) a good deal to blame as he left the camp in such a bad place to defend. As far as I can make out there are about 700 killed white and black. They say there were about 20,000 Zulus and I think that there must have been quite that number. We shot hundreds of them but it seemed to make no impression they still came on. Here we are now with nothing, all I saved was my mackintosh which was on the saddle. I have got one shilling left today. We have got to patrol the country with my troop and the Edendale troop, the only ones left. We are very down about the affair (that is what are left of Colonel D's column) and without our head there seems no-one here to look after us. Directly all the troops are withdrawn out of Zululand I think the Zulus will then cross into Natal. I hear the Carbineers are going to Maritzburg to get another outfit and recruit. Neither Adam nor Bootlegs have turned up and tell Arthur Shepstone I think Lulu must have been killed. I cannot write to anyone else so you must tell them. I will come home in about two or three weeks time if I can get leave. Tell Kate that George was sent with another lot of men and I never saw him the whole day.

With the best love to all I remain your
affectionate son,

A.F.H.

Much about Isandlwana, nothing about Rorke's Drift. The descendants have been asked about other letters, but without success. In short, Hall's and Henderson's letters present an historical conundrum. Perhaps some day further documents will come to light, which will explain something more of what happened to the NNC that day at Rorke's Drift.

[Previously published in Ian J. Knight (ed.), *There will be an Awful Row at Home about This*. Victorian Military Society, 1987.]

The Active Defence after Isandlwana

British raids across the Buffalo, March–May 1879

P. S. THOMPSON

The impression exists that after its defeat by the Zulu at Isandlwana the British army in northern Natal remained inert, and that almost six months later, the arrival of reinforcements from abroad enabled Lord Chelmsford to resume the offensive. It is a deceiving impression, for the panic after Isandlwana lasted only a few weeks, and the British went over to an active defence about two months after the battle. From the end of March 1879, the British demonstrated and raided along the border of Natal and Zululand, and the withdrawal of the harassed Zulu from the exposed country on the left bank of the Buffalo (Mzinyathi) River, during April and May, attests to the British ascendancy in the northern sector.[1] This account describes the British actions that secured this ascendancy.

Within a fortnight after the battles of Isandlwana and Rorke's Drift the British forces in northern Natal had recovered from the shock of defeat. They introduced regular patrolling and occasional scouting on their front, and on 14 March a small party even made a fleeting visit to the Isandlwana battlefield.[2] Meanwhile the bulk of the imperial forces, in garrison at Helpmekaar, Rorke's Drift, and near Msinga, immediately concerned themselves with fortification and sustenance against daunting logistical difficulties. Settler units there and at Fort Pine, and the Native Border Guard near the river, also restored their confidence and discipline.

The situation along the northern border soon stabilized. Lord Chelmsford would resume the offensive there in due course; but first he must act in the south. The Zulus' investment of a British force at Eshowe obliged him to lead a relief column thither at the end of March. In order to facilitate his advance he ordered a demonstration all along the border to distract and confuse the Zulu.

On 26 March Major Wilsone Black, of the 2/24th, crossed the Buffalo at Rorke's Drift with 35 Natal Mounted Police and 10 officers who remained from the defunct 3rd Regiment, Natal Native Contingent. They rode 10 miles (16 km) in Zululand, apparently going round the Zulu Chief Sihayo's stronghold without encountering an enemy, although for a time they saw a Zulu force moving along a ridge two miles (3 km) distant. At the same time Major Harcourt M. Bengough, commanding the 2nd Battalion of the 1st Regiment, Natal Native Contingent, led most of his men from Fort Bengough, near the Msinga magistracy, to the Buffalo downstream. They were joined by part of the Native Border Guard, but the river was too high for any of them to cross.[3] Whether or not the demonstration had the effect that Lord Chelmsford desired is impossible to determine in the absence of Zulu reports. In any event he was able to relieve the force at Eshowe.

Heartened by this measure of success, Lord Chelmsford ordered the demonstration along the border to continue, and authorized raids across it where practicable.[4] Accordingly there assembled a force of over 2 000 men at Rorke's Drift, which consisted of Natal Mounted Police, Natal Carbineers, and mounted Native troops from Helpmekaar; the 2/1 NNC from Fort Bengough; two detachments of the Native Border Guard from downriver; and a mounted Native detachment from the Msinga magistracy. Major John G. Dartnell, commander of the NMP and commandant of colonial defence in Klip River County, was in charge. About 5 a.m. on 9 April the force crossed the Buffalo. Dispositions were made against an enemy surprise and trap, and then the NMP, the NNC and some of the mounted Natives advanced into the Batshe valley and burnt Sihayo's and several others' abandoned kraals, as well as crops. A strong Zulu force was rumoured to be at Isandlwana, but the raiders saw only two Zulu, who fired three or four shots at long range. The expedition returned to the Natal side without mishap about 2.30 p.m.[5]

It would seem then that the British could come and go across the Buffalo if they pleased, but Lord Chelmsford and Sir Henry Bulwer, the Lieutenant-Governor of Natal, had fallen out over how they should do so. Lord Chelmsford argued that British raids would throw the Zulu off balance and reduce their ability to resist. Sir Henry argued that they would benefit little and provoke retaliation. Eventually the home authority ruled in favour of Lord Chelmsford, by which time he doubted if the colonial troops really were suitable and imperial troops were sufficient for the purpose. He did order one more general effort, ostensibly to disconcert the enemy on the eve of his second invasion of Zululand,[6] and Major-General Frederick Marshall, who commanded the cavalry of the column forming in the north, determined that the demonstration would culminate in an expedition directed to Isandlwana.[7]

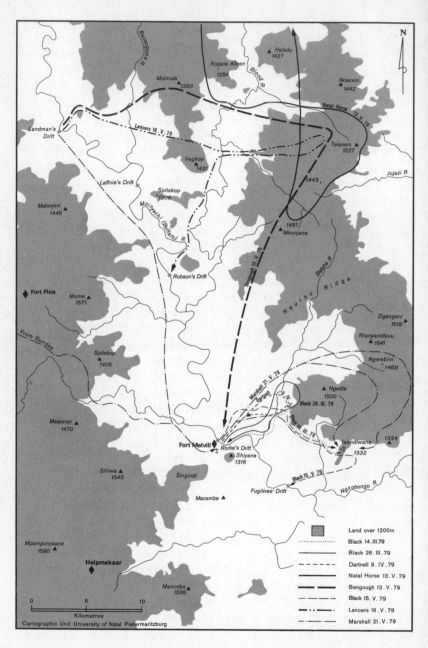

British raids into south-western Zululand, March – May 1879.

On 13 May Bengough's battalion, which had moved to Landman's Drift, crossed the Blood River near Koppie Alleen and scoured Itelezi Hill, reputedly the lair of a hundred Zulu spies. Detachments of the 17th Lancers screened, and the Natal Horse co-operated in, this action.[8] On 16 May Colonel D. C. Drury Lowe made a similar reconnaissance with two squadrons of the 17th Lancers from Landman's Drift, crossing the Blood and burning a large number of kraals.[9]

On 15 May Lieutenant-Colonel (promoted from Major) Black and a small party rode to Isandlwana. A Zulu force, estimated at 30 to 40, followed the party as it returned by way of Sotondose's (Fugitives') Drift, where its crossing was covered by part of Bengough's battalion.[10] Then, on 19 and 20 May, General Marshall concentrated the mounted imperial and colonial units at Rorke's Drift. The imperial units were the Lancers and the King's Dragoon Guards; a section of N Battery, 5th Brigade, Royal Artillery; and some of the Army Service Corps. The colonial units were the Natal Mounted Police, the Natal Carbineers, Carbutt's Rangers, probably the Buffalo Border Guard, and the Newcastle Mounted Rifles, and some Native scouts. At 4 a.m. on 21 May Colonel Drury Lowe led a wing of the Lancers, and another of the Dragoons, along with ten Carbineers and some scouts, across the drift and up the Batshe valley, then over the Nquthu ridge into the valley beyond, in a wide sweep around and onto the Isandlwana battlefield. At 5.30 a.m. Marshall led the rest of the Lancers and Dragoons, Bengough's battalion, and some of the colonial troops, across, and followed the advance as far as the high ground, which his force then swept down to a junction with Drury Lowe's cavalry on the battlefield. Meanwhile Black posted the four

*British cavalry returning to Fort Melvill at Rorke's Drift
on 21 May 1879 with military equipment
retrieved from Isandlwana.*

companies of the 2/24th (which were the garrison at the drift) at the head of the Batshe valley to secure the return route. The main forces reached the battlefield about 8.30 a.m. Troops searched the site and buried some of the dead, and they burnt abandoned kraals in the area. There was no opposition, although a Zulu force was reported later to have gone to meet the expedition and reached the field too late. Marshall brought back the troops in the early afternoon. The next day he returned to Dundee, but the troops remained at Rorke's Drift while a squadron of the Lancers scouted across Sotondose's Drift. On 23 May the units returned to their original posts.[11] Within the week those which comprised the invading column gathered at Landman's Drift and moved across the Buffalo to Koppie Alleen, whence they advanced into Zululand on 31 May 1879.

The British demonstrations and raids along the Buffalo in March, April, and May indicate that the British had regained the initiative along the northern border of Natal and Zululand. Whether or not these actions contributed to the successes of the relief of Eshowe and the second invasion of Zululand is debatable. At least they dispel the impression that the British forces on this front did little or nothing during the long interval between the two invasions of Zululand.

[Previously published in *Military History Journal*, 5, 3, 1981.]

Notes

1. On the Zulu withdrawal see reports dated 10 and 11 April in *The Natal Mercury*, 14 and 16 April 1879, respectively, and CSO 1927, Minute 3470/1879: J.S. Robson to the Colonial Secretary, 10 July 1879. It must be stressed that there was no similar evacuation further down the river, in the Qudeni region.

2. See War Office, *Narrative of the Field Operations Connected with the Zulu War of 1879*, London, 1881, p. 62; C.L. Norris-Newman, *In Zululand with the British throughout the War of 1879*, London, 1880, p. 122; and L.T. Jones (ed.), *Reminiscences of the Zulu War by John Maxwell*, Cape Town, 1979, p. 12.

3. Report dated 27 March in *The Natal Mercury*, 16 April 1879; CSO 1926, Minute 1762/1879: H. F. Fynn (Resident Magistrate, Umsinga) to the Colonial Secretary, 28 March 1879; Richard Wyatt Vause, Diary, 26 March 1879. John Stalker, *The Natal Carbineers*, Pietermaritzburg and Durban, 1912, p. 108; H. P. Holt, *The Mounted Police of Natal*, London, 1913, p. 76.

4. CSO 1926, Minute 1871/1879: Colonel Crealock to Officer Commanding, Lower Tugela [4] April 1879.

5. Reports dated 10 and 11 April in *The Natal Mercury*, 14 and 16 April 1879, respectively; 11 April in *The Natal Witness*, 17 April 1879; and 15 April in *The Natal Colonist*, 19 April 1879; CSO 1926, Minute 1951/1879: Fynn to the Colonial Secretary, 10 April 1879.

6. See *B.P.P.* (C. 2454), enc. 2 in no. 21: W. D. Wheelright (Colonial Commandant, Defensive District No. 7) to the Colonial Secretary, 21 May 1879; (C. 2374) enc. in no. 26: Bulwer to the High Commissioner, 24 May 1879; and reports in *The Natal Mercury*, 29 May 1979.

7. H. J. Watson, Letters from South Africa, 1879–1880 (TS), p. 86; F. E. Colenso, *History of the Zulu War and its Origin*, London, 1880, p. 400; E. Durnford (ed.), *A Soldier's Life and Work in South Africa, 1872–1879*, London, 1882, pp. 268–9.

8. CSO 723, Minute 4612/1879: enc., General Edward Newdigate to Captain Claude Bettington, 10 and 14 May 1879; Watson, Letters, pp. 79–82, passim.

9. Sonia Clarke, *Invasion of Zululand 1879*, Johannesburg: Brenthurst Press, 1979, p. 187, quoting from St. Vincent Journal.

10. Report dated 15 May in *The Natal Colonist*, 22 May 1879; Norris-Newman, *In Zululand with the British*, pp. 179–81; CSO, 1926; Minute 2549/79: Fynn to the Colonial Secretary, 17 May 1879. Fynn adds that after Black's and Bengough's men left, the Zulu force increased to about 100, and the Native Border Guard stationed nearby came down to guard the crossing; a lively but harmless exchange of shots ensued and the Zulus retired.

11. Clarke, *Invasion of Zululand*, pp. 187–9. Watson, Letters, pp. 86–92, passim. Report dated 22 May in *The Natal Colonist*, 27 May 1879. W. O., *Narrative of the Field Operations*, pp. 91–2; Colenso, *History of the Zulu War*, p. 400; Durnford, *A Soldier's Life*, p. 26. Norris-Newman, *In Zululand with the British*, pp. 181–4. J. P. Symons, in My Reminiscences of the Zulu War (TS), pp. 9–11 and Letter (TS) dated 25 May 1879. John Maxwell wrote (*Reminiscences*, p. 15) that the Native Border Guard Reserve from the Msinga magistracy participated in the affair; however, its participation is mentioned only by him, and he may be confused with the expeditions to the battlefield in June (cf. p. 16 and Norris-Newman, *In Zululand with the British*, p. 220.)

Bulwer, Chelmsford and the Border Levies

The dispute over the defence of Natal, 1879

J.P.C. LABAND

'Sir H. Bulwer', remonstrated Lieutenant-General Lord Chelmsford in a long and self-exculpatory despatch to the Commander-in-Chief of the British Army, the Duke of Cambridge, 'from my first arrival in Natal has thrown every obstacle in my way.'[1] Those lines were written in April 1879, by which date relations between Chelmsford, the General Officer Commanding in South Africa, and Sir Henry Bulwer, the Lieutenant-Governor of the Colony of Natal, had reached their absolute nadir. Not that they had ever been completely unclouded. When in August 1878 Chelmsford had arrived in Natal bent on making the necessary military arrangements for an apparently impending campaign in Zululand, he had found Bulwer unconvinced of the necessity, or even the justice, of the contemplated war. Such a divergence of attitudes did not make for easy co-operation, though initially Chelmsford and Bulwer had been able to discuss several issues 'in the most friendly spirit and without reservation.'[2] The atmosphere of goodwill had rapidly dissipated, however, and Bulwer had come to resent the bellicose and impatient tone of Chelmsford and his military staff, and to find them 'not very pleasant to deal with'.[3] Over the coming months many areas of friction were to develop between the military and civil authorities. Yet none was to be more vexed than the dispute over the deployment and command of the Natal border levies, for the issue came to represent the essence of the struggle between the Lieutenant-General and the Lieutenant-Governor for dominance in the Natal sphere of military operations related to the war in Zululand.

On setting up his headquarters in Pietermaritzburg, Chelmsford was at once appalled to encounter the Natal government's insouciance and lack of military preparedness in the face of what he considered the likelihood of a sudden Zulu raid into the colony. He was only too conscious that once the three columns of his army had invaded Zululand, the whole extended and ill-defended Natal border with that kingdom would be exposed to a devastating counter-attack. To meet this threat, the colonial authorities seemed to be relying solely on the passive defence of the white community, who during such an emergency would take to the various laagers and fortified posts then in the process of improvement or construction about Natal, while the unfortunate black population was to be left to take care of itself as best it could.[4] Faced with the prevalent belief that the idea of a Zulu invasion was in any case 'absurd', Chelmsford indignantly undertook to disabuse the Natal government, to chivvy its members out of the 'fools' paradise' where he was convinced they had taken refuge, and to force them to take up the pressing question of their own defence.[5]

In this task the Lieutenant-General had needs of an ally, and in Sir Bartle Frere, the British High Commissioner in South Africa, he was assured of the staunchest support. Frere had come to South Africa in 1877, specifically commissioned by the British government to speed up the process of confederation. He had rapidly come to the conclusion that the independent Zulu kingdom posed an obstacle to his plans, and had therefore to be eliminated. Consequently Chelmsford, in making preparations for a war against Zululand, which Frere was trying to engineer, was acting in strict accordance with the High Commissioner's intentions.[6] But it would not have suited Frere at all to have Natal ravaged by the Zulu. Therefore Chelmsford felt perfectly justified in writing to Frere, representing that his presence in Pietermaritzburg was absolutely essential if Bulwer and his advisers were to be persuaded to take adequate measures against a possible Zulu on-slaught.[7]

Frere, as the Imperial Agent in South Africa, and in his capacity as High Commissioner and military Commander-in-Chief,[8] was superior to both Bulwer and Chelmsford, and so was ideally placed to arbitrate between them. He was also, if it became necessary, in a position to support one against the other. Frere was unable to arrive in Pietermaritzburg before 28 September 1878. Nevertheless by that date Chelmsford had succeeded, unaided, in bringing the Natal government around to his way of thinking. The Lieutenant-General was staying at Government House as a guest of Bulwer's, and though the two men were increasingly at variance with each other on any number of issues, they still managed in their many private conversations to maintain a 'most amicable manner'. Gradually, these discussions paved the way for a meeting on 10 September of the Defence Committee of the Natal Government's Executive Council. Invited to attend,

Chelmsford grasped the opportunity to speak out freely. The Committee had met frequently in the past but, to Chelmsford's mind, Bulwer had on those occasions sabotaged any positive consequences through excessive bureaucratic pedantry. This time, though, he allowed all of Chelmsford's suggestions to be adopted,[9] and by 26 November the Executive Council had finalized their arrangements for the defence of the colony.[10]

Natal was divided into seven Defensive Districts and two Sub-Districts,[11] each under the command of a Colonial District Commander, responsible to the Natal government. These officers had command of the laagers and fortified posts in their districts, as well as whatever forces they could raise, until such time as their districts might be placed under direct military command.[12] Very few whites, though, would be available for military service in their districts, as the Natal Mounted Volunteer Corps and the bulk of the Natal Mounted Police had been placed at the disposal of the military authorities invading Zululand, while those that remained would be needed to man the laagers. This meant that the real defence of the border districts would have to be left in the hands of the black population.[13]

Despite much settler disquiet over the wisdom of arming the 'natives', Chelmsford had from the outset been determined to augment the imperial troops under his command with black auxiliaries, to be raised from Natal's Native Reserves. During November and December 1878 nearly 8 000 were drafted, either into the seven battalions of the Natal Native Contingent, or into Pioneer, Transport and Hospital corps. All of these units fell under the command of the military, and not colonial authorities, and were intended for service in Zululand. On the other hand, it was agreed that the additional levies that the Colonial District Commanders would have to raise for the defence of the border once the British troops and their colonial supports had marched into Zululand, would be maintained by the Natal government.[14] Chelmsford had initially held extravagant plans for these border levies, envisaging a standing force of some 6 000. But Bulwer was able to fend him off, pleading that his government had not the desire nor, most likely, the financial wherewithal to keep such a large body of men in the field. Instead, he proposed a scheme whereby all the blacks living along the border with Zululand would constitute the force guarding it. Each Colonial District Commander would raise a small standing Border Guard of a few hundred men, posted under white levy-leaders at strategic drifts along the river. These would be supplemented by a Reserve of fighting-men furnished by each chief in the vicinity of the border. The Border Guard and Reserves would be able to relieve each other at intervals, thus enabling them without too great a disruption to continue with their normal occupations. Bulwer's

Sir Henry Bulwer (left) and Lieutenant-General Lord Chelmsford (below).

plan had what was, to his mind, the three-fold advantage of saving his government the cost of rations, clothing and shelter because the border levies would be spending so much time at their homes; of actually mobilizing more men along the border than could have been achieved with a standing force as envisaged by Chelmsford; and of allowing the blacks to fight as they preferred, employing their traditional tactics, which they would not have been able to do if organized into regular British-style units as was the Natal Native Contingent. After considerable debate, Chelmsford gave way to Bulwer in late December 1878.[15] In reality he had been left with but little option, for the Zululand campaign was about to open and arrangements, even unsatisfactory ones, had to be finalized. There was just time enough in hand. By the first week of January the Colonial District Commanders had called out their levies along the Thukela and Buffalo frontier and, just a few days later – on 11 January 1879 – the British began their invasion of Zululand.

Almost at once, on 22 January, disaster overwhelmed Lord Chelmsford's Centre Column at Isandlwana and forced him to retire over the Buffalo into Natal. By this action the Left Column under Colonel Wood was also constrained to fall back; but the Right Column, which had fought its way to the mission-station at Eshowe, was blockaded in its hastily fortified position. After the first thunderstruck spasms of panic at this totally unanticipated turn of events had subsided somewhat, Chelmsford feverishly set about restoring the military situation. During February and March he toured the border improving the defensive posts, and began deploying the reinforcements rushed out to him by the appalled imperial government at Westminster. His plan was first to relieve Colonel Pearson's garrison at Eshowe, and then to launch a major new offensive deep into the heart of the Zulu kingdom.

To Chelmsford, about to commit a major part of his available forces to the Eshowe Relief Column, it seemed axiomatic that not only should he have the final say in deciding on the dispositions of the colonial troops left manning the border to his rear, but that they should also actively assist his advance on Eshowe by making diversionary raids across the Thukela River line.[16] Bulwer instantly and vigorously opposed the Lieutenant-General's requirements as far as they concerned the border levies. For one thing, he stood firmly by the prerogatives, vested in him as Lieutenant-Governor, as Supreme Chief of the 'native population' of Natal. In terms of these, Bulwer alone was empowered to call up the blacks in time of war, and he was adamant that 'no provision is made for the supersession of the Lieutenant-Governor by any military or other authority.'[17] He could, of course, make over the command of any black troops raised in Natal to the military, as had been the case with the Natal Native Contingent. But the border levies had not been, and were (as we have seen) maintained by the Natal colonial authorities rather than by the British military ones. It was perfectly true that the three Colonial Defensive Districts along the Buffalo and Thukela had in early January been placed under overall military command,[18] and Bulwer had then conceded that the military would be assured of the right to give any directions 'regarding the distribution and disposal' of colonial troops which 'for military reasons may at any time appear necessary for the better defence of the District';[19] but that did not mean that Bulwer had abandoned his ultimate authority over the border levies nor, more immediately, that he had ever sanctioned their employment on military service in Zululand. There was the nub. If the Lieutenant-General planned to use the border levies in a way which the Lieutenant-Governor considered foolhardy or ill-advised, then Bulwer was prepared to invoke his powers to prevent him. And indeed, Bulwer gravely doubted the wisdom of allowing his border levies to make raids into Zululand. In his stand Bulwer received the unexpected support of Sir Bartle Frere, though for reasons rather different from his own. The High Commissioner merely feared that the 'raw' border levies would be 'next to useless' if used for 'offensive purposes', and should rather be reserved for passive defence along the border line.[20] The nature of Bulwer's objections was succinctly expressed in a Resolution of 1 March 1879, adopted by the Executive Council of the colony. In it, 'raiding expeditions' were stigmatized 'as being an impolitic and undesirable system of war . . . calculated to provoke retaliation, and . . . tending to demoralize the people engaged in it.'[21] Bulwer was willing to grant, however, that in the event of a Zulu raid into Natal, the border levies were 'free' to pursue the raiders back over the border.[22]

Chelmsford was not prepared to countenance the reservations of the civilian authorities. He persisted in his conviction that if the forces defending the border were to be effective, they must on occasion be prepared to go over to the offensive and to strike at the Zulu facing them across the river. In the short term such action would serve to create a useful diversion in favour of the column advancing to the relief of Eshowe; while in the long term it was supposed that a vigorous adoption of what Chelmsford termed the 'active defence' would force the Zulu to abandon the border zone altogether, thus significantly diminishing their ability to mount raids against the colony.[23] Confident of the wisdom of such a strategy, and contemptuous of the colonial authorities' craven and unproductive reliance on passive defence centred around the settlers' laagers, the Lieutenant-General resolved to proceed regardless with his plans for the border levies and to employ them as he thought best. If by doing so he acted without the prior sanction of the Lieutenant-Governor, then the consequences would simply have to be faced as best they could once Bulwer discovered what he had done. The obvious drawback with such an approach was that it required duplicity, but Chelmsford no doubt considered that the circumstances warranted it. Perhaps it was Frere's departure from Natal on 15 March to deal with pressing problems in the Transvaal[24] that spurred Chelmsford on in the underhand course he was about to adopt. Although Frere had not favoured the use of border levies for raiding Zululand, he was not opposed to raids as such and advocated, moreover, the prospect of a military man taking charge of Natal and of subordinating everything there to the conduct of the war.[25] For Chelmsford the loss of his sympathetic and powerful support at Bulwer's very elbow was certainly calculated to make it very difficult, if not impossible, to win the Lieutenant-Governor over to his conception of the proper role for the levies stationed along the border.

That Chelmsford had early determined on proceeding behind Bulwer's back was borne out by his letter of 3 March to Colonel Wood, in which he confided that as soon as he was in a position to move on Eshowe he hoped to be able 'to send in large raiding parties with a hooroosh.'[26] Yet within a fortnight of writing that letter he met Bulwer at Pinetown and left him with the most distinct impression that he had bowed to the Lieutenant-Governor's insistence that the border levies should be employed exclusively for the defence of the border, and should not raid into Zululand. He certainly let Bulwer know that he might require them to demonstrate along the river in order to create a diversion, but he made no reference to sorties into the enemy's country.[27] The Pinetown meeting, aimed ostensibly at clearing up the differences between the Lieutenant-General and the Lieutenant-Governor concerning the employment of the border levies, had in fact been exploited by Chelmsford to allay Bulwer's suspicions as to his real, and unexpressed, intentions. Once Bulwer found out that he had been misled, what had passed at the meeting became a matter for intense recriminations. Meanwhile, Bulwer proceeded in good faith. In accordance with what he understood to be the Lieutenant-General's requirements, he issued instructions on 15 March ordering the Colonial District Commanders along the border to move their levies up to the river, not preparatory to leading them across it, but to make demonstrations along the Natal bank should the military authorities request this.[28]

While Bulwer fulfilled his part of the Pinetown accord, Chelmsford proceeded with his cynically disguised preparations. In his letter of 17 March to Wood, concerning his imminent march on Eshowe, he bluntly declared:

> . . . I shall tell the border Commandants to make demonstrations all along the line . . . and if the river admits to raid across.[29]

Word was accordingly passed along the border to the various commanders to demonstrate and raid across the river in order to divert attention from Chelmsford's advancing column. Major A.C. Twentyman, the military commander of the Middle Border, began his demonstration on 24 March, and on 2 and 3 April sent small raiding parties over the flooded river, which burned a couple of deserted Zulu homesteads.[30]

Bulwer was absolutely ignorant of these developments. The first intimation he gained of Twentyman's sorties across the Thukela was on 7 April, when he received a copy of a military telegram. Sent from Eshowe, which Chelmsford had just relieved, it called for 'raids to be made across the border wherever feasible.'[31] Bulwer's initial reaction was to suppose that the instructions concerned only those troops under direct military authority, such as the Natal Native Contingent and Natal Mounted Volunteers. He simply could not believe that they were intended also to apply to the border levies who, as Chelmsford had apparently conceded at Pinetown, were to serve only within Natal, and whose employment over the border Bulwer had never authorized. But that very evening he was disabused, when a report written on 2 April by Mr W.D. Wheelwright, Colonial Commandant of District VII, was handed to him.[32] In it Wheelwright reported that Major Twentyman, under whose overall military command Colonial District VII fell, had indeed requested him and his border levies to participate with the other units under his direct command in demonstrating, and in making raids into Zululand. But, Wheelwright went on to write, although perfectly willing to assist Twentyman by supporting him with his levies along the Natal bank, he had refused to send any of the troops under his command across the river without the prior and explicit 'sanction of the Government'. In taking that decision he had been acting in full knowledge of the government's expressed disapproval of raids into Zululand, and consequently expected the government's support for his action, should Lord Chelmsford object to his conditional compliance with Twentyman's request for his co-operation.[33] Wheelwright was not destined to be disappointed in his petition, for the Lieutenant-Governor heartily endorsed his refusal to allow his levies to cross into Zululand without the government's sanction.[4] Furthermore, on 9 April he wrote to both Frere and Chelmsford officially supporting Wheelwright's stand, and roundly deploring the likely adverse consequences of the raids.[35] He phrased his objections most forcibly in his letter to Frere:

> 'The burning of empty kraals', he wrote, 'will neither inflict much damage upon the Zulus, nor be attended with much advantage to us; whilst acts of this nature are, so it seems to me, not only calculated to invite retaliation, but to alienate from us the whole of the Zulu nation . . . including those who are well disposed to us . . . [W]e run a risk of driving every Zulu into a desperate defence of his country, and thereby incur the further risk of making the war a long and tedious one'.[36]

For his part, Chelmsford adopted the strategy of taking extreme exception to what he was pleased to view as Bulwer's unwarranted interference with his military arrangements. In doing so, one suspects, he was merely practising his own repeatedly proclaimed preference for the 'active defence', for in all truth his position was an untenable if not dishonourable one. But this did not prevent him on 11 April from writing a very effective, disingenuous complaint to the Duke of Cambridge. Despite his intimate knowledge that since January the military command along the border had been by arrangement with Bulwer an essentially divided one, he protested with a show of righteous indignation to the Duke that 'the Lieutenant-Governor of Natal . . . actually sent orders without consulting me, or my Staff forbidding any native to cross the border.'[37] Having hopefully secured a vital ally, the following day he carried the attack directly into the enemy's camp. He informed Bulwer in the starchiest of terms that the Lieutenant-Governor's refusal to allow his orders to the 'native forces' to be carried out was 'fraught with such dangerous consequences' that he considered it necessary to refer the whole question of military command in South Africa to the Home Government.[38]

Bulwer, understandably, could accept neither Chelmsford's invidious complaints nor the aspersions they cast upon his integrity as Lieutenant-Governor. In his spirited rejoinder of 15 April, he pointed out to Chelmsford that he had done no more than to approve of Wheelwright's stand in refusing to raid across the Thukela subsequent to the event. Considering, moreover, that the position adopted by Wheelwright was perfectly in line with the terms of the Pinetown accord, as they were understood by him and his Government, Bulwer was furthermore quite justified in firmly making clear that he considered the part the Lieutenant-General had played in the affair had hardly furnished him with adequate grounds for taking the moral tone he had in his various letters of complaint. Having parried Chelmsford's thrusts, Bulwer then proceeded to prepare the ground for his own counter-attack. He concluded his letter with the ominous observation that Chelmsford's ordering of the levies over the border was 'at entire variance' with the understanding they had arrived at at Pinetown, and that he had proceeded without Bulwer's authority, or 'any reference' to him whatsoever.[39]

The very next day, 16 April, Bulwer followed up his riposte to Chelmsford with an enormous, 11-page despatch to Sir Michael Hicks Beach, Secretary of State for the colonies. During the course of it he rehearsed all his reservations over the policy of raiding over the border, his understanding of the terms of the Pinetown conversation, and the unfairness of Chelmsford's allegations concerning his 'interference' with military affairs. He then went on to reiterate that the border levies had never been placed under the Lieutenant-General's command, and that he had never authorized their employment over the border. That being the case, he insisted vehemently that Chelmsford, in ordering them into Zululand

> without any authority, without my concurrence, and positively without any reference to me, – has exceeded his powers and acted without due regard for the authority of this Government.[40]

While the government in London proceeded to digest the counter-accusations hurled at each other in their despatches, and to attempt to judge between them, Bulwer and Chelmsford, now both thoroughly aroused, continued with their mutual battle of words. In his response to Bulwer's letter of 15 April, Chelmsford succeeded in fanning the flames of dispute yet higher. He flatly denied that at Pinetown he had ever agreed to the border levies' 'exclusive employment *within* the border' on the logical, but specious grounds, that such an undertaking would have been 'diametrically opposed' to his well-known advocacy of the strategic advantages of the 'active defence'. Yet if such sophistry were calculated to provoke the Lieutenant-Governor, how much more so was Chelmsford's explanation, which he now set out, for keeping his instructions for raids over the border secret from the Natal government. It was the presence of 'numerous spies that are believed to infest the colony', claimed the Lieutenant-General, and from whom by imputation the Natal government was incapable of withholding any information of value, that had forced him to take the course he had. Chelmsford had at least admitted that he had kept Bulwer in the dark about the projected raids; but his explanation, besides being insulting, was clearly nothing more than a conscious attempt to divert attention from the fact that he had deliberately flouted Bulwer's known attitude towards raiding. Chelmsford concluded his provocative and dishonest letter with what was nevertheless a clear articulation of what had by then emerged as the central issue in his exchange with the Lieutenant-Governor:

> 'If I am to be considered fit to be entrusted with the conduct of the war,' he wrote, 'I contend that the command of the colonial forces assembled along the border of Natal for its defence should be placed unreservedly in my hands, and that I should be permitted to employ them within or without the border in whatever manner I may consider best in the interests of the Colony'.[41]

In his final letter to Frere before setting off for the front on 22 April for his second, and ultimately successful invasion of Zululand, he underlined the same point, stating vehemently that it was high time that 'the danger of divided command . . . be done away with'.[42] The letter that contained those words had been an attempt to elicit Frere's aid in gaining the sole command of the troops along the border; but Bulwer had not been idle either in marshalling his support. On 23 April he laid Chelmsford's contentious letter of 18 April before his Executive Council for their consideration.[48] Their conclusions he reported to Chelmsford in an impeccably polite, but extremely cool despatch, which he prefaced with his reiterated and categorical statement that at Pinetown he had never given Chelmsford leave to send the levies over the border. As for the Executive Council, while emphatically objecting to the expediency of further raids across the river (mainly on the original grounds that they would provoke retaliation and harden Zulu resistance), they had nevertheless conceded that Chelmsford might indeed employ the border levies in sorties into Zululand if he thought it 'imperatively necessary for military reasons.' Though prepared through his Executive Council to compromise so far, Bulwer would not abandon his claim to exclusive command of the border levies, nor could he refrain from emphasising to Chelmsford that his Executive Council's concessions had been most reluctant, and against their 'decided opinion'.[44] Neither did Bulwer fail to communicate their position to Frere.[45]

While the Natal government was working out its grudging and circumscribed semi-capitulation to Chelmsford's demands, the Lieutenant-General himself was undergoing a change of mind over the dependability of the border levies, and their ability to raid effectively.[46] Reports emanating from the middle border opened his eyes to their lack of morale and low military capability – as shown during the demonstrations and raids of March and April – and persuaded him, as Frere had been as early as February, that they were really useless instruments with which to wage the 'active defence'. Picture then Bulwer's astonishment when, after all the Lieutenant-General's previous vehemence over the absolute necessity of raiding across the river with the border levies, he received Chelmsford's letter of 7 May, in which he was informed that with troops of such inferior calibre 'it would be absurd to attempt any military operations across the border', and that it would now be 'only under very exceptional circumstances' that they would ever be called upon to serve in Zululand.[47]

But Bulwer's partial concessions, and Chelmsford's sudden change of front concerning the employment of the border levies, by no means resolved what persisted as the fundamental issues at stake. It had not as yet been proven that Chelmsford's policy of raiding had been a mistaken one, as Bulwer and his supporters would have had it; while the question of the ultimate command of the border levies still remained open. It was this latter which first received a definitive answer, and both Bulwer and Chelmsford were humiliated. On 19 May Hicks Beach sent Bulwer a telegram, informing him that it was the British government's decision that the 'full command of any forces, whether European or Native . . . must of course be with the General, with whom the responsibility for the operation rests.'[48] Yet Chelmsford's triumph was destined to be almost instantly blighted. The British government had also decided to solve once and for all the problems inherent in a divided command in Natal by creating a single, unified command: and it was not Chelmsford who was selected to fill the post. Hicks Beach again telegraphed Bulwer on 28 May, this time to let him know that the chief civil and military authority in South-East Africa was to be placed into the hands of General Sir Garnet Wolseley.[49] As a full General he out-ranked Chelmsford; as Governor of Natal he subordinated Bulwer; and as Governor of the Transvaal and High Commissioner for South East Africa he displaced Frere from his supervision of affairs in Natal and Zululand.[50]

Hicks Beach wrote to Frere in an attempt to soften the blow of the proconsul's demotion, and in doing so spelled out his government's reasons for its decision. He explained that the obvious ineffectiveness of the Pinetown meeting between Bulwer and Chelmsford, coupled with their subsequent barrage of mutually recriminatory despatches, had shown

> the danger that must result from such a state of affairs, the mischief that must, I fear, already have been done, and the urgent necessity for change. In fact, a dictator is required.[51]

Wolseley, the British government's choice for the post of dictator would, however, still be some time in arriving in South Africa. This allowed sufficient space for the original protagonists, who had wrangled themselves out of their independent commands, to bring the outstanding issue of their smouldering dispute to an appropriate conclusion.

On 20 May, Major Twentyman, in command of the forces stationed along the middle border, led a full-scale raid into Zululand. Clearly, he must have been unaware of Chelmsford's revised estimation of the quality of his troops, for it was on his own initiative, yet in accordance with the Lieutenant-General's apparently still unrescinded commands of March and April to raid across the river whenever possible, that he decided to create a diversion in favour of the Second Division, then about to commence its advance on Ulundi. In the course of his operation he did considerable damage to Zulu homesteads directly across the river; but in the estimation of Mr Wheelwright, whose border levies significantly had remained on the Natal bank while the other units crossed to make their raid, the exercise had been unlikely to achieve anything except to stir up a frontier that had in fact relapsed into quiescence.[52] Bulwer was predictably aghast at news of Twentyman's raid, but this time so too was the officer to whose discretion Chelmsford had delegated the option of making further raids into Zululand while he was away with the Second Division. Major-General the Hon. H.H. Clifford had been as unaware of Twentyman's intentions to make a raid as had Bulwer, and came out firmly against any repetition. But as

Bulwer lamented in his indignant report to Frere, the raid had already had the effect of provoking minor retaliatory Zulu forays over the border, and more could now be anticipated.[53] Nor was he mistaken. On 25 June the Zulu launched a well co-ordinated and destructive counter-raid into the Thukela valley near Middle Drift which pitilessly exposed the inadequacy of the Natal border defences and the impossibility of doing much to rectify the situation, especially since the border levies had been left utterly demoralized.[54] Bulwer's longstanding and dire predictions, about which he might be excused for reminding Hicks Beach,[55] had been amply vindicated. Chelmsford's policy of raiding had finally provided to be as self-defeating as Bulwer had always feared it would.

Sir Garnet Wolseley arrived in Pietermaritzburg on the afternoon of 28 June, and was welcomed by Bulwer whom he immediately discovered to be 'charming', 'pleasant' to work with, and altogether 'a Gentleman'. Nor could he find much to fault in the Lieutenant-Governor's handling of affairs during the crisis brought on by the war, except his treatment of the border levy issue. There Wolseley considered him to have made the 'mistake of rather trying to interfere with military matters.' Though rather indulgently confiding to his journal that Bulwer's 'conduct on this point was silly', he nevertheless jotted down that in mitigation he considered the Lieutenant-Governor to have been 'so bullied' by Frere and the military over the border levies that he could be forgiven for rather having 'lost his head'.[56] Be that as it may, Wolseley was fully prepared to endorse the stand Bulwer had taken over the inadvisability of mounting raids across the river, and stated so officially. The commencement of raids into Zululand from Natal, he declared both to Bulwer and to the Home Government, 'was objectionable and mistaken in policy.'[57]

If Chelmsford had won a Pyrrhic victory in his demand for an undivided command over the troops stationed along the border, then Bulwer had emerged resoundingly justified in his condemnation of the Lieutenant-General's policy of the 'active defence'. Yet Bulwer, as the thorough gentleman that he undoubtedly was, resisted the temptation to crow. At a dinner given at Government House in Pietermaritzburg in honour of Chelmsford, then on his way home to face his many critics in England, Bulwer sat next to the Lieutenant-General. 'We are on very good terms,' he wrote afterwards to his brother, 'but of course we did not touch on the subject of our difference.'[58]

[Previously published in *Theoria*, 57, October 1981.]

Notes

1. Chelmsford to the Duke of Cambridge, 11 April 1879, quoted in Maj. the Hon. Gerald French, *Lord Chelmsford and the Zulu War*, London, 1939, p. 181.

2. Chelmsford to Frere, 11 August 1878, quoted in ibid., pp. 42–3.

3. Bulwer to Maj.-Gen. E.E.G. Bulwer, 8 December 1878, quoted in Sonia Clarke, *Invasion of Zululand 1879*, Johannesburg, 1979, pp. 213–4.

4. Chelmsford to Frere, 11 August 1878, quoted in French, *Lord Chelmsford*, p. 43; Chelmsford to Frere, 11 September 1878, quoted in ibid., p. 47; and extract from letters from Chelmsford to Frere, no date, quoted in ibid., pp. 51–2.

5. Chelmsford to Frere, 11 September 1878, quoted in ibid., p. 48.

6. J.P.C. Laband and P.S. Thompson, *A Field Guide to the War in Zululand 1879*, Pietermaritzburg, 1979, pp. 1–2.

7. Frere to Hicks Beach, 20 August 1878, quoted in Basil Worsfold, *Sir Bartle Frere*, London, 1923, pp. 86–7.

8. John Benyon, *Proconsul and Paramountcy in South Africa*, Pietermaritzburg, 1980, pp. 152, 154, 358–9.

9. Chelmsford to Frere, 11 September 1878, quoted in French, *Lord Chelmsford*, pp. 47–9.

10. CSO 1972, no. 4237/78: Lt.-Governor to Colonial Secretary, 15 November 1878; and *Natal Government Gazette*, vol. XXX, no. 1739, 26 November 1878.

11. The two Sub-Districts consisted of the Colony's two metropolitan centres, Pietermaritzburg and Durban. The other Districts were based on the Counties into which Natal had been divided for administrative purposes, and were essentially rural.

12. CSO 2629, no. 4237/78: Circular, Instructions for the Colonial District Commanders, 21 November 1878.

13. *B.P.P.* (C. 2318), enc. 18 in no. 1: Minute by Bulwer, 28 February 1879.

14. GH 1221, no. 67/79: Bulwer to Hicks Beach, 16 April 1879.

15. GH 1413, no. 4909/78: Bulwer to C.B.H. Mitchell, 20 December 1878; and GH 1326, no. 160/78: Chelmsford to Bulwer, 30 December 1878.

16. GH 1423, enc. in no. 1222/79: Memorandum by Chelmsford, 20 February 1879.

17. *B.P.P.* (C. 2318), enc. 7 in no. 1: Bulwer to Chelmsford, 7 February 1879. Bulwer was not served well on this score by his Attorney-General, who subsequently advised him that in his opinion the Lieutenant-General was justified in directing the Colony's blacks to perform 'any military service which the General Commanding in Chief may assign to them or order them to engage in.' (Attorney-General's Office 1/16/1, p. 405: Memorandum by M.H. Gallwey, 14 March 1879).

18. GH 1326, no. 6/79: Bulwer to Chelmsford, 13 January 1879.

19. CSO 1926, no. 1356/79: Bulwer to Chelmsford, 28 February 1879.

20. *B.P.P.* (C. 2318), enc. 10 in no. 1: Minute by Frere, 11 February 1879.

21. Ibid., enc. 19 in no. 1: Extracts from the Minutes of the Proceedings of the Natal Executive Council, 1 March 1879.

22. Ibid. (C.2374), enc. in no. 9: Bulwer to J.W. Shepstone, 8 March 1879.

23. Ibid. (C.2318), no. 18: Chelmsford to Bulwer, 18 April 1879; and J.P.C. Laband and P.S. Thompson, *War Comes to Umvoti*, Durban, 1980, p.45.

24. J. Mathews, 'Lord Chelmsford and the Problems of Transport and Supply During the Anglo-Zulu War of 1879' (unpublished M.A. thesis, University of Natal, 1979). p.87.

25. Frere to Hicks Beach, 15 February 1879, quoted in Worsfold, *Frere*, p.194.

26. WC II/2/2: Chelmsford to Wood, 3 March 1879.

27. GH 1326, no. 40/79: Bulwer to Chelmsford, 15 April 1879; GH 1221, no. 67/79: Bulwer to Hicks Beach, 16 April 1879.

28. Greytown Correspondence 21/3, no. 168/79: Minute by Chelmsford, 15 March 1879.

29. WC II/2/2: Chelmsford to Wood, 17 March, 1879.

30. Laband and Thompson, *Umvoti*, pp. 47–9. Downstream in Colonial Defensive District VI, Captain G.A. Lucas called out his border levies on 27 March and demonstrated at the flooded Thukela drifts (P.S. Thompson 'Captain Lucas and the Border Guard: The War on the Lower Tugela, 1879', *JNZH*, III, 1980, pp. 39–40).

31. GH 1221, no. 67/79: Bulwer to Hicks Beach, 16 April 1879.

32. GH 1221, no. 67/79: Bulwer to Hicks Beach, 16 April 1879.

33. CSO 1926, no. 1880/79: Wheelwright to Colonial Secretary, 2 April 1879.

34. CSO 1926, no. 1880/79: Minute by Bulwer, 9 April 1879.

35. GH 1326, no. 32/79: Bulwer to Frere, 9 April 1879; and *B.P.P.* (C.2318), enc. 1 in no. 13: Bulwer to Chelmsford, 9 April 1879.

36. GH 1326, no. 32/79: Bulwer to Frere, 9 April 1879.

37. Chelmsford to Duke of Cambridge, 11 April 1879, quoted in French, *Lord Chelmsford*, p.181.

38. *B.P.P.* (C.2318), enc. 2 in no. 13: Chelmsford to Bulwer, 12 April 1879.

39. GH 1326, no. 40/79: Bulwer to Chelmsford, 15 April 1879.

40. GH 1221, no. 67/79: Bulwer to Hicks Beach, 16 April 1879.

41. *B.P.P.* (C.2318), no. 18: Chelmsford to Bulwer, 18 April 1879.

42. Chelmsford to Frere, 21 April 1879, quoted in French, *Lord Chelmsford*, pp. 212–3

43. *B.P.P.* (C.2367), enc. 3 in no. 44: Extracts from the Minutes of a Meeting of the Executive Council, 23 April 1879.

44. GH 1326, no. 54/79: Bulwer to Chelmsford, 25 April 1879.

45. GH 1326, no. 63/79: Bulwer to Frere, 30 April 1879.

46. WC II/2/2: Chelmsford to Wood, 25 April 1879.

47. GH 500, no. 2526/79: Chelmsford to Bulwer, 7 May 1879.

48. *B.P.P.* (C.2318), no.11: Hicks Beach to Bulwer, 19 May 1879.

49. Ibid., no.19: Hicks Beach to Bulwer, 28 May 1879.

50. Ibid., Appendix: Commission issued to Sir Garnet Wolseley, 28 May 1879. See also Edgar Brookes and Colin Webb, *A History of Natal*, Pietermaritzburg, 1965, pp.143–4; and Benyon, *Proconsul and Paramountcy*, p.165.

51. Hicks Beach to Frere, 29 May 1879, quoted in Worsfold, *Frere*, p.258.

52. Laband and Thompson, *Umvoti*, pp.56–62. In District VI during the first two weeks of May, the border levies had made a number of limited sorties into Zululand, and raided again on 28 May. (Thompson, 'Captain Lucas', pp.40–1).

53. GH 1326, no.88/79: Bulwer to Frere, 24 May 1879.

54. Laband and Thompson, *Umvoti*, pp.67–77.

55. GH 1221, no.124/79: Bulwer to Hicks Beach, 2 July 1879.

56. Wolseley's Journal: 28 June 1879.

57. *B.P.P.* (C.2482), enc.3 in no.37: Wolseley to Bulwer, 26 July 1879; and ibid., no.37: Wolseley to Hicks Beach, 27 July 1879.

58. Bulwer to E.E.G. Bulwer, 26 July 1887, quoted in Clarke, *Invasion of Zululand*, pp.220–1.

Captain Lucas and the Border Guard

The war on the lower Thukela, 1879

P.S. THOMPSON

Panic on the Border

The outbreak of war in January 1879, between Britain and the Zulu kingdom, alarmed the inhabitants of the Lower Tugela Division of Natal Colony. When the British column in the area advanced into Zululand, it left them with little but the prospect of an early British victory as assurance against some Zulu counterstroke across the Thukela. The British column did defeat a Zulu force at the Nyezane and go on to occupy Eshowe, but the very day of the battle (22 January) two large forces of Zulu appeared on the left bank of the Thukela above Forts Pearson and Tenedos. F.B. Fynney, the Border Agent responsible for intelligence and police in the Lower Tugela Division, reported that the Zulu king had ordered them to invade Natal.[1] The Resident Magistrate of the division as well as the District Commandant advised colonists to move to places of safety in the villages of Stanger, Williamstown (Umhlali), and Verulam.[2] The British commander at the forts and the Commandant turned out local tribesmen to reinforce those already watching the river drifts. The Commandant also held three groups, each approximately 150 men, on the high ground to move to threatened points, as well as a strong reserve at Thring's Post, near an important intersection of the road between Stanger and Greytown.[3]

The Zulu forces soon vanished, but the colonists' fear increased at the news of the British Centre Column's defeat at Isandlwana. Rumours of invasion abounded. The Natal Native Contingent supporting the small British garrisons at the forts melted away.[4] Fynney explained the British setback as best he could to the chiefs in the division, and they pledged loyalty and continued to furnish men for the border guard, but it was evident that popular resolve would collapse if the Zulu were to cross the river in strength.[5] Colonel Pearson, the coastal column commander, found his position at Eshowe precarious, sent back his few mounted troops and entrenched the rest, while Zulu forces gathered round to besiege them.

In these circumstances defence of the lower Thukela line was the immediate responsibility of Captain Gould A. Lucas, Commandant of Colonial Defensive District No. VI. How he acted in these and subsequent difficult circumstances is the subject of this article.

Defensive District No. VI

On 31 December 1878 Lucas had been appointed to command Colonial Defensive District No. VI.[6] Lord Chelmsford, commander of the imperial forces in South Africa, had criticized the colonial defensive preparations, and consequently Sir Henry Bulwer, the Lieutenant-Governor, had divided the colony into seven defensive districts (see Map 1) and two sub-districts (Pietermaritzburg and Durban) and instructed their commandants on the raising or rallying of the inhabitants, according to the development of the Zulu threat.[7] The three districts on the Zululand border, including No. VI, were most vulnerable. The selection of Lucas to command one of them presumably owed to his early military career (in the 73rd Regiment), perhaps to his experience in the Langalibalele 'rebellion', and probably his acquaintance with local customs and temper as Resident Magistrate of Alexandra County. A decisive – perhaps too decisive – manner may also have encouraged expectations of positive performance under duress.[8] In June 1878 the colonial government had circularized resident magistrates with new plans for defence, and Lucas had sent them a plan of his own for Alexandra County, one which he had *already* drafted and which they accepted.[9] Subsequently he was put down for a commandancy, and when Major Shapland Graves, 3rd Regiment (the Buffs), in charge of the North Coast, was transferred to the Natal Native Contingent, his territory (excluding Durban), now styled Colonial Defensive District No. VI, was given to Lucas.[10]

Lucas arrived at Stanger to take command between Christmas and New Year, and received a copy of the Lieutenant-Governor's latest instructions on defence. Lucas looked at the border and decided that the instructions were unrealistic. Earlier Sir Henry had envisaged at least 2 000 tribesmen as a Border Guard against possible Zulu incursions, but now he proposed a standing force of only 200, and the rest to come out at short notice at half a dozen or so designated posts only when the commandant called them to meet an actual incursion. Lucas wrote to the Colonial Secretary, who dealt with the administration of defence, on 2 January that the full defensive force must be embodied *before* any Zulu incursion, otherwise it could not be got together at all; and he asked for authority to raise it at once and to post it along the border, if possible to stop the enemy in the very river. Above all he urged that this be done speedily, for he had to defend a line extending along fifty miles (80 km) of a river which rose and fell fitfully, with at least nine good drifts and innumerable lesser ones.[11] He telegraphed twice on 3 January for the authority to raise the full force and once again on 4 January, pointing out that Colonel Pearson had told him that the imperial forces could afford no protection of the border after they had advanced into Zululand.[12] When John Dunn (the white *induna* who had just brought about a thousand of his people out of Zululand for safety) offered 250 armed men for border defence, Lucas accepted them at once on his own authority.[13]

Bulwer remarked to the Colonial Secretary that Lucas's messages were 'highly coloured' and 'very exaggerated', that Lucas had exceeded his authority in accepting Dunn's offer, and even that he had erred in appointing Lucas to the command and wished that he could remove him.[14] Bulwer did not answer Lucas directly, but referred the matter to Sir Henry Bartle Frere, the High Commissioner. Frere referred it to Colonel Bellairs, Deputy Adjutant-General, whose view presumably would reflect Lord Chelmsford's. Bellairs suggested that British officers be appointed 'Inspecting Field Officers' to supervise the border defensive districts. Frere agreed and Bulwer readily accepted the suggestion,[15] even though it meant that control of part – and by implication, all – of the colonial military would be directly under imperial military authority. Lucas, still pressing for the immediate levy and reporting that a hostile force had formed across the river, was now referred to Major Walker, 99th Regiment, who would be in charge of the imperial line of communications between Stanger and the lower Thukela.[16] Meanwhile Walker was warned to discount Lucas's extravagant assessments of the situation.[17] On 15 January Lucas reported to Walker at Stanger.[18] Although Lucas had only 428 men at hand[19] Bulwer soon noted how satisfactorily he was organizing his district. None the less Bulwer decided that he should give him a piece of his mind – but in the wake of the Isandlwana disaster this was left 'to stand over awhile'.[20]

Reinforcements and Recriminations

Circumstances seemed to vindicate Lucas after all. Before Isandlwana Chelmsford and Bulwer attached no great importance to defence. After Isandlwana Lucas's importunities seemed reasonable. What now, if the Zulu attacked? Defeat compelled Chelmsford to a defensive strategy pending the arrival of reinforcements and the accumulation of supplies and transport in

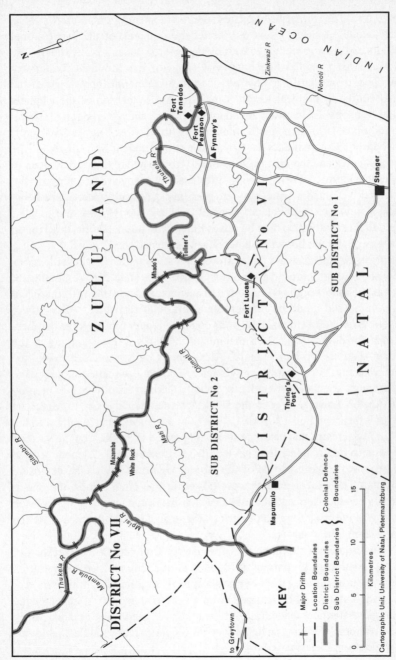

The Natal-Zululand border along the lower Thukela, 1879.

the colony. The military authorities soon were abetting rather than abating Lucas's calls. Indeed, a few days after the outbreak of the war Colonel Bellairs had already seemed to be moving towards Lucas's point of view. He informed the Colonial Secretary that some of the Mounted Volunteers (members of settler units, now attached to the imperial forces) and of the Natal Native Contingent would remain on the Natal side of the Thukela while Pearsons's column advanced into Zululand, and also suggested raising an additional 500 men for the defence of the Lower Tugela Division.[21] Perforce the Colonial Secretary instructed the Resident Magistrates of the Lower Tugela and the Inanda Divisions to call up and to forward the men to Lucas at Thring's Post.[22] Then, after Isandlwana, several corps of the Mounted Volunteers were put into the line.[23] Major Walker asked that Lucas's numbers be doubled.[24] Scarcely a week later Chelmsford himself urged that at least 2 000 men be put at Lucas's disposal, and his description of the perils on the border matched Lucas's earlier one.[25]

Bulwer began a canvass for reinforcements. Along the Thukela the tribes were already committed to the Border Guard.[26] The Natal Native Contingent had taken in most of the willing men elsewhere, and now many of these had gone home and could be reassembled only with difficulty.[27] The Lower Tugela, Inanda and Umlazi Divisions could no longer furnish large numbers of men for duty.[28] What men the inland divisions had were going to the border districts upriver.[29] Only Alexandra County could provide the reinforcements for its absent magistrate. With patience and diplomacy the government persuaded the reluctant chiefs there to send over 900 men by mid-April.[30] Lucas's force in the field increased quickly. On 15 March he had 993 men[31] and on 12 April 1 795.[32] On 16 April Lucas reported to the Colonial Secretary that his force was being raised to 3 500,[33] but he was too sanguine: a return in late June gave only 33 officers and 2 323 men.[34] (Even so, his was the largest force of the Border Guard in any of the defensive districts.) The reinforcements were posted in two main camps, the one at Lucas's headquarters and the other (which had a fort) near Thring's. Each camp was the base for a sub-district, whose first line of defence were the guards along the river.[35]

Notwithstanding the imperial prerogative, Colonial Defensive District No. VI continued to present problems to the colonial government. A telegram (brought over from Fynney's agency) to Lucas might wait days at his headquarters until he returned from a visit to some part of his extended line.[36] And absences aside, Lucas seems to have been weak at paper work. The cavalier administration in District No. VI periodically rankled fastidious officialdom in Pietermaritzburg.

Anticipating a large reinforcement, Lucas put in a requisition for a large supply of arms and equipment, which threw the commissary and ordnance officers as far as Durban into some confusion. Evidently the government had not fully informed them about Lucas's force and its status. An embarrassed Colonial Secretary wrote to Lucas that at least he could tell his civil superiors of such a large (and expensive) requisition in advance. Lucas replied blandly that he had not done so since he did not deem it necessary.[37] When the government called on him to plot his dispositions on a map which they sent for the purpose, Lucas did so tardily, then explained that anyway the map was inaccurate (which was true) and that he would make a better one and send it. At length he sent a large, colourful thing which was even more egregious for its oversimplification.[38] Late in April the Colonial Secretary called on the various district commandants for copies of their defence regulations; a month and a reminder later Lucas produced the desired papers and an apology for the delay, which he blamed on a lack of paper, envelopes and minute jackets at his headquarters![39]

When the Acting Secretary for Native Affairs instructed him to furnish drivers and leaders to the military transport service from his force, Lucas called for volunteers, got none, and received a sharp reprimand from the Acting Secretary, who had written nothing about 'volunteers' in the instructions.[40] Lucas complied faithfully with similar instructions thereafter, but still failed to report the fine details upon which the meticulous Bulwer insisted.[41]

The Border Guard required white leaders, for which the colonial government made modest provision. As a former military man in a quasi-military assignment, Lucas proceeded to create a small staff, to which Bulwer at first objected as superfluous. Then Lucas distinguished his leaders with officer ranks, which, the Colonial Secretary claimed, had no basis in the defence regulations. Bulwer was also concerned at the seemingly excessive (and therefore expensive) number of such officers. Lucas was obliged to justify his officering policy, which, it turned out, was in keeping with Major Walker's orders.[42]

Lucas also fell foul of the civil authorities when it came to the enforcement of discipline. In the weeks after Isandlwana, when the Zulu king sought to suborn Natal border chiefs, Lucas became suspicious, and then convinced, that one chief, Mkonto, was a traitor; he sought to punish him, but the government insisted on an investigation, which Fynney carried out to the exoneration of Mkonto. This did not soften Lucas, who for long refused to have any of Mkonto's men under his command.[43] Somewhat later, Lucas asked for a magistrate's authority to punish serious breaches of discipline, notably instances when men fell asleep at their posts. Bulwer would not have it: 'the real fact is that Captain Lucas wants to get all the power into his own hands.'[44]

Taking the War to the Enemy

In the absence of reliable Zulu testimony the deterrent effect of the Border Guard on the lower Thukela can only be conjectured. Threats and shots were exchanged across the river, and rumours flew concerning Zulu activities and intentions. The Border Guard could not be indifferent to these; yet it had no real tests of arms.[45] The Mounted Volunteers became bored.[46] The settlers returned to their private and public interests − an election to the Legislative Council was in the offing, and the new railway between Verulam and Durban would open soon − and the presence of so many troops, chiefly the Imperial reinforcements, created an artificial prosperity.[47]

Lord Chelmsford was aware that inactivity might impair the efficiency of the static forces, and therefore he proposed a modicum of activity for them in his new strategic plan. In the latter part of February he suggested raids over the border; this set off a bitter dispute between himself and Bulwer, who stubbornly opposed such raids. Both had good reasons, which can be supported by certain evidence.[48] Of importance here is Lucas's involvement in the matter.

A priority for Chelmsford was the relief of Pearson's beleaguered force at Eshowe. He ordered a vigorous demonstration by imperial and colonial forces all along the Thukela, beginning in the last week of March.[49] If they could cross and raid, then so much the better: the more the Zulu would be distracted and off balance when the relief column advanced from the lower Thukela.

Lucas called out the reserves of the border tribes on 27 March. The tribesmen responded to the call cheerfully; they were under the impression that they were going to meet a possible Zulu invasion, and since they had many more firearms than before, they were confident of success. Also, the river was rather too high for a serious crossing. Lucas's show of force at least frightened the Zulu living along the left bank − they abandoned their homes and fled with their livestock to the hills − but whether or not it produced confusion or distraction among any Zulu forces is practically impossible to determine.[50] In any event, Chelmsford's relief column advanced into Zululand on the 29th, repelled and routed a large Zulu attacking force at Gingindlovu on 2 April, reached Eshowe the following day, and then engaged in some forays of its own in the vicinity. On 4 April Chelmsford

The Border Guard stationed at White Rock Drift, lower Thukela.

ordered raids wherever feasible along the border.[51] Lucas could do no more than keep his Border Guard posted menacingly above the unfordable drifts. After several weeks the Zulu lost their fear and returned to their homes on the left bank.[52]

Chelmsford returned to Natal and conferred with Bulwer. Neither relented on the matter of raids, but Chelmsford received an interesting letter, whose substance he had his chief of staff impart to the Lieutenant-Governor in a tantalizing manner: a certain officer, who should not be named (since his letter was private), under his command but entrusted by the Lieutenant-Governor with defence of the border, was under the impression that earlier orders were still in force and had expressed his intention to cross the border at the first opportunity. In deference to His Excellency's views on the subject, Chelmsford inquired whether or not he should instruct that officer to do so. Bulwer replied that he preferred to have a higher authority decide on raiding in general and not to treat specific cases; but that since the Lieutenant-General had inquired, he desired that the officer be instructed not to cross.[53]

The anonymous officer almost certainly was Lucas. A Volunteer at the lower Thukela wrote to the *Natal Mercury* on 15 April: 'Raids seem in prospect all along the border.'[54] The same day that Chelmsford wrote to Bulwer (19 April), Border Agent Fynney reported to the Acting Secretary for Native Affairs that he had just returned from a visit along the border, where several chiefs and headmen told him of its being whispered about that they would be called on to participate in a raid or raids into Zululand: they asked if the government expected them to do so, and said that while they were ready to defend the border against invasion, they were loath to cross unless supported by regular troops.[58]

Evidently Lucas was instructed to check his aggressive designs, for the month passed without further important incident. He was told to start building a large fort at his headquarters, and this earthwork, appropriately named 'Fort Lucas', took most if not all of May to complete.[56]

Yet some crossings did occur, mostly in Sub-district No. 2, the remoter part of Lucas's territory, the charge of 'Captain' Robert Woolley.[57] Official reports of these incidents have not been found, and the information on them is sparse and somewhat confusing. Apparently on 2 May 'Lieutenant' J. Rapson crossed with a small force at the Mazembe Drift and brought back nine head of cattle.[58] Two days later about 500 of the Border Guard crossed at an unnamed place to frighten away a body of Zulu reported to be threatening some refugees that had gone back to the left bank to gather crops.[59] On 9 May 'Lieutenant' W.E. Boast covered a small force which crossed at the White Rock Drift and brought back 21 beasts.[60] A few days later some of the Mounted Volunteers crossed, probably at the Mhadu Drift, skirmished with a Zulu force, and returned with an unspecified number of cattle.[61]

Imperial reinforcements were gathering on the coastal plain between the lower Thukela and the Nyezane, constituting the new First Division under Major-General H.H. Crealock which was preparing for a second invasion of Zululand. In northern Natal a Second Division also readied for invasion. Probably to throw the expectant Zulu off balance, Chelmsford, who had at last won his point against Bulwer,[62] again ordered raids all along the border.[63] On the morning of 28 May Lucas sent across a contingent in each sub-district, at Tollner's and the White Rock drifts, respectively. The first, under 'Captain' R.D. Browne, went upstream and burnt two kraals and returned in the afternoon; but the second was warned of an ambush by scouts and returned to the right bank at once.[64]

That was the last instance of raiding by the Border Guard. Chelmsford was now with the division in the north, and Major-General H.H. Clifford was left in charge of the forces remaining in Natal. Clifford shared the sentiments of Bulwer, who wrote to him: 'Will you give to Captain Lucas such instructions on this subject as you may consider necessary.' To which Clifford replied: 'I have given the necessary orders.'[65]

Changed circumstances also dictated prudence. After the First Division advanced into Zululand, the same kind of forces, however more numerous, would be left to watch the lower Thukela frontier. The last elements of the First Division departed from the lower Thukela on 17 June. At once rumours and scares beset the troops left behind – not least the British garrisons in Forts Pearson and Tenedos.[66] If the raids had provoked the Zulu, then the absence·of the great majority of the regular troops (the only ones that they really feared) now invited retaliation. Early in June there had been strong indications that the Zulu would raid across the river between Forts Lucas and Pearson;[67] but the blow did not fall until 25 June, when two Zulu forces made a destructive sweep on the right bank that surpassed any which colonial forces had made. The Zulu raid occurred upriver, against tribes in Defensive District No. VII (Umvoti County). However, the crossing of one force at the Mambula Drift suggests that, if provocation was a factor in the selection of targets, then the forays at the nearby Mazembe and White Rock drifts had had an effect. A small portion of Lucas's force, that just below the Mpisi, hastened to assist their attacked neighbours in driving back the enemy. (The initiative in doing so was that of the local leader, E. Walford, a mere sub-leader of less than three weeks service!)[68] Of course, the moral impact of the Zulu raid in Defensive District No. VI was enormous: for at least a week the Border Guard was on the *qui vive* day and night.[69] Only the news of Lord Chelmsford's victory at Ulundi seems to have restored a measure of the old confidence.

End in Obscurity

Sir Garnet Wolseley arrived at the end of June to pacify the Zulu nation. The various chiefs submitted in due course to the new British Commander-in-Chief and the war ended officially on 1 September. Long before that date Lucas's army had dwindled to company strength. The divisions in Zululand could go no further without adequate transport – the lack of oxen and wagons, drivers and leaders was acute. Wolseley took readily to a circumvention of the problem: switching from four-legged to two-legged transport, i.e. the Natal blacks should form a Carrier Corps. On 30 June the assembled chiefs acquiesced. Wolseley, supposing that Lucas had 3 500, decided that he should send some 2 000 to Crealock's column, and the Secretary for Native Affairs telegraphed that he should turn over this number as soon as possible to the military authorities at Fort Tenedos.[70]

Lucas protested that he would be left with 82 men for defence of the border. He hinted strongly that a Zulu force again threatened across the Thukela, and insisted on further explicit instructions in these circumstances.[71] He notified to the Resident Magistrate at Stanger the development and suggested that arrangements at once be made to remove women and children and cattle from the border. In consequence the Magistrate also demanded specific approval of the instruction,[72] and an anxious Justice of the Peace telegraphed that the inhabitants of the division were greatly alarmed at the prospect of losing the bulk of the Border Guard.[73] The Secretary dutifully referred Lucas's plaint to Bulwer, who consulted Clifford, and none of them was moved by it.[74] Wolseley ordered Lucas to comply.[75]

It took some time to get the men together, but on 15 July they were turned over at Fort Tenedos to form the 'armed carrier corps' of Crealock's First Division.[76] The men were unhappy at the transfer, even though they were allowed to keep their guns. Those from the Lower Tugela Division worried about leaving their families unprotected against possible Zulu raids. Lucas would not let these men have even a few days' leave to make personal arrangements[77] – perhaps he believed that once gone they would not return to the ranks. Within a short time after their departure the carriers were deserting in numbers, but Clifford decided not to act against them,[78] perhaps because the war was virtually over.

Lucas remained at his post with his token force. Fynney, who was seconded to the general in Zululand at the end of June, suggested that Lucas take charge of the Frontier Border Police in his absence, but Bulwer would not allow it.[79] During the first week of August the regiments of Crealock's division recrossed the Thukela *en route* to Durban. A company of the 99th remained at Fort Pearson, while three soldiers looked after Fort Tenedos.[80] The Mounted Volunteers were disbanded, with dinners and speeches at the home-comings in Stanger and Verulam.[81] Walker departed, and Lieutenant-Colonel Thynne, Grenadier Guards, took his place.[82]

The date on which the Border Guard in Defensive District No. VI was disbanded has not been found, but probably it was in early September.[83] Lucas faded from the war along with it.

A letter from H. Laing of Glendale, who had been a leader in the Border Guard in District No. VI, appeared in the *Natal Mercury* on 19 September 1879. Laing referred to the official receptions for the returning Volunteers and the Edendale Horse, as though these were invidious compliments when the Border Guard equally deserved congratulation. He cited Captain Lucas and his Border Guard in particular. The editor of the newspaper endorsed the sentiments, 'every word'; but if any official praise for Lucas or his men was forthcoming, it has yet to be found.

Laing was inexact in equating the service of Lucas' *ad hoc* militia with that of volunteer units which had been in battle, but his sense of slight was understandable. The colonial authorities' irritation with Lucas's efforts seemed to exceed any appreciation, whereas no evidence has been found to suggest that his military superiors were so dissatisfied.

The significance of the colonial forces' operations on the lower Thukela need not be magnified, but the vicissitudes of the commandant and the men of that district point up the fact that the Natalians made a determined if mixed effort in the war. They also reveal some of the difficulties inherent in the relationship between civil and military authorities in war-time. After all Lucas's task proved thankless not so much for his doing wrong as for his being impolitic.

[Previously published in *Journal of Natal & Zulu History*, III, 1980.]

Notes

1. *NGG*, vol. XXX, no. 1749, 28 January 1879: Government Notice no. 50, 22 January 1879, Major Walker, Lower Tugela, to Deputy Adjutant-General; Colonial Secretary to Resident Magistrate [Stanger], 23 January 1879, reproduced in *Natal Colonist*, 25 January 1879. Cf. telegrams from Lieutenant Kingscote, Lower Tugela, to the Commodore, Durban, 22 January 1879, in *Natal Colonist*, 23 and 25 January 1879; and from F.B. Fynney to Colonial Secretary, 23 January 1879, GH 1421, Minute 480/1879.

2. Unsigned letter, dated New Guelderland, 23 January 1879, reproduced in *Natal Colonist*, 25 January 1879. For defence of the villages named see Public Notice, 23 January in CSO 690, Minute 2195/1879.

3. *NGG*, vol. XXX, no. 1749, 28 January 1879: Government Notice no. 50, 22 January 1879: Major Walker to Deputy Adjutant General; SNA 1/1/33, no. 52: Fynney to Acting Secretary for Native Affairs, 24 January 1879. GH 1421, Minute 483/1879: C.B.H. Mitchell (Colonial Secretary) to Sir Henry Bulwer, 23 January 1879.

4. Lieutenant Kingscote, Lower Tugela, to the Commodore, Durban, 30 January 1879, reproduced in *Natal Mercantile Advertizer*, 31 January 1879. Also see correspondence concerning the Natal Native Contingent in this sector in CSO 1926, Minute 613/1879 and SNA 1/1/33, no. 65.

5. SNA 1/1/33, nos. 52, 63 and 68: Fynney to ASNA, 24 January 1879, 7 and 10 February 1879, respectively.

6. *NGG* vol. XXX, no. 1743, 24 December 1878: Government Notice no. 398.

7. See Chelmsford to Frere, 11 September 1878, quoted in Gerald French, *Lord Chelmsford and the Zulu War*, London, 1939, pp. 46–7, *NGG* vol. XXX, no. 1739, 26 November 1878: Government Notice no. 356; and CSO 2629, Minute 4237/1878: 'Instructions for the Colonial District Commanders'.

8. See the synopsis of his career in GH records and H.C. Lugg, *A Natal Family Looks Back*, Durban, 1970, pp. 28–30.

9. The correspondence is in SNA 1/4/2, no. 46.

10. CSO 679, Minute 124/1879: Bulwer to Colonial Secretary, 5 January 1879.

11. CSO 679, Minute 124/1879: Lucas to Colonial Secretary, 2 January 1879.

12. CSO 1925, Minute C3/1879: Lucas to Colonial Secretary, 3 and 4 January 1879.

13. CSO 679, Minute 122/1879: Dunn to Lucas, 4 January, and Lucas to Colonial Secretary, 5 January 1879; and ibid., Minute 124/1879: Lucas to Colonial Secretary, 4 January 1879 (telegram).

14. CSO 1925, Minute C3/1879: Bulwer to Colonial Secretary, 4 January 1879; and CSO 679, Minute 124/1879: Bulwer to High Commissioner, 5 January 1879.

15. CSO 690, Minute 124/1879: Bulwer to High Commissioner and reply, 5 January; Bellairs' and Frere's comments, 6 January: and Bulwer to Colonial Secretary, 7 January 1879.

16. CSO 690, Minute 124/1879: Bulwer to Colonial Secretary, 7 January; and CSO 680: 230/1879: 12 January 1879.

17. GH 1421, Minute 271/1879: Lucas to Colonial Secretary (telegram) and Bulwer to Colonial Secretary, 13 January 1879.

18. CSO 680: Minute 232/1879: Lucas to Major Huskisson, Durban, 16 January 1879.

19. CSO 679, Minute 124/1879: Bulwer to Colonial Secretary, 15 January 1879.

20. CSO 679, Minute 124/1879: Bulwer to Colonial Secretary, 15 and 17 January 1879.

21. GH 1421, Minute 27/1879: Bellairs to Colonial Secretary, 14 January 1879.

22. SNA 1/1/33, no. 41: Mitchell to RM Inanda, 16 January 1879.

23. The Isipingo Mounted Rifles were ordered up from Durban (see correspondence in GH 1422, Minute 618/1879), and the Alexandra, Stanger and Victoria Mounted Rifles returned from Zululand (see Eric Goetzsche, *'Rough but Ready'*, Durban [n.d.], pp. 33, 36).

24. SNA 1/1/33, no. 62: RM Lower Tugela to SNA, 9 February 1879; and SNA 1/6/12, no. 8: Bulwer to Colonial Secretary, 12 February 1879.

25. SNA 1/6/12, no. 12: Chelmsford to Bulwer, 15 February (telegram); as well as the ensuing correspondence in GH 1422, Minute G169/1879, 16 February; and GH 1423, unnumbered minute, 20 February 1879.

26. SNA 1/1/33 RM Lower Tugela to SNA, 9 February 1879.

27. GH 1423, unnumbered minute: Bulwer to Colonial Secretary, 6 March 1879. Cf. SNA 1/6/12, no. 12, Bulwer to Chelmsford, 15 February; and SNA 1/6/14, nos. 10 and 11: RM Lower Tugela to ASNA and Captain Barton to SNA, 19 March 1879.

28. SNA 1/1/33, no. 62: RM Lower Tugela to SNA, 9 February 1879; SNA 1/6/12, no. 68: RM Inanda to SNA, 6 March 1879; and nos. 55 and 69: RM Umlazi to SNA, 6 and 8 March 1879 respectively; and SNA 1/6/13, no. 15: William Campbell to ASNA, 18 March 1879.

29. Those from Klip River and Weenen Counties went to District No. 1 and those from Pietermaritzburg and Umvoti Counties to District No. VII.

30. SNA 1/6/12, nos. 17, 51 and 58: Acting RM Alexandra to SNA, 22 February, 3 and 6 March 1879, respectively; SNA 1/6/14, nos. 21 and 44, 14 and 21 April 1879, respectively. Also cf. SNA 1/6/14, no. 22: W. T. Arbuthnot to [SNA], 12 April 1879.

31. In SNA 1/6/14, no. 6.

32. In CSO 1927, Minute 2133/1879.

33. CSO 699, Minute 2182/1879: Lucas to Colonial Secretary, 16 April 1879.

34. SNA 1/6/15, no. 69: A. S. Windham (ASNA) to Major-General Clifford, 27 June 1879.

35. CSO 699: Minute 2182/1879: Lucas to Colonial Secretary, 16 April 1879.

36. See SNA 1/6/13, no. 15 and SNA 1/6/15, no. 59: Lucas to Colonial Secretary, 29 March, and to SNA, [11] June 1879, respectively.

37. The correspondence (9–23 March 1879) is in CSO 693, Minute 1523/1879.

38. The principal correspondence (28 February – 25 April 1879) is in CSO 690, Minute 1287/1879; 695, Minute 1709/1879; and CSO 699, Minute 2182/1879. The two maps are with the first and last minutes.

39. The correspondence (29 April – 28 May 1879) is in CSO 690, Minute 1287/1879.

40. The principal correspondence (21 April – 31 May 1879) is in CSO 703, Minute 2580/1879.

41. The principal correspondence (9 June – 2 July 1879) is in SNA 1/6/15, nos. 55, 58, 59, 63 and 77.

42. The principal correspondence (4 March – 16 April 1879) is in CSO 696, Minutes 1875 and 1876/1879; and CSO 699, Minute 2182/1879; and SNA 1/6/13, no. 50.

43. The principal correspondence and reports (26 February – 14 April 1879) are in SNA 1/1/33, nos. 6, 35, 86 and 122; SNA 1/6/12, nos. 48, 49, 71, 72 and 75; SNA 1/6/13, no. 14; and SNA 1/7/12, p. 80. The rolls of men transferred to the Carrier Corps include some of Mkonto's tribe (cf. SNA 1/6/16, nos. 3 and 12).

44. The principal correspondence (19 April – 16 May 1879) is in SNA 1/6/14, no. 46.

45. The various incidents are reported by Fynney in SNA 1/1/33 and SNA 1/6/13 passim.

46. See especially correspondents' reports in *Natal Colonist*, 18 and 20 March, 26 April, 3 and 29 May 1879.

47. See especially correspondents' reports in ibid., 20, 22, 23 and 31 May, and 2 September 1879.

48. The principal correspondence is scattered. For the published material and commentary see *B.P.P.* (C. 2318): encs. nos. 10 and 11: Frere to Bulwer, 11 February 1879 and Chelmsford to Bulwer, 20 February 1879, and no. 17: Bulwer to Frere, 2 March 1879 and no. 19: Extract from Executive Council's Minute of Proceedings, 1 March 1879, in no. 1; and enc. in no. 18: Chelmsford to Bulwer, 18 April 1879; and (C. 2367): enc. 2 in no. 37: Frere to Bulwer, 19 April 1879, and no. 44, Bulwer to Frere, 26 April 1879; (C. 2374): no. 9, including Minute from Bulwer to ASNA, 8 March 1879, and no. 29: Bulwer to Hicks-Beach, 22 May 1879, enclosing Minute from Chelmsford to Bulwer, 7 May 1879; and (C. 2482): no. 37: Wolseley to Hicks-Beach, 27 July 1879. Also see F. E. Colenso, *History of the Zulu War and Its Origin*, London: 1880, pp. 387–93, and French, *Lord Chelmsford and the Zulu War*, pp. 82, 84–5, 181–2, and 212–13. For manuscript material see GH 1422, Minute 668/1879, and GH 1423: 143 and 1257/1879, as well as the unnumbered minute with memoranda by Chelmsford (20 February) and Bulwer (6 March 1879); CSO 1926, Minute 1356/1879, and CSO 1973, Minute 1880/1879; Greytown Correspondence 21/3, Minute 168/1879, and AGO 1/16/1, p. 405.

49. H. P. Holt, *The Mounted Police of Natal*, London, 1913, p. 76; John Stalker (ed.), *The Natal Carbineers*, Pietermaritzburg and Durban, 1912, p. 108. Cf. CSO 1926, Minute 1880/1879: W. D. Wheelwright to Colonial Secretary, 2 April 1879.

50. See SNA 1/1/33, no. 122: Fynney to ASNA, 31 March 1879.

51. CSO 1926, Minute 1871/1879: Colonel Crealock to Officer Commanding, Lower Tugela, 4 April 1879.

52. See SNA 1/1/33, no. 8: Fynney to ASNA, 19 April 1879.

53. The correspondence is in CSO 698, Minute 2054/1879.
54. Issue of 18 April 1879.
55. SNA 1/1/33, no. 8: Fynney to ASNA, 19 April 1879.
56. Reports in *Natal Colonist*, 6 May, and *Natal Mercury*, 4 July 1879.
57. See report in *Natal Mercury*, 4 July 1879. For more on Woolley (late of the 2/20th), whom Lucas called his second-in-command, see SNA 1/6/13, no. 50, and SNA 1/6/14, no. 31: Lucas to Colonial Secretary, 29 March and to SNA, 26 April 1879, respectively.
58. Report in *Natal Mercury*, 7 May 1879.
59. Report in *Natal Colonist*, 6 May 1879.
60. Report in *Natal Mercury*, 14 May 1879.
61. Report in *Natal Colonist*, 15 May 1879.
62. See *B.P. P.* (C.2318), no. 11: Hicks-Beach to Bulwer, 19 May 1879.
63. See *B.P. P.* (C.2454), enc. 2 in no. 21, and (C.2374), no. 46: W.D. Wheelwright to Colonial Secretary, 21 May, and Bulwer to High Commislsioner, 24 May 1879, respectively; also reports in *Natal Mercury*, 29 May 1879.
64. SNA 1/16/34, no. 79: Fynney to ASNA, 29 May 1879, with statement by Frontier Border Policeman Folozi.
65. *B.P. P.* (C.2454): encs. 4 and 5 in no. 31: Bulwer to Clifford and reply, 4 June 1879. On Clifford's command see (C.2374): no. 26: Bulwer to High Commissioner, 24 May 1879.
66. Report in *Natal Mercury*, 7 July 1879.
67. Letter in ibid., 19 September 1879.
68. See *B.P. P.* (C.2454): enc. 10 in no. 60: W.D. Wheelwright to Colonial Secretary, 26 June 1879. On Zulu movements upriver cf. SNA 1/6/15, no. 76: Lucas to SNA, 1 July 1879 (telegram). Walford's appointment is in *NNG*, vol. XXXI, no. 1771, 1 July 1879: Government Notice no. 217, 28 June 1879.
69. Report in *Natal Mercury*, 4 July 1879.
70. A. Preston (ed.), *The South African Journal of Sir Garnet Wolseley 1879–1880*, Cape Town, 1973, p. 48.
71. Cf. ibid. and SNA 1/6/15, no. 76: Lucas to SNA, 1 July 1879 (two telegrams).
72. SNA 1/6/15 no. 76: Lucas to RM Lower Tugela, 1 July, and RM to SNA, 2 July 1879.
73. SNA 1/6/15, no. 80: J.L. Hulett to Colonial Secretary, 3 July 1879 (telegram).
74. See CSO 1927, Minute 3248/1879: Mitchell to SNA, 4 July 1879; also the comments on Lucas' telegrams in SNA 1/6/15, no. 76.
75. CSO 1927, Minute 3399/1879: RM Lower Tugela to Colonial Secretary, 15 July 1879; however, Wolseley (see n. 70) does not mention this.
76. SNA 1/6/16, nos. 1 and 3 and no. 10: W.F. Ashley to SNA, 27 July and 8 August 1879, respectively. The enclosed rolls give 1 005 men from Sub-district no. 1 and 941 from Sub-district no. 2.

77. CSO 1927, Minute 3399/1879: RM Lower Tugela to Colonial Secretary, 15 July 1879.

78. See the correspondence (4–6 August 1879) in SNA 1/6/16, no. 9.

79. CSO 1927, Minute 3399/1879: RM Lower Tugela to Colonial Secretary, 15 July 1879.

80. Report in *Natal Colonist*, 14 August 1879.

81. See reports in *Natal Mercury*, 28 July, 1 and 22 August; and *Natal Colonist*, 19 August 1879.

82. Report in *Natal Colonist*, 4 September 1879.

83. Cf. reports in *Natal Mercury*, 19 September; and *Natal Witness*, 27 September 1879.

Mbilini, Manyonyoba and the Phongolo River Frontier

A neglected sector of the Anglo-Zulu War of 1879

J.P.C. LABAND

In the South African context the frontier, which may be defined as a zone of interpenetration between two previously distinct societies, began rapidly to close in the late 1870s as white settlers (backed by British imperial power) consolidated their political authority over the indigenous peoples.[1] Yet in some regions this process was less advanced than in others: not all white settlers who had intruded themselves along the margins of black polities had yet fully established their hegemony, with the consequence that disputes over land and political jurisdiction were still the norm, and endemic warfare the consequence. No frontier in the 1870s better exemplified this disturbed condition than that along the upper reaches of the Phongolo River, wedged as it was between the conflicting claims of the Zulu and Swazi kingdoms and the Boer Transvaal Republic.

It is a region of high relief, where the river systems have cut deep valleys through the terrain. The beautiful, red-earthed valleys of the Assegai (Mkhondo), Ntombe, Phongolo and Bivane rivers contrast with the great granite flat-topped mountains and the rugged, broken countryside between. The landscape is open and grassy, with forests crowning some of the higher peaks, and bush filling the kloofs. A region of reasonable rainfall, the summers are wet and warm, the winters dry and cold. Significantly, considering that Zulu, Swazi and Boer were pastoralists, it is an environment suitable for livestock. The sourveld grasses of its sandy highlands are nutritious only in the growing season, while the tall grassland types of its valley systems are nutritious and palatable throughout the dry winter. Mixed and intermediate types grow between the two, and can be grazed for six months of the year. The transitional nature of the grazing requires the free movement of cattle. Herds should spend the spring in the high country, and move down as summer advances to the sweet valley floors for the winter.[2] In other words, effective management of herds necessitates the control of large and varied tracts of land. Zulu, Swazi and Boer understood this well.

The Zulu kingdom of the 1870s was becoming increasingly congested and its natural resources were under growing strain. Expansion to the south and south-west was blocked by the British Colony of Natal. To the north, across the Phongolo, lay the Swazi kingdom. From the beginning of his reign King Cetshwayo focused on Swaziland and its resources. Since the late 1860s Zulu homesteads had been expanding across the Phongolo to shore up Zulu influence in the area. The process proceeded at an accelerating pace during the 1870s into the lands north and north-east of Zululand. Yet King Cetshwayo stopped short of an actual invasion of Swaziland, despite his preparations in 1875. He was prevented by the complex interaction between internal Zulu politics (powerful chiefs in northern Zululand had independent interests in Swaziland and feared the repercussions of war with Swaziland), and pressure from abroad from Natal and the Transvaal. The north-west, at the headwaters of the Phongolo, whose boundaries were still unclear, seemed a possible vent for Zululand's excess population. The expansion of Zulu homesteads paralleled the process further downstream.[3] Yet in this region competition for resources came not so much from the Swazi, but from the much more formidable Boers.

Transvaal territory formed an arc around north-western Zululand, but the Boers' suzerainty was ill-defined. The fact that there were not enough Boers physically to occupy the land they claimed always made their territorial rights difficult to uphold. In 1848 King Mpande had accorded grazing rights between the Buffalo (Mzinyathi) and Blood (Ncome) rivers to the resolutely republican Boers who had trekked out of British Natal west of the Buffalo. On the strength of this ambiguous grant, the Boers had proclaimed their Republic of Utrecht, and remained on their farms on Zulu sufferance. With decided relief this tiny republic had submerged itself in September 1859 into the larger polity of the South African Republic, and had become the Utrecht District of the Transvaal. By 1878 there were 248 whites in the little village of Utrecht and 1 352 in the district as a whole. Of these, 375 were able-bodied men. Despite these tiny numbers, there was almost no free land still available, for by 1880 the district had been surveyed and 163 farms delineated. Land-hungry Boers had consequently encroached on the grazing east of the Blood River, and their right to this territory was disputed by the Zulu.[4] North of Utrecht, and abutting both the Zulu and Swazi kingdoms, lay the Transvaal District of Wakkerstroom. It had not been settled by whites until 1853, and only by 1859 had there been sufficient of them for it to be proclaimed a separate district. Thereafter immigrants had poured in, for it was considered the healthiest horse district in the Transvaal, and there was a rapid expansion in wool farming. By the 1870s free land was no more available than in Utrecht, and the Boers were spilling southwards over the Phongolo, in direct confrontation with the Zulu expanding northwards.[5]

Only at the end of 1864 did the Boers first set up beacons asserting what they conceived to be their boundary with Zululand. The line stretched between Rorke's Drift in the south and the confluence of the Phongolo and Bivane rivers in the north. In 1875 they proclaimed a new boundary line that took in a large tract of territory south of the Phongolo.[6] The Zulu could naturally accept none of these land claims. They insisted on a western border running up the Buffalo to its sources in the Drakensberg and along the watershed to the Assegai River in the north. In all these regions were people who had *khonza*'d (given their allegiance) to the Zulu king, and it was this that the Zulu considered as the definition of the limits of their kingdom.[7] The British annexation of the Transvaal on 12 April 1877 gave greater force to Boer claims in what had come to be known as the Disputed Territory, and it was to avoid a confrontation with Zululand that the Lieutenant-Governor of Natal offered to mediate in the dispute. His Boundary Commission duly began its sittings in March 1878. It only scrutinized Boer claims beyond the Blood River, which its findings were not to uphold. The disputed area in the upper reaches of the Phongolo it did not consider, though Transvaal claims north of the Phongolo were strong, and official opinion in Natal held that Zulu suzerainty terminated at the river.[8] The commission's findings were not made public until December 1878. Meanwhile, tension remained high in the vicinity of the upper Phongolo, and there were a number of incidents between white settlers and the Zulu.

These confrontations centred around the little German settlement of Luneburg, some 3 km (nearly 2 miles) *north* of the Phongolo. Boers had first encroached on the area in the latter years of King Mpande's reign. They had come to cut timber, and the king had let them be, only asserting his right to the region.[9] In November 1869 Lutherans from the Hermannsburg Mission Society in Natal established themselves below Ngcaka Mountain between the Phongolo and Ntombe rivers. Since 1862 settlers of the Hermannsburg community had been entitled to own land individually, and some left the mission stations to start their own farms, though remaining part of the mission congregation, and accepting the authority of a pastor. Such a one was the Revd Mr P. Filter who arrived in 1870 with his family to take charge of the tiny community. Since Luneburg lay in territory to which the Boers laid claim, the community was only established with the permission of the

Transvaal government. To be safe, however, the Luneburgers also gained Mpande's permission to settle. It was ever their policy to give obedience to the earthly powers while pursuing the conversion of the heathen through the example of their godly lives and fruitful labour. Soon their valley was highly cultivated, and they were breeding sheep with rams imported from Germany in 1875.[10]

Cetshwayo was less prepared than his father Mpande to accept the unchallenged presence of the Luneburgers in a region into which he was expanding. In May 1877 there were reports that the Zulu were building a military homestead on the Phongolo as a demonstration of the king's authority, and that Cetshwayo had instructed the *induna* near Luneburg (presumably Manyonyoba) to cease paying taxes to the Transvaal government as he had been doing for the past three to four years.[11] These orders can be seen as Cetshwayo's response to the implications of the advent of British rule in the Transvaal, and his attitude was made very clear on 18 October 1877 when a Zulu delegation met the Administrator of the Transvaal, Sir Theophilus Shepstone, at Conference Hill. The Zulu declared that they would never give up their claim to the Luneburg district.[12]

In order to confirm this point, in mid-November 1877 at least 2 000 Qulusi arrived to erect a military homestead within 5 kms (3 miles) of Luneburg. Their behaviour was not aggressive, and they explained that the establishment of a military homestead was merely to enable the king to control the Zulu in the area.[13] The implication was plain, nevertheless: Cetshwayo was laying formal claim to the area infiltrated by his people. His employment of the Qulusi on this mission was equally significant. EbaQulusini was a military homestead established near present-day Vryheid by King Shaka. The people of various clans attached to it occupied the valley of the Bivane, and regarded themselves as personal adherents of the king. Thousands strong, they were not drafted into conventional age-grade regiments (*amabutho*) where they would be amalgamated with the other young males of their age from throughout the kingdom, but fought together as a royal section. They were in charge of *izinduna* appointed by the king to represent the royal house, the principal ones in 1877 being Sikhobobo and Mahubulwana.[14] Action by the king's most loyal adherents could only be construed as a manifestation of the king's will.

The Qulusi had withdrawn again by the end of November 1877, but they left great uncertainty among the settlers, and the conviction with Shepstone in the Transvaal that Cetshwayo was being deliberately provocative regarding the Phongolo frontier and that by implication he was putting the settlers of Utrecht and Wakkerstroom into jeopardy.[15] Shepstone's belief

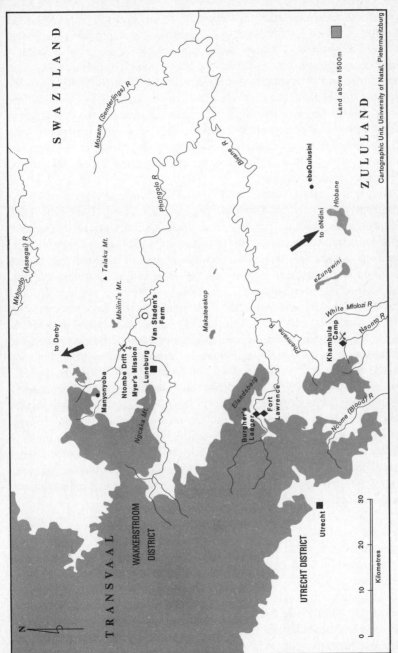

North-western frontier of Zululand, 1879.

was reinforced when during the same period the king established a number of cattle posts north of the Phongolo to reinforce his claim; while the Qulusi *induna* Sikhobobo and his men nearly came to blows with a party of Boers when constructing a homestead on the Ngwempisi River near present-day Piet Retief. An encounter was only averted when a Swazi force in the vicinity upheld the Zulu claim that their land was Cetshwayo's and the Boers, outnumbered, withdrew.[16] In yet another incident, the king asserted his authority in the region when in January 1878 he sent his men north of the Phongolo to execute a man accused of a crime in Zululand, but who was now living on a Boer's farm, and to carry the transgressor's wives, children and cattle back to Zululand.[17]

During the uneasy months of 1878, while Zulu and Boer awaited the report of the Boundary Commission, and Sir Bartle Frere, the High Commissioner, moved towards a final confrontation with the independent Zulu kingdom, further occurrences in the upper Phongolo region exacerbated the increasingly tense situation. At the end of May the Zulu served notice on Boer farmers along the Assegai River in Wakkerstroom to move, and seemed intent on building a homestead on the Swazi border. Besides provoking the Boers and Swazi, the Zulu again upset the Luneburgers. Some 150 Zulu from homesteads in the vicinity began cutting wood towards the end of May in order to resume building the military homestead begun and abandoned the previous November on the farms owned by Mrs Röhrs and Bernhard Bohmer.[18] As it turned out, the homestead was only the size of a private one, sufficient to accommodate Faku, the king's representative, and a small force. The fears of the settlers for their personal safety might rapidly have subsided on realizing this, but the meaning of establishing a royal homestead was clear: the king was declaring his right to administer the Zulu settled in the area.[19] This was borne out on 7 June when Mguni, a petty Qulusi *induna*, claimed to be acting on the king's instructions when he evicted a Zulu living on C. van Staden's farm near Luneburg and established his own homestead in his place.[20]

Yet Faku, as the king's eyes and ears, and therefore nominally in charge of the local inhabitants, was in something of an embarrassing position. His instructions were not to antagonize the whites, yet the Qulusi *izinduna* were reproaching him for not evicting the settlers. Indeed, they took matters into their own hands, and in early September sent messengers to farmers, especially those near the sources of the Phongolo, instructing them to leave at once for Natal where there was plenty of grass, and to cease ploughing. His authority flouted, Faku went to the king for instructions.[21] Cetshwayo, who was busy from July in building new homesteads up to the Swazi royal graves and the strongholds of Ngwavuma, [22] apparently decided to support the Qulusi's initiative. Consequently, when Faku returned in late September, he ordered the settlers of Luneburg to leave in the king's name as the land was required for the king's cattle being sent from Zululand, and for cultivation by the local Zulu. Moreover, he ordered the few Boer farmers remaining in the Bivane River area to vacate at once. The Zulu started building their homesteads on their deserted farms, [23] stealing stock, and harassing white travellers along the routes over the Bivane and Phemvana rivers. [24] Despite some uncertainty and the denials of the king's officials, who protested that they did not know that the Luneburgers were British subjects, it is quite clear that Faku was acting on Cetshwayo's express instructions. He would never have dared otherwise to have taken such provocative action. [25]

Yet all these alarms were nothing compared to that which occurred on 7 October 1878. An attack was made on four or five Swazi homesteads on the lower Makosini koppies near the Mozana (Senderling's) River north of the Phongolo. At the same time, the homestead of Swazi subjects of Cetshwayo close to Luneburg was also raided. The Swazi began to concentrate and threatened to retaliate, farmers in the vicinity of the Assegai River prepared to trek, and the Luneburgers got ready to go into the stone-walled laager which they had built around their church. Further raids were anticipated, and a general conflagration along the border was feared. [26]

The leader of the raiders was Mbilini kaMswati, who was reputed at the age of twelve to have had the fresh pelt of a dog which had been skinned alive pulled over his head in order that the animal's vicious nature might be transferred to him. [27] Certainly, his cruelty was proverbial, though to those who knew him he appeared kind, if shrewd and wily, and he was appropriately an acknowledged expert at the game of *Sokhexe*, where a contestant tries to trace his way out of a labyrinth scratched on the floor of a hut by his opponent. [28] Small of stature and of dark complexion, and wearing the headring of a homestead head although unmarried, [29] he was the eldest son of laMakhasiso, the Swazi king Mswati's chief wife at the royal homestead of Hhohho in northern Swaziland. Mswati died in August 1865 when Mbilini was about twenty. Although his father had favoured him as his heir, he was debarred according to Swazi custom because his mother had been the king's first wife. Nevertheless, he was the only adult candidate. The choice lay with the royal family and regents, and because they distrusted his rash temperament, in November 1865 they installed the minor Ludvonga, whose mother was of the right status. Mbilini would not accept their decision, but his rebellion collapsed in the absence of sufficient support. In April 1866 he fled to the South African Republic to seek aid. The Boers saw him as a potential pawn in their conflicts with Swaziland, but as no large-scale influx of supporters followed him into exile, his value proved to be limited, and his presence thus unwelcome. At the end of 1866 or the beginning of 1867 Mbilini consequently proceeded to Zululand, where he hoped to find backing for his claim to the Swazi throne.[30]

The Zulu king certainly had use for him. Having tendered his allegiance, Mbilini was allowed to settle in the upper reaches of the Phongolo. There he gathered about him adherents, chiefly of Swazi extraction, who did not form part of the regular Zulu military system, but operated as a guerrilla force of auxiliaries.[31] From his caves and rocky fastnesses Mbilini maintained a degree of turbulent independence, raiding his neighbours on all sides, but particularly the Boers of the Disputed Territory and the Swazi of the faction who had ousted him.[32] In doing so, he aided the covert Zulu action against Boer and Swazi alike and the infiltration of Zulu settlers across the Phongolo, for it is inconceivable that Mbilini would have been allowed to continue to operate as he was if he had not been furthering the king's aims.[33] Yet his relative autonomy made him doubly useful as a cat's paw, for the king could always disown him if it became necessary.

In July 1870, and again in April 1874, Mbilini launched raids on the south-western corner of Swaziland through the Wakkerstroom District. On the latter occasion Cetshwayo denied complicity and gave the Boers permission to retaliate.[34] He did so again after two further attacks made by Mbilini north of the Phongolo on 30 December 1876 and 2 January 1877 against Swazi of his faction who had become Transvaal subjects, and which caused Boers to trek away in alarm from the Assegai River. The Boers would have preferred that the king should hand Mbilini over to them, but negotiations broke down when an unauthorized commando raid by Field Cornet Kohrs and the Wakkerstroomers attacked Mbilini on 24 February 1877 at his homestead on Sithebe Hill. Mbilini managed to escape to the king for sanctuary, who henceforth refused to hand him over to the Boers.[35] Shortly before the raids of October 1878, Mbilini established a new homestead in the Qulusi country near ebaQulusini itself. It was on the south side and half way up Hlobane Mountain and called iNdlabeyitubula – 'they (the Boers) gave my home a shove.'[36]

Mbilini's provocative raids of October 1878 were intended by him to rebuild the herds that he had lost to the Boers in February 1877, though the British, whether colonial officials or the military, saw in them Cetshwayo's means of gauging how far he could push the British in the Disputed

Territory.[37] It seems, though, that on this occasion Cetshwayo was furious with Mbilini. He was in negotiation with the Swazi for rain in that time of drought, and they refused to allow the necessary ceremonies at the graves of the Zulu ancestors in Swaziland on Mbilini's account.[38] Yet once again the king refused to punish Mbilini. For one thing, Mbilini had *khonza'd* to him, and he feared his failure to protect him would put off others who wished to tender their allegiance.[39] For another, Mbilini was difficult to take action against when in his natural fastnesses, and at that time when war was clearly on the horizon, it seemed idiotic to waste strength on alienating so bold and skilful a leader, whose talents would soon be required in the Zulu cause.[40]

For the already apprehensive settlers of the upper Phongolo region, Mbilini's October raids were the final straw. It was clear that unless they were reassured by the presence of British troops, both Luneburgers and Boers would abandon the area.[41] The distinct possibility alarmed Sir Bartle Frere, who wrote to Colonel Evelyn Wood, the commander of the British troops stationed at Utrecht, making it clear that Wood's troops should be used to dissuade the Zulu from meddling any further with the 'Lunebergers' [sic].[42] Wood consequently despatched the garrison at Utrecht (which consisted of two companies of the 90th Regiment under Major C.F. Clery) to Luneburg. The soldiers arrived on 19 October and immediately set about strengthening the stone laager around the church and fortifying the adjoining churchyard. During November they built their own earthwork fort nearby, calling it Fort Clery.[43]

Wood's action in moving the Utrecht garrison to Luneburg and replacing it with the garrison at Newcastle alarmed his commander, Lieutenant-General Lord Chelmsford. Chelmsford was busy at that stage building up his forces along the Zulu border preparatory to the anticipated invasion of the kingdom, and feared a pre-emptive Zulu strike. He was consequently concerned about the possible consequences of dissipating his concentration of troops in the north-west, especially since Colonel Rowlands, who was to invade Zululand from the Transvaal, was operating without success against Sekhukhune and the Pedi, and because the Swazi seemed reluctant to co-operate.[44] Yet Wood felt he had taken a justifiable risk in that he had prevented the abandonment of the Phongolo valley to the Zulu, which would have had the adverse strategic effect of separating the British from the Swazi.[45] Frere endorsed this view, pointing out that the district was full of caves and other natural strongholds which would have cost many lives to retake, leaving aside the government's obligation to protect British subjects.[46]

Yet there was the danger, envisaged by Chelmsford, that Wood's move might provoke the Zulu, especially since the boundary question had not been settled. Indeed, Cetshwayo was severely put out. The arrival of troops in Luneburg he perceived as part of the aggressive British strategy of hemming him in, and proof that they were not keeping faith over the boundary issue.[47] Realizing this, the Natal government attempted at the end of October to allay the king's not unjustified suspicions, and in a message tried to clarify that there were no aggressive intentions behind the movement of troops, but only a desire to protect threatened British subjects.[48] Yet the damage was done. On 11 November 1878 Sikhobobo, a senior *induna* of the Qulusi, went to Luneburg accompanied by 40 or so adherents, whom he left out of sight. He declared he came with a message from the king insisting that the troops must return at once to Utrecht as the area was claimed by the king as his. He was not allowed into the laager as the general opinion was that he was a spy. The local blacks insisted that he came not from the king, as he claimed, but had been sent by Mcwayo kaMangeda, the *induna* of the ebaQulusini military homestead, to collect military information.[49] This view was propounded in particular by Manyonyoba, the local *induna* who, in Faku's absence, acted as Cetshwayo's representative. He was reputed nevertheless to be secretly faithful to the British, and at the close of 1877 had indeed tried to curry favour by revealing what he knew of Cetshwayo's plans to Transvaal officials. The knowledge that Manyonyoba was at least willing to hedge his bets emboldened Colonel Wood, accompanied only by an interpreter, to visit the *induna* at his homestead in the Ntombe valley some 8 kms (5 miles) from Luneburg to assure him that the presence of troops was a purely defensive and temporary measure.[50]

Manyonyoba, though like Mbilini a typically self-serving and independently minded chieftain living on a turbulent frontier, was much longer established in the region than his notorious friend. His father, Maqondo (Magonondo), had been an independent chief who had put himself without fighting under Shaka's rule. Manyonyoba therefore owed Cetshwayo his allegiance, and the Swazi had never exercised any authority over him.[51] His adherents were described as the débris of various chiefdoms conquered by Shaka and Dingane – Zulu, Swazi, Sotho – who had gone begging for land until the king, out of compassion, had allowed them to settle north of the Phongolo, along both banks of the Ntombe River. There they lived in almost inaccessible caves in the steep hillsides that dropped down to the Ntombe valley, which was covered in thousands of ant-hills constructed of the bright red earth, and which was cut across by great dongas. From his rocky fastnesses Manyonyoba raided the surrounding countryside, and on one occasion in the past had been seized and imprisoned for some time by the Boers for stock theft.[52]

Manyonyoba's position, then, was an ambiguous one. If undecided which side to take, the presence of Wood's troops at least persuaded him for the time being to profess friendliness towards the British.[53] And the British were clearly not intending to abandon their hold on Luneburg. In December 1878 two companies of the 1/13th Light Infantry and the Kaffrarian Rifles relieved the two companies of the 90th.[54] Then in late December Mbilini obeyed the king's orders to leave his position in the Ntombe region and to occupy Hyentala Mountain, some 65 kms (40 miles) away from Luneburg, with 200 of his armed adherents. Cetshwayo's instructions were clearly a response to the British ultimatum of 11 December, one of the terms of which stipulated that Mbilini be surrendered for punishment for his raid of October.[55] Manyonyoba was left feeling exposed and uncertain what to do. The king apparently promised him aid if the British attempted to drive him from his lands. On Christmas day his fighting men were doctored for battle, which left the Luneburgers in their turn uncertain of his intentions.[56]

In early January 1879, on the eve of the expiry of the British ultimatum on 11 January, tension heightened in the area. Myer's thriving mission station in the Ntombe valley was plundered and partly destroyed, and he and his family fled to the Luneburg Laager. The Zulu were engaged in storing grain in their caves against the coming conflict, and building kraals for their cattle in inaccessible places. The Swazi along the frontier were also moving their cattle out of harm's way, while the Swazi king, Mbandzeni, was preparing to hold the First Fruits ceremony, after which his men were to guard the drifts and paths into Swaziland.[57] Under the leadership of their pastor, the Revd Mr Filter, whom Commandant Schermbrucker of the Kaffrarian Rifles described as 'a severe specimen of the Lutheran Pastor type of the 16th century', the Luneburg flock prepared to be led 'spiritually to heaven or bodily against the Zulu'.[58] By the third week of January all the local farmers and their families had come in and the laager was fully occupied. They mustered among them 28 men capable of bearing arms. In addition 78 black farmworkers from the vicinity cheerfully undertook patrols under the command of Nkhosana, one of their number, and worked as scouts and sentries.[59]

In the first week of January the Left (No. 4) Column of 2 278 men under the command of Colonel Wood assembled on the banks of the Blood River in the Utrecht District. Once hostilities opened on 11 January it marched in support of the Centre (No. 3) Column which was to advance on oNdini from Rorke's Drift. Fighting several small skirmishes against the Qulusi, Wood had reached the White Mfolozi when word of the disaster that had befallen the Centre Column at Isandlwana on 22 January caused him to draw in his patrols by 25 January. On 31 January he marched to Khambula Hill at the headwaters of the White Mfolozi, where he set up camp. From this fortified position he proceeded to send out mounted patrols against local pockets of Zulu resistance. His position was a good one, for not only did he shield the Utrecht District from a possible Zulu attack, but was also able to maintain communication with Colonel Rowland's No. 5 Column with its headquarters at Derby on the Transvaal border with Swaziland, and a detachment at Luneburg.

Chelmsford had originally intended that Rowland's column should join the others in the advance on oNdini. However, as a consequence of Rowland's unsuccessful operations during September–October 1878 against the Pedi, the general decided that the No. 5 Column should remain in garrison on the Phongolo frontier to keep Sekhukhune and the predatory local chiefs like Mbilini in order, and to protect Wakkerstroom from Zulu inroads. Consequently, Rowland's column did not advance from its posts at Derby and Luneburg except to take part in localized military expeditions. The column consisted of 1 565 officers and men, made up of the 80th Regiment (Staffordshire Volunteers), seven little corps of irregular horse raised mainly in the eastern Cape and Transvaal, and some Swazi levies. When on 26 February the hostile attitude of the Boers necessitated the return of Rowlands and his staff to Pretoria, No. 5 Column was attached to Wood's command.[60]

Luneburg was alarmed on 22 January by rumours that Mbilini was moving on the settlement. Schermbrucker sent out patrols which learned that far from attacking Luneburg, Mbilini and his forces had joined the Qulusi to the south at eZungwini Mountain. There, on the very same day as the battle of Isandlwana, Wood had taken eZungwini and driven off Mbilini and the Qulusi. The partial eclipse of the sun that fatal 22 January was looked upon by the Zulu in the Phongolo region as a sign that Mbilini's power, which was associated with the sun, was in decline.[61] And indeed, on 24 January Wood's forces again scattered the Qulusi (probably including Mbilini) to the north of Hlobane Mountain, and on 1 February Lieutenant-Colonel Buller proceeded on a mounted patrol from Khambula to destroy ebaQulusini itself, the rallying point for Qulusi resistance.[62] No wonder that Mbilini and the Qulusi sent to Cetshwayo complaining that they could not manage Wood's forces and begging that an army be sent to assist them.[63]

As for Manyonyoba, all his fighting men, which could not have numbered more than a thousand, were involved on 26 January in a skirmish with a patrol of Schermbrucker's south of Luneburg. On news of their defeat, Manyonyoba took to his caves with his women, children and infirm, as well as his own cattle, while royal cattle in his care were driven towards oNdini. Schermbrucker intercepted these at the junction of the Ntombe and Phongolo rivers, capturing 365 of them and some 200 goats besides. Half of Manyonyoba's discomforted fighting men joined the Qulusi opposing Wood; while the remainder, operating in groups of one to two hundred, kept up raids from the Ntombe caves and made the Luneburg-Derby road unsafe for small parties of British. The garrison at Luneburg was too well fortified for them to attempt to attack it, however, while in its turn the garrison was too small to risk assaulting the caves.[64] This apparent stalemate persuaded Manyonyoba to persist in playing a 'shuffling part' concerning negotiations with the British. He seemed prepared, despite the recent military encounters, to come to some agreement, but was apparently overborne by his chief *induna*, Sityuwabunto/Situwabemba, who was determined to fight on and to intensify the raiding.[65]

This determination was put into practical effect on the night of 10–11 February. Manyonyoba himself led as strong a force as he could muster to join a war party, led by Mbilini himself, mounted on a brown horse, and the Qulusi *induna* Tola kaDilikana, which had advanced from Hlobane and, skirting 5 km (3 miles) to the east of Luneburg, had crossed the Phongolo.[66] The small mounted patrols sent out from Luneburg were inadequate for the area and failed to intercept the combined Zulu force, which numbered about 1 500. Its objective was the Christianized Africans and black farmworkers and servants of the Ntombe region, whose masters were in the Luneburg Laager. These Africans had been learning the Christian life of hard and honest labour under the example of the Lutherans,[67] and were alienated from Manyonyoba's people, as evidenced by their willingness to serve the British as auxiliaries. Significantly, some of the Wakkerstroom Boers who owned farms in the region had clearly entered into a pact with the Zulu king's representatives, whereby in return for their co-operation as guides, the Zulu undertook to spare their property. Thus when Mbilini's force began to ravage the Ntombe valley, certain designated Boer farms were carefully left untouched.[68]

At 3.30 a.m. on the morning of 11 February Mbilini's men arrived at Wagner's mission station some 6 kms (3 and-a-half miles) north-north-east of Luneburg, burning *kholwa* (Christianized African) houses and killing 2 men, 6 women and 7 children. The war party then divided into four groups, which killed a further 2 men, 11 women and 15 children on Benneke's farm, and another 2 men, 11 women and 3 children on Laarse's and Klingenber's farms, also burning down the latter's house. The bodies of the killed were fearfully mutilated with assegai thrusts (which seemed particularly barbarous to the indignant settlers); but it was the exclusive use of assegais which ensured that the sentries at Luneburg were not alerted to the raid.[69] At full daylight the war party began to retire towards Manyonyoba's caves, driving before them several hundred cattle, thousands of sheep and goats, and a number of captured children. A small patrol of seven Kaffrarian Rifles under Lieutenant Schwartzkopf intercepted one of the Zulu groups of about 300 men as it was crossing the Ntombe around 9 a.m. With the aid of a few 'native police' and the thoroughly aroused inhabitants of the valley (whose number swelled to almost 700 in the ensuing encounter), they killed 15 of the raiders and recaptured some of the stock. The rest of Mbilini's men made good their escape to the Ntombe caves. Their audacious raid left the valley in an uproar, and was the immediate cause of a retaliatory raid by the British.[70]

On 13 February Lieutenant-Colonel Buller with the Frontier Light Horse and Dutch Burghers (recruited in the Utrecht District) left Khambula for Luneburg. They were reinforced the next day by Wood's Irregulars (black levies) and Schermbrucker's black auxiliaries. Buller resolved to attack Manyonyoba's caves the following day, though with the calibre of the forces available he did not expect to make much of an impression.[71]

In the small hours of 15 February Buller's force of 13 Frontier Light Horse, 33 Burghers, 417 Wood's Irregulars, 8 Kaffrarian Rifles, 100 Luneburg Natives and a 6-pounder gun moved out of Luneburg. After several hours of successfully quiet marching they were in position in the Ntombe valley below the rocky ledges on both sides of the river where Manyonyoba had his homesteads. A shell fired at sunrise hit his principal homestead and caused the wildest consternation. Half the mounted men, under Buller himself, charged up from below, cutting off the cattle feeding on the slopes. Manyonyoba's men fired a volley and fled up to the caves and rocky strongholds where the horsemen could not follow. Piet Uys (the Burghers' commander) and the rest of the horse moved along the high ground, above the caves. They could effect nothing, though, and the Zulu hid in the caves until the raiders retired, firing after them. The engagement had lasted about half-an-hour, during the course of which five homesteads at considerable distances from each other along the lower slopes of the hillsides had been destroyed, and 34 Zulu killed, including two of Manyonyoba's sons. The British withdrew with the loss of 2 black auxiliaries killed, 3 wounded and 1 missing. They arrived back at Luneburg after nine hours in the saddle with booty consisting of 375 cattle, 254 goats and 8 sheep. The following day Buller marched back to Khambula, leaving Manyonyoba still ensconced in his caves but with the score in death, destroyed dwellings and captured stock more even.[72]

Colonel Rowlands had not been available to aid Buller in his raid as he would have wished, for on 15 February he was involved in his own aggressive action while between Derby and Luneburg. Constant raiding from Khambula had caused many of the local Zulu to abandon the open country for the relative security of Hlobane and Ngongama mountains and the broken terrain of the confluence of the Phongolo and Bivane rivers. One such stronghold was Talaku Mountain, which lies some 32 kms (19 miles) north-east of Luneburg, and abounds in caves, firewood, water and grazing. Some of the Qulusi had moved there, into the Swazi zone, hoping to find safety for themselves and their cattle.[73] Rowlands attacked two homesteads on rocky ledges on the south side of the mountain with 103 Transvaal Rangers, 15 Boers, 75 Vos's Natives (black levies) and 240 Fairlie's Swazi auxiliaries. In the running skirmish two Zulu were killed (including Mozalane, an *induna* who had come from Cetshwayo the day before), and 197 cattle, 70 goats, and 44 sheep captured for the loss of 6 Swazi wounded. About 40 women and some children surrendered and claimed protection from the British. Yet, in all, Rowland's attack was as equivocable a success as Buller's, for he had to leave the Qulusi, strongly posted in other caves, in possession of the mountain.[74]

On 20 February 250 Swazi auxiliaries under Captain Harvey from Rowlands's forces at Luneburg attacked Makateeskop, a mountain 16 kms (10 miles) south-east of their base which, because Zulu cattle were being driven there daily, was considered a vital depot. It was held by 40 members of the iNgobamakhosi age-grade regiment, who were driven off with 9 killed, and 1 taken prisoner, besides the loss of 25 cattle, 1 horse, 20 sheep and 100 goats. But the very next day, once Harvey withdrew, the Qulusi re-occupied the mountain, nullifying the effect of his attack.[75] In similar vein, on 25 February Rowlands made another attempt at Manyonyoba's caves about the Ntombe, but failed to dislodge him.[76]

It had become clear to the British that despite the losses inflicted during February on the Zulu in the upper Phongolo region, none of the encounters had had any decisive result. And while there were encouraging reports that the king had ordered Mbilini to leave the Ntombe valley and take up position to the south of the Phongolo, others indicated that Manyonyoba had been promised Cetshwayo's support should the British again try to drive him out.[77] Perhaps the greatest indication of lack of British success, though, was the fact that the road between Derby and Luneburg remained unsafe in their estimation for all except strong parties, as the Zulu continued to infest the route and fire on those passing by.[78]

Yet, as Mbilini was to demonstrate, not even large parties were secure. On 9 February five companies of the 80th Regiment under Major C. Tucker had relieved the existing garrison at Luneburg, and Schermbrucker's Kaffrarian Rifles had gone to reinforce Wood at Khambula.[79] Supplies for the new garrison were forwarded from Derby, and on 7 March a company of the 80th under Captain D. Moriarty moved out of Luneburg to meet a convoy of 18 wagons carrying ammunition and supplies, and to escort it in. By 9 March the convoy and escort had reached the north bank of the Ntombe, but the rain-swollen river prevented all but two wagons crossing the drift. While waiting for the river to subside, Moriarty and 71 men pitched camp on the north bank and formed a V-shaped laager. A detachment of 35 men under Lieutenant H.H. Harward encamped on the south bank.[80] Moriarty's defensive arrangements were inadequate, as gaps were left between the wagons and the flanks of the laager were not secured on the river.[81]

The soft target Moriarty presented was evidently a sore temptation for Manyonyoba, who called on Mbilini to help him in attacking it.[82] His appeal came at the right moment, for Mbilini was in any case preparing for a new offensive, and had been collecting men from all parts of the surrounding countryside.[83]

On the evening of 11 March Mbilini himself is reputed to have come into the unsuspecting laager and, while eating mealies, to have spied out the British dispositions.[84] Before dawn on 12 March, and under cover of a thick river mist, Mbilini and a force of at least 800 (though estimations go as high as 9 000), advanced the 5 kms (3 miles) from his fastness, a huge, flat-topped mountain north-east of the sleeping camp.[85] His men approached unchallenged to within 65 m (70 yards) of the laager, when they fired a volley and rushed upon the panicking British with their assegais. A detachment crossed the river to attack Harward's men and to cut off the retreat from the north bank. Colour-Sergeant Booth managed to rally a few of the fugitives and to conduct a fighting retreat, which caused the Zulu to give up their pursuit after about 5 kms (3 miles). In the camp they had overrun, the Zulu ritually disembowelled the dead, killed the dogs, broke open and looted the boxes of ammunition, scattered about mealies and flour, shredded the tents (very much as they had done at Isandlwana)[86] and drove off 250 cattle.

On being alerted of the disaster, Major Tucker immediately marched on the Ntombe with 150 men of the garrison, but lacking mounted men was unable to prevent Mbilini's force from withdrawing at the trot and in a dense mass to Mbilini's mountain. They were able to carry off most of their

Mbilini kaMswati (right) with his induna *Mbambo.*

wounded, and the British later found only 30 Zulu bodies on the banks of the river.[87] The British themselves had lost 1 officer and 60 men, a civil surgeon, 2 white wagon conductors and 15 black drivers. After Isandlwana and Hlobane (still to be fought on 28 March) these were the greatest casualties suffered by the British in an engagement during the course of the war.[88]

Mbilini returned to his homestead on Hlobane with his captured rifles and ammunition,[89] doubtless well satisfied with his success. But in Luneburg, all sorts of precautions were taken at Fort Clery by the stunned and thoroughly apprehensive garrison against possible Zulu attack.[90] The Zulu, however, remained completely inactive,[91] though rumours abounded that Mbilini intended to raid the region once more, and to fall upon Luneburg itself, which was much more vulnerable than the impregnable camp at Khambula.[92] Meanwhile, in retaliation and to keep spirits up, on 25 March a mounted patrol from Khambula once more ravaged the homesteads and mealie fields in the Ntombe valley belonging to Manyonyoba's adherents, and encountered no resistance in doing so.[93]

Greater events, though, were brewing at the end of March. Word reached the British that Mbilini had reported his recent victory to the king, and that he was daily expecting the arrival of a great army from oNdini.[94] This did not deter Colonel Wood from proceeding with plans to launch a major raid on 28 March against Hlobane, Mbilini's stronghold and the Qulusi's cattle depot. The raid was in response to Chelmsford's instructions to create a diversion in favour of his intended march to the relief of the Eshowe garrison, beleaguered since January. It was also hoped that it would draw off part of the Zulu army facing Chelmsford along the coast and, alternatively, prevent Mbilini from reinforcing the coastal Zulu.[95]

Meanwhile, the main Zulu army had set out from oNdini on 24 March in order to deliver a knock-out blow against Wood, whose activity and success had convinced Cetshwayo that he was a deadlier adversary than Chelmsford. Unaware of the approaching Zulu army, Buller and 675 men started to scale the eastern slopes of Hlobane at 3.30 on the misty morning of 28 March, while Lieutenant-Colonel J. Russell's 640 men moved onto the adjoining Ntendeka Mountain from the west. Buller moved his men across the flat crown of Hlobane, brushing aside the Qulusi and Mbilini's men and rounding up their cattle. But it is most probable that the Zulu, who must have known of the near presence of their army, were drawing Buller into a trap. For when at 9 a.m. Buller was ready to descend with his booty, resistance was steadily increasing and the British being effectively harassed. Then, at that moment, Buller became aware of the Zulu army advancing across the plain on Hlobane from the south-east. In the ensuing precipitate retreat down the mountain, the British were mercilessly harried by Mbilini and the Qulusi, and many of them cut off at its base by an age-grade regiment detached from the Zulu army. Altogether some 2 000 Zulu might have been engaged, and their losses are unknown. The British, on the other hand, lost 15 officers and 79 men, as well as over 100 of their black auxiliaries, and fell back in disorder on Khambula.

Perhaps the most significant battle of the war occurred the next day when, in a bitter engagement that began at 1.30 p.m. and lasted until nightfall, the Zulu army was finally thrown back in complete rout from Khambula. Its defeat was pregnant with implications for the further course of the war. The morale of the Zulu regiments was badly shaken, and in future they were only prepared to attack the British if they could be brought to fight in the open. As for Cetshwayo, he realized that he could no longer hope to win the war in the field, and that his only salvation lay in negotiation.[96]

It is not certain whether Mbilini took part in this crucial battle, though it is known that the Qulusi irregulars lost particularly heavily in the flight.[97] In any event, he suffered a superficial wound to the forehead, though whether this was inflicted at Hlobane or Khambula is unresolved, though Hlobane seems the likelier.[98] What is sure, though, is that Mbilini was dead in a skirmish before his wound would have had time to heal.

After the battle, Wood's force remained undisturbed at Khambula, and his operations remained confined to sending out mounted patrols which engaged in several light skirmishes with the Zulu.[99] All of the Qulusi and Mbilini's adherents had gone from Hlobane by 3 April.[100] They moved north to raid the Phongolo region once again, accompanied by Mbilini who reportedly travelled in a cart because of his wound. Once there, they broke into several small parties, one of 150 men even crossing into the Assegai valley where they were intercepted and dispersed by the local black population.[101] On the night of 4 April several parties from Hlobane, making up a force perhaps 1 200 strong, came into the valley of the Phongolo opposite Luneburg, burning the huts of the blacks and driving off their cattle. Preparations were made once again to defend the Luneburg Laager against imminent attack, and patrols were sent out to keep track of the Zulus' movements. The Zulu, however, retired rapidly in the direction of Makateeskop with their booty. On the way, they came across two companies (150 men) of the 2/4th (King's Own Royal) Regiment under Major W.F. Blake from Khambula, who were marching to relieve the five companies of the 80th at Luneburg, whom Wood wished to proceed to Utrecht to increase his own available forces.[102] Major Blake at once formed laager, and the Zulu, who had learned their lesson well at Khambula, left them unmolested and broke into several small parties which proceeded to clear the countryside of stock as they went, and to burn the homesteads.

Captain Prior of the 80th with seven mounted men of his regiment, as well as Pastor Filter's son, while following up one of these small parties on 5 April, came across a few mounted Zulu near the Ntombe who were moving in the direction of the Phongolo with captured horses and cattle. In the course of the ensuing skirmish the Zulu party scattered. Captain Prior and Private Bowen, whose horses were the freshest, followed up two of the Zulu who had doubled back in the direction of the Ntombe. They exchanged shots with them, and both Zulu were wounded.[103] One fell and was assegaid by blacks friendly to the British, while the other escaped. The dead man was Tshekwane, a younger son of Sihayo the Qungebe chief whose homestead was near Isandlwana, and who had often accompanied Mbilini on his marauding expeditions.[104] The other horseman was Mbilini himself, and he had been shot in the back through the right shoulder, the bullet coming out below his waist.[105] He died of this dreadful wound within a few days, and before he could regain his homestead at Hlobane.[106] The death of the veritable hyena of the Phongolo left his adherents leaderless. They were reported by May to have been ordered by the king to leave Hlobane and to move to the Ngwegwe Hill over the Phongolo.[107]

As for Manyonyoba, constant patrols during May from Luneburg and by Commandant J.A. Rudolph, whose Burghers operated from their laager on the Bivane River close by Fort Lawrence (which had been built by a company of the 2/4th),[108] kept him in his caves on the defensive.[109] In fact, the British considered that the Zulu of the north-west, who had shown such little enterprise since the death of Mbilini, could be safely contained by the existing garrisons in the area. This was vital, for Chelmsford was preparing for his second invasion of Zululand, and Wood's forces, which were required for the renewed advance on oNdini, could hardly have been employed if moving them were to leave the Transvaal frontier open to Zulu raids. Confident, then, that little risk to the frontier communities would be incurred, on 5 May Wood moved south from Khambula to join Chelmsford and his Second Division. On 28 May the men of the 80th from Utrecht caught up with him, and on 17 June he effected his rendezvous with Chelmsford.[110]

The British assessment of the situation along the Phongolo frontier now that Mbilini was dead and the Qulusi cowed was only reasonably accurate. The Boers of the Wakkerstroom District were unwilling to take the field against the Zulu as requested and patrol the border, even when it was rumoured that Manyonyoba was intending to raid towards the Assegai.[111] This could be compensated for, and 20 mounted black auxiliaries, under Giligili, a 'trustworthy native', were found who were willing to patrol, which they did with some zeal as their own homesteads were at stake.[112] Yet, as ever, the lack of mounted men proved to be the greatest handicap in the effective defence of the region, despite the occasional success. On the morning of 4 June 50 Zulu attacked the blacks living on William Craig's farm on the Bivane. Thomas van Rooyen and 12 Burghers from Fort Lawrence cut them off as they were retiring over the Elandsberg (kwaLembe) to Makateeskop, and friendly blacks with them killed 18. The British hoped that after this setback the Zulu would be discouraged from further raids,[113] but on 7 June they struck with vigour. A large Zulu force, quite possibly Qulusi and Mbilini's adherents, swept off the cattle from Niebuhr's farm near Luneburg. Young H. Filter, the pastor's son and Zulu interpreter to Major Blake, tried to retrieve the cattle, but was cut off and killed near the Ntombe with 6 black border policemen. The 25 mounted infantry of the 2/4th at Luneburg and the 18 troopers of Schermbrucker's Horse were insufficient to act against the raiders. The Zulu sensibly made no attempt to attack Luneburg, and at sunset went off with their booty towards the Ntombe. The blacks friendly to the settlers took to the mountains and caves, and left their enemy master of their mealie gardens.[114] From 7 until 21 June, when they finally passed back across the Phongolo, large forces of Zulu raiders swept with impunity between the Ntombe and Assegai, attacking the homesteads in the area and driving off thousands of cattle and sheep. Manyonyoba's men occupied the hills opposite Luneburg, and were able to remain there through June with impunity.[115] They continued to constitute the greatest danger to the other blacks living in the vicinity, for after the great raids of June no further serious Zulu activity occurred elsewhere in the upper Phongolo region.[116]

Nevertheless, a potential threat from quite another quarter lay over the British and their black allies along the Phongolo.[117] The Wakkerstroom Boers, as has been noted, were unwilling to aid the British militarily and were clearly in communication with the Zulu. So blatant had this become, that in late June official enquiries were made by the responsible landdrosts concerning treasonable relations between Van Staden and other Boers of the Assegai River region with Zulu deputations who had come to treat with them.[118] These Boers made no secret of their resistance to British rule, nor of being in league with the Zulu. Some had reputedly gone to see Cetshwayo, and more Boers than usual that June were wintering along the border, some close to the Phongolo among the Zulu homesteads. That they felt safe to do so simply confirmed British suspicions – not that the British had the forces available to prevent them doing as they pleased. In fact, as has been shown above, the Boers had found it expedient to guide the Zulu raiding parties, and it became known that in the latest series of raids from 7 June onwards they had led the Zulu against local homesteads which would not *khonza* to them, and had indicated which farms should be spared their ravages.[119] On that occasion the Zulu had made no bones about their intention to 'kill all the English . . . and their Kaffirs', but not the Boers, who were their 'friends'.[120] This relationship was confirmed by an incident of 4 August when the Zulu warned Hendrik Versagie 'to shift over' as an *impi* was coming to kill the blacks friendly to the British. The Boers north of the Phongolo consequently trekked into laager until the threat of a raid was past.[121] Three weeks later, Conrad Potgieter was reported to be camped in the ruins of Kohrs's farm near Luneburg, on the best of terms with Manyonyoba who had burnt it, and who still threatened the British garrison.[122]

Yet the Boers stopped short of actually taking up arms against the British. In any case, the situation had been dramatically changed by the battle of Ulundi which was fought on 4 July. The defeated Zulu army scattered, not to reassemble, while Cetshwayo fled as a fugitive to the north. Sir Garnet Wolseley, who superseded Lord Chelmsford, set about capturing the king and pacifying Zululand. A column, made up of Wood's disbanded forces, was put under the command of Lieutenant-Colonel Baker Russell and detailed to achieve the pacification of north-western Zululand, where it was feared that the Zulu, especially the Qulusi, might attempt a last-ditch resistance.[123] Wolseley determined that Baker Russell, when operating towards the headwaters of the Black Mfolozi from the south, should be supported by a simultaneous advance from the north across the Phongolo by Swazi forces and by British troops from the Transvaal operating through Luneburg, both of whom would clear Baker Russell's front. The Transvaal troops were under the command of Lieutenant-Colonel the Hon. G. Villiers, and were to consist of mounted Burghers and of the adherents of Prince Hamu kaNzibe, whose chiefdom was south-east of Luneburg, and who had deserted to Wood in March 1879, living since then in the safety of Utrecht. While the Swazi's specific objective was to ensure that Cetshwayo did not slip across the upper Phongolo into Swaziland, Villiers's, as Special Commissioner to Hamu, was to obtain the submission of the turbulent and semi-independent Zulu of the Phongolo frontier.[124]

Wolseley's strategy for north-western Zululand did not succeed, however.[125] The Boers of Wakkerstroom, not the least surprisingly in the light of their recent record, refused to volunteer for Villiers's force. They even went to the extent of preventing local blacks from serving as auxiliaries, and helped the Zulu by forwarding them information of British movements.[126] Hamu's men proved initially unwilling to advance further into hostile territory than midway between Utrecht and Luneburg.[127] As for the Swazi, though they were happy to loot Zulu homesteads along the Phongolo, they were still too afraid of Zulu power to risk their army far into Zululand.[128] Their dereliction did not much concern Wolseley, though, who was by this stage satisfied that Cetshwayo was not heading in their direction, and who was in any case reluctant to let loose an army in Zululand which he might not be able to control.[129] Besides that, he felt that Villiers was in no danger, as the Zulu against whom he was to operate (in particular Manyonyoba), would offer 'no formidable opposition'.[130]

Villiers therefore advanced on the Assegai with what forces he had managed to raise: 300 mounted whites and 700 black auxiliaries. Hamu's men, who had begun to recover their nerve, also started to join him, and wasted no opportunity in looting the countryside.[131] By 14 August Villiers was approaching the Assegai, and though he feared some resistance from the local blacks,[132] none materialized, and on 21 August he crossed the river without opposition. He reached Luneburg on 25 August. On 27 August the mounted men of Baker Russell's column, which had also encountered some unfriendliness on their march, but no outright resistance, pushed ahead and reached eZungwini. The Qulusi *izinduna* and Manyonyoba, situated as they were between Baker Russell and Villiers, were in a clearly vulnerable position and were faced with the dilemma of whether or not to submit.[133]

Two sons of the Qulusi *induna* Msebe informed Baker Russell on 28 August that both their father and Manyonyoba wished to surrender.[134] Msebe gave himself up the next day. Meanwhile, the intelligence that Cetshwayo had been captured by a British patrol in the Ngome forest on 28 August had an immediate effect on those Qulusi still holding out. At a council held on 30 August they decided to surrender, and on 1 September Mahubulwana kaDumisela, the principal *induna* of the Qulusi, submitted on behalf of his people.[135] Baker Russell then advanced across the Bivane and made for Luneburg.[136]

Manyonyoba, though apprehensive of Villiers's 'awful rabble' who were plundering left and right, and with whom his men had exchanged some shots, nevertheless persisted with his expressed intention of submitting. On 3 September he sent word to Major Elliott at Luneburg that at sunset on 4 September he was prepared to lay down his arms.[137]

This intention, which would have ended the war in the north-west without the loss of any more blood, was tragically frustrated. On 4 September Baker Russell received Wolseley's instructions to 'clear Manyonyoba out'.[138] Accordingly, and sceptical of Manyonyoba's intention of surrendering that very day at Luneburg, he ordered Colonel Black to march for his stronghold on the banks of the Ntombe with a force consisting of Teteleku's Mounted Natives and some mounted infantry. Force, though, was not to be used unless necessary, and seven Zulu men in one of the caves were allowed quietly to surrender and, with the promise that their lives would be spared, were put in charge of some of Teteleku's men. The rest of Black's force went further up the hillside, where there were many men, women and children sheltering in other caves with their cattle and fowls. One of Manyonyoba's men panicked and fired a shot. The moment they heard it, Teteleku's men guarding the prisoners, who were not being supervised by one of their own white officers, fell on them with their assegais and butchered the lot. After that, the other Zulu were naturally quite unwilling to come out of their caves and surrender, and shouted down that they were no longer prepared to believe the white man's word. Teteleku's men were unrepentant, and marched back to their bivouac singing victory songs, but by their action they had ruined the chance for negotiating with Manyonyoba, and had left room only for the employment of brute force.[139]

Consequently, on 5 September Baker Russell despatched a large patrol to take Manyonyoba's principal cave, which was on the left bank of the Ntombe. While the King's Dragoon Guards skirted the base and Irregular Horse made their way around to the north side of the mountain to cut off any fugitives, infantry of the 94th Regiment scrambled in single file up to the caves. As the British came up the Zulu set light to the grass and bush, and soon the whole mountainside was ablaze. Most of Manyonyoba's adherents had already slipped away, though, and there were only a few still remaining in the caves. These refused positively to come out. So the British piled up wood, mats and mealies and set these and the huts at the entrances to the caves alight in an effort to smoke the Zulu out. They had no success, however, so they withdrew with the few cattle, goats, fowls and mealies that were still left to loot.[140]

The next day Manyonyoba's brother and a few adherents were captured,[141] though on Sunday, 7 September, the British remained inactive.[142] During the early hours of 8 September they began a determined effort to finish the business. While Baker Russell's force (the 94th Regiment, Lonsdale's Horse, some of Teteleku's men and Natal Police) returned to the caves they had attempted to smoke out on 5 September, Colonel Bray with men of the 2/4th from the Luneburg garrison proceeded to Mbilini's mountain across the Ntombe, where there was some Zulu activity. Little resistance was anticipated, as that very morning 14 men with their wives and children had surrendered themselves at Luneburg. Russell's men encountered only four poor starved old women who crawled out of a cave. The soldiers then blew up the caves with three charges of dynamite, presuming there were no more Zulu still inside. There was resistance, though, at Mbilini's mountain, where two NCOs of the 2/4th were shot by Zulu firing from the caves. When the troops threatened to blow up the caves in retaliation with all inside them, the Zulu's only reply was to swear at the British interpreter. The caves were then duly blown up under the direction of Captain Courtney, R.E. with at least 30 people still sheltering in their depths

This act of barbarity ended resistance. Manyonyoba's son, an *induna* and a few others were rounded up.[143] Manyonyoba himself eluded the British and escaped to a cave near the head of the Ntombe valley. Irregular cavalry hunted for him there without success.[144]

Despite Manyonyoba still being at large, Wolseley concluded that resistance in the Ntombe valley was effectively over. He therefore decided to break up Villiers's force of 'riff-raff' and send them home.[145] Russell he ordered on 10 September to proceed immediately to Lydenburg in the Transvaal in order to make a demonstration of force against the Pedi in the hope that Sekhukhune might surrender.[146]

Enough troops were left in Luneburg to control the Ntombe valley, and fear of starvation at length compelled Manyonyoba to give himself up on 22 September with his wife and principal *induna*. His remaining adherents, on their surrender, were allowed to remain in their caves pending removal.[147] On 1 September Wolseley had announced the division of the Zulu kingdom into thirteen fragments, each to be ruled by a chief to be appointed for his dependability. One of these was Hlubi, whose Tlokwa had fought with the British during the war. He was thus considered particularly reliable,[148] and for that reason Wolseley decided to relocate Manyonyoba to his territory on the borders of Natal at the junction of the Buffalo and Thukela rivers. Under his rule, Manyonyoba would be rendered quite harmless.[149]

Manyonyoba and 94 of his adherents were escorted out of the valley which had been their home, and going by way of Utrecht reached Fort Mclvill on the Buffalo on 8 October. They were permitted to build a new homestead in the Batshe Valley, between Rorke's Drift and Isandlwana, close by the site of what had been Sihayo's Sokhexe homestead.[150] Sihayo himself had been relocated from the focus of his former authority. Predictably, Manyonyoba and his people were hardly greeted with much enthusiasm by their new neighbours. Manyonyoba's reputation for being a freebooter, worse even than Mbilini, went before him, and his neighbours took immediate precautions to safeguard their stock from his anticipated depredations.[151]

With the death of Mbilini and the removal of Manyonyoba, an element which for many years had troubled the Phongolo frontier was eliminated. Yet what finally closed the frontier, and brought a form of tranquility to the region, was Wolseley's settlement of September 1879 which eliminated the territorial claims of the defunct Zulu kingdom. For when drawing the boundaries of the 13 chiefdoms, he made the northern limit of Hamu's territory the Bivane, and that of Sekethwayo the Phemvana. The whole disputed territory between the confluence of the Phongolo and Bivane, including the Ntombe valley and Luneburg, consequently went to the Transvaal,[152] and the political authority of the settlers was confirmed at last.

[Previously published in *Journal of Natal & Zulu History*, X, 1987.]

Notes

1. H. Lamar & L. Thompson (eds.) *The Frontier in History: North America and Southern Africa Compared*, New Haven & London, 1981, pp.7–10; C. Saunders, 'Political Processes in the South African Frontier Zones', in ibid., pp.149–50, 164–6, 170–1.

2. T.S. Van Rooyen, 'Die Verhouding tussen die Boere, Engelse en Naturelle in die Geskiedenis van die Oos Transvaal tot 1882', *Archives Year Book for South African History, 1951 (I)*, Cape Town, 1951, p.39; J.P.H. Acocks, *Veld Types of South Africa Map*, Pretoria, 1951; *Natal Regional Survey, No.1: Natural Resources of Natal*, Oxford, 1951, pp.33, 63, 66, 78; Jeff Guy, *The Destruction of the Zulu Kingdom*, Great Britain, 1979, pp.4–8.

3. M.A. Monteith, 'Cetshwayo and Sekhukhune 1875–1879' (unpublished M.A. thesis, University of the Witwatersrand, 1978), pp.24,66–7; P. Bonner, *Commoners and Concessionaires: The Evolution and Dissolution of the Nineteenth-Century Swazi State*, Johannesburg, 1983, pp.131, 133, 147, 151, 216–7.

4. Van Rooyen, 'Boere, Engelse en Naturelle', pp.43–4; F.J. Potgieter, 'Die Vestiging van die Blanke in Transvaal (1837–1886) met Spesiale Verwysing na die Verhouding tussen die Mens en die Omgewing', *Archives Year Book for South African History, 1958 (II)*, Pretoria/Cape Town, 1958, p.68; S.J. Reynecke, 'Utrecht in die Geskiedenis van die Transvaal tot 1877' in ibid., 218, 242–3; J.P.C. Laband and P.S. Thompson with Sheila Henderson, *The Buffalo Border 1879*, Durban, 1983, pp.19–20.

5. Van Rooyen, 'Boere, Engelse en Naturelle', pp.45, 78; Potgieter, 'Blanke in Transvaal', pp.66–8, 119; Bonner, *Commoners and Concessionaires*, p.135.

6. Van Rooyen, 'Boere, Engelse en Naturelle', p.43; J. Laband and J. Wright, *King Cetshwayo kaMpande (c. 1832–1884)*, Pietermaritzburg and Ulundi, 1983, pp.7–8, 11–12.

7. C. de B. Webb and J.B. Wright (eds.), *A Zulu King Speaks*, Pietermaritzburg and Durban, 1978, pp.xii–xiii.

8. Ibid., pp. xiii–xv; *B.P. P.* (C. 2220), Appendix II, enc. 1 in no. 1: Secretary of the Transvaal and Zulu Boundary Commission to Bulwer, 20 June 1878; ibid., enc. in no. 2: Report by Acting Secretary for Native Affairs on the country north of the Pongola River and relations between the Zulu and the Swazi, 28 June 1878; ibid., Bulwer to Frere, 17 July 1878.

9. Webb and Wright, *Zulu King Speaks*, pp. 21, 24.

10. P. Schwarz, 'Gemeinde Lüneburg, Natal' in Pastor J. Schnackenberg (ed.), *Geschichte der Freien en.-luth. Synode in Südafrika 1892–1932*, Celle, 1933, pp. 24–5; Van Rooyen, 'Boere, Engelse en Naturelle', p. 376; Potgieter, 'Blanke in Transvaal', p. 119; A. H. M. Leuschke, 'The Hermannsburg Mission Society in Natal and Zululand, 1854–1865 (unpublished B.A. Hons. thesis, University of Natal, 1985) pp. 17, 19–20, 54–5.

11. SS 236, no. R1769/77: Rudolph to State Secretary, Transvaal, 3 May 1877.

12. R. L. Cope, 'Shepstone and Cetshwayo 1873–1879' (unpublished M.A. thesis, University of Natal, 1967), pp. 226–34, 237–9.

13. Ibid., pp. 242–5; GH 789: Shepstone to Bulwer, 16 November 1877; *Times of Natal*, 16 January 1878.

14. C. Vijn (tr. and ed. J. W. Colenso), *Cetshwayo's Dutchman*, London, 1880, p. 127: Bishop Colenso's notes; *JSA*, vol. IV, pp. 277–8: Testimony of Ndukwana kaMbengwana; J. Y. Gibson, *The Story of the Zulus*, London, 1911, p. 194: Guy, *Zulu Kingdom*, p. 36.

15. TS 25: Bulwer to Shepstone, 18 November 1877; GH 789: Theophilus Shepstone to Bulwer, 23 November 1877.

16. *JSA*, vol. IV, pp. 136–7: Testimony of Mtshayankomo kaMagolwana.

17. *B.P. P.* (C. 2222), enc. 2 in no. 43: Theophilus Shepstone to Bulwer, 26 January 1878; ibid., 29 January 1879.

18. AU 13, no. 108/78: Rudolph to Secretary for Native Affairs, Transvaal, 26 May 1878.

19. AU 13, no. 115/78: Rudolph to Secretary to the Transvaal Government, 1 June 1878; SS 281, no. R1999/78: Rudolph to State Secretary, Transvaal 25 May 1878; SS 291, no. R2365/78: Bernhard Böhmer to T. Shepstone, 8 July 1878.

20. SS 286, no. R1986/78: Rudolph to State Secretary, Transvaal, 18 June 1878.

21. *Times of Natal*, 23 September 1878: Utrecht Correspondent, 12 September 1878.

22. Bonner, *Commoners and Concessionaires*, p. 150.

23. SS 306, no. R3466/78: Rudolph to State Secretary, Transvaal, 27 September 1878.

24. AU 13, no. 225/78: Rudolph to Secretary for Native Affairs, Transvaal, 2 October 1878; AU 13, no. 247/78: Rudolph to Secretary for Native Affairs, Transvaal, 27 October 1879.

25. SNA 1/6/11, no. 6: Report of Acting Secretary for Native Affairs on communication from Landdrost Utrecht of 27 September, 4 October 1878; *B.P.P.* (C. 2260), enc. 2 in no. 6: Memorandum by Bulwer accompanying Papers relating to Zulu Affairs during the month of October 1878, 16 January 1879; ibid., sub-enc. 20 in enc. 2 in no. 6: Reply by Cetywayo to Message of Lt.-Gov. of Natal conveyed by Sighla and Tapula, 29 October 1878.

26. AU 13, no. 242/78: Rudolph to Secretary for Native Affairs, Transvaal, 12 October 1878; *B.P.P.* (C. 2222), enc. in no. 26: Rudolph to Secretary for Native Affairs, Transvaal, 27 October 1878; ibid. (C. 2260), enc. 2 in no. 6: Bulwer's Memorandum on Zulu Affairs, 16 January 1879; J.P.C. Laband and P.S. Thompson, *Field Guide to the War in Zululand and the Defence of Natal*, Pietermaritzubrg, 1987, p. 83.

27. Paulina Dlamini (comp. H. Filter, tr. & ed. S. Bourquin), *Servant of Two Kings*, Durban and Pietermaritzburg, 1986, p. 67; notes, p. 124: Testimony of Jacob Mkwanazi.

28. Capt. W.R. Ludlow, *Zululand and Cetywayo*, London & Birmingham, 1882, pp. 148–9.

29. Dlamini, *Two Kings*, p. 68.

30. Bonner, *Commoners and Concessionaires*, pp. 103–9, 212, 261 (note 5).

31. Vijn, *Cetshwayo's Dutchman*, p. 107: Colenso's notes; F. Schermbrucker, 'Zhlobane and Kambula', *The South African Catholic Magazine*, III, 30, (1893), p. 338.

32. Major Ashe & Capt. the Hon. E.V. Wyatt Edgell, *The Story of the Zulu Campaign*, London, 1880, pp. 11, 99; F.E. Colenso, assisted by Lt.-Col. E. Durnford, *History of the Zulu War and its Origin*, London 1880, pp. 203–4; Vijn, *Cetshwayo's Dutchman*, p. 104: Colenso's notes; Bishop J.W. Colenso & H.E. Colenso, *Digest of Zulu Affairs*, series no. 1, part 1, Bishopstowe, 1881, pp. 323–4; Gibson, *Zulus*, p. 156; Webb and Wright, *Zulu King*, p. 22; Dlamini, *Two Kings*, pp. 67–8.

33. Bonner, *Commoners and Concessionaires*, p. 134.

34. Ibid., pp. 120, 129–30, 134.

35. Ibid., pp. 147–8; *Times of Natal*, 16 January 1878; Colenso, *Digest*, series no. 1, part 1, pp. 323–5; Webb and Wright, *Zulu King*, pp. 22–3.

36. *B.P.P.* (C. 2374), enc. in no. 10: Statement of Trooper Grandie, a Frenchman, Weatherley's Horse, made before Brig.-Gen. Wood, 16 April 1879; Dlamini, *Two Kings*, p. 68.

37. AU 13, no. 242/78: Rudolph to Secretary for Native Affairs, Transvaal, 12 October 1878; TS 33: Thesiger to T. Shepstone, 21 October 1878; Alison Collection, p. 59: J.N. Crealock to Alison, 22 October 1878.

38. AU 13, no. 247/78: Rudolph to Secretary for Native Affairs, Transvaal, 27 October 1878; Vijn, *Cetshwayo's Dutchman*, pp. 105–6: Colenso's notes; Colenso, *Digest*, series no. 1, part 2, p. 630; Webb and Wright, *Zulu King*, p. 23.

39. *Natal Colonist*, 29 October 1878; CO 879/14: *African Confidential Print* 164, p. 32: Memorandum on the Zulu Question by E. F[airfield], 19 March 1879.

40. F. Colenso, *Zulu War*, pp. 204–6.

41. AU 13, no.246/78: Rudolph to Secretary for Native Affairs, Transvaal, 14 October 1878.

42. WC II/2/4: Frere to Wood, 7 October 1878.

43. AU 13, no.259/78: Rudolph to Secretary for Native Affairs, Transvaal, 22 October 1878; Sir E. Wood, *From Midshipman to Field Marshal*, London, 1906, vol.II, pp.9–12; Laband & Thompson, *Field Guide*, p.83.

44. J. Mathews, 'Lord Chelmsford: British General in Southern Africa 1878–1879' (unpublished D. Litt. et Phil. thesis, University of South Africa, 1987), pp.91–3.

45. Wood, *Midshipman to Field Marshal*, vol.II, p.11.

46. *B.P.P.* (C. 2367), enc. 6 in no.39a: Memorandum by Frere, 29 October 1878.

47. Ibid., enc. 4 in no.39a: John Dunn to Secretary for Native Affairs, Natal, 20 October 1878; ibid., enc. 5 in no.39a: Minute by Bulwer, 28 October 1878.

48. Ibid. (C. 2260), sub-enc. 23 in enc. 2 in no.6: Message to Cetywayo from the Lt.-Gov. of Natal, conveyed to Mquazi and Umfolozi by J.W. Shepstone, 30 October 1878.

49. AU 25: Statement by Rudolph, 11 November 1878; AU 13, no.294/78: Rudolph to Secretary for Native Affairs, Transvaal, 13 November 1878.

50. AU 13, no.259/78: Rudolph to Secretary for Native Affairs, Transvaal, 22 October 1878; AU 13, no.294/78: Rudolph to Secretary for Native Affairs, Transvaal, 13 November 1878; Wood *Midshipman to Field Marshal*, vol.II, pp.12–13: Monteith, 'Sekhukhune', p.135.

51. Colenso Collection, Box 2, p.258: Colenso to Bulwer, 26 March 1879; Colenso, *Digest*, series no.1, part 1, pp.118, 331.

52. *Natal Mercury*, 17 February 1879: Lüneburg correspondent, 6 February 1879; Schermbrucker, 'Zhlobane and Kambula', p.338; Ashe and Wyatt Edgell, *Zulu Campaign*, p.99; Wood, *Midshipman to Field Marshal*, vol.II, p.12; Capt. W.E. Montague, *Campaigning in South Africa*, Edinburgh and London, 1880, p.337.

53. Colenso, *Digest*, series no.1, part 1, p.331.

54. Laband and Thompson, *Field Guide*, p.83.

55. SNA 1/6/3, n.n.: Original Draft of the Ultimatum, signed by Bulwer, 4 December 1878.

56. CP 9, enc. d in no.4: Wood to Military Secretary, 30 February 1879: Extract from Commandant Schermbrucker's report of 28 December 1878.

57. *Times of Natal*, 10 January 1879.

58. Schermbrucker, 'Zhlobane and Kambula', p.336.

59. *B.P.P.* (C. 2260), enc. 2 in no.13: Schermbrucker to Wood, 23 January 1879.

60. Intelligence Branch of the War Office, *Narrative of the Field Operations Connected with the Zulu War of 1879*, London, 1881, pp.8–10, 19–20, 50–2, 67–8, 143–5; C.L. Norris-Newman, *In Zululand with the British throughout the War of 1879*, London, 1880, p.92; Schermbrucker, 'Zhlobane and Kambula', p.337; Laband and Thompson, *Field Guide*, p.21.

61. *B.P.P.* (C. 2260), enc. 2 in no. 13: Schermbrucker to Wood, 23 January 1879.

62. War Office, *Narrative*, pp. 51, 67.

63. CP 8, no. 49: Bishop Schreuder to Chelmsford, 10 February 1879.

64. CP 9, no. 10: Schermbrucker to Wood, 26 January 1879; Fairlie's Diary: 26 and 27 January 1879; Woodgate's Military Diary: 1 February 1879; *Natal Mercury*, 17 February 1879: Lüneburg correspondent, 6 February 1879.

65. Woodgate's Military Diary: 9 February 1879; *Natal Mercury*, 17 February 1879: Lüneburg correspondent, 6 February 1879.

66. TS 38: Rudolph to H.C. Shepstone, 16 February 1879.

67. Leuschke, 'Hermannsburg Mission Society', pp. 32, 64.

68. *Natal Mercury*, 18 October 1879: Utrecht Correspondent, 7 October 1879.

69. Ashe and Wyatt Edgell, *Zulu Campaign*, p. 98.

70. For accounts of the raid of 11 February, see TS 38: Rudolph to H.C. Shepstone, 13 February 1879: Statement of Tupuswana; WO 32/7715: Diary of Operations, Major Spalding's Report to Quartermaster-General, 23 February 1879; Woodgate's Military Diary: 15 February 1879; *Natal Mercury*, 21 February 1879: Lüneburg correspondent, 11 February 1879; *Times of Natal*, 3 March 1879: Report from Schermbrucker, 11 February 1879; *B.P.P.* (C. 2308), enc. 5 in no. 14: enclosed in Schermbrucker to Wood, 11 February 1879: Lt. Schwartzkopf to Schermbrucker, 11 February 1879.

71. Ibid., enc. 3 in no. 14: Buller to Wood, 14 February 1879; Woodgate's Military Diary: 15 February; War Office, *Narrative*, pp. 67–8.

72. For Buller's raid of 15 February see Woodgate's Military Diary: 16 February 1879; WO 32/7715: Diary of Operations, Major Spalding's Report to the Quartermaster-General, 23 February 1879; *Times of Natal*, 24 February 1879: Colonel Rowlands's Report; *Natal Mercury*, 25 February 1879: Lüneburg correspondent, 16 February 1879; *Natal Colonist*, 1 March 1879: *Natal Witness* correspondent with Wood's Column, 17 February 1879; War Office, *Narrative*, p. 68; Ashe and Wyatt Edgell, *Zulu Campaign*, pp. 93–5.

73. Woodgate's Military Diary: 17 February 1879; *Times of Natal*, 10 March 1879: Kambula correspondent, 3 March 1879.

74. WO 32/7715: Diary of Operations, Major Spalding's Report to the Quartermaster-General, 23 February 1879; *Times of Natal*, 24 February 1879: Colonel Rowlands's Report; ibid., 24 March 1879: Derby correspondent, 6 March 1879; War Office, *Narrative*, p. 68; Ashe and Wyatt Edgell, *Zulu Campaign*, p. 95.

75. WO 32/7715: Diary of Operations, Major Spalding's Report to the Quartermaster-General, 23 February 1879; *Times of Natal*, 28 February 1879; ibid., 10 March 1879: Kambula correspondent, 3 March 1879; War Office, *Narrative*, p. 68; Ashe and Wyatt Edgell, *Zulu Campaign*, pp. 95–8.

76. *Times of Natal*, 10 March 1879: Kambula correspondent, 3 March 1879; War Office, *Narrative*, p. 68.

77. CP 9, no. 4: Wood to Military Secretary, 30 February 1879.

78. MacLeod Letters, Bundle B, no. 19: MacLeod to Father, 9 March 1879; War Office, *Narrative*, p. 68.

79. Ibid., p. 69.

80. For accounts of the engagement, see ibid., pp. 69–72; D. C. F. Moodie (ed.), *The History of the Battles and Adventures of the British, the Boers and the Zulus in Southern Africa*, Sidney, Melbourne and Adelaide, 1879, pp. 263–9; F. Emery, *The Red Soldier*, London, 1977, pp. 157–62; *Marching over Africa*, London, 1986, pp. 74–7; Laband and Thompson, *Field Guide*, pp. 84–5.

81. See especially Booth Papers: Major C. Tucker to Booth's father, 19 March 1879.

82. WO 32/7720: Diary of Military Operations, Spalding to Quartermaster-General, 29 March 1879; *Natal Colonist*, 25 March 1879: Newcastle correspondent, 18 March 1879.

83. Woodgate's Military Diary: 13 March 1879; Ashe and Wyatt Edgell, *Zulu Campaign*, p. 106; W. M. Laurence, *Selected Writings*, Grahamstown, 1882, p. 29: Letter IV, 20 March 1879.

84. Booth Papers: Interview with Sergeant-Instructor Booth, V.C. in *County Express*, 9 April 1898.

85. Montague, *Campaigning in South Africa*, p. 336.

86. J. Laband, *Fight Us in the Open*, Pietermaritzburg and Ulundi, 1985, pp. 18–19.

87. Booth Papers: Booth to Wife and Children, 14 March 1879; Tucker to Booth's father, 19 March 1879.

88. Laband and Thompson, *Field Guide*, pp. 57, 85, 105.

89. CP 14, no. 7: Tucker to Staff Officer, No. 4 Column, 27 March 1879.

90. Moodie, *British, Boers and Zulus*, pp. 266–7: from a letter in the *Transvaal Argus*.

91. WO 32/7720: Diary of Military Operations, 22–27 March 1879, Major Spalding's Report to Quartermaster-General, 29 March 1879.

92. CP 14, no. 7: Tucker to Staff Officer, No. 4 Column, 27 March 1879; CP 14, no. 9: Report by L. H. Lloyd, Political Assistant, submitted by Wood to Military Secretary, 27 March 1879; *Natal Colonist*, 15 March 1879.

93. Woodgate's Military Diary: 25 March 1879.

94. CP 14, no. 7: Tucker to Staff Officer, No. 4 Column, 27 March 1879.

95. For the battle of Hlobane, see Laband and Thompson, *Field Guide*, pp. 104–5; John Laband 'The Battle of Khambula, 29 March 1879: A Re-Examination from the Zulu Perspective', in Ian Knight (ed.), *There will be an Awful Row at Home about This*, Shoreham-by-Sea, 1987, pp. 21–2.

96. For the battle of Khambula, see ibid., pp. 23–9.

97. Ibid., p. 29.

98. Woodgate's Military Diary: 8 April 1879; *Natal Colonist*, 24 April 1879: Kambula correspondent, 10 April 1879; SNA 1/1/3, no. 73: Statement of Sibalo, son of Ribana, taken by J. W. Shepstone, 1 June 1879.

99. War Office, *Narrative*, pp. 84–5.

100. Woodgate's Military Diary: 1 and 3 April 1879.

101. Woodgate's Military Diary: 7, 8 and 17 April 1879.

102. Laband and Thompson, *Field Guide*, p. 83.

103. AU 13, no. 120/79: Rudolph to Secretary for Native Affairs, Transvaal, 17 April 1879; AW 4, no. 5/1879–81: James Clark to Landdrost Wakkerstroom, 26 May 1879; *Natal Mercury*, 19 April 1879: Utrecht correspondent, 11 April 1879; ibid., 25 April 1879: Utrecht correspondent, 17 May 1879; ibid., 3 May 1879: *Times of Natal* correspondent, 23 April 1879; *B.P.P.* (C. 2374), no. 10: Frere to Hicks Beach, 29 April 1879; Vijn, *Cetshwayo's Dutchman*, pp. 123–4: Colenso's notes; War Office, *Narrative*, p. 85.

104. Dlamini, *Two Kings*, pp. 68–9. See also SNA 1/1/34. no. 73: Statement of Sibalo taken by J.W. Shepstone, 1 June 1879. For doubts expressed concerning the dead man's identity, see Vijn, *Cetshwayo's Dutchman*, p. 124: Colenso's notes.

105. *Natal Colonist*, 24 April 1879: Kambula correspondent, 10 April 1879; *Natal Mercury*, 3 May 1879: *Times of Natal* correspondent, 23 April 1879; Ashe and Wyatt Edgell, *Zulu Campaign*, p. 301.

106. Woodgate's Military Diary: 17 April 1879; War Office, *Narrative*, p. 85.

107. CP 16, no. 14: Statement of a Zulu employed by General Wood, who returned to camp on 12 May 1879.

108. Laband and Thompson, *Field Guide*, p. 83.

109. AU 13, no. 154/79: Rudolph to Landdrost Wakkerstroom, 9 May 1879; SS 346, no. R1946/79: Landdrost Wakkerstroom to Secretary of State, Transvaal, 26 May 1879.

110. War Office, *Narrative*, pp. 100–3.

111. AU 14, no. 243/79: Rudolph to Colonial Secretary, Transvaal, 30 June 1879.

112. Ibid.

113. SS 346, no. R1932/79: Rudolph to Colonial Secretary, Transvaal, 5 June 1879.

114. *B.P.P.* (C. 2482), enc. 1 in no. 17: Border Policeman Gruhla's statement to Rudolph, 10 June 1879; ibid., (C. 2454), enc. 1 in no. 42: Chelmsford to Secretary of State for War, 16 June 1879.

115. CP 9, no. 61: Schermbrucker to Colonel Bray, 21 June 1879; *Natal Mercury*, 28 June 1879: Lüneburg correspondent, 16 June 1879.

116. AU 14, no. 243/79: Rudolph to Colonial Secretary, Transvaal, 30 June 1879; SS 352, no. R2421/79: Rudolph to Colonial Secretary, Transvaal, 10 July 1879.

117. *B.P.P.* (C. 2482), enc. B (2) in no. 48: MacLeod to Rudolph, 16 June 1879.

118. SS 346, no. R1945/79: Landdrost Wakkerstroom to Secretary of State Transvaal, 26 May 1879; AU 14, no. 243: Rudolph to Colonial Secretary, Transvaal, 30 June 1879.

119. *Natal Mercury*, 28 June 1879: Derby correspondent, 12 June 1879; ibid., 18 October 1879: Utrecht correspondent, 7 October 1879.

120. *B.P. P.* (C. 2482), enc. B (2) in no. 48: MacLeod to Rudolph, 16 June 1879.

121. AU 14, no. 385/79: Rudolph to Colonial Secretary, Transvaal, 7 August 1879.

122. *Natal Mercury*, 30 August 1879: Swazi correspondent, 18 August 1879.

123. AU 14, no. 264/79: Rudolph to Colonial Secretary, Transvaal, 24 July 1879; Wolseley's Journal: 18 July 1879.

124. WO 32/7756: Telegram, Wolseley to Secretary of State for War, 21 July 1879; WO 32/7773: Wolseley to Secretary of State for War, 2 August 1879; WO 32/7766: Wolseley to Secretary of State for War, 22 August 1879; WO 32/7780: Wolseley to Secretary of State for War, 3 September 1879; Wolseley's Journal: 18 July 1879; *The Graphic*, 30 August 1879, p. 198; Ashe and Wyatt Edgell, *Zulu Campaign*, p. 379.

125. Wolseley's Journal: 10 August 1879.

126. *B.P. P.* (C. 2482), no. 81: Wolseley to Hicks Beach, 20 August 1879.

127. WO 32/7775: Wolseley to Secretary of State for War, 13 August 1879; *Natal Mercury*, 15 August 1879: Utrecht correspondent, 10 August 1879.

128. MacLeod Letters, Bundle E, no. 2: General Colley to Lt.-Col. Villiers, 24 August 1879; Bonner, *Commoners and Concessionaires*, pp. 153–4.

129. Wolseley's Journal: 18 August 1879.

130. *B.P. P.* (C. 2482), no. 8: Wolseley to Hicks Beach, 20 August 1879.

131. Watson Letters, p. 164: 3 September 1879; *B.P. P.* (C. 2482), enc. 2 in no. 57: Villiers to Bulwer, 15 September 1879.

132. Wolseley's Journal: 15 August 1879.

133. WO 32/7777: Telegram, Wolseley to Secretary of State for War, 2 September 1879; *B.P. P.* (C. 2482), enc. 3 in no. 78: Clifford to Frere, n.d.; ibid., enc. in no. 84: Wolseley to Secretary of State for War, 27 August 1879; *Natal Mercury*, 30 August 1879: Swazi correspondent, 18 August 1879; War Office, *Narrative*, pp. 129–30.

134. Woodgate's Private Diary: 28 August 1879.

135. WO 32/7782: Diary of Baker Russell's Column: 29 and 30 August, 1 and 3 September 1879.

136. War Office, *Narrative*, p. 131.

137. Watson Letters, p. 164: 3 September 1879; p. 166: 4 September 1879; *Natal Witness*, 9 September 1879: *Natal Mercury* correspondent at Utrecht, 6 September 1879; *Natal Mercury*, 17 September 1879: Correspondent with Villiers's Column, 7 September 1879.

138. Wolseley's Journal: 6 September 1879.

139. Woodgate's Private Diary: 4 September 1879; Watson letters, pp. 165–7: 4 September 1879; Vijn, *Cetshwayo's Dutchman* p. 102: Colenso's notes; Montague, *Campaigning in South Africa*, p. 337.

140. Woodgate's Private Diary: 5 September 1879; WO 32/7782: Journal of Baker Russell's Column: 5 September 1879; Watson Letters, p. 167: 5 September 1879; Montague, *Campaigning in South Africa*, pp. 337–41.

141. Woodgate's Private Diary: 7 September 1879; WO 32/7781: Wolseley to Secretary of State for War, 11 September 1879.

142. Watson Letters, pp. 167–8: 7 September 1879.

143. Woodgate's Private Diary: 8 September 1879; Watson Letters, pp. 168–70: 8 September 1879; *Natal Witness*, 27 September 1879: Correspondent with Baker Russell, Luneburg, 9 September 1879; 'H' [W. Heron-Maxwell], *Reminiscences of a Red Coat*, London, 1895, pp. 37–8; Vijn, *Cetshwayo's Dutchman*: Colenso's notes, pp. 100–2.

144. Woodgate's Private Diary: 10 September 1879; Montague, *Campaigning in South Africa*, p. 341.

145. Wolseley's Journal: 8 September 1879.

146. Ibid.; WO 32/7778: Wolseley to Secretary of State for War, 8 September 1879; Watson Letters, p. 170: 9 September 1879.

147. CO 179/132, p. 356: Telegram, Wolseley to Secretary of State for War, 22 September 1879; Montague, *Campaigning in South Africa*, p. 342.

148. J. P. C. Laband, 'The Cohesion of the Zulu Polity under the Impact of the Anglo-Zulu War: A Reassessment', *JNZH*, VIII, 1985, p. 58.

149. *B.P.P.* (C. 2482), enc. in no. 130: Wolseley to Secretary of State for War, 3 October 1879.

150. SNA 1/1/35, no. 87: Fynn to Secretary for Native Affairs, Natal, 10 October 1879; ZA 21, enc. in G728/79: Report on the Relocation of Manyonyoba, 15 October 1879.

151. SNA 1/1/35, no. 73: Robson to Secretary for Native Affairs, Natal, 9 October 1879.

152. ZA 19, enc. in Herbert to Osborn, 25 February 1880: Report of the Zululand Boundary Commission, Lt.-Col. G. Villiers, Capt. J. Alleyne and Capt. H. Moore, 5 December 1879.

The Griqua and Mpondo Marches

Natal's southern border during the Anglo-Zulu War

P. S. THOMPSON

The imperial authorities and colonial government in Natal had more than the Zulu border to consider as war loomed in 1878. To the west, over the Drakensberg, lived the BaSotho, now nominally under the Cape government; their chiefs were divided and variously hostile to the innovations of the alien administration. To the south-west, below the Drakensberg, lived the Griqua of the late Adam Kok, a portion of whom had reacted violently against Cape administration, which reaction moved the Cape Colony formally to annex East Griqualand in 1879. To the south, occupying the coastal country were the Mpondo, now divided into two polities because of a contentious succession; the senior chief, Mqikela, who ruled eastern Pondoland, retained his independence, but at some cost. Frustrated at his refusal to relinquish Port St. John's, where the Mzimvubu meets the ocean, the British High Commissioner, Sir Bartle Frere, simply discountenanced his paramountcy and purchased the port from his western rival, thus depriving Mqikela of the customs revenue. A company of the 1/24th Regiment fortified a position near the mouth of the river. If the hostile and disgruntled elements along the borders of Natal could co-operate then they might upset the British strategy, focused on Zululand.

The government of Natal must take into account the threat of a possible Griqua or Mpondo irruption. The situation along the southern border differed from that along the northern one in several important respects. White settlement was so thin as to be almost negligible. In the Ixopo Division (including Ipolela) of Pietermaritzburg County and in Alfred County, which marched in order with East Griqualand and Pondoland, there were only 266 and 168 Europeans, respectively, according to the magistrates' estimates in November 1878. The same returns put blacks in the Ixopo Division at 30 471 and in Alfred County at 20 974, and the number of their fighting men – presumably disposed towards the colonial authority – at 8 706 and 4 579, respectively.[1] The only organized white forces in this borderland were a detachment of the Natal Mounted Police (37 men) at Harding, the seat of the Alfred magistracy, and the Ixopo Mounted Rifles (27 officers and men),[2] based at the new Ixopo magistracy. Otherwise there was nothing. Field cornetcies were administrative rather than military features, and an infant Alfred County Rifle Association apparently could not be counted as a paramilitary force.[3] There was some talk of calling out other Natal Volunteer Corps for duty in the south in early December 1878,[4] but those that were called out in fact went north; however, the Ixopo Mounted Rifles were not called out, presumably being left to meet an emergency in their division.

The Natalian strategy in the south was obviously defensive. The southern part of the colony was organized for war along with the whole: the Ixopo Division, along with the Upper Umkomanzi Division of Pietermaritzburg County, was designated Colonial Defensive District No. IV, under Major Arthur C. Hawkins, the Resident Magistrate of the latter division; and Alfred County, along with Alexandra County, was designated Colonial Defensive District No. V, under Captain Gould A. Lucas, late of the 73rd, the Resident Magistrate of the latter county.[5] The commandants were instructed to select and prepare places of refuge for the white settlers and to sound out chiefs and arrange for levies to turn out from the reliable ones in time of need.[6]

The organization of the blacks appears to have been a perfunctory task for the commandants, who listed the numbers of fighting men but otherwise left the chiefs to their own devices. European levy leaders and places of assembly were designated. The levies would turn out to fight in their own style; however, provision was made that a tenth of their numbers should be supplied with government firearms.[7] Protection of the whites, who lacked strength in numbers while scattered, consisted of congregating them in fortified places where they could be armed and equipped to defend themselves. Stone-walled laagers had been built by the government in 1878 at Richmond and Umzinto, the magistracies of the Upper Umkomanzi Division and of Alexandra County, respectively. A public notice, signed by Hawkins and dated 18 January 1879, announced that the Richmond laager would be the central post of defence in Colonial Defensive District No. IV.[8] Probably the laager at Umzinto was similarly nominated in No. V.[9] These laagers could be held for some time; however, their distance from the borderland left the white settlers there at a relative disadvantage. Laagers farther forward were needed, and the government took belated steps for their erection.

In Ixopo the Resident Magistrate, Marthinus Stuart, having made arrangements for the black levies (tentatively fixed at 2 980), turned to the

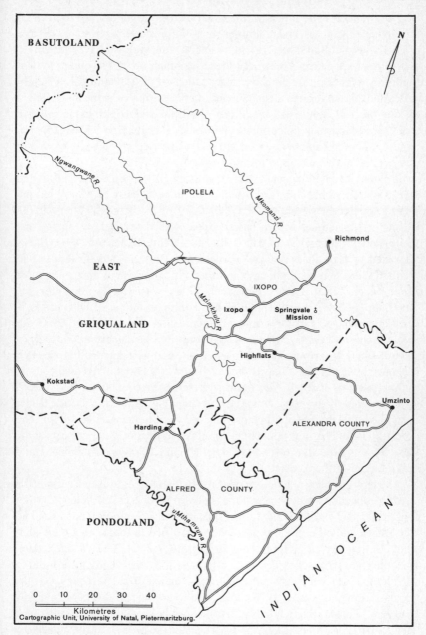

Southern Natal border, 1879.

white populace. (The Ixopo Mounted Rifles were reported now to have 28 dependable members, and might get 35 or 36 for active service; and to have 30 carbines and 8 500 ball cartridges and 40 revolvers and 1 200 revolver cartridges.) On Stuart's notice 29 men assembled on 12 December to deal with the defence of the division. They called on the government to supply rifles and ammunition to the inhabitants, to be distributed at the magistrate's discretion, and nominated the Ixopo township and Highflats as rallying points. If it came to a choice of one or the other, then that should be the Ixopo, where a sod embankment and ditch should be dug around the Wesleyan church and a Mr Greer's to form a laager.[10]

Progress at Harding was less satisfactory. A laager connected to the court-house had been mooted by the authorities as early as May,[11] but the matter apparently was not pressed. In January, on the very eve of the war, the Resident Magistrate, Major James Giles, was distracted by having the command of Colonial Defensive District No. V thrust upon him, when Lucas departed to take charge of the district on the lower Thukela. Lucas had warned Giles that he might have to turn over command to him, but almost three weeks after Lucas' departure, Giles was still waiting for the appointment to be gazetted.[12] Giles had an impossible task: District No. V was an L-shaped territory, and communication was difficult across the broken coastal country. Umzinto, the ostensible headquarters, is 80 kilometres (48 miles) from Harding in an air line and was practically twice that distance by land track. Giles had enough to worry about in his own county, although Lucas had left Alexandra with defensive measures incomplete.[13] Not surprisingly, he concentrated on his own, though the matter of a laager remained in abeyance, until plans were drawn in September of 1879.[14] The court-house at Harding would have to suffice as the one defence post for the few whites of the county, and the Natal Mounted Police detachment could afford them further protection.

The news of the Zulu victory over the British forces at Isandlwana had a varied impact on the populace of the southern border. On 24 January, Major Hawkins, the No. IV District Commandant, sent to Stuart in Ixopo to call up the Bhaca and other loyal tribesmen to his office to throw up a bank-and-ditch as quickly as possible, and to Captain Randall W. I. Walker, commanding the Ixopo Mounted Rifles, to have his corps ready to turn out to defend the laager the instant the magistrate called. The consequence of the defeat, Hawkins wrote to Walker, would be 'incalculable' among the natives.[15] Indeed, like many Natalians, he probably felt there was as much danger from disorders among the blacks inside the colony as from attacks by those outside.

The colonial records have not yielded any report from Stuart of his preparations against the perceived dangers at this time. A semi-fictionalized account of the whites' shock and alarm in Ixopo tells of the village carpenter's wife, a Mrs Mitchell, in an old pink print with flounces, riding a plough horse through the night up to the magistracy on Highbury's Hill, where Stuart was still working at his desk while the children were being put to bed, and calling out that 'the kaffirs' had massacred the people at Isandlwana and asking if he would call out the Rifles. The corps assembled and remained, much to the relief of the womenfolk. Rumours flew about, and the men worked all day on earthworks at the magistracy and the church, while the women cooked food, bundled up clothing and medicines, and buried the silverware, in case they had to go into laager in a hurry.[16] So much for the story. At Springvale, 18 kilometres (11 miles) to the east, the missionary Thomas Jenkinson recorded in his diary that a telegraph report on the 25th stated that two large Zulu forces were in rear of the British armies in Zululand and seeking to raid Natal on orders from the Zulu king Cetshwayo.[17] He recorded on the 26th:

> Another alarming message from the magistrate, mentioning the Ixopo as the rallying place and laager. Most deeply depressed that now for the first time we were in danger . . . I was never afraid before; I should not be so now, if our troops were defending us here in Natal.[18]

Harding Court-House. (Photograph taken in 1884.)

It may have been about this time too, that Gold's store, at Highflats, was barricaded and loopholed for defence.[19]

In Alfred County news of Isandlwana was spread from the postcart, before Giles received an official telegram about it, at 8.30 p.m., Saturday, 25 January. He decided to disseminate the official account, which by that time was less terrifying than some of the exaggerated rumours. There was great consternation among the whites, but he observed no panic; among the blacks apparently there was some excitement, but he did not perceive any danger from it. After all, they were remote from the action, and he represented Isandlwana to them as the surprise of a wagon guard, and stressed the repulse of the Zulu at Rorke's Drift.[20]

Of course, the Zulu did not invade Natal, and their victory at Isandlwana did not lead to disturbances directed at whites in the colony. In due course the fear among the settlers faded. There was still reason for vigilance, particularly in the south, for Zulu spies and emissaries were reported among the Mpondo and the BaSotho;[21] and the temporary military ascendancy of the Zulu may have conduced to Moorosi's rebellion against the Cape authorities in southern Basutoland. At the beginning of February the Lieutenant-Governor of Natal, Sir Henry Bulwer, sent further instructions to the colonial defensive district commandants. He remarked that those in Districts Nos. IV and V had not been called out, but they very likely would be, and at some length enjoined upon all the necessity of reassuring the black populace of the government's good intentions and solicitude.[22] Later in the month, at a meeting called by Hawkins and Stuart at Highflats, a Cape official arrived with a mounted force of 50 or 60 and addressed the assemblage: when he learned of it, Bulwer expressed great displeasure at this unwanted 'demonstration' in the Ixopo Division.[23] By that time, however, the feeling seems to have prevailed that the south was safe. Neither Hawkins nor Giles evinced serious apprehension about their districts. In early February members of the Natal Mounted Police detachment at Harding petitioned to be sent to the Zulu front, too, but their request was refused.[24] The colonial government was even willing to call up southern levies for service on that front. Hawkins' statements showing the defensive state of his district from mid-March to mid-April 1879 tell that the Ixopo Mounted Rifles, 28 strong, were not called out at the time.[25] Twelve levies of black fighting men, collectively known as the Ixopo Native Contingent, under the command of 'Major' Walker, were sent to the Zulu border in March; they numbered about 1 500, foot and horse, although initially diminished much from desertion.[26] In his statements Hawkins remarked: 'There ought to be about 6 000 fighting men left [in the district] but I do not think they would answer to any further call, unless under compulsion.'[27] Giles' statements, for March and mid-April, give 6 624 blacks probably available for service,[28] but do not mention that the Alexandra Mounted Rifles, based at Umzinto, and levies from Alexandra County amounting to about 900 men, were actually in service on the Zulu border.[29]

There was no menacing movement across the southern border. The beaten Griqua seem to have been oblivious to affairs in Zululand. If Mqikela's Mpondo were not, then their excitement translated to action directed at the Cape rather than Natal; the chief pursued a truculent line toward other Bhaca and the Xesibe, small peripheral tribes of the interior, which culminated in some bloodshed the following winter. By this time the war in Zululand was practically over, and Frere apparently hoped to inflate the outbreak into a crisis in order to reduce Pondoland. Imperial troops moved to the southern border in the spring, but the new High Commissioner for Southeast Africa, Sir Garnet Wolseley, would not be drawn on the scheme. The Mpondo were troublesome but their military prowess was not regarded highly, and the crisis soon dissolved.[30]

And so the war in Zululand had affected the southern reaches of Natal. It had tested the moral if not the physical courage of the white settlers, and had tested the government's policy towards the blacks. The loyalty of the latter to the colonial authority seemed proved, even to the extent that over 2 000 served the Queen on the northern front. And for those it had been a 'good' war, an experience with some excitement and no casualties. The men of the Ixopo Native Contingent marched through the streets of Pietermaritzburg on 15 August. They were returning home from the front, evidently in high spirits. They chanted several songs, and a bystander caught and approximately translated the refrain of one of them:

> The white chief has banded our several chiefs –
>   Against Cetywayo, the curse of the Zulus;
> He has got no place, he has got no power, he has got no men –
>   Cetywayo, the curse of the Zulus;
> He's put his tail at last between his legs –
>   Cetywayo, the curse of the Zulus;
> The white army now is coursing him down,
>   and they'll catch him yet –
>   Cetywayo, the curse of the Zulus.[31]

[Previously published in Ian J. Knight (ed.) *There will be an Awful Row at Home about This*, Victorian Military Society, 1987.]

Notes

1. See the returns in GH 1412, Minute 4550/1878.

2. GH 1412, Minute 4550/1878.

3. Cf. CSO 1971, Minutes 3124 and 3125/1878.

4. See the *Natal Colonist*, 10 December 1878, and the *Natal Witness* 14 December 1878.

5. See *NGG*, vol. XXX, nos. 1739, 26 November 1878, and 1740, 3 December 1878, for Government Notices nos. 356 and 368 of 1878, respectively.

6. See CSO 2629, Minute 4237/1878, and the earlier General Instructions in SNA 1/4/2, no. 46.

7. See Richmond Correspondence 2/14/6, Minute 153/1878. Cf. CSO 681, Minute 356/1879 and CSO 1972, Minute 4821/1879, which leaves this much to inference concerning Colonial Defensive District No. V.

8. Richmond Correspondence 2/14/6, Minute 153/1878.

9. The notice (see above) is printed, and blanks were left so that the appropriate locations could be written in. Presumably one was furnished to Lucas or Giles (see below) just as to Hawkins, but it has not been found.

10. Richmond Correspondence 2/14/6, Minute 153/188.

11. GH 1411, Minute 1541/1878.

12. CSO 681, Minute 356/1879.

13. Cf. 681, Minute 356/1879, and the *Natal Mercury*, 15 February 1879.

14. GH 1413, Minute 4666/1879.

15. CSO 699, Minute 2195/1879.

16. V. M. Fitzroy, *Dark Bright Land*, Cape Town, 1955, p. 308.

17. Thomas B. Jenkinson, *Amazulu*, London, 1882, p. 78.

18. Ibid.

19. See 'Defensive District No. IV: Statement showing defensive state of district, 15 March 1879', in SNA 1/6/14, no. 6.

20. CSO 684, Minute 615/1879.

21. See e.g. reports in the *Natal Mercury*, 9 December 1878; *Times of Natal*, 7 February 1879; *Natal Colonist*, 3 March 1879, and *Natal Witness*, 15 April 1879; and cf. *Natal Colonist*, 4 March 1879.

22. GH 1422, p. 35.

23. SNA 1/1/33, no. 82.

24. *Times of Natal*, 14 and 19 February 1879.

25. SNA 1/6/13, no. 34; SNA 1/6/14, nos. 6 and 30; CSO 1927: Minutes 2133 and 2163/1879.

26. GH 1423, Minute 1626/1879; SNA 1/6/12, nos. 44 and 52; SNA 1/6/13, nos. 26 and 47; SNA 1/6/14, nos. 2, 28 and 29; and SNA 1/7/12, pp. 74, 88–9; CSO 693, Minute 1574/1879, and CSO 694, Minute 1607/1879.

27. See as given above.
28. Ibid., and also CSO 1926, Minute 1381/1879.
29. See SNA 1/6/14, no. 21.
30. See C. C. Saunders, 'The Annexation of the Transkeian Territories', *Archives Year Book*, 1976, p. 77; and cf. the *Natal Colonist*, 12 and 14 June, 5, 9, and 12 August 1879.
31. *Times of Natal*, 18 August 1879.

Town and Country and the Zulu Threat, 1878–9

The Natal government's arrangements
for the protection of settlers

P.S. THOMPSON

The Colony's Defences

The government of the Colony of Natal provided for the protection of the white settlers against a possible Zulu incursion and related dangers prior to and during the Anglo-Zulu War of 1879. The colonial government, while concerned with the safety of the blacks, the mass of the colony's population, could do little to guarantee it; also it should be remembered that this government was an institution of the intrusive people of the region, and therefore gave primacy to their, the white settlers', interests. Thus the policies towards whites and blacks diverged.

The government's policies towards the rural and urban whites also diverged. The government regarded with greater urgency the need to afford protection to the more numerous but scattered and vulnerable countryfolk. It gave relatively scant regard to the protection of the townsfolk. Of course, Natal was not invaded and the white settlers were not attacked; but one may wonder how they would have encountered a mighty Zulu *impi* raiding the upper Thukela valley or falling upon Pietermaritzburg or Durban, acts deemed quite possible at different times during the war.

The colonial government had authority and responsibility with regard to defence. The matter was of particular concern to the Executive Council's Defence Committee. Defence included provision for local military or paramilitary units, for places to receive and shelter non-combatants, and for adequate logistical supports to both, and, of course, collaboration with the imperial military forces present in the colony. The concern here is chiefly with its arrangements to receive and shelter the non-combatants: most of the white settlers were non-combatants, and even the few who were not looked to their defence.

Throughout the colony there were places, usually at administrative or commercial centres, where non-combatants could rally and, with some official direction, defend themselves. These places might be a fortified building or group of buildings, but most common was the 'laager'. By the 1870s 'laager' meant an enclosure, of permanent or temporary construction, in which people assembled for security. The defensive perimeter might consist of wagons, earth ramparts, or brick or stone walls.

The colonial government had commenced a system of defences, in conjunction with the imperial military, during the 1860s, when it assumed some financial responsibilities for the stone blockhouse of Fort Nottingham and the earthworks Forts Buckingham and Williamson. Also it had set about construction of permanent laagers at outlying settlements, Greytown and Ladysmith and subsequently Estcourt, but not in the towns, Pietermaritzburg and Durban, where there were adjacent forts with imperial garrisons.[1] If local people wished to set up defences of their own, the government did nothing to hinder them − thus the building (but not completion) of 'Bester's Laager' in the Weenen Division and the 'Malakoff Tower' at Victoria (now Tongaat).[2] As conflict between the British and Zulu crowns developed, the colonial government applied funds for the improvement of its existing laagers and the construction of new ones at Newcastle and Stanger, in 1877, and at Richmond, Umzinto, Verulam and near Dundee, in 1878.[3]

These laagers were at administrative centres, where the Resident Magistrates could take charge of the incoming countryfolk seeking refuge. This provision was not altogether satisfactory, for in certain country districts there was a demand for additional laagers. The government met this demand by agreeing to match the local initiative with funds, but it is not clear that it complied in most cases. The results were mixed. In Klip River County settlers beyond the Biggarsberg commenced three and completed two laagers, and in the upper part of Weenen County built one on the farm Strydpoort, apparently about this time. In Umvoti County farmers erected laagers overlooking the Umvoti River bridge, near the Hermannsburg Mission, and at Rietvlei. Laagers were also mooted for Kearsney and Noodsberg, but nothing was done. Referring to the former, Captain A.H. Hime, the Colonial Engineer, wrote that he was opposed to the construction of many small laagers which would have the effect of dissipating the defensive strength of the colonists. By mid-1878 the government no longer encouraged the private initiatives.[4]

It is interesting that in most cases the motivation for private laagers came from the Dutch-speaking white settlers, who evinced a distrust of the government's intentions touching on their safety. One might even go so far

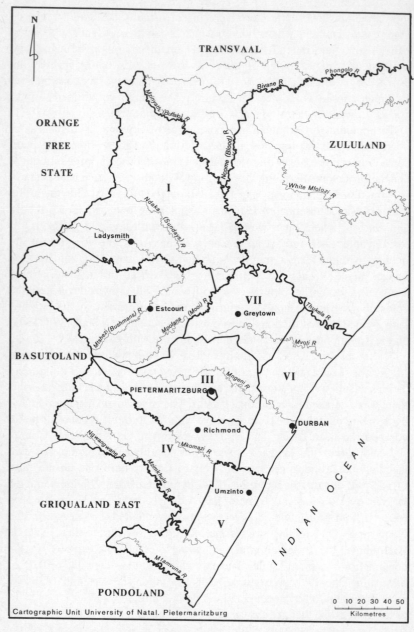

Colonial Defensive Districts, Colony of Natal, 1879.

as to say that the government built laagers for the British settlers, and the Dutch-speaking settlers built laagers for themselves, although this was certainly not as the government intended things to be. When fear mingled with distrust, some of the Boers preferred flight. In Klip River County there were cases of farmers leaving their farms for their interior, but it is not possible to give the number, and when the war came there were enough left to repair to the completed laagers of the Biggarsberg.[5] As the war broke Bulwer remarked that Dutch farmers in Weenen County were expressing fears that the government was abandoning them, and apparently some did flee from the county, especially the eastern portion,[6] but this may have been due to the lack of a defensible laager in the area. There was no such flight from the western part.

Organization for War

During the winter of 1878 war between Britain and the Zulu kingdom seemed increasingly likely. The Lieutenant-Governor, Sir Henry Bulwer, circularized the Resident Magistrates of the colony with regard to the prospects of defence in June,[7] and Lieutenant-General Sir Frederick Thesiger – Lord Chelmsford from October – the commander of imperial forces, arrived and first advised the government on more elaborate preparations for defence in August.[8] The Defence Committee of the Executive Council duly considered the matter in September and October.[9] Meanwhile the imperial forces were taking positions along the border, and the General became impatient with the Lieutenant-Governor's reluctance to alarm the colonists with active measures for their involvement in the impending war. By November this could not be put off longer; on the 2nd the Natal Mounted Police were put under the General's orders; on the 16th the High Commissioner, Sir Henry Bartle Frere, ordered mobilization of colonial forces required, and on the 26th eight of the colony's eleven Mounted Volunteer Corps were taken into the imperial service.[10] The colonial government yielded to the exigencies of the situation, and on the 28th the Resident Magistrates were circularized to supply returns of fighting men in their divisions.[11] It had, of course, pressed building operations on the various laagers. By the outbreak of war the new laagers at Newcastle, Richmond, Umzinto, and near Dundee were practically complete. Work was still needed on ones at Verulam and Umhlali, and was supposed to have commenced on another at Oliviershoek. There were plans for works at Harding and Ixopo. The government also faced a rising demand for munitions and was hard pressed to supply what was needed for the armouries and by the rifle associations. Demand for firearms temporarily exceeded supply when town guards were organized, not only in Pietermaritzburg and Durban but in some of the larger villages, but this was limited by official insistence on strict control over issue and practice.[12]

Under pressure of events and from the General, Sir Henry moved to systematize the defence of the colony. The Executive Council approved of its division into seven Colonial Defensive Districts under appointed commandants, which was gazetted on 26 November. Instructions to the commandants followed on the 29th.[13]

The defensive districts and commandants were as follow –

I	Klip River County	Major J.G. Dartnell
II	Weenen County	Maj.-General W.P. Lloyd
	Pietermaritzburg County	
III	Umgeni Division	Major W. Boycott
IV	Upper Umkomanzi and Ixopo Divisions	Major A.C. Hawkins
V	Alexandra and Alfred Counties	Captain G.A. Lucas
VI	Durban and Victoria Counties	Major S.H. Graves
VII	Umvoti County	Mr W.D. Wheelwright

It will be noticed that the military divisions corresponded with civil ones, and in the cases of Districts IV, V and VII the commandants were Resident Magistrates. The ranks indicate past rather than present military service, except in the case of Dartnell and Graves. Only Wheelwright appears to have lacked some military background. Pietermaritzburg and Durban were designated sub-districts, under Lieutenant-Colonel C.B.H. Mitchell, R.M., who was the Colonial Secretary, and Major J.W. Huskisson, 56th Foot, who was commander of the imperial forces' base of operations. The instructions directed the commandants to take control of all Mounted Police and black levies and such other forces assigned them, all public laagers and fortified posts and the main lines of communication, and government arms and ammunition in their districts. In the event of hostilities they would, in co-operation with the Resident Magistrates, take the necessary measures to assure the safety of the inhabitants of their districts.

Where the Commandant and the Resident Magistrate was the same person, arrangements for defence should have proceeded relatively smoothly. Indeed, they did in Districts IV and VII. They should have done also in District V, where Captain Lucas had devised a plan of defence for Alexandra County as early as September; however, he antagonized the local settlers at a meeting to discuss its implementation in mid-December. A week later he was transferred to command District VI, in place of Graves now with an imperial command, and left District V to Major J.G. Giles, the Resident Magistrate of Alfred County. At Harding Giles, keeping a sharp watch on the Mpondo over the southern border, could not give much attention to affairs at Umzinto. Meanwhile Lucas concentrated his attention on defending the lower Thukela line with black levies, and neglected the settlements in lower Victoria and Durban counties.[14] Thus the two defensive districts on the coast were really four defensive zones, the two contiguous ones left to the supervision of lower officials. In Districts II and III there were some delays,[15] and in District I, whose commandant was also in charge of the colonial forces with the imperial Centre Column invading Zululand, much discretion was perforce left to the district magistrates.[16]

The commandants proceeded to supervise the provision of laagers and the organization of local defence forces. In early January several notices were drafted which designated the central posts of defence and carried instructions for their inmates; however, it seemed unlikely anyone would have to go into laager and these were not published until after the war began. Similarly, the organization of ad hoc defence units lacked a sense of urgency. The Dutch-speaking settlers organized their own laager guards, but in the predominantly English-speaking villages response varied greatly. In Newcastle the villagers petitioned to form a town guard in the Resident Magistrate's absence, and in Ladysmith a guard was established, but whether at this time or later is not clear. At Estcourt and Ixopo, meetings to organize local defence broke up without any consequent organization. Stanger and Umzinto seem not to have had town guards. In spite of some chaotic meetings the mixed community at Greytown provided not only a guard but patrols for the neighbourhood. At Verulam and Pinetown local units formed, apparently without difficulty, while at Howick, New Hanover, York, and possibly Harding, rifle associations assumed defensive roles.[17]

Lord Chelmsford was anxious that the border of the colony be protected against possible Zulu incursions which would threaten his lines of communication once the imperial forces had entered Zululand, and pressed Sir Henry particularly to organize blacks for this purpose. The result was the formation of the Native Border Guard. So important did it seem to defence that Lucas and Wheelwright became almost exclusively concerned with it, and the Resident Magistrate at Umsinga likewise in District I. In addition, the government appointed special border agents and police to monitor the border. In these circumstances it was natural that the three border defensive districts – I, VI, VII – should be subordinated directly to the imperial command. Their subordination took place on 13 January 1879.[18] Thereafter their real military commanders were not Bulwer's appointees but Chelmsford's – Major A.S. Walker, 99th Foot, in charge of the base at Stanger, for District VI, and Major A.C. Twentyman, 2/4th, at Greytown, for District VII. Colonel R.T. Glyn, 1/24th, was responsible for District I, but when the imperial column advanced, Glyn and Dartnell with it, W.H. Beaumont, the Resident Magistrate of Newcastle, was left temporarily in charge.[19]

The sub-districts were obviously anomalous cases, instances of urban areas requiring special attention. Major Mitchell, the Colonial Secretary, exercised greater control over Pietermaritzburg than did Major Huskisson, the base commander, over Durban. The reasons are fairly obvious: Mitchell had civil as well as military authority and, when required, could attend to military matters without distraction; Huskisson had no civil authority, arriving in Durban a month before the war began, and he had to devote much of his time to the all-important organization of the port through which flowed the life blood of the imperial forces. It is also important to note the Durbanites displayed an independence, indeed almost a fractiousness, when it came to self-defence, exacerbated by a sense that Pietermaritzburg was receiving better treatment than their town.[20]

The local authorities proceeded to organize Town Guards, though in the case of Pietermaritzburg so hesitantly that the movement almost aborted, and again this owes largely to Sir Henry Bulwer's injunction not to alarm people needlessly. But in neither town did the guard attain a number considered sufficient, and it was obvious that the local Volunteer Corps must supplement it. Again much of the problem lay with the government. It did not specify clearly whether the guard should be a police or a militia, and was niggardly in providing firearms and practice facilities. Reflecting Bulwer's reluctance to be precipitate, some residents saw no need to organize when no crisis was likely, and if one should arise, then they would do so. Also, burgesses were inclined to consider first the safety of their families, from whom guard duty might take them in the hour of danger.[21] In the case of Pietermaritzburg it was not made clear where the non-combatants would go in a crisis; in Durban a few central buildings were designated. At this stage there was no plan, at least publicly, for a laager of any kind. The sense of danger that existed among the white settlers in the countryside seems to have been missing in the towns.

The Isandlwana Crisis

The test of the colonial government's scheme of defence came with the British defeat at Isandlwana. Just after the battle a fear of invasion and disorder swept Natal, and as it was subsiding, another alarm swept the Midlands. The Zulu did not invade, nor did the black populace disrupt the colony; yet the white settlers (and many blacks, too, it would seem) saw that there was the opportunity for such action, and they reacted accordingly. Their apprehension lasted through February, until the Zulu defensive strategy and the blacks' passivity were obvious to all, and vanished in March with the arrival of the imperial reinforcements that enabled Lord Chelmsford to regain the strategic initiative.

The news of the Isandlwana defeat reached the colonial authorities in Pietermaritzburg on 24 January. Of course, the word of it spread quickly throughout the colony, and the government issued a terse official version to scotch rumours the next day.[22] It also put the defensive districts in a state of alert. In the case of the border districts under military control notice was superfluous, although the Lieutenant-Governor sent special notice to the Commandants and Resident Magistrates in Districts I and II, apprising them of the untoward events and urging them to take proper measures for defence.[23] No such notice seems to have been given for District III, but probably it was not necessary with the capital at its centre. There was no need to call out defenders in Districts IV and V. On 28 January the government notified rules for the provisioning of public defensive posts, and on 1 February further instructions in order to standardize defensive measures throughout the colony. The commandants should secure the posts and complete arrangements for their defence. It was made clear, too, that the laagers and posts were primarily for the use of the white settlers, and other arrangements, which were not spelt out, should be made for the black population.[24]

The return of Lord Chelmsford to the capital enabled the civil and military authorities to co-ordinate defensive policies; however, under stress neither party seemed to regard the other as fully comprehending or complying with its own needs. A memorandum giving the military's view of defence was sent to the District Commandants and Resident Magistrates on 10 February. It stated that the black levies of the colony could not be counted on to resist a Zulu invasion, which would by-pass the established posts of defence and sweep the country in between. In that event the available colonial forces, black and white, would have to hang on the flanks of the invader and harass him. Of course, no consequential force of white males could be expected to come forward before they had secured their families, so the Resident Magistrates should urge removal of white women and children from threatened districts to safe ones, leaving the menfolk to take the field.[25] The magistrates do not appear to have pressed such a removal. The burghers did not come out, mounted and armed as the General would have them, and he turned to raising levies from among the blacks, whose reserve of manpower was much greater. Perhaps at the military's instigation, the government required the commandants to furnish weekly statements of the strength and disposition of forces and the character and amount of the public arms and ammunition in their districts.[26] In late February Bulwer aired the possibility with the High Commissioner and Lieutenant-General of transferring Districts II and III to the imperial military, but the latter did not see the necessity.[27] On 15 March the government simply instructed the commandants to co-operate closely with each other and with imperial military authorities in their districts.[28]

Let us turn now to the particular defensive arrangements in Natal during the Isandlwana crisis, looking first at the country districts and then at the town sub-districts. The defences in the countryside consisted of the government laagers, including permanent and improvised buildings, and private laagers; however, in addition to these there were fortified 'posts', largely extempore adaptations of private buildings to defence. Manning of all these was provided for the most part by those who took refuge in them, under the supervision of government officials (usually the Resident Magistrates) in the public laagers, and under that of elected leaders in the private ones; in the case of the small posts, which accommodated relatively few whites (and, along the coast, many Indians), command belonged usually to the proprietor of the place. In most instances the able-bodied white men who had horses were also required for duties outside the laagers, particularly for patrols.

The most convenient way of surveying these arrangements is to take the Colonial Defensive Districts in turn, beginning with those along the border with Zululand.

The Border

District I (Klip River County). The government had provided three laagers, two at the chief centres of population, Ladysmith and Newcastle, and one near Dundee, on the middle border, now called Fort Pine. All these were in a state of readiness for refugees when the war broke out. In addition to these, the Boers had two laagers, Pieters', between Fort Pine and Rorke's Drift, and the Ermelo 'fort', between Dundee and Newcastle. Fort Pine and the Ermelo Fort were occupied in the aftermath of Isandlwana. It is not clear from surviving records whether or not Pieters' Laager was occupied then. At Ladysmith and Newcastle the resort to laager was not so urgent, for the settlers of those neighbourhoods would have ample time to come in with timely notice of a Zulu *impi* across the Thukela. An effort was made to fortify the Umsinga magistracy after the outbreak of war, but news of Isandlwana put the few settlers in the division to flight and the building was abandoned.[29]

District VII (Umvoti County). The government laager at Greytown accommodated the people of the village and the surrounding area. There were the three private laagers as well – the Hermannsburg, Rietvlei and Umvoti laagers. The Dutch farmers in the eastern part of the county, towards Kranskop, occupied and strongly manned the first of these. The other two were abandoned, that at Rietvlei because no doors for the gates had arrived, and that at the Umvoti Bridge because the District Commandant believed that it could not be manned in sufficient strength and refused to provide government munitions for it. After Isandlwana the white settlers from the countryside flocked into the three, and then the two laagers, and just as their sense of well-being was returning, they were frightened on the night of 2–3 February by a false report that the Zulu had crossed the Thukela in strength and were moving towards Greytown. At Rietvlei those who remained in the neighbourhood fortified a shed on the farm Bellevue for defence.[30]

District VI (Victoria County). The government had built laagers at Stanger and Verulam, and had work well-advanced on another at Umhlali. The laager at Stanger was occupied in the wake of Isandlwana, but apparently those at Verulam and Umhlali, still incomplete, were not.[31] It is doubtful if these were large enough to shelter both whites and Indians, numbers of whom worked in the district and could not be left to their own devices after the fashion of the blacks; thus, with a view to protecting his work force, J. Liege Hulett erected a stockade at Kearsney.[32]

In the border defensive districts there was a sufficient, perhaps even an excessive number of laagers to which white settlers could resort, and those nearest Zululand were actually occupied in late January and February, and in some cases longer. It should be noted that authority and discipline varied in the laagers. Where different-speaking groups mixed there appears to have been difficulty. The English field cornet at Fort Pine evidently could not enforce his authority among the Boers and consequently the two local mounted Volunteer Corps had to be sent over from Helpmekaar to carry out duties which the inmates in the laager at Hermannsburg performed, albeit with some reluctance.[33] At Greytown initially there was considerable friction between Dutch- and English-speaking burghers, the former distrustful of government authority and the latter resentful of their unco-operativeness, and a large number of the former went off to the Hermannsburg laager.[34] There also seems to have been friction at Stanger, where some

Dutch immigrants considered themselves ill-treated when they resorted to the laager.[35] Some of the German settlers at Hermannsburg chose to defend themselves at their mission rather than go into laager with their Dutch-speaking neighbours.[36]

Small detachments of imperial troops – British regulars – were stationed in the border districts, and in the case of No. VII, two battalions of the Natal Native Contingent. Also, the mounted Volunteer Corps were there. The burghers in laager at Greytown and Hermannsburg occasionally sent out mounted patrols.[37] In addition a large part of the Native Border Guard was embodied at strategic places along the border, and was augmented subsequently by contingents raised in the interior. These black forces constituted the great majority of fighting men in service at the border by the end of March.

Collaboration between imperial commanders, Colonial Commandants and Resident Magistrates did not always work as smoothly as the government wished. The District Commandants had been subordinated to imperial military officers, who assumed overall responsibility for defence but also concerned themselves in the first instance with the imperial forces in the districts. It was probably natural that Colonel Glyn, in District I, should devote himself to sustaining the dejected No. 3 Column and developing its defences at Helpmekaar and Rorke's Drift. Major Dartnell, the District Commandant, also with the column, had his hands full with the Mounted

Inside the laager at Greytown.

Police and Volunteers who had been called up. Fortunately, the Resident Magistrates at Ladysmith and Newcastle had their communities well in hand for the occasion.[38] In District VII Major Twentyman, with headquarters at Greytown, had firm control over both imperial and colonial forces under his command. Indeed, the District Commandant, Resident Magistrate Wheelwright, took personal charge of a large native reserve levy close by the Thukela and left most business in Greytown to his clerk; thus he had little influence on civil defence at the county seat.[39] The situation was similar in District VI. The imperial commander, Major Walker, was at Stanger, and the Resident Magistrates there and at Verulam remained at their posts to supervise defensive arrangements, while the District Commandant, Captain Lucas, took himself off to the Thukela and so closely attended the activities of the black levies there that some settlers at a distance from the front even complained of neglect, and consequently the government removed Durban County from his jurisdiction.[40]

The Interior

In the areas far from Zululand the white settlers generally feared a sympathetic rising among the Natal blacks or attack from blacks across other borders more than an invasion by Zulu; but these fears should not be exaggerated. They varied considerably from place to place. It is fair to state, however, that the government's recent preparations for defence in these quarters were found insufficient, not because the laagers could not accommodate the settlers seeking refuge but because they were few and far between, leaving many in the newly settled regions exposed unless they abandoned their properties and lands in anticipation of a crisis and not at its occurrence.

District II (Weenen County). There was the government laager at Estcourt, an enclosure which took in the blockhouse (now called 'Fort Durnford') and Mounted Police stables as well as other small buildings on a spur overlooking the Bushman's River. The enclosure was large enough for all the white settlers of the county; however, it was not used.[41] The Boers in the upper part of the county did use the Strydpoort Laager, but whether simply as a base for their mounted 'corps' or as a refuge for their families as well is not quite clear.[42] The Boers in the lower part of the county had no such laager, and many apparently fled the district.[43] The English-speaking settlers in the vicinity of Mooi River remained and decided to fortify the church and enclosure at Weston in an emergency,[44] which did not occur. The government, particularly concerned about the BaSotho, belatedly commenced a proper laager at Oliviershoek, even though the Resident Magistrate of the Upper Tugela Division doubted that it could be properly manned.[45]

District III (Umgeni Division).   No post was ready for defence, but this doubtless was because the focus of the district was Pietermaritzburg, even though it was a separate sub-district. It was expected that many country people would go to the city, where the District Commandant had his office and charge of a quarter of the city laager.[46] After Isandlwana the people at Howick erected a stone laager, while several smaller defensive posts were selected (and in at least one case, at Baynes' Drift, prepared) for defence in the northern part of the district.[47]

Districts IV (Upper Umkomanzi and Ixopo Divisions) and V (Alexandra and Alfred Counties).   There were good stout laagers at Richmond and Umzinto, respectively, but they were far from the southern border, threatened by turbulence among the Griqua, BaSotho, and Mpondo. In haste earthwork laagers were thrown up in connection with the magistracies at Ixopo and possibly Harding,[48] while civilian initiatives resulted in fortified posts at Highflats and Ifafa[49] – at the latter place John Bazley built a stockade and ordered a small cannon for it.[50] Whether or not these extemporized defences could have been held against an enemy in large numbers is debatable; fortunately for those who sought refuge (as at Ixopo) or might have to (as at Harding) their defensibility was not tested.

The Towns

It has been pointed out that the colonial government had not given much attention to defensive preparations in Pietermaritzburg and Durban, although their designation as sub-districts indicates its awareness of special conditions attaching to their defence. As mentioned earlier, the commandants of both were military men – but they had other duties which left relatively little time to superintend defensive arrangements. There had been no preparations of defensive positions as such. Members of the town councils had taken the initiative in enrolling town guards, but enrolment had lagged for want of enthusiasm and urgency and the government's reluctance to leave public firearms to the guardsmen's care. In Durban an infantry and an artillery Volunteer Corps remained in the town and were available for its defence, in Pietermaritzburg an infantry Volunteer Corps. There were also the small detachments of imperial troops at the forts on the outskirts of the towns.

The news of Isandlwana shocked the townspeople. The sensation seems to have been amplified by their numbers and proximity. In Pietermaritzburg there was also the sense of personal loss, for the Natal Carbineers, based in the city, had suffered relatively heavy casualties in the battle; indeed, the closest Natalians came to panic in the interior was at Pietermaritzburg in the few weeks after Isandlwana.

In *Pietermaritzburg* Colonel Mitchell took charge of defensive measures with a certain aplomb, and the townspeople fell in with them with alacrity. The centre of the town was converted into a laager, a block and half being enclosed by barricades between the buildings, which were pierced or shuttered according to requirements, and those who should take refuge there were assigned to different parts of the enclosure and their menfolk told off to defend these quarters under specified officers. The usual prescriptions for food and personal articles were made. The plans were publicized and there is little reason to doubt that the Maritzburgers would have given a good account of themselves in the event of an attack.[51]

In *Durban* the situation was somewhat different. A defence committee convened consisting of several town councillors and notables, some of whom seemed unduly eager to defend the town. Major Huskisson deployed the Volunteers in front of the town and allocated expected refugees to certain buildings in the centre of the town. When it became obvious the Zulu were not at the gates, the Volunteers were brought back, and with the Town Guard and members of the local rifle association and some of the imperial troops, were allocated buildings to defend, and the lot was called a laager. Initially Huskisson planned to erect barricades as well, but they seem not to have been got ready or placed, as in Pietermaritzburg. Each building thus would be a stronghold protected by its garrison and its neighbours' cross-fire. Members of the committee deprecated this arrangement, and agitated for a continuous line of earthworks outside the town. In vain Huskisson pointed out that there were not enough men to build and then to man the circumvallation, but public meetings pressed the government to authorize and to help pay for it. The Lieutenant-Governor listened to the Commandant and not the committee and there was much bitterness. On the matter of placing non-combatants, Huskisson and the committee did reach agreement. Parcelling them out among buildings would be dangerous, especially in the event of a windswept fire, and besides, there also would be a rush of Indians and others from the countryside, for which there had been no allowance. Therefore a palisade was erected across the Point, where the non-combatants could take refuge.[52]

Huskisson's patience with the agitators was remarkable. He went about his military business without undue distraction and without discourtesy to the more offensive burgesses. At the government's request, he added to his sub-district the County of Durban, which Lucas had neglected. The additional territory did not cause him much worry: local initiative, supported by the government railways department, built a laager at Pinetown, while the settlers at New Germany made a fortified post of their church.[53] His work was enormously increased with the arrival of imperial reinforcements, beginning in March, but their arrival at least dissipated the fears of the committee men and the matter of defending Durban was dropped on both sides. The Volunteer Corps were stood down, and an Indian Corps took over fatigue duties. The Town Guard became a paper organization.[54]

It is difficult to believe that Huskisson's plans for defence of Durban would have saved the town against a large and determined enemy. His defensive points were reasonably well placed, but very much depended on their mutual support. It was pointed out that buildings might be taken separately and the whole position lost in detail. Barricades would have linked the buildings and afforded a co-ordinated defence. Perhaps Huskisson envisaged this, but he did not emphasize it. Of course, the popular plan for earthworks around the town was impracticable. One gets the feeling that once the Point palisade was built, all the civilians – the ad hoc soldiers and refugees alike – would have made for that sanctuary.

Conclusion

The arrival of imperial troops not only put Durban at ease, but the rest of the colony as well. The Zulu strategy had shown itself to be defensive, the local blacks remained pacific, and no threats materialized across the other borders.

The matter of civil defence was not left at once, however, for Lord Chelmsford wished to mobilize the able-bodied men of Natal for a vigorous defence of the border while his imperial forces invaded Zululand again. His insistence on using black levies in demonstrations from late March to late May exasperated Sir Henry Bulwer, who considered his prerogative as Supreme Chief was being violated and that the General was promoting a dangerous retaliatory warfare. The matter was referred to London, where it was decided in the General's favour, but also served to prompt his supersession by Sir Garnet Wolseley.[55] Lord Chelmsford also believed that the white settlers had not done enough on their own behalf, and wished mounted units to be fielded. He was demanding too much, as Sir Henry made clear. Inquiries were made with the District Commandants at the end of May, and the few responses found suggest that the manpower in the countryside was fully extended, while that in the towns was limited, probably for want of mounts.[56] In short the white settlers would rally in their locales and defend themselves as best they could; they could not be integrated in an offensive plan to Lord Chelmsford's satisfaction. Sir Henry had perceived this all along, and the Natal government's policy from the outset had been geared to the reality. In most respects the government had done well; most of the defensive posts were prepared by the time of the war, and steps had been taken to arm and to organize the settlers, although it must be admitted rather belatedly and imperfectly.

If the government's arrangements for defence were sound in conception but varied in implementation, then the judgement must be qualified in one important respect, viz. the government was concerned with defending the people in the country; it was almost blind to the problem of defending those in the towns – real towns, Pietermaritzburg and Durban, and not villages, such as Greytown, Ladysmith, and Stanger. Perhaps the rural bias of the assembly, the immense scope of the field and the urgency to act, or the frightening prospect of country-folk 'eaten up' in isolation account for this. Perhaps the presence of imperial garrisons, or the notion that already congregated townspeople could be co-ordinated quickly in an improvised defence, caused the government to discount or to defer preparations for their defence. In any case, when the war came, the country had laagers and the towns had none.

[Paper for the South African Historical Society. Conference at the University of Cape Town, 1985.]

Notes

1. See the annual *Blue Books for the Colony of Natal* 1861–1873, Sections G and H, passim.

2. See the reports in CSO 1925, Minute C5/1878.

3. CSO 2621, p.237; *Blue Books* for 1877 and 1878, J 2–3. See *NGG*, vols. XXIX, no. 1660, 31 July 1877, and vol. XXX, no. 1715 and 1728, 25 July and 17 September 1878, respectively, for the estimates for the defensive works.

4. *Natal Mercury*, 2 July 1878; CSO 648, Minute 1855/1878 and CSO 1925, Minute C50/1878. For the Klip River County laagers, see J.P.C. Laband and P.S. Thompson, *The Buffalo Border 1879*, Durban, 1983, pp. 22–6, 92 and 95; and for those in Umvoti, idem., *War Comes to Umvoti*, Durban, 1980, pp. 18, 95 and 97.

5. Laband and Thompson, *The Buffalo Border*, p.41.

6. CSO 681, Minute 349/1879 and CSO 699, Minute 2195/1879.

7. Cf. the instructions in CSO 1925: unnumbered Minute, and in SNA 1/4/2, no. 46.

8. See the General's memorandum (unnumbered but dated 24 August 1878) in GH 1424, and remarks in Gerald French, *Lord Chelmsford and the Zulu War*, London, 1939, pp. 42–5.

9. GH 1424, Minute 109/1878; CSO 2610, Minute C27/1878; French, *Lord Chelmsford*, pp. 46–9.

10. CSO 2610, Minute 166/1878 and CSO 2621, p.403; *NGG*, vol. XXX, no. 1739, 26 November 1878.

11. CSO 1972, Minute 4417/1878.

12. CSO 666, Minute 4195/1878; CSO 686, Minute 819/1879 and CSO 688, Minute 1100/1879; GH 1411, pp. 30–49, passim; SNA 1/4/2, no. 46; CE, Minute 2142 of 1878; Richmond Correspondence, 2/14/6 Minute I53/1878; *Natal Mercury*, 7 November 1878, and 4 and 9 January, and 4 February 1879; Laband and Thompson, *The Buffalo Border*, pp. 27, 28, 52, 103; P.S. Thompson, "'The Zulus Are Coming!' The Defence of Pietermaritzburg, 1879", *JNZH*, VI, 1983, p. 34.

13. GH 1411, pp. 165–93; CSO 1972, Minute 4440/1878. Cf. *NGG*. vol. XXX, nos. 1739 and 1740, 3 December 1878; and CSO 2629, Minutes 4440 and 4417/1878.

14. GH 1411, Minute 1541/1879; CSO 681, Minute 356/1879 and CSO 683, Minute 516/1879; *Natal Mercury*, 15 February 1879; P.S. Thompson, 'Captain Lucas and the Border Guard: The War on the Lower Tugela, 1879', *JNZH*, III, 1980, pp. 33–4.

15. Cf. CSO 681, Minute 357/1879 and CSO 1972, Minutes 4525 and 4587/1878.

16. CSO 678, Minute 90/1879; CSO 680, Minute 241/1879; and CSO 699, Minute 2195/1879.

17. CSO 680, Minute 241/1879; CSO 681, Minute 357/1879; CSO 699, Minute 2195/1879; 715, Minute 3830/1879; CSO 1971, Minutes 3124 and 3125/1878; and CSO 1972, Minutes 4647 and 4800/1878; Richmond Correspondence, Minute I53/1878; *Natal Colonist*, 5 November and 7 December 1878; *Natal Witness*, 10 December 1878; Laband and Thompson, *War Comes to Umvoti*, pp. 35 and 97; Laband and Thompson, *The Buffalo Border*, p. 52 and cf. p. 54.

18. GH 1326, p. 209; *Times of Natal*, 15 and 17 January 1879. Cf. *Natal Witness*, 11 January 1879.

19. Laband and Thompson, *The Buffalo Border*, p. 38; Laband and Thompson, *War Comes to Umvoti*, pp. 36 and 47; Thompson, 'Captain Lucas and the Border Guard', p. 34.

20. See Durban Corporation Public Meetings 1871–1903; Minutes of the Durban Town Council, vol. 10; Durban Corporation Letter Books, vol. 705 and 706 passim. See also the *Natal Mercury*, 6, 9 and 16 January 1879; *Natal Colonist*, 9 January 1879; and *Natal Advertizer*, 16 and 18 January 1879.

21. Thompson, 'The Zulus Are Coming!', pp. 31–2; Durban Corporation Public Meetings, 1871–1903, p. 71: a copy of the notice referred to is at the Local History Museum in Durban.

22. GH 1421, Minute 505/1879; CSO 686, Minute 819/1879. See also *NGG*, vol. XXXI, no. 1749, 28 January 1879.

23. GH 1421, Minute 505/1879; CSO 686, Minute 819/1879 and CSO 1972, Minute 505/1879.

24. GH 1421, Minute 564/1879 and GH 1422, p. 35; CSO 2630, Minute 668/1879.

25. CSO 2553, Minute C36/1879.

26. CSO 1972, Minute 852/1879.

27. CSO 1926, Minute 1356/1879; GH 601, Minute 1345/1879.

28. CSO 2630, Minute 1345/1879.

29. Laband and Thompson, *The Buffalo Border*, pp. 41, 49, 52, 54, 90, 93 and 104.

30. Laband and Thompson, *War Comes to Umvoti*, pp. 35–41 passim, 95–7.

31. GH 1421, Minute 480/1879; *Natal Colonist*, 25 January and 20 February 1879; *Natal Mercury*, 4 and 7 February 1879.

32. R.F. Osborn, *This Man of Purpose: Pioneer of Natal and Zululand: A Biography of Sir James Liege Hulett*, Umhlali, 1973, p. 33.

33. Laband and Thompson, *The Buffalo Border*, pp. 53 and 105; Laband and Thompson, *War Comes to Umvoti*, p. 97.

34. Laband and Thompson, *War Comes to Umvoti*, pp. 36–7.

35. *Natal Mercury*, 21 February 1879.

36. Laband and Thompson, *War Comes to Umvoti*, p. 96.

37. Ibid., pp. 40 and 97.

38. Laband and Thompson, *The Buffalo Border*, pp. 51–9 passim.

39. Laband and Thompson, *War Comes to Umvoti*, p. 33 et passim.

40. CSO 683, Minute 516/1879 and 685, Minute 722/1879.

41. CSO 715, Minute 3830/1879; *Natal Colonist*, 27 February and 1 March 1879.

42. *Natal Colonist*, 11 February 1879.

43. *B.P.P.* (C.2318), no. 7; CSO 699, Minute 2195/1879.

44. GH 569, Minute 1254/1879; CSO 699, Minute 2195/1879; *Natal Mercury*, 13 February 1879.

45. CSO 686, Minute 819/1879.

46. CSO 699, Minute 2195/1879; GH 1423, Minute 1222/1879.

47. GH 1423, Minute 1222/1879; CSO 682, Minute 429/1879; CSO 711, Minute 3450/1879; and CSO 715, Minute 3830/1879; *NGG* vol. XXXI, no. 1750, 4 February 1879; George Morris Sutton diary for 1879, entries for 26 January–12 February passim.

48. Cf. CSO 699, Minute 2195/1879; T.B. Jenkinson, *Amazulu*, London, 1882, p. 78; and V.M. Fitzroy, *Dark Bright Land*, Cape Town, 1955, p. 308; CSO 1973, Minute 2300/1879 and CSO 1974, Minute 4666 and 5035/1879.

49. Cf. Richmond Correspondence 2/14/6, Minute I53/1878; and SNA 1/6/14, no. 6 with regard to Highflats; and SNA 1/4/2, no. 46 and the *Natal Colonist*, 6 March 1879, with regard to Ifafa.

50. CSO 1972, Minute 931/1879.

51. Thompson, 'The Zulus Are Coming!', pp. 39–43 passim.

52. See the sources mentioned in n. 23. The particular items detailing Durban's defence are too numerous to cite conveniently here.

53. CSO 685, Minute 722/1879; *Natal Mercury*, 14, 15, 19 and 21 February 1879.

54. *Natal Mercury*, 6, 11 and 13 March 1879; *Natal Advertizer*, 6 March 1879; *Natal Colonist*, 11, 15 and 29 March 1879; John Robinson, *A Life Time in South Africa*, London, 1900, p. 137; C.L. Norris-Newman, *In Zululand with the British Throughout the War of 1879*, London, 1880, pp. 125–7.

55. See J.P.C. Laband, 'Bulwer, Chelmsford and the Border Levies', *Theoria*, vol. LVII, 1981, pp. 1–15.

56. CSO 715, Minute 3830/1879; CSO 1973, Minute 3076/1879; and CSO 2631, Minute 2790/1879; and also the report for the Klip River Division, in Ladysmith Correspondence, 12/1/3.

Weenen County and the War, 1879

P.S. THOMPSON

Colonial Defensive District No. II

On 13 November 1878, with the British Crown obviously about to make war on the Zulu kingdom, the Natal government, responding belatedly to Lord Chelmsford's proddings to elaborate defensive arrangements for the colony, established seven Colonial Defensive Districts, and instructed the commanders with regard to the placement and protection of the white settler population and the information and preservation of the more numerous black population.[1]

Weenen County was designated Colonial Defensive District No. II, under the command of Major-General B.P. Lloyd, who had retired from a civil following a military career to the farm Brynbella (near Estcourt). He far outranked any of the other defensive commandants, in terms of past or present rank, and the charge to one so exalted could have been intentional. The government had followed administrative boundaries closely in the delimitation of the defensive districts, which embraced whole counties (save in the case of Pietermaritzburg County), which is understandable since the few white officials perforce added the military responsibilities to their administrative ones.

Weenen County, District No. II, posed special problems, somewhat different from the others. The geography made effective control if not unified command difficult. The county extended from Basutoland in the west almost to the Zulu border in the east; in both marches were large black populations, which the Natal government regarded with a mixture of solicitude and doubt. The chief lines of communication were the main road from the coast to the interior, from which roads branched off at Estcourt, east to Weenen and on to Greytown in Umvoti and west to the upper Thukela and the Free State. There were, of course, lesser roads, but these were hardly more than tracks, and the country was very broken at the eastern and western extremes. The county had three separate administrative divisions, Weenen,

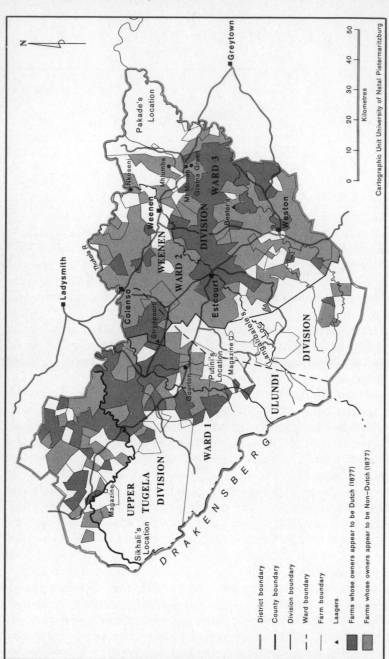

Colonial Defensive District No. II: Weenen County and part of Klip River County.

Ulundi and Upper Tugela. Practically all the white population was in the Weenen Division which, however, contained a large number of blacks in the Mpafana Location. The Ulundi and Upper Tugela Divisions were virtually all-black reserves. The population was rural and agrarian, the only villages of note being the old administrative centre, Weenen town, and its successor, Estcourt. General Lloyd, working closely with the Resident Magistrates, especially the senior one in Estcourt, Peter Paterson, would be hard pressed to look after the differing peoples of his far-flung district in the event of a Zulu irruption or internal disorder.

In November 1878, returns of population for the various counties and divisions were furnished to the Defence Committee of the Executive Council. Those for Weenen County estimated 1 000 whites and 29 584 blacks in the Weenen Division (including Ulundi) and 201 whites and 7 756 blacks in the Upper Tugela Division.[2] Thus whites constituted 3,1% of the county's inhabitants; none the less their protection was foremost in the minds of the colonial authorities. Certainly they were the most vulnerable. The 1879 *Blue Book*, whose statistics the Resident Magistrate considered more reliable than that of 1878, gives 1 086 whites and 25 945 blacks in the county, and classifies 217 white persons by occupation and profession: of these 181 (84%) were farmers, and thus would be fairly dispersed. The return of the ecclesiastical establishment for 1878 indicates that about two-thirds were Dutch.[3] It also tells that of the 604 white males, only 283 (47%) were between 15 and 50[4] and thus probably suitable for active defensive service. On the other hand, the Defence Committee's returns estimated 8 523 black fighting men in the Weenen and Ulundi Divisions and 2 732 in the Upper Tugela Division.[5] (See Tables for detailed statistics.)

Lloyd began work on protection of the whites. Taking into account popular feelings and the local circumstances, he chose to do this by means of personal contacts with community leaders and public meetings. He thought that the issuing of orders and regulations otherwise might be misunderstood and give umbrage.[6] This view is plausible, for the Dutch-speaking farmers apparently did not see eye-to-eye on defence. The preceding year they had pressed the Resident Magistrate at Estcourt, Peter Paterson, to take measures for their protection, and he had called meetings, at which it was suggested that the 'Weenen Burgher Force' be reorganized and the Field Commandant of the county, Johannes Stephanus Boshoff, who had been appointed in 1855, be replaced by an 'energetic' younger and popular leader. Paterson had asked the government if he should involve himself in the matter, evidently with a negative response,[7] for Boshoff remained Field Commandant. One might also infer some discontent in a recent turn-over in field

TABLE I

WEENEN COUNTY: NATIVE SOCIETY
STATISTICS FOR 1877–1880

	1877	1878	1879	1880
Population	36 375	25 700	25 945	27 587
Male	17 031	11 290	11 550	12 277
Female	19 344	14 410	14 395	15 310
Christians (congregations)				
Dutch Reformed	–	–	–	–
Anglican	80	80	30	–
Lutheran	292	330	308	184*
Agriculture				
Acres reaped	15 002	12 634¾	10 170	17 559
Sorghum				
Acres reaped	9 860	8 136	5 309	9 280
Production (muids)	22 386	29 850	36 644	21 539
Average market value (muid)	12s	20s	20s	35s
Maize				
Acres reaped	5 140	4 482	4 850	8 124
Production (muids)	12 760	17 697	23 425	19 196
Livestock				
Horned cattle	30 086	29 029	27 199	33 421
Goats	20 619	16 623	20 018	31 853
Wool-bearing sheep	5 628	3 514	1 077	4 910
Horses	1 391	1 329	1 866	2 578

Source: Blue Book for the Colony of Natal, 1877–1880

*The return would appear to be incomplete.

TABLE II

WEENEN COUNTY: SETTLER SOCIETY
STATISTICS FOR 1877–1880

	1877	1878	1879	1880
Population	1 106	839	1 086	1 376
Male*	616	456	604	784
Under 15	284	214	267	305
15–49	264	220	283	349
50 and older	27	44	54	58
Female	490	383	482	592
Occupation				
Government	16	17	25	93
Farming	162	147	181	197
Retailing	20	14	21	25
Crafts	35	18	17	24
Church ˙	11	8	8	7
Medicine	1	–	1	1
Law	1	1	1	3
Religion (congregations)				
Dutch Reformed	600	600	650	650
Anglican	300	300	200	–
Lutheran	47	54	61	55

Source: Blue Book for the Colony of Natal, 1877–1880

*The total given does not equal the sum of the numbers of persons given in
the various age-groups in every case.

TABLE III

WEENEN COUNTY: THE SETTLER ECONOMY STATISTICS FOR 1877–1880

	1877	1878	1879	1880
Agriculture				
Crops: Acres reaped/amount produced *(muids)*/average market value *(muid)*				
Total acres reaped	–	1858 ¼	2179 ¼	2630
Maize	1199 / 3483 / 13s	967 / 5506 / 30s	1251 / 8095 / 16/8	1488½ / 1424 / 37s
Wheat	420 / 1704 / 2716	225 / 1797 / 36/6	147 / 623 / 35s	242½ / 5130 / 32s
Oats	436 / 935 / 22s	517 / 137 / 35s	714 / 489 / 35s	733½ / 909 / 23s
Oat-hay	– / 294 / 8/6	– / 489 3/4 *(tons)/*	– / 638 *(tons)/*	– / 757 3/4 *(tons)/*
		22/6 (100lbs)	10/4 (100lbs)	9s (100lbs)
Tobacco	9 / 17300 *(lbs)* / £10 (cwt)	13½ / 9150 *(lbs)/* £11–4 (cwt)	11 ³/₄ / 2090 *(lbs)/* £12–8 (cwt)	15½ / 4648 *(lbs)/* £7–15(cwt)
Livestock: Head/*average market value				
Horned cattle	22622 / £8–10	17275 / £10–10	19834 / £12–10	24154 / £7
Wool-bearing sheep	4627 / 18s	126977 / 17/6	59089 / 16s	55736 / 13s
Angora goats	18378 / 14/6	3292 /-	18869 / 15s	23436 / 13s
Horses	2494 / £7–10 *(draught)* / £22 *(saddle)*	1749 / £25 *(draught)* / £23 *(saddle)*	1866 / £25 *(draught)* / £20 *(saddle)*	2719 / £25 *(draught)* / £20 *(saddle)*
Labour				
Average no. of native servants employed	936	755	901	621
Wages (p.a.)				
Praedial servants	£50	£24	£30	£19
Natives with rations (p.m.)	8s	15s	10/-	15s
Domestic (female) servants	£28	£18	£24	£16
Farm Implements				
Ploughs	349	438	421	574
Harrows	27	25	29	5
Wagons	26	28	49	56
Carts	2	6	18	34

Source: Blue Books for the Colony of Natal, 1877–1880

TABLE IV

WEENEN COUNTY: THE SETTLER ECONOMY COMPARATIVE STATISTICS FOR 1877–1880

	1877	1878	1879	1880
Perishables: Prices in Weenen County/Durban County (1877 and 1878) and Durban Borough (1879 and 1880).				
Foodstuffs (lb)				
Beef	5d / 7d	7d / 9d	6d / 9d	6d / 9d
Wheaten flour (196 lbs)	£1–8 / £2–10	£2–5 / £1–10	£2–1–6 / 15s	49s / 32s
Wheaten bread	5d / 3d	5d / 3d	5d / 3d	5d / 3d
Salt (cwt)	14s / 17s	15/7 / 7s	14/8 / 12s	16s / 7s
Sugar	4½d / 4d	6d / 4d	5d / 4d	5d / 3s
Tea	4s / 3/9	4s / 3/9	3/4 / 3/6	3/4 / 3s
Coffee	1/6 / 1/6	2/6 / 1/6	1/5 / 1/4	1/3 / 1/3
Tobacco	2s / 2s	1/6 / 3s	2s / 1/6	1/4 / 2/6
Beverages				
Rum (gallon)	10/6 / 4/6	12s / 3/9	12s / 3/6	12/6 / 3/6
Brandy (bottle)	6s / 6/6	8s / 6s	6/8 / 5s	6s / 5s to 7/6
Beer (bottle)	2s / 1/9	3s / 1/6	2/6 / 1/6	2/6 / 1s to 1/6
Semidurables: Prices in Weenen County/Durban Borough.				
Sheets (pair)	NA	NA	NA	8/4 / 5/6
Blankets (pair)				17s / 18s
Boots (pair)				14s / 12s
Calico (yard)				6d / 5d
Flannel (yard)				2s / 1/9
Jacket				17/6 / 10s

Source: Blue Books for the Colony of Natal, 1877–1880.
NA: detailed information not available.

cornets. In 1876 resignations and new appointments occurred in all the wards, and in the case of Nos. 2 and 3 men with English surnames (H. Daniel Winter and John Button), respectively, replaced ones with Dutch (Johannes C. and Johannes P. Buys), and in 1879 the old field cornet (Gert van der Merwe) in Ward No. 1 was reappointed.[8]

The Boers

In Ward No. 1, the upper part of the Weenen Division, the Dutch farmers organized themselves and Lloyd simply endorsed the arrangements. They had a strong stone-walled laager on the farm Strydpoort. A meeting was held on 2 December to form a laager defence corps, and the old Field Cornet, Gert van der Merwe, enrolled 23 members. Andries W. J. Pretorius, 'with his usual generosity', placed his house, which adjoined the laager, at the disposal of those also wishing to use it in an emergency. Pretorius owned Strydpoort, and the local report of the meeting refers to him as 'Commandant'. A committee was formed to add to the roll of members. The meeting was adjourned till the 9th, when the nascent unit met at Sterk Spruit to adopt rules, to elect officers and to attend to other business. A letter from General Lloyd was read, which heartily approved the steps already taken and offered assistance – and the colonial government in due course proved willing, almost eager, to endorse this manifest self-reliance. The men styled themselves the Upper Tugela Defence Corps, with at least 34 members, and elected Pretorius captain, van der Merwe first lieutenant, and William Gray and D. Hulme second lieutenant and quartermaster, respectively. The first muster and drill was scheduled for 19 December. A local reporter was sanguine with respect to the corps – 'a fine body', including some of the best shots in the division. (He wrote that one or two at the first meeting had professed astonishment at receiving a notice from the Messenger of the Court warning them that they had overshot their mark this time in potting elands.) He (or she) remarked that they were armed with Swinburne Henrys;[9] if so, then they must have provided all their own ammunition, for the returns of arms and ammunition at the laager in March and April give 15 Snider carbines and 20 Snider rifles and 7 500 Snider cartridges, and 3 500 Westley Richard cartridges and 500 percussion caps.[10]

On 29 December Lloyd attended a meeting in Ward No. 3, the lower part of the division, where most of the Dutch farmers lived. It was held at the house of the Field Commandant and it would seem that the ward's old and new field cornets were present. About 30 men in all were present, most of them Boers from the Mooi River neighbourhood. They chose Bester's Laager, a stone walled enclosure on the adjacent farm Twyfelfontein, as the local place of defence and refuge. It had been built some 20 years before but never completed, apparently for want of funds. Lloyd pointed out that an enemy with firearms would command it from nearby higher ground. The men then appointed a committee, apparently including both the field cornets, to find a place for another laager, and Boshoff offered to help however he could and to keep arms and ammunition for a laager till they were needed at his farmstead, Kruisfontein. Since some of the men complained that they lacked ammunition for their Westley Richard rifles, Lloyd directed that 1 500 rounds and 2 000 percussion caps be sent for Boshoff to store, and gave notice that cartridges could also be bought in Estcourt; in addition he directed that 20 Snider rifles and 10 Snider carbines, with proportional ammunition, be sent to the commandant.[11] The committee seems never to have selected a new laager site, but the Sniders arrived for storage at Kruisfontein, along with 7 500 cartridges.[12]

The English

It was natural that Lloyd's primary attention should be to the central ward, No. 2, in which lay Estcourt. The military organization was characteristic of the English rather than the Dutch settlers. The Weenen County Rifle Association, based on Estcourt,[13] was not a militia organization but a means to enable local men to buy arms and ammunition at discount from the government in order to gain proficiency in marksmanship. For those who wished to be martial, but on a part-time basis, there was a volunteer corps, the Weenen Yeomanry based at Weston, a mounted unit formed in 1876. It numbered just 19, but General Lloyd was the captain, with W.F. Popham first lieutenant and Herbert Blaker quartermaster. (The second lieutenancy was vacant.)[14] Along with the other 14 volunteer corps in the colony it undertook to train regularly and was liable to be called up in an emergency, the kind of fixed arrangement the government seems to have preferred to the old commando system. Obviously the two government-sponsored organizations could not provide much protection, certainly not on an extempore basis – the little corps of yeomanry was not even called into service as the war approached.[15] Estcourt was also the station of a detachment of Natal Mounted Police, which in July numbered 61,[16] but now, having been placed under imperial command,[17] much less.

The central defensive post was the blockhouse perched on a hill just south of Estcourt. This was built in 1874–1875, at the direction of the then Major Anthony Durnford, R.E. (and today it is called 'Fort Durnford').[18] In the autumn of 1878 the adjacent Mounted Police camp was enclosed by high loopholed stone walls between the blockhouse and the stable.[19] This became

Estcourt Laager. The blockhouse, 'Fort Durnford', is on the right.

known as the Estcourt Laager, and it was large enough to take in easily most of the white inhabitants of the division, if not the county. Lloyd would have a problem providing a garrison for the town, the laager, or even the blockhouse. Rather late, Lloyd and Paterson called a meeting to consider defence in Estcourt. At this meeting, on 4 January 1879, it was proposed that the rifle association should act as a town guard, but only three members actually enrolled! A little over a week later Lloyd complained to the Defence Committee that the police detachment was too small to secure the blockhouse, especially since the magistrate had sentenced two out of the eleven to imprisonment, and he suggested to Paterson that eight blacks be called up to augment it.[20] Meanwhile he drafted a notice proclaiming the Estcourt Laager the central post of defence and refuge in the event of danger and disturbance, of which he or Paterson would apprise the people as early as possible.[21]

It is tempting to criticize Lloyd for ineffectual efforts in Wards Nos. 2 and 3, and to credit what was done in Ward No. 1 to local initiative. It should be remembered, however, that he could not compel the burghers to take action, and that the burghers themselves were distracted by the extraordinary circumstances of the impending war. In his official report for the county as a whole in 1878, Paterson points out that the imperial military build-up prior to invasion of Zululand created exorbitant demands for certain produce and especially transport, and the latter drew many able-bodied men into the lucrative business of transport-riding. He states, too, that until the end of the year 'very little alarm was felt' with respect to the imminent hostilities. Evidently this complacency gave way to uncertainty, for when the field cornets began collecting the statistics for the year, they found 'a great many residents were absent from their homes, having either left the county or withdrawn to less exposed localities than those in which their farms are situated.'[22]

Black levies

Lloyd had thus dealt with the white settlers by the time the war began. He had not dealt with the blacks who constituted 97% of the county's population, but there was little practically that he could do for them, and the government continued to rely on the Resident Magistrate, Peter Paterson, when it came to military matters affecting them. The commandant and magistrate were ordered indeed to collaborate. The government had decided that the blacks should have an active role in defence, and had circularized instructions to magistrates as early as September for the calling up of levies by clan or tribe under white leaders at specified places when they were required.[23]

There survive two tables, dating at latest to November, which describe the levies envisaged in the Weenen and Ulundi Divisions. One is in Paterson's handwriting and the other in that of another – it almost looks like the Lieutenant-Governor's, but it is unlikely he would be drafting tables – presumably a clerk. Which is the later and authoritative one has not been determined, although it is tempting to suppose that it is Paterson's.[24] The tables agree in most matters. In the Weenen Division there were four chiefs who would turn out men for defence – Faku, chief of the Basu tribe; Ndomba, of the Bhele; Mganu, of the Thembu; Pakade, of the Mchunu; and the ci-devant Zulu, Mkhungu, of the Xhosa (isiQoza). It was estimated that they had 2 250, 1 086, 1 228, 2 011 and 603 able-bodied men, respectively; but Paterson noted that no more than half could be considered available for service. The Basu levy would gather at the blockhouse at Estcourt, and the Thembu at Weenen town. Paterson's table states that the Bhele would also gather at Weenen, and the Mchunu at Mhlumba and the Xhosa at Monási's kraal, while the other table gives their stations as the Estcourt blockhouse, Mhlunuta, and Weenen, respectively. The tables also state that levies would assemble at Ulundi from the BaSotho Hlubi's Hlongwe, Teteleku's Mpumuza, the Ngwe, and several small unnamed tribes with 106, 162, 572 and 305 able-bodied men, respectively. Paterson noted that about 50 of Hlubi's mounted men would probably be required for special service. Apart from discrepancies concerning place of assembly and the notes, the tables have two different lists of levy leaders; the one in the clerk's hand notes that all those named have declined (although there is a question mark for one) to serve, whereas the other with other names, in Paterson's hand, does not. The matter of levies was largely an administrative exercise in paper-work at this stage, for the men were not to be called out unless the Supreme Chief, i.e. the Lieutenant-Governor, really wished them to defend the colony.

Levies were called up, but not to defend the county. Colonel Durnford pressed for the formation of the Natal Native Contingent with European-style organization and under imperial military control. So Paterson was told now to call on the loyal chiefs for a different purpose. The account in his official report[25] is interesting for its insights:

> . . . In November, I received instructions to raise Native Levies for military service, either within or without the Colony, as might be required. Some reluctance was exhibited by the natives at first in obeying the order to muster, not so much from any feeling of disloyalty, as partly from their usual dilitariness [sic], partly from the conflicting claims of the Government on the one hand and on the other of their landlords and employers – many of the natives residing on private farms – and partly also from their dread of the warlike prowess of the Zulus. However, without very much delay, all the men called for by the Government were forthcoming, and the following are about the numbers supplied for military service from Weenen County:– Men of Umkunga's, Umdomba's, Umganu's, and U'Pagadi's Tribes, forming the late 3rd Regiment Natal Native Contingent, under Commandant Lonsdale, about 1 500; Jahu's [Faku's] men, and men of the Amangwe Tribe (late Putini), forming part of the 1st Regiment N.N. Contingent; of the former 225, of the latter 300; Basutos, under Hlubi, all mounted men, about 50; in all considerably over 2 000 men. When the men were once mustered and prepared to start for the front, they showed no lack of military spirit or enthusiasm; indeed, at the end, more men of some tribes turned out and joined the Levies than were called for. U'Pagadi, for instance, was required to find 600 men, but he actually supplied about 730. The Chiefs themselves evinced the utmost loyalty, and an earnest desire to carry out, as far as possible, the wishes of the Government: but their power over their people is being gradually, but surely weakened, and they no longer possess any despotic authority over them, at least, in this County; although when, as in this case, they are acting under the distinct orders of the Government, they are necessarily supported in carrying out such orders, so far as they do so fairly and justly.

Approximately 2 800 men from the county joined the contingent at the front by 11 January 1879.[26]

The BaSotho enigma

In October and November it was reported that three messengers from Cetshwayo had been detained in the Leribe district of Basutoland,[27] and again in December that the Zulu king sought to send mounted men to communicate with the chief Molapo.[28] It seemed prudent then, considering the somewhat disturbed conditions in the Cape protectorate, to take certain defensive precautions in the Ulundi and Upper Tugela Divisions of the county. On instructions from the government, in early January the Administrator of Native Law and Acting Resident Magistrate at Ulundi, Charles Boast, inspected the mountain passes which Durnford had closed several years before and reported that they were negotiable only by men on foot.[29] The government pressed the Resident Magistrate at Oliviershoek, in the Upper Tugela Division, Albert B. Allison, to get on with the building of an earthwork laager at the magistracy. The government had decided one was necessary in May[30] and the Colonial Engineer had issued instructions for building in July;[31] Durnford had inspected the site and reported in November, and Chelmsford approved the construction in order to give a sense of security in the neighbourhood.[32] Allison wanted protection but wrote early on that a hasty work would do in an emergency, and pointed out later to Lloyd that whatever arms and ammunition were in store at the magistracy, it could hardly be defended when there were only 19 white men within a radius of 20 miles (32 km), and some of them had already enrolled in the Upper Tugela Defence Corps.[33]

This then was the situation in Weenen County when the Anglo-Zulu War began. A Colonial Defensive District, No. II, had been created, and a retired general given command of it. His attention was directed to the protection of the minuscule white settlement, in the main dispersed over one division. In the circumstances, he did about as well as could be expected. With slight exaggeration it may be said that the English followed his lead and the Dutch their own. The massive black population, concentrated near the borders, and therefore susceptible to foreign agitations, remained primarily the responsibility of the Resident Magistrate. They remained docile; very probably their chief concern was survival under conditions of prolonged drought. In any event, an appreciable number of the presumably warlike had been drafted to the front in the imperial service, and therefore were in no position to disrupt life in the county.

War and a reverse

War against the Zulu apparently evoked no jubilation among the inhabitants of Weenen County. Indeed, the Lieutenant-Governor wrote to the Colonial Secretary on 16 January 1879, that he had heard that the Dutch in Weenen County feared that the government was abandoning them.[34] The Resident Magistrate wrote to the Colonial Secretary on the 13th that false reports about the Zulu were starting to circulate: he asked for authentic information of importance in brief that he could post for general information and thus prevent panic. The Secretary replied that he would send important news, but not necessarily on a daily basis. Paterson undertook to keep in communication with the magistrates at Greytown and Ladysmith for the same purpose.[35] Lloyd augmented the nine police at the Estcourt Laager with some mounted blacks, as earlier requested, and despatched two detachments of ten each under white leaders to patrol between Weenen and Pakade's location and between the location and the Zulu border, respectively.[36]

The news of the Zulu victory at Isandlwana gave rise to alarm. It is not quite clear when and how the first information came to the county. If it came as in other parts, then it came among the blacks first. Paterson wrote on 27 January that the unsettled state owed to reports spread by the men from the Natal Native Contingent[37] – the 3rd Regiment had been disbanded at Rorke's Drift on the 24th, and the mounted units had deserters. The effect may have been greater since some of the units had suffered heavy losses, notably Pakade's Mchunu and Mkhungu's Xhosa.[38] For all the uncertainty there was, wrote Paterson in his annual report, 'no such panic as that which appears to have arisen in Pietermaritzburg and Durban and other parts of the Colony,' and stressed the point:[39]

> Nothing could exceed the calm and quiet bearing of the people, both European and Native, under the trying circumstances under which we were placed during the period intervening between the disaster of Isandhlwana and the arrival at the front of such reinforcements as obviated to a great extent the risk of invasion by the Zulus.

The colonial government issued a terse statement on the British reverse on the 24th, and directed it to the magistrates in Weenen and Klip River Counties on the 27th, also enjoining them to co-operate with the District Commandants for the defence of their posts.[40] This was followed on the 28th by rules for provisioning the posts,[41] and on 1 February by a minute to all the commandants and magistrates urging them to secure and to complete arrangements for their posts.[42]

The Estcourt Laager

The Resident Magistrate directly called a public meeting at Estcourt. Both Lloyd and Paterson urged those present to come forward and take steps to protect themselves; yet the meeting did nothing and broke up in confusion. No one said it, but Paterson believed that the men would not commit themselves to service which might take them into the field before they had first secured their families.[43]

Lloyd requested the Colonial Secretary on the 28th to have the notice concerning the laager, which he had drafted earlier, published in the Government Gazette and the Pietermaritzburg newspapers, and to have 50 copies of it sent to him. The notice appeared in the *Times of Natal* on the 31st and in the *Natal Witness* on 1 February. It stated that the commandant of the laager (presumably Lloyd himself) would give the orders and make the regulations and enforce them strictly and that every able-bodied man would have to serve in the defence, even outside the walls. Those coming into laager should bring as much food as possible, as well as cooking utensils, and would be allowed to send as much as a fortnight's provisions, clearly marked, for storage at their own risk, although Lloyd did have some provisions stored in the laager. They should also bring their own firearms and ammunition, but the notice made it clear that the laager was stocked with arms and munitions.[44] Wagons should go to the north gate to be admitted, but with no more than eight oxen, and arranged inside in order of arrival.

There does not seem to have been a rush into the laager at Estcourt; indeed, there is no record that any families took refuge there. It was enough for Lloyd that all heads of families had been informed where to go and what to do in case of emergency.[45] The circumstances thus enabled Lloyd to improve its defences without interference. Paterson called up a hundred men from Mkhungu's and Ndomba's NNC veterans[46] and they were put to work under Lloyd's direction, levelling off a hillock about 180 metres (196 yards) distant which commanded the laager and cutting away the surrounding brush, raising the banquette inside and sloping the glacis outside the walls, where glass from broken bottles was sprinkled.[47]

The improvements mentioned might make the laager impregnable against a Zulu assault, but as observers of the work remarked, the laager would need a garrison variously estimated at 300, 300–400 men, and 100 white men and 600 or 800 loyal blacks.[48] These were not likely to be had, and Lloyd carried on alterations in the laager with that in mind. If the garrison proved unable to hold the walls, then the inmates should fall back to the blockhouse and the stables, on opposite sides of the enclosure – more precisely, the whites would hold the blockhouse and the blacks would man the walls and retire to the stables, if necessary. A ditch was dug and a loopholed sandbag rampart erected in front of the blockhouse, which probably resembled a mini-laager. The stables were prepared by blocking all but one of the doorways to a height of about 1,8 metres (2 yards) with boxes filled with earth; the remaining openings could then be filled in with sandbags and loopholed in half an hour. The number of loopholes along the rear wall (part of the laager perimeter) was increased, and they were cut to permit rifle barrels angles of altitude as well as azimuth.[49]

All this work was probably completed by the end of February or early in March. Meanwhile munitions were sent up from Pietermaritzburg.[50] The returns from mid-March to April show that the laager was stocked with 136 Snider rifles and 14 Snider carbines, with 30 800 rounds of ammunition; 180 Enfield rifles, with 15 100 rounds; 8 Swinburne Henry carbines, with 28 800 rounds; and 5 500 rounds of Westley Richards rifle ammunition.[51] The whites arriving armed would probably have Swinburne Henrys or Westley Richards. The Sniders probably were reserved for the other whites who would defend the blockhouse. The obsolete Enfields were meant for the blacks.

Outlying posts

If Ward No. 2 was secure, then Ward No. 1 was overprotected. The number of men ready to join in the Upper Tugela Defence Corps at Strydpoort under Pretorius was estimated between 70 and 100. There may even have been a surfeit of men for the laager. It was reported that the Boers were sending most of their women and children away, chiefly to the Free State.[52] The reverse was true of Ward No. 3. It really was too late for the laager committee there to carry out its task, and Kruisfontein remained a rendezvous for the farmers to take up such arms and ammunition as were in store there. Poor defences and proximity to the Zulu border may have precipitated a flight. It may have been the area the High Commissioner had in mind when he remarked (to the Secretary of State for Colonies) on 28 March after travelling up from Howick to Ladysmith: 'All the Dutch farmers we saw told us of neighbours and friends who since the war alarms had trekked to the Orange Free State so that by far the larger portion of the Dutch and many of the English farms were wholly or partially deserted.'[53] And on 3 May Lloyd mentioned (to the Colonial Secretary) that Weenen township was practically deserted, and that the very few persons still there would come to Estcourt for protection.[54] The High Commissioner remarked as well that the Boers' fear had spread to the English settlers,[55] but enough of them remained to organize an alternative defensive post. A group meeting at

Weston church on 3 February decided to convert the church and yard to one when the need arose, and appointed a commander, George Turner, of Warley Common, assisted by W. Liversage and A. Knopwood, to look after preparations. Lloyd approved the measure, and sent 25 Snider rifles with 5 000 cartridges to the church.[56] At Colenso the 11 whites working on the new bridge over the Thukela reported that they would take up the ends of the bridge and defend themselves in the middle. Mr F. Dickenson, a former army officer, would take command. Lloyd approved and sent them 10 Snider rifles and 1 500 cartridges.[57]

Lloyd did not omit the border areas. He continued the mounted patrols by blacks in the easternmost part of the county, until, about the beginning of February, he called on the Weenen Yeomanry to replace or possibly to supplement them. The corps had volunteered to cross the border at the beginning of the war and been rebuffed. Now Lieutenant Popham and his two officers (apparently a second lieutenant was found) and thirteen men, plus four mounted blacks, found themselves posted at Gretna Green, a farm near where the track from Weston entered the road from Weenen to Greytown and close to the Mpafana location and the Zulu border. Here the little corps remained 'under canvas' at least until the third week in April, and very likely longer – indeed, it is not clear when it was relieved of its lonesome vigil. It was reported that the men wished to join the forces at the front for the second invasion of Zululand;[58] however, the wish was not to be realized. Lieutenant Popham had other ideas, for in mid-April he tendered his resignation, which was gazetted on the 22nd.[59]

At the Upper Tugela magistracy on the morning of 31 January Allison received the Colonial Secretary's message about the British reverse and the directive to prepare the defence of his post in co-operation with the Defensive District Commandant. He wrote to Lloyd the same day that Oliviershoek was in fact indefensible. Lloyd recommended that he be allowed to abandon it if it were seriously endangered, but the Lieutenant-Governor retorted crossly that Allison had misled him earlier so that plans had been drawn up and money allocated for a laager and Allison had not yet thrown up even an earthwork. Lloyd smoothed the matter out: the Upper Tugela Division was so remote that a large raid from Zululand or Basutoland was unlikely, and if one were made, the whites in the division could retire to the Strydpoort Laager; however, if a small raid were made, then Allison might defend the magistracy behind a small earthwork. The Lieutenant-Governor grumbled that Allison should have taken the initiative with an earthwork instead of waiting for the government to construct a proper laager, on which work commenced in March.[60]

Hard Times in the Thorns

The Lieutenant-Governor, in his minute to the magistrates and commandants on 1 February, urged that the black population should be given every
assurance that the government was solicitous of their security and
well-being.[61] In his official report Paterson stated that through their chiefs
they were given appropriate directions for their protection.[62] Many of the
blacks needed such assurance. The 3rd Regiment of the Natal Native
Contingent had had a disastrous career, and now there was a possibility the
Zulu might raid the locations along the middle border. More than the war
oppressed these people. The drought in the colony had affected the county
unevenly, sparing the upper divisions and parching the lower parts. Paterson
reported for 1878:[63]

> The Natives in the lower or thorn districts suffered very severely from
> scarcity of food; their grain crops failed even more completely than
> during the previous years, and this was the fourth succeeding year of
> deficient crops. Fortunately the crops in the Upper Districts were
> remarkably good, and the Natives there had, consequently, consider-
> able quantities of grain to dispose of, but the demand being
> considerably greater than the supply, and many of the wagons which,
> in ordinary times, would have been employed in carrying mealies to
> the distressed Districts for sale being more profitably employed
> elsewhere, the prices naturally rose very considerably – a good cow
> being sometimes bartered for a single sack of grain. To aid those who
> were most distressed, I was authorised to procure mealies for sale to
> such Natives as desired them, using my discretion as to requiring cash
> payments or giving credit. A good many muids were sold for cash, and
> a considerable quantity also on the credit of the Chiefs or heads of
> kraals. Some of the debts thus incurred have been already discharged,
> and I have no doubt that by the end of the present year all will be
> honestly paid off. I cannot finish this part of my Report without again
> recurring to the unshaken loyalty and trust in the Government which
> has been evinced by the Native population, and to the absence of any
> marked increase of crime among them, notwithstanding the unsettled
> state of the County, and the great scarcity of food under which so many
> have been suffering.

And for 1879:[64]

> The great scarcity of food amongst the Native population which
> prevailed in some parts of the Division during the previous year

continued during the first half of the past year; but, although doubtless hard pushed in many cases, the Natives with the aid afforded them by the Government as stated in my Report for 1878, and the kindly help in many cases of their European masters who supplied them with mealies on credit and at reasonable rates, or lent them money to purchase food with, managed to get through the season previous to reaping without actual starvation; and their last crops, although by no means up to the average, have been sufficient to place them above want – indeed were it not for the recklessness with which they waste large quantities of grain in making beer to be consumed at gatherings which are too often scenes of drunkenness, riot and debauchery, they would probably have had sufficient grain to place them beyond want for some time to come, notwithstanding the prospect of another failure of crops in the Midland and Lower Districts.

It is not surprising then that Paterson urged postponement of collection of the hut tax among the Basu, Bhele, Mchunu and Xhosa from April and July, to which the government reluctantly consented.[65]

The colonial government had adopted a policy of receiving Zulu refugees, who would return to Zululand after the war. Paterson pointed out that those quartered in the county would be a strain on its resources, but the government agreed to pay for their food in that event. The Zulu chief Gamdana, brother of Sihayo, came over to Msinga with about 90 of his people, mostly old men, women and children, who were moved to Estcourt at the end of February. It was said that Mkhungu wanted Gamdana, with the 33 members of his family, to live with him. The rest who could, should earn their keep on white farms for a term of six months. White settlers reacted angrily, fearing the introduction of Zulu spies and arguing that the apprentices' term was too short to be economical. A meeting was held at Stock's Royal Hotel on 3 March, at which over a hundred persons signed a memorial, protesting against the squatting of refugees among the local blacks. Messrs Pretorius, Bernard and Ralfe were deputed to carry the memorial to Pietermaritzburg. None the less the refugees remained for the duration of the war, indeed of the year.[66]

The Weenen Contingent

The imperial military authorities, finding themselves on the defensive strategically, decided that a Zulu invasion could best be met by a kind of guerrilla warfare. Rather than confront an *impi*, bands of whites and loyal blacks should hang upon the flanks and harass it. The military realized by this time that no white men would be forthcoming for such service until their families were absolutely safe, and thus urged that defensive measures be completed in this respect. The military's view, set out in a communication to the High Commissioner on 8 February, was incorporated in a minute which the government distributed to the magistrates and commandants.[67] The Lieutenant-Governor opined that Colonial Defensive District No. II (as well as No. III) could be placed under an imperial military officer, as had happened in the three districts bordering Zululand. The military evidently did not believe this was necessary; however, it did exert pressure for a greater call-up of colonial forces in support, and attention was thus drawn to the disbanded veterans of the 3rd Regiment of the Natal Native Contingent. The Lieutenant-Governor and Lieutenant-General then became involved in a protracted dispute over the command, disposition, and application of black levies, which the latter won.[68] Thus in early March further levies were called for, which included men from the tribes in eastern Weenen.

Lloyd and Paterson had meanwhile persisted in their original task of organizing black levies for defence in the county. White levy leaders had been found and Lloyd had warned them in December to be ready to turn out at short notice; however, he wrote rather vaguely to the Colonial Secretary on 4 January that he was waiting for further instructions to clarify the government's directive to 'place' them.[69] The flurry of directives after Isandlwana refocused his thoughts: towards the end of February he reported that the establishment of the levies was under way.[70] The places of assembly were on the eastern edges of the white settlement and in the location. Pakade's levy, which was supposed to be the largest, was to assemble under N. H. Robinson at Mhlumba, in the location, and Mganu's, under T. Wheeler, at or near Nkaseni. Ndomba's levy would gather under C. B. Cooke on the Weenen town lands, while Faku's, under F. Birkett, and Mkhungu's, which still lacked a leader, would assemble on farms a few kilometres west of Weenen, probably Sterk Spruit and Onverwacht respectively.[71] The men evinced the greatest reluctance to service. Those who had served in the NNC wanted an assurance that they would not be organized and drilled in the European fashion or be sent into Zululand again. Paterson reported, too, that the white farmers on whose lands many of them resided in return for labour, threatened them with breach of contract if they left, which often appeared more persuasive than the Supreme Chief's appeal. All but five or six kraals of Faku's Basu and about fifty kraals of Mganu's Thembu were on private land. It may seem curious that Faku should have mustered his quota first; but then his men were allowed to return home.

Ndomba's Bhele were about equally divided between private and public lands. Mkhungu had bought a farm for himself and his Xhosa, but many of them still lived on private land adjoining it. Only Pakade's Mchunu resided for the most part in the location; yet large numbers also lived on private land, to which many had moved recently because of the drought. Almost all the men living on private land were under labour contracts. Paterson added that, irrespective of tenure, many men were absent, having gone as far as Pietermaritzburg or the Diamond Fields for work.[72] He had to admit in due course that his pre-war estimates of fighting strengths had been too high.

Most of March passed while the levy leaders and chiefs were assured and assembled. Lloyd probably indulged in some wishful thinking when he estimated that 1 500 were 'in the Field, on patrol or otherwise', in his return for 15 March. He was more realistic in the return on the 29th, which stated that 250 of Pakade's Mchunu were out and probably 250 were available in reserve, and accounted similarly for 250 and 200 of Faku's Basu, 250 and 200 of Mkhungu's Xhosa, 200 and 150 of Mgana's Thembu, and 100 each of Ndomba's Bhele.[73] The government, yielding to the military, now ordered those in the field to proceed to the border in the Msinga Division, where they would come under the Commandant of Colonial Defensive District No. I. Accordingly the 'Weenen Contingent' or 'Weenen Corps', estimated at 600 men, assembled at Estcourt to receive government blankets and firearms, and marched off on 8 and 9 April for the Msinga magistracy.[74] Lloyd's return for 19 April shows a residue of 90 men in the field in his District No. II.[75] There was no effort to raise similar numbers in the Upper Tugela or Ulundi Divisions; however, some mounted men of the Ngwane who had served under Durnford rejoined the imperial service under Captain Theophilus Shepstone, jr., in May.[76]

Drakensberg patrols

The Ulundi and Upper Tugela Divisions remained peaceful after Isandlwana, but there was a report that the BaSotho were encouraged by the news of the British disaster to raid Free State farms for cattle.[77] Allison suggested to Lloyd that a small patrol be established on the Free State border of his division to discourage cattle rustlers and horse thieves. The Lieutenant-Governor liked the idea, especially for catching Zulu spies, but left Allison to propose the method to Lloyd.[78] Reports, apparently of a portentous nature, of cattle drives along the Drakensberg, especially towards the Bushman's River pass near the Giant's Castle, were also current and prompted Paterson to instruct Boast at Ulundi to investigate in mid-

February. The Resident Magistrate sent a party up the pass and another to the top of the escarpment near the Giant's Castle, and both proceeded several kilometres in Basutoland. They encountered a solitary bull, which fled at their approach. Boast concluded consequently that the reports were untrue. Paterson sent out some of Hlubi's BaSotho to investigate as well, and they returned with rumours from among the people below the escarpment about drives whose origins he could only guess. The passes were still closed to all but foot traffic, but the people none the less were told to watch and to report any movements.[79] Allison meanwhile consulted chiefs and headmen on the best ways to stop raids in his division.[80]

In the latter part of February Moorosi led the Phuthi in southern Basutoland into 'rebellion' against the Cape authorities. Greater vigilance was required along the Drakensberg, and patrols commenced 1 March at the behest of the colonial government.[81] Allison put out patrols, presumably on lines he had suggested.[82] Boast disposed of one group of six stationed at Cathkin, another of eight about midway between the Giant's Castle and Bushman's River pass, and a third, of six, about midway between the two – for patrolling.[83] Reports seemed to justify the action. On 8 March the *Natal Witness* stated that Moorosi had received messengers from Cetshwayo, who had promised assistance, even though the Zulu king had urged him not to fire the first shot! Another report, on the 18th, stated that Moorosi and his men might be trying to make their way to Zululand by way of the Drakensberg.[84] Patrols were doubled in consequence and the Upper Tugela Defence Corps and Weenen Yeomanry were alerted to be ready to move thither at once.[85] At Oliviershoek Allison made arrangements to defend the Upper Tugela Division as best he could. Lloyd asked him to establish double patrols, too, if he deemed them necessary, but Allison apparently descried no hostile movements until mid-April, when he dispatched a scouting party to ascertain information on Moorosi's movements.[86]

Recovery

In February the fear of a Zulu irruption or a black disturbance within the colony abated. There was no funk in Weenen County, a local correspondent wrote in the *Witness* of 22 February. Another wrote from Estcourt in the *Colonist* of 6 March that no one anticipated a Zulu attack, the laager work notwithstanding, and that some of the most intelligent chiefs ridiculed the idea of a Zulu invasion in force and the natives were not in the least alarmed. There were signs that the whites were falling back into their routines – evidently enough farmers were in the third ward now to inhibit the magistrate's efforts to raise levies,[87] and in the first ward the Upper Tugela Defence Corps was soon reduced by absenteeism to about 40 men;[88] the second lieutenant, William Gray, went off to join the forces for Zululand.[89]

The imperial military authorities recovered the initiative at the front, and the build-up of reinforcements presaged the second invasion of Zululand. These developments made Natalians complacent, just when the imperial military wished to make them aware of their continuing vulnerability. The advance could not provide a closed front, and Zulu forays between the invading columns and especially across the border would be an unwanted distraction. The military pressed the colonial government to canvass the districts for able-bodied men who would take the field in an active defence. The results were disappointing, nowhere more so than in Weenen County. Both Lloyd, reporting in late June, and Paterson, in mid-July, made it quite clear that the white population was extended to the limit of its power.[90] They stated that there were only 45 able-bodied Europeans who could ride and had horses and take the field in Ward No. 2, and 108 in Ward No. 3. Lloyd could only estimate 40 men in the Upper Tugela Defence Corps in Ward No. 1, while Paterson gave the total number of effectives in the ward as 50. Of course, there were other men, either infirm or horseless, who could defend posts – 12 of them in Ward No. 1, 18 (according to Lloyd) or 24 (according to Paterson) in Ward No. 2, and 17 in Ward No. 3. There was no point in the military's pressing civil defence further; anyway, by this time the campaign in Zululand was practically over.

The war had had a bracing effect upon the people of Weenen County, quite apart from its economic aspects. Apprehension gave way to alarm when it was learned that British arms had suffered a reverse at Isandlwana. The whites did not panic, the blacks did not rise. Defensive measures were accelerated, especially with regard to the white settlers, but the black population was not ignored and presently was drawn into defence of the vulnerable border areas. Of course, when it became apparent that Zulu strategy was defensive and that the BaSotho posed no threat, and British reinforcements arrived in the colony, local defence measures eased. By March fear had dissipated with regard to the Zulu, by April with the BaSotho. A brief Zulu invasion scare in Msinga in May and a small Zulu raid in Umvoti in June seem to have had no repercussions in Weenen. Cetshwayo was captured at the end of August, and a British peace was then forced upon Zululand. Moorosi's rebellion died with him in November. Long before then the white settlers of Weenen County were at peace. The Weenen Yeomanry returned and disbanded, indeed the corps ceased to exist after 1879.[91] The

Weenen Contingent returned to Estcourt and was mustered out in July.[92] The last men of the Natal Native Contingent returned in October, when at the instigation of Paterson the Lieutenant-Governor as Supreme Chief issued an address, specially thanking the chiefs who had supported the government and delivered over their men for service.[93]

[Paper presented at the Workshop on Natal History, University of Natal, Pietermaritzburg, 1984.]

Notes

1. See GH 1411, pp. 165–93; and CSO 1972, Minute 4237 of 1878; and *NGG*, vol. XXX, nos. 1739, 26 November and 1740, 3 December 1878, Government Notices nos. 356 and 368 of 1878, respectively.

2. CSO 1925, Minutes 4417/1878 and W65/1879; GH 1412, Minute 4550/1878.

3. *Blue Book for the Colony of Natal. 1878*, Pietermaritzburg, Section H, pp. 18–21.

4. *Blue Book. 1879*, V: 2–3. The Resident Magistrate's remarks on accuracy are in the first paragraph of his report in JJ: 18–21, and the last paragraph of his report in the *Blue Book. 1878*, JJ: 14–16.

5. GH 1412, Minute 4550/1878.

6. CSO 699, Minute 2195/1879: Lloyd to the Colonial Secretary, 3 May 1879.

7. CSO 2552, Minute C8/1878: Paterson to the Colonial Secretary, 2 January 1878.

8. Cf. *Blue Books. 1876*, B: 3 and 4, C: 22 and 24; *1878*, C: 24; and *1879*, C: 24.

9. *Natal Witness*, 7 and 26 December 1878. See also C5O 1925, Minute C50/1878: Paterson to the Colonial Secretary, 3 August 1878; and CSO 1972, Minute 4640/1878: Lieutenant-Governor to the Colonial Secretary, 7 December 1878, et seq.

10. SNA, 1/6/14, nos. 6 and 30, and CSO 1927, Minutes 2133 and 2163/1879: 'Statement[s] showing defensive state of district' for Colonial Defensive District No. II, 15 and 29 March and 12 and 19 April 1879, respectively.

11. CSO 678, Minute 90/1879: Lloyd to the Secretary of the Defence Committee, 2 January 1879.

12. See statements in note 10.

13. See CSO 1971, Minute 3566/1878: Weenen County Rifle Association to the Colonial Secretary, 24 September 1878.

14. Cf. *Blue Books. 1876 and 1878*, I: 7 in each.

15. See *NGG*, vol. XXX, no. 1739, 26 November 1878: Government Notice no. 365 of 1878.

16. According to the return, 6 July 1878, in CSO 1911, Minute 2848/1878.

17. General Orders no. 188 of 1878, in the *Times of Natal*, 8 November 1878.

18. The building of the blockhouse is described in detail in the booklet *Estcourt and the old fort [:] Fort Durnford Museum* [n.p., n.d.], recently printed and available at the museum.

19. See the correspondence in CSO 2552, Minute C11/1878, and the reports in the *Times of Natal*, 25 February 1878, and the *Natal Advertizer*, 16 June 1878.

20. CSO 680, Minute 241/1879 and CSO 681, Minute 336/1879: Lloyd to the Secretary of the Defence Committee, 9 and 13 January 1879, respectively. Cf. CSO 715, Minute 3830/1879: Paterson to the Colonial Secretary, 16 July 1879.

21. Public Notice, January 1879, enclosed in CSO 699, Minute 2195/1879.

22. *Blue Book. 1878*, JJ: 14–15.

23. CSO 1925, Minute C177/1878.

24. Ibid.

25. *Blue Book. 1878*, JJ: 15.

26. See the returns in SNA 1/6/11, no. 20.

27. Cf. CSO 1925, Minutes 4400 and 4015/1878 and the report in the *Natal Witness*, 12 November 1878.

28. CSO 1972, Minute 4887/1878: Resident Magistrate, Newcastle, to the Colonial Secretary, 19 December 1878.

29. Weenen Letter Books, vol. 6/1/2, 1875–1882, p. 353: Boast to Paterson, 11 January 1879.

30. GH 1411, pp. 30–31: Lieutenant-Governor to the Colonial Secretary, 20 May 1879.

31. In CSO 686, Minute 819/1879.

32. See the correspondence in CSO 666, Minute 4195/1878.

33. CSO 686, Minute 819/1879: Allison to the Colonial Secretary, 20 July 1878, and to Lloyd, 31 January 1879.

34. CSO 681, Minute 349/1879: Lieutenant-Governor to the Colonial Secretary, 16 January 1879.

35. In CSO 680, Minute 285/1879.

36. CSO 681, Minute 345/1879: Lloyd to the Colonial Secretary, 14 January 1879. Cf. SNA 1/6/11, no. 20: Lloyd to Acting Secretary for Native Affairs, 20 February 1879.

37. In CSO 1925, Minute 23/1879.

38. *NGG*, vol. XXXI, no. 1764, 8 August 1879: Government Notice no. 155.

39. *Blue Book. 1879*, JJ: 19.

40. In GH 1421, Minute 505/1879; and CSO 686, Minute 819/1879 and CSO 1972, Minute 505/1879.

41. In GH 1421, Minute 564/1879.

42. In GH 1421, p. 35; and CSO 2630, Minute 668/1879.

43. CSO 715, Minute 3830/1879, sub–enc. Minute 3472/1879: Paterson to the Colonial Secretary, 16 July 1879.

44. In CSO 699, Minute 2195/1879. Also see CSO 684, Minute 601/1879 and CSO 1972, Minute 704/1879.

45. CSO 699, Minute 2195/1879: Lloyd to the Colonial Secretary, 3 May 1879.

46. SNA 1/6/13, no. 49: Paterson to the Colonial Secretary, 8 February 1879. SNA 1/6/11, no. 20: Lloyd to the Acting Secretary for Native Affairs, 20 February 1879.

47. Report in the *Natal Colonist*, 6 March 1879.

48. In ibid., 27 February and 1 March 1879; CSO 715, Minute 3830/1879, sub–enc. Minute 3472/1879: Paterson to the Colonial Secretary, 16 July 1879. The second report estimates that the main buildings and stables were defensible by a hundred.

49. Report in the *Natal Colonist*, 6 March 1879.

50. Paterson's report in the *Blue Book. 1879*, JJ: 19.

51. See the statements in note 9. Lloyd was also keen to obtain bayonets for the Enfields (see the correspondence in CSO 690, Minute 1299/1879).

52. Report in the *Natal Colonist*, 11 February 1879. Cf. Paterson's report in the *Blue Book. 1879*, JJ: 19.

53. In *B.P.P.* (C. 2318), no. 7.

54. In CSO 699, Minute 2195/1879.

55. *B.P.P.* (C. 2318), no. 7.

56. CSO 685, Minute 735/1879 and CSO 699, Minute 2195/1879: Lloyd to the Colonial Secretary, 3 February 1879; GH 569, Minute 1254/1879: Lloyd to the Colonial Secretary, 20 February 1879; CSO 699, Minute 2195/1879: Lloyd to the Colonial Secretary, 3 May 1879.

57. GH 569, Minute 1254/1879: Lloyd to the Colonial Secretary, 20 February 1879; CSO 699, Minute 2195/1879: Lloyd to the Colonial Secretary, 3 May 1879.

58. Cf. the reports in the *Natal Colonist*, 1 April 1879, and in GH 1423, Minute 1222/79, and the statements in note 10.

59. *Times of Natal*, 23 April 1879. Cf. CSO 1973, Minute 2018/1879.

60. See the correspondence in CSO 686, Minute 819/1879.

61. See p. 262.

62. *Blue Book. 1879*, JJ: 19.

63. *Blue Book. 1878*, JJ: 15–16.

64. *Blue Book. 1879*, JJ: 20.

65. Ibid., JJ: 21; SNA 1/1/33, no. 76.

66. Paterson's report, in the *Blue Book. 1879*, JJ: 20; Reports in the *Natal Colonist*, 1, 4 and 13 March 1879.

67. In CSO 2553, Minute C849/1879.

68. This matter is treated in J. P. C. Laband, 'Bulwer, Chelmsford and the Border Levies', *Theoria*, no. 57, October 1981, pp. 1–15.

69. CSO 678, Minute 96/1879: Lloyd to the Colonial Secretary, 4 January 1879.

70. GH 1423, Minute 1222/1879: Lieutenant-Governor to the Lieutenant-General [n.d.].

71. This is from a collation of the information in the correspondence in SNA 1/6/12, no. 88, the statements on the defensive state of the district (see note 10), and Lloyd's map showing the defensive posts, 3 March 1879, in CSO 690, Minute 1282/1879.

72. SNA 1/6/12, no. 77: Paterson's 'Report upon the raising of a Native Levy for the defence of Weenen County,' 11 March 1879.

73. See note 10.

74. CSO 696, Minute 1884/1879: Lloyd to the Secretary to the Defence Committee, 3 April 1879; Reports in the *Natal Colonist*, 27 March and 1 April 1879.

75. See note 10.

76. SNA 1/6/15, no. 15: Allison to the Secretary for Native Affairs, 14 May 1879.

77. CSO 1926, Minute 1008/1879: Allison to the Colonial Secretary, 11 February 1879; reports in the *Natal Colonist*, 23 and 25 January 1879.

78. See the correspondence in CSO 686, Minute 819/1879.

79. See the correspondence in SNA 1/1/33, no. 21.

80. CSO 686, Minute 819/1879: Allison to Lloyd, 2 March 1879.

81. Weenen Letter Book 6/1/2 p. 357: Boast to Paterson, 4 March 1879.

82. CSO 686, Minute 819/1879: Allison to Lloyd, 2 March 1879.

83. Weenen Letter Book 6/1/2 p. 357: Boast to Paterson, 3 March 1879.

84. *Natal Witness*, 20 March 1879.

85. CSO 696, Minute 1884/1879: Lloyd to the Secretary of the Defence Committee, 3 April 1879.

86. Ibid., and CSO 1926, Minute 2062/1879: Allison to [Colonial Secretary], 15 April 1879.

87. Cf. Paterson's reports in the *Blue Book. 1879*, JJ: 19, and in SNA 1/6/12, no. 77.

88. CSO 715, Minute 3830/1879: Lloyd to the Colonial Secretary, 26 June 1879.

89. Report in the *Natal Colonist*, 13 March 1879.

90. See CSO 715, Minute 3830/1879: reports to the Colonial Secretary of Lloyd, 25 June 1879, and Paterson, 16 July 1879.

91.   It is not clear when, but the Volunteer Corps in the imperial service were disbanded in July, and it seems unlikely the Weenen Yeomanry would have remained in the field any later, indeed if that long.

92.   Report for 1879 of the Resident Magistrate, Umsinga Division, in the 'Natal Blue Book for Native Affairs' (in the Natal Archives), p. 31.

93.   In SNA 1/6/16, no. 77.

'The Zulus are Coming!'

The defence of Pietermaritzburg, 1879

P.S. THOMPSON

On the morning of Friday, 24 January 1879, the white residents of Pietermaritzburg found themselves with a temporary scarcity of domestic servants. About seven o'clock Barbara Buchanan went into the kitchen, where she met a servant of several years service who remained. 'Oh, Inkosazan, you will be very sad today.' 'Why, Tembu?' she asked. He replied: 'Wait till Master goes to the office.'[1] During the night two officers had ridden down from Greytown with the report of the British army's defeat at Isandlwana to the government authorities.[2] If Buchanan is correct, then the news of it must have spread informally and quickly in advance among the black population. They could expect scant protection in the event emboldened Zulu raided the enemy seat of power, and fled to families and refugees in the country.[3] The outflow of blacks was followed by an inflow of whites into the city. On Sunday one householder wrote, as though there were nothing atypical in it at the time, that he had just lodged a friend with five children, in from the border, and let two rooms to another country family.[4] Some white persons found the city unsafe in any case, and apparently left for Durban and the sure safety of a ship ready to sail.[5]

The fact is that the arrangements for defence of Pietermaritzburg were meagre and imperfect. Apparently no one had believed that the Zulu posed a threat – certainly not with British forces martialed against them. So undaunting had Lord Chelmsford's prospects been that the civic leaders had not even considered defence against the Zulu. Instead, they had appealed to citizens to organise against the possibility of disorder among local blacks misled by false rumours of a British reverse.

To be fair to the city's leaders, it must be added that the colonial government had not greatly inspired their effort. The Lieutenant-Governor of Natal, Sir Henry Bulwer, loath to abet a war fever, feared that any elaboration of defensive preparations might generate insecurity among the colony's inhabitants rather than otherwise. When pressed by Lord Chelms-ford, commander of the imperial forces, he did make them, in connection with the imperial offensive preparations.[6] He divided the colony into seven defensive districts and detailed advice for their protection.[7] At that time (3 December 1878) he designated the city of Pietermaritzburg a separate sub-district, and then (24 December) placed it under Lieutenant-Colonel Charles Bullen Hugh Mitchell, R.M., the new Colonial Secretary and Acting Commandant of Volunteers.[8]

By this time the Town Council of Pietermaritzburg had decided to act on its own. The passage of imperial troops through to the front created excitement amongst the townspeople, while the concomitant reduction of the imperial garrison at Fort Napier, at the west end of the city, caused some uneasiness. The *Times of Natal*, the evening newspaper, remarked (4 November 1878): 'Nearly all the troops in town have been sent on to near the Tugela River. . . . We have only a company of the 2–24th in garrison . . .'. More troops were on the way – and also would pass through – and very probably the colonial units, the Volunteer Corps, would be called out to follow them. The city correspondent of the Durban *Natal Advertizer* recorded his foreboding:

> Today is the anniversary of the Bushman's Pass affair [in 1873] – the Natalian Waterloo. The monument on the Market Square to the volunteers who lost their lives on that occasion, has been suitably decorated with evergreens [,] flowers etc. There is a strong probability that by the 4th of next November other volunteers will have died for their country and we may have need of more marble.[9]

The Mayor of Pietermaritzburg, Wesley Francis, and one of the Town Councillors, Mr Topham, interviewed the Lieutenant-Governor. Sir Henry agreed that they should take defensive precautionary steps, but asked that they do so quietly, in order not to cause unnecessary excitement.[10] They convened a meeting at the Town Office on Friday, 8 November, and those assembled unanimously resolved in favour of a temporary increase of police supervision, through the Mayor's enrolment of a city guard or special constables. When at least 50 men were enrolled, the guard would meet to adopt rules and regulations for the organization. The Mayor advertised this resolution and the opening of the roll to volunteers at the Town Office.[11]

The leaders of the guard movement had proceeded perhaps too quietly. The meeting was small and no notice had been posted for it in advance[12] – and so it appeared secretive. Resentment was expressed in the press.[13] By the end of the month only 15 men had enrolled.[14] At the current rate, the *Natal*

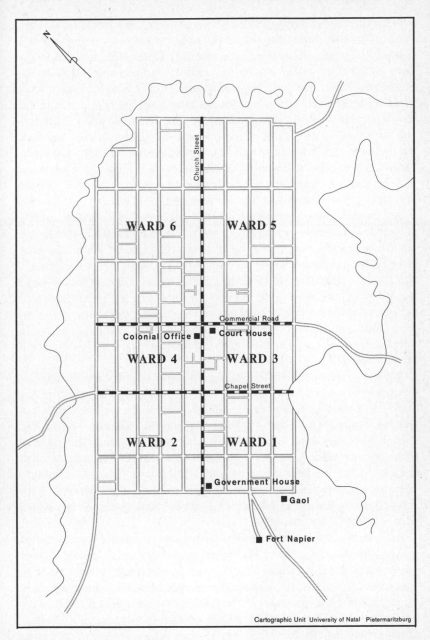

Pietermaritzburg ward boundaries, 1879.

Witness (the city's morning paper) observed dryly, the City Guard was not likely to become formidable before the end of the century.[15] But war was imminent. The Natal Carbineers, the mounted Volunteer Corps in the city, were called into service on 23 November;[16] and it seemed as if the Maritzburg Rifles, their infantry counterpart, might follow to the front.[17] Their departure would leave the city without any organized protective unit. It turned out that the Rifles stayed; however, they numbered just 109 officers and men,[18] and they were trained to conventional military warfare and were not available for constabulary duty. There was the Natal Rifle Association, for which no statement of numbers has been found; it consisted of burghers, too, but functioned primarily to enable them to practice shooting.[19] Neither organization was a substitute for the envisaged City Guard.

A requisition placed in the Market House at the end of November quickly garnered more signatures than the guard roll, and obliged the Mayor to call another, genuinely public meeting to consider defence.[20] An enthusiastic crowd filled the Theatre Royal the evening of Friday, 6 December. Francis explained his past action, and then the meeting opened. Several men spoke to the matter at hand, also to the imprudence or not of the Volunteer Corps being sent to the front, which occasioned some sharp exchange; however, the assemblage endorsed the establishment of a city guard – and straight away a table was brought into the hall and a roll laid upon it, which more than 50 men signed.[21]

The list was transferred to the Market House the next day, and the number of signatures soon reached more than 90.[22] The evening of Monday the 9th, there was a meeting to organize the guard. Francis resisted the suggestion that he actually lead the City Guard; indeed, he was shown not even to have signed the roll, and hastily did so in bad grace. The majority then voted to exclude from decisions those who had not enrolled. Francis had the latter leave the hall, which created a brief but ugly scene. Finally a committee was elected to draft a plan of organization.[23] They met on the 11th and presented rules and regulations to a general meeting on the 16th, which approved with slight changes.[4]

As formally constituted, the City Guard was a burgher force, divided among four districts. District No. 1 comprised city wards 1 and 3; District No. 2 wards 2 and 4; District No. 3 ward 5; and District No. 4 ward 6. Residents in each district organized their own sub-unit, whose members elected a leader and sub-leader.[25] The leader (or sub-leader) kept a list of the men and their residences, and had to be notified of a change of address or absence from the city for any length of time. When directed to do so, the leader embodied a sixth of the guard in his district for patrol duty, and attempted to insure that this duty fell equally. When a leader or sub-leader was not present, the others on duty elected one of themselves acting leader. Only in the emergencies were there night patrols, and no one had to patrol then longer than three hours. A room or tent in the district was designated the rendezvous or rallying place of the guard, and it was occupied nightly. Provision was made as well for special mounted patrols in the immediate neighbourhood of the city.[26]

The leaders and sub-leaders of the districts elected a general leader, with whom they constituted a permanent committee which framed by-laws, according to which they could make regulations to carry out their duties. The general leader convoked the committee or the entire guard, and decided, the Mayor concurring, when to call up the guard.[27] The leaders and sub-leaders elected were, respectively, E. Owen and W. Lister in District No. 1; J.H. Spence and J. Baverstock in District No. 2; W. Francis and M. Pincus in District No. 3; and J. Ashmore and W. Hodgkins in District No. 4. They elected Lieutenant-Colonel Mitchell the general leader.[28] In the circumstances Mitchell had appreciable power. His other positions bespoke his authority in civil affairs and his experience in military matters; and, judging from the recriminations that had characterized the defence movement, the jealousies of the burghers were such that a man of his social status was needed to give the guard cohesion.[29] All in all, he was likely to get his way in arrangements for defence. The Mayor and Town Council seemed quite ready to acquiesce. If guardsmen were not, then 20 or more of them could requisition a general meeting.[30] No record of their having done so has been found.

The purpose of the City Guard was also clarified. The initial resolution in favour of the guard had referred vaguely to sustaining 'the existing condition of things within and on the Border of the Colony'.[31] Attention was soon directed to very much within. The *Advertiser's* correspondent wrote on 5 December:

> The natives here are getting restless, and evidently cannot properly understand matters. They are leaving service in large numbers; once they make up their minds to go, nothing, apparently will stop or dissuade them. Everyone of the Corporation Kafirs has gone, and the advisability of obtaining some of the newly-arrived Coolies is being considered.[32]

(He noted particularly the absence of those employed by the Sanitary Committee.[33]) Lieutenant-Colonel Mitchell told the City Guard meeting which approved the by-laws (30 December):

It is undoubtedly considered necessary that we should have such an organisation as was proposed, in order to prevent confusion in case of a little feeling getting up among the Kafirs from the idea that they were not getting the worst of it on the other side of the border.[34]

Little more than a fortnight later the *Witness* stated that the City Guard was aimed at countering disruption by certain local blacks inspired by rumours of a military defeat.[35] At a guard meeting on 23 January Mitchell again spoke to the point: the purpose was 'to protect the City internally in case of any disturbance arising possibly from [a] slight reverse being magnified in the report made of it to the natives or some other like case.'[36]

Of course, it is impossible now to gauge the feeling of apprehension among the white population of the city; nor is it clear whether a rising or a riot was uppermost in their minds in this case. Their sense of vulnerability is not surprising. An official statement to the Defence Committee of the Legislative Council, dated 22 November 1878, reckoned there were 4 724 Europeans and 2 839 Natives in the city;[37] however, a statement for the surrounding Umgeni Division of Pietermaritzburg County reckoned 2 364 and 52 020 inhabitants, respectively.[38] A British visitor put it succinctly a few years later: 'There is one great peculiarity which must strike a traveller on coming into Natal, and to which not even the dust of Pietermaritzburg can avail to blind his eyes – I mean the predominance of the black race over the white. Here you are really among the Kafirs and Zulus.'[39]

The City Guard should have been set to prosper, but it did not. Members had to take the oath as special constables. Mitchell and 61 men did so promptly,[40] but others hung back, so that by 23 January with 108 men enrolled,[41] probably just over half had taken the oath.[42] What inhibited the growth of the organization? The *Witness* described the major objections to it under five heads: (1) The guard was unnecessary. (2) Enrolment could wait until such time as it became necessary. (3) The special constable's oath also made one liable for ordinary police duties. (4) In an emergency the men would be obliged to leave their families when they should remain to protect them. (5) The Lieutenant-Governor could get all the men needed if only he would proclaim martial law. The *Witness* explained that the third and fifth points were untenable legally, and that the fourth was specious in fact. The City Guard, it argued, was a force for a contingency and to be effective must be organized now and not during the contingency.[43]

The real block to further enrolment apparently was indifference. 'Only Waiting To Be Asked' wrote to the *Witness* to find out where he could read a copy of the regulations and take the oath[44] – and so, fulminated the *Times of*

Natal, Maritzburg deserved to be called 'Sleepy Hollow', if recruits had to be personally canvassed.[45] The authorities could be slow, too. The City Guard was not required to drill, but it was supposed to develop a practical knowledge of the rifle.[46] The Mayor, go-between for the Town Council (representing the guard) and the colonial authorities,[47] arranged for the storage of rifles and ammunition in the Town Office; however, they had to be transferred to the Police Station for security.[48] An instructor was engaged from the military at the fort for practice weekdays at 6 a.m. and 5 p.m. and Saturdays at 3 p.m.[49] The first Saturday (18 January) a large number of the guard arrived at the Police Station, when it was discovered that there was in fact no ammunition. The men went home in a bad humour. The following Monday the committee of the guard learned that the ammunition had been ordered but somehow gone astray! Lieutenant-Colonel Mitchell promised to look into the matter.[50]

The City Guard seemed to be foundering. On 13 and 20 January the committee met to consider its continuance or dissolution,[51] and on the 23rd a public meeting urged that the guard continue. Mitchell pointed out that he needed at least 216 men to implement his arrangements. Captain Albert Henry Hime, the Colonial Engineer, led 28 more men to enroll. Mitchell said that he would gladly continue, but in the circumstances he would have to fall back on a different organization than that originally proposed.[52]

* * * * *

Ever since the commencement of the Anglo-Zulu War on 11 January the atmosphere in Pietermaritzburg had been tense with expectation. Rumours of Zulu forces at the Thukela, even of their getting an upper hand, flew about so that the *Witness* complained that the government did not publicize the earliest correct information from the front to scotch them.[53] Now there was correct information. Friday the 24th dawned still and bright. Walter Stafford and Harry Davis, officers of the Natal Native Contingent who had been at Isandlwana, arrived with the first official report of the defeat. Stafford later wrote:

> It was at daybreak, tired and dead beat that Maritzburg was reached and we arrived at the Government House just as the native was preparing to light the fire. I woke up the Hon. W. Lyttleton and handed him the despatches who led us up to Sir Bartle Frere's room. After a detailed description we were instructed to go to our hotel and not say a word.

In those days the post cart ran from Maritzburg to Kokstad and passed through my father's farm at Stafford's Post and as I met Baartman Uys the driver I asked him to tell my people we had met with a disaster but that Harry Davis and myself were well.

He must have told the news to one or two friends as the news spread through Maritzburg like wildfire . . .[54]

The report of Isandlwana produced a memorable sense of fear and alarm.

The whole thing is at this moment as distinct as if it were only yesterday. The dim feeling of undefined awe, when it was whispered that news had been brought of the disaster. Then the questions hurriedly asked of the highest colonial official obtainable; the answer, 'The news is just as bad as it can be;' the question as to who was known to be killed; the reply again, 'Durnford's killed for certain, and Scott, and at least half the Carbineers.'[55]

The government issued a short account of the defeat, based on the recent report of the two officers from Lord Chelmsford's column. Again Saturday morning, the 25th, groups of people gathered on the streets and little business was transacted.[56] At the behest of a civic deputation the authorities issued a summary of a despatch received from the General himself,[57] which was posted at the Colonial Office on Church Street. Late in the afternoon the post-cart arrived from Greytown, and out climbed the ill, tired correspondent of the London *Standard*, Charles Norris-Newman, with authentic information from the General's army.[58] A crowd pressed round and would not let him go until he had related, however briefly, what had happened. He then delivered letters for Sir Bartle Frere, the High Commissioner, and other officials. The *Times of Natal*, for which Norris-Newman was special correspondent, got to work on an extra with his news.[59] In a few hours both the government and the newspaper issued lists of the missing among the Volunteers and Mounted Police.[60] Of the Carbineers who had gone into Zululand, nearly two-fifths were lost.[61] The correspondent observed: 'Crowds gathered about the newspaper office, eager to scan the printed list and see whether any of those known and dear to them were among the lost, and the scene was sad and striking for those who witnessed it.'[62] Barbara Buchanan has explained: 'Pietermaritzburg was a small town and its people were linked by close friendship ties, and a very large percentage of families had sent a member to the front.'[63]

The civic leaders had envisaged nothing more than disorder among the local blacks; now they had that as well as the contingency of a Zulu invasion to anticipate. The City Guard turned out, also for night patrol, but they, along with the Maritzburg Rifles, the Natal Rifle Association and possibly the troops at the fort, could scarcely defend the city against a marauding Zulu *impi*. In this crisis Lieutenant-Colonel Mitchell implemented his new arrangements for defence. Doubtless he consulted his colleagues, especially those also with military experience and responsibilities, but it seems that he alone made the decisions which counted for the defence of Pietermaritzburg. He established a laager in the centre of the city, where the townspeople could take refuge and provide for their own protection.

At that time 'laager' meant an enclosure, a wall behind which settlers with firearms could repel more numerous blacks with spears. The wall might be of wood, as when the Boers had drawn up their wagons at Blood River; or of brick, stone, even earth thrown up, as communities, Boer and British, constructed when they had settled. Such laagers existed in the veld, or in country centres, where they were joined to magistrates' buildings. None had been constructed in a town the size of Pietermaritzburg. The city posed special problems. It was not a case of rural folk in small numbers gathering in a narrow enclosure, but of city folk – and probably some rural folk, too – gathering in relatively great numbers, so that the enclosure must be large. Mitchell planned in terms of city blocks.

On Saturday, the 25th, he had posted at the Colonial Office a notice, 'A Few Hints to the Inhabitants of the City',[64] which named certain buildings which should be combined in a laager, whither the burghers should repair in the event of an emergency: 400 men, women and children into the magistrate's offices, the nearby Treasury and Presbyterian church; 500 into the court-house; 700 into the Native High Court and the adjacent stone building; 800 into the Colonial Office and adjoining stores along Commercial Road; another 800 into the houses along Church Street from the Colonial Office to Timber Street and down to Pietermaritz Street; and finally 800 into those along Longmarket Street between the Native church and Timber Street. The guns which normally signalled the mails and other occasions were to cease (with the sole exception of the eight-o'clock gun); henceforth three guns fired in rapid succession would be the call to laager, with two or three hours to spare; but a fourth gun would mean come in with all speed. Preparations for a stay in the laager should be made in advance, including items such as bedding and cooking and eating utensils packed each evening for instant dispatch, and food, already cooked if possible, to last a week. Entry to the laager should be calm and orderly, and inside all must obey the reasonable orders of the commandant or his deputy. Sanitation would be enforced strictly – each family should bring a small broom and scrubbing brush, a supply of disinfectant, and two pails (one for water, the other for night soil) – and the 'hints' ended with the warning that the inmates of the laager must prepare themselves for many unwonted and irksome domestic duties, and that 'a display of cheerfulness under the novel and trying circumstances will serve to lighten their difficulties.'[65]

The posting of this memorandum added to the popular alarm, as some supposed that it was prompted by more unfavourable news which the government had not imparted.[66] After all, the colonial authorities in the offices at the upper end of the city would go to the strong stone gaol for protection, and, of course, the military would look after themselves in the fort.[67]

The Sunday morning services, in churches hung in black, were accompanied by the noise of work on the laager.[68] The Maritzburg Rifles turned out as a fatigue party, and Chinese carpenters, coloured government labourers, and a large number of convicts sent down from the gaol, joined them in the erection of barricades and alterations to buildings for defence. Wagons rattled along the street with ammunition and stores for the laager strongholders. The intense activity was at once alarming and assuring to anxious onlookers.[69] Towards evening Lord Chelmsford and part of his staff arrived, which increased anxiety but then eased it, for he brought news that the Zulu had retired from the border.[70] None the less the work on the laager continued through the night, the next day and the following night, while business remained almost totally suspended. At last the block bounded by Church and Longmarket Streets, Timber Street and Commercial Road, and most of the buildings on block to the north, were enclosed. Between buildings packing cases filled with earth or sacks similarly filled were laid up on each other to make the barriers; but where communication required covered ways, obstructing walls were broken down. Gaps were left for traffic on Church Street, but with material close by to fill the archways quickly. The buildings were barricaded and loopholed, and heavy shutters fitted for the larger government ones. Of course, doorways were left to be closed up at the last minute.[71] The Colonial Engineer saw to the sinking of three wells inside the laager, and checked two tanks, which together could hold three thousand gallons (12 270 litres), on top of the court-house.[72] The Town Council consulted Mitchell about food stores, and duly provided 300 sacks of mealie-meal, 140 tons of mealies, 10 tons of rice and 10 tons of salt, and the sellers agreed to hold them in readiness free of charge (for the first month); they also had the dead trees in the park cut and brought to the rear of the Town Office for firewood.[73]

Mitchell issued another memorandum on the 28th, describing the extent of the laager and dividing it into wards congregating the residents of the

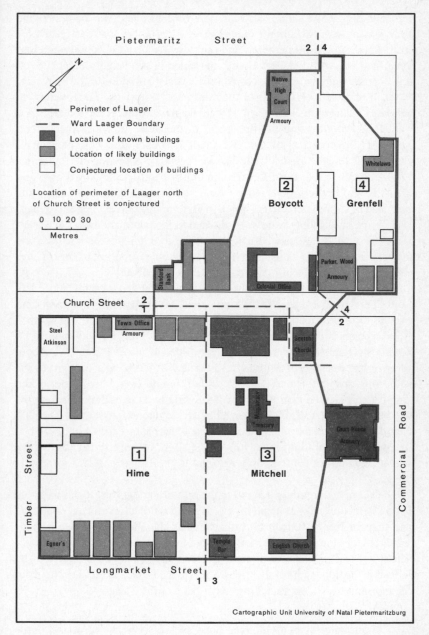

Pietermaritzburg Laager, 1879.

corresponding City Guard districts.[74] A fortnight later he perfected the arrangement with two further memoranda. An armoury was designated for each of the four 'ward laagers', and each ward laager was subdivided into three sections, with the City Guard integrated in the laager defence. Each ward laager was placed under a military officer; in addition to the whole, Mitchell himself took charge of the third one, comprising the government buildings adjacent to Commercial Road; Captain Hime, R.E., took the first ward laager, comprising the remainder of the block up to Timber Street; Major W. Boycott, late of the 29th (and, curiously, also commandant of Colonial Defensive District No. 3), the second, comprising the buildings across Church Street from the Colonial Office to the Standard Bank; and Major F. W. Grenfell, 60th Rifles, the fourth, comprising those along the west side of Commercial Road down to Pietermaritz Street. The City Guard leaders and sub-leaders were subordinated to the commandants. Each ward laager also had an orderly officer, an officer to complete the barriers, two officers to distribute arms, and the three section superintendents. These officers were named and their special duties described.[75]

The laager was not quite finished when it seemed that it might be needed. Lord Chelmsford had been in the city a week. Mitchell's latest memorandum seemed to relieve fears, and work on the laager evidently slowed down.[76] (Lord Chelmsford wrote privately: 'The townspeople, although in a fright, are however terribly apathetic, and give little or no assistance.'[77]) About seven in the evening of Monday, 3 February, a messenger brought to the authorities disquieting news, which spread abroad several hours later, when the post-cart arrived from Greytown: the Zulu had crossed the Thukela the day before, the people of Greytown had already gone into laager! The City Guard was out and patrolled the night; the Maritzburg Rifles stood watch at the government buildings; the work on the laager was pressed again.[78] There was no signal, but some people resorted to the laager and had to be sent home.[79]

The alarm apparently extended to the military at the fort. It was said that Lord Chelmsford stayed up all night, his horse saddled for any eventuality;[80] and that Sir Henry Bulwer and his staff had their bedding as well as the Government House records moved to the fortified gaol for safe-keeping.[81] The story is told of the wife of an officer (himself in besieged Eshowe), who lodged in the upper part of the town. She was awakened in the early hours of the morning by violent knocking at the door of the house.

'Who's there?'

'*I* am here; open the door at once, please!' was the response, in the well-known voice of a staff officer of the garrison.

'What in the name of goodness can you or anyone want at this hour?' asked the lady.

'I have come on purpose to escort you and your family to the jail – the Zulus are coming!' (this in a very loud voice indeed), 'and his Excellency the Governor and nearly everybody else are there already!' said the staff officer.

'Indeed, I cannot come!' replied the lady.

'Indeed, you must!' said, in earnest and broken tones, the staff officer.

'Indeed, then, I will do nothing of the kind! I am in bed, and intend to stay there!'

This ended the exchange. The officer rushed off elsewhere, but not before he roused the lady's two servants, thrust horse-pistols into their hands, and, tears in his eyes, abjured them to defend their mistress and her babies with their lives.[82]

The excitement increased in the morning. The shutters were fixed in the laager – ostensibly to forgo any confusion in the event of the alarm! And then, in the evening, a notice was posted outside the Colonial Office, which stated that in fact all was quiet at the border.[83]

On Wednesday the work on the laager and the patrols and watches continued.[84] Although the city was again peaceful, morale had been shaken – the *Witness* remarked that only strong military reinforcements would restore the feeling of confidence and security.[85]

Reinforcements soon began to arrive in the colony, but even before they could be an assurance to the colonists, Sir Henry Bulwer suggested toward the end of February that Mitchell might be subordinated to the military commander at the fort,[86] Lieutenant-Colonel W. Lambert (of the 88th Regiment),[87] in the same way that the commandants of the colonial defensive districts at the border had been subordinated to the imperial military officers in charge of the lines of communication; however, no record of the Pietermaritzburg sub-district having been similarly assigned has been found. It is likely that Lieutenant-Colonel Lambert preferred not to have the added responsibility.

* * * * *

The Pietermaritzburg laager probably was finished about the middle of February, when Lieutenant-Colonel Mitchell issued the last directives for manning and occupation. According to returns for March it contained 740

Swinburne Henry rifles and 428 Swinburne Henry carbines, with 319 200 rounds of ammunition. At the gaol were 184 Snider rifles and 381 Snider carbines, with 83 000 rounds. At his immediate disposal were the Maritzburg Rifles, under Captain G.O. Matterson, with 4 officers and 98 men, and 4 to 9 Mounted Police.[88] Probably the local rifle association was subsumed in the City Guard, which, augmented by the other able-bodied men there, would man the laager.

There were no more near-panics. On 27 February several people thought that they heard the report of the signal guns, but these proved to be three detonations from blasting work on the Town Hill.[89] At another time some mischievous person reportedly struck a large tank thrice to make sounds like the guns and frightened a few people in the immediate vicinity from their beds.[90]

The passage of time demonstrated that the Zulu strategy was defensive and that the local black population was passive. Apropos of the latter, the City Guard was regarded as a deterrent to their disorder. Early in February it was reported to have captured two blacks, mounted and carrying ten rounds apiece; however, they were let go when they proved not to be Zulu.[91] Later on a guard chased a mounted and armed black man down West Street to Government House. The man explained that he had escaped at Rorke's Drift and got a government horse at Ladysmith, and he was also allowed to go.[92] The *Times of Natal* praised the City Guard for having caught many blacks who might have been intent on robbery.[93] How many has not been ascertained, but the two specific reports cited suggest that suspects were treated leniently.

A few days after the first excitement, Barbara Buchanan asked Tembu, the family servant who had stayed, if he would not go home. He answered that his brother was taking care of his wife, and said that his people were on the alert and would be warned in ample time of any Zulu inroad.[94] The *Natal Colonist*'s Pietermaritzburg correspondent wrote on 28 January: 'Our own natives have shown loyalty and determination to defend their homes, and see little threat, though many still being savage [,] deceit and treachery is their stock-in-trade.'[95] This ambivalence seems to have carried over to the official arrangements for their protection. The laager was constructed with a view to protecting the whites, and yet it soon became apparent that it must accommodate others. In his memorandum of 28 January Mitchell permitted each family to bring in one reliable servant – all other blacks should go to Fort Napier or the gaol. Indians and coloured would be admitted to the laager without regard to number; however, neither they nor the black servants would occupy any part of the buildings reserved for whites – a place would be set apart for them.[96]

By the end of February, when black auxiliaries began passing through the city to reinforce the troops (white and black) at the border, the matter of protecting the black populace struck an ironic chord for the authorities. Sir Henry Bulwer inquired after it, and Mitchell asked Colonel W. Bellairs, the Deputy Adjutant-General, how many could be taken in at Fort Napier. Bellairs suggested 500, but Mitchell estimated that there might be as many as 5 000, of whom two-fifths would be able-bodied men. Bellairs suggested that 500 come to the fort, an equal number go to the gaol, and the rest enter the city laager. This would be impracticable, according to Mitchell – not

Lieutenant-Colonel Charles Bullen Hugh Mitchell, R. M.

Pietermaritzburg from Fort Napier.

even a quarter of that number could be admitted to the laager. Mitchell also rejected an alternative proposal that the men be armed and posted, under white leaders, to defend other important buildings around the city. At last Bellairs agreed that the 4 000 blacks could take refuge at the fort, but their protection there seems to have received no further attention.[97]

The Maritzburg Rifles continued to mount guard at the court-house throughout February.[98] The City Guard continued to patrol the streets, even at night, until the last week of the month;[99] however, mounted patrols in the outskirts of town seem to have ceased at least a week before then.[100] Enthusiasm was getting so thin that some men avoided duty on the slenderest pretexts.[101] The leaders were so disgusted that they decided to post the shirkers' names for public derision.[102] Obviously there was no longer real need for the patrols, and they were discontinued; however, it was agreed that the guard would remain in existence and hold meetings, shooting competitions and the like from time to time.[103]

Captain Hime, commandant of the first ward laager, heard that some able-bodied bachelors intended to go to the fort instead of the laager in an emergency, and asked that they be assigned to defend detached outbuildings there, if that were the case. Mitchell was concerned, and warned that chaos could result in the laager if the manning problem were not settled; however, Sir Henry reminded him that the military commander at the fort no doubt would assume overall command in an emergency, and there would be time enough for Mitchell and him to dispose of the matter satisfactorily then.[104] Second thoughts about Mitchell's defensive arrangements were also expressed in letters to the newspapers. These scored abandonment of most of the city in favour of defending its inner precinct. There were calls for the fortification of selected buildings around town, without regard to an enclosure, as was the case in Durban.[105] Lieutenant Robert Holliday, of the Maritzburg Rifles, proposed a system of inner and outer defences, as though the city could expect a European-style siege.[106]

These examples of revision betoken the restoration of a sense of confidence and security, even the imminence of peace. At length the *Witness* opined (26 April): 'The defensive arrangements in the City are regarded as belonging to the pre-historic period. The City Guard has ceased to patrol the streets. The provisions [for the laager] collected by the municipal authorities are being sold off, at a great sacrifice.'

The war was distant. Involvement in it consisted chiefly in occasional moral demonstrations, such as the launching of and contributing to a fund for the relief of the widows and children of those who had been lost at Isandlwana,[107] and then other memorial funds and testimonials,[108] which probably affected only a stratum of white society. By mid-July the war was virtually over. The government authorities and public servants had gone through the motions of greeting Sir Garnet Wolseley and taking leave of Lord Chelmsford. The Town Council and citizens of Pietermaritzburg prepared to welcome home the Natal Carbineers from the front,[109] and there were complaints of the disorderliness of other soldiers, now passing back through the city to the coast.[110] On 12 July the sacks of earth around the court-house were being removed,[111] and within a few days the barricades were coming down. The arches across Church Street fell, and the heavy shutters for the government buildings were taken away.[112] (The *Witness* wondered if the dismantling of the laager was not premature[113] and asked rather plaintively: 'Could not some portion be left as a monument?'[114]) The last of the arms and ammunition was taken from the court-house.[115] The return of these to the military would also signify the end of the City Guard. Finally, it was announced that from 22 July signals for the mails would be resumed by the cannon at Fort Napier.[116]

The defence of Pietermaritzburg is a peripheral episode of the Anglo-Zulu War. None the less it is instructive, for an account sheds light on the acts and reveals something of the attitudes of the city's inhabitants – or at least of the white settlers. These inhabitants seem to have been slow to consider organizing for self-defence. The imperial garrison at Fort Napier had probably been an assurance for so long that when it was reduced for war at the border, the townspeople still retained some of the old sense of security. A City Guard was promoted by conjuring with their fear of an admittedly unlikely local black irruption, and nearly collapsed because of the maladroitness of the promoters. On the eve of the war the Colonial Secretary, an officer whom the squabbling burghers could respect, intervened and gave it belated credibility. Suddenly, within a fortnight of the war's commencement, the city was apparently threatened not only by disorder at home but by attack from across the border. In consternation the settlers submitted to the same officer, now commandant, who established a laager and directed measures for their security. (The laager served for the protection of whites, and of the relatively few Indians and coloureds as an afterthought; it excluded the mass of blacks, who might have been represented as a kind of Trojan horse in the circumstances.) This system of defence was never tested – the twin threats soon dissolved – yet it was a sensible, military arrangement, and probably would have stood a test.

[Previously published in *Journal of Natal & Zulu History*, VI, 1983.]

Notes

1. Barbara I. Buchanan, *Pioneer Days in Natal*, Pietermaritzburg, 1934, p. 113.

2. Walter H. Stafford, 'Stirring Days of Old Times: A Story of Isandhlwana', (manuscript in the Killie Campbell Africana Library), pp. 13–14; Allan F. Hattersley, *Pietermaritzburg Panorama*, Pietermaritzburg, 1938, p. 69; Charles L. Norris-Newman, *In Zululand with the British throughout the War of 1879*, London, 1880, p. 74. Buchanan states that the officers came late the preceding evening.

3. See Buchanan, *Pioneer Days*, pp. 113–14.

4. From a private letter, dated Pietermaritzburg, 26 January 1879, quoted in *The Graphic*, 15 March 1879, reproduced in *The First Six Months of the Zulu War As Reported in 'The Graphic'*, compiled by S. Bourquin, Durban, 1963, p. 30. Cf. Marina King, *Sunrise to Evening Star. My Seventy Years in South Africa*, London, 1935, p. 139.

5. See Frances E. Colenso, *History of the Zulu War and Its Origin*, London, 1880, p. 310; W. E. Simons, 'When Maritzburg Stood to Arms', in *Reminiscences of the Zulu War*, I, 55; and Stafford, 'Stirring Days of Old Times', p. 14.

6. Cf. Gerald French, *Lord Chelmsford and the Zulu War*, London, 1939, pp. 42–9 passim; and Sonia Clarke, *Invasion of Zululand 1879*, Johannesburg, 1979, pp. 213–14. The worsening relations between Chelmsford and Bulwer are treated succinctly in J. P. C. Laband, 'Bulwer, Chelmsford and the Border Levies,' *Theoria*, vol. 57, 1981, pp. 1–15.

7. See CSO 1925, Minute 4144/1878, and CSO 2629, Minute 4237/1878; and GH, volumes 1326, pp. 184–5, 194–5, and GH 1411, pp. 165–93. Also *NGG*, vol. XXX, nos. 1739: Government Notices 356 and 365, and 1740: Government Notice 368.

8. See NGG, vol. XXX, no. 1740: Government Notices 368 and 398, respectively.

9. *Natal Advertizer*, 6 November 1878.

10. *Times of Natal*, 9 December 1878.

11. Ibid., 11 November 1878.

12. Ibid., 13 November 1878.

13. See e.g. ibid., 13, 15, 18, 25, 27, 29 November, and 2, 4 December 1878.

14. *Natal Colonist*, 30 November 1878.

15. *Natal Witness*, 21 November 1878.

16. *NGG*, vol. XXX, no. 1739: Government Notice 365. The Natal Carbineers' and Maritzburg Rifles' strengths were given as 53 and 109 respectively, on 31 December 1878, according to the *Blue Book. 1878*, I 6 and 8.

17. See *Times of Natal* 22, 25, 27 November, and 9 December 1878.

18. *Blue Book. 1878*, I 8.

19. See Law no. 19 of 1862, in the third volume of the *Statutes of Natal*, 3v. Pietermaritzburg, 1902.

20. *Natal Colonist*, 30 November 1878.
21. *Times of Natal*, 9 December 1878.
22. Ibid., and 11 December 1878.
23. Ibid., 11 December 1878.
24. See ibid., 13 and 20 December 1878; and *Natal Colonist*, 17 December 1878.
25. *Times of Natal*, 13 December 1878.
26. Ibid., 6 January 1879.
27. Ibid., and 13 December 1878.
28. Ibid., 25 December 1878. Also, cf. ibid., 1 January 1879.
29. Cf. ibid., 20, 22, 24 January 1879; and *Natal Witness*, 11 January 1879.
30. *Times of Natal*, 6 January 1879.
31. Ibid., 11 November 1878.
32. *Natal Advertizer*, 6 December 1878.
33. Ibid., 9 December 1878.
34. *Times of Natal*, 1 January 1879.
35. *Natal Witness*, 16 January 1879.
36. *Times of Natal*, 24 January 1879.
37. GH 1412: Minute 4550/1878.
38. Ibid.
39. J.J. Aubertin, *Six Months in Cape Colony and Natal . . .*, London, 1886, p. 102. Rowland J. Atcherley, who visited Maritzburg in the winter of 1877, wrote in *A Trip to Boërland*, London 1879, p. 40: 'The coolies are not so numerous as they are in Durban, but the Kafirs are more so.'
40. *Times of Natal*, 1 January 1879.
41. Ibid., 24 January 1879.
42. *Natal Witness*, 25 January 1879.
43. Ibid., 16 January 1879.
44. Ibid., 9 January 1879.
45. *Times of Natal*, 10 January 1879.
46. Ibid., 13 December 1878.
47. Ibid.
48. Ibid., 1, 8, 15 January 1879. No statement of the exact number of arms supplied at this time has been found; however, on 24 December Francis applied for and Mitchell agreed (27th) to sixty stand of arms (CSO 674, Minute 4929/1878).
49. *Natal Witness*, 9, 21 January 1879; *Times of Natal*, 10 January 1879.
50. *Natal Witness*, 21 January 1879; *Times of Natal*, 20 and 22 January 1879.
51. See ibid., and 15 January 1879; and *Natal Witness*, 14 and 21 January 1879.

52. *Times of Natal*, 24 January 1879.

53. *Natal Witness*, 23 January 1879.

54. Stafford, 'Stirring Days of Old Times', pp. 13–14.

55. F.R. Statham, *Blacks, Boers, & British*, London, 1881, p. 175. Marina King also writes vividly of the state of alarm (*Sunrise to Evening Star*, p. 143), but the sequence of events is so broken and muddled in her chapter on the war period that her account generally is questionable.

56. *Natal Witness*, 28 January 1879.

57. Norris-Newman, *In Zululand*, pp. 73–4.

58. *Natal Witness*, 28 January 1879.

59. Norris-Newman, *In Zululand*, p. 73.

60. *Natal Witness*, 28 January 1879.

61. See *Narrative of the Field Operations connected with the Zulu War of 1879*, London: HMSO, 1881, pp. 156–7.

62. Norris-Newman, *In Zululand*, p. 74.

63. Buchanan, *Pioneer Days*, pp. 113–14. Captain Henry Hallam Parr arrived in the city from Rorke's Drift during the second week of February. He briefly describes white morale then in *A Sketch of the Kafir and Zulu Wars*, London, 1880, pp. 271–2: 'The little town had quite lost its comfortable and homelike look. Anxious and care-worn faces were common in the streets; every other woman seemed to be in mourning, and almost every other man, if not in mourning, wore a slip of crape on his left arm *en militaire*, showing how many had been killed . . . at Isandhlwana.'

64. *Natal Witness*, 28 January 1879.

65. Ibid.; and *Times of Natal*, 29 January 1879.

66. Norris-Newman, *In Zululand*, p. 75; *Natal Colonist*, 28 January 1879; *Natal Witness*, 28, 30 January 1879.

67. Colenso, *Zulu War*, p. 310; J.F. Ingram, *The Story of an African City*, Pietermaritzburg, 1898, p. 59.

68. Hattersley, *Pietermaritzburg Panorama*, p. 69.

69. *Natal Witness*, 28 January 1879; *Natal Mercury*, 27 January 1879.

70. Norris-Newman, *In Zululand*, p. 76.

71. See ibid., p. 75; *Natal Witness*, 28 January 1879; *Natal Colonist*, 30 January 1879; and *Graphic*, 15 March 1879. Cf. later accounts in Buchanan, *Pioneer Days*, p. 115; Simons, 'When Maritzburg Stood to Arms'; and R.E. Gordon, *The Place of the Elephant*, Pietermaritzburg, 1981, p. 63. A description of the apparently completed laager is in *The Illustrated London News*, 28 June 1879. This includes: 'The whole front of the position can be raked from a couple of bastions placed at two opposing angles, however, the laager has not been provided with artillery yet.' It is difficult to envisage 'bastions' in the conventional military sense or even an unconventional sense, given the other information about the laager.

72. CSO 685, Minute 717/1879.

73. CSO 683, Minute 537/1879; *Natal Witness*, 28 January and 6 February 1879; Pietermaritzburg Town Council Minute Book: PC 1/1/4, for special meeting, 28 January, and ordinary meeting, 4 February 1879.

74. *Natal Witness*, 30 January 1879.

75. CSO 699, Minute 2195/1879.

76. *Natal Advertizer*, 31 January 1879; *Natal Mercury*, 3 February 1879.

77. WC II/2/2: Chelmsford to E. Wood, 3 February 1879.

78. *Natal Witness*, 4, 5, 6 February 1879; *Natal Colonist*, 6 February 1879; *Natal Advertizer*, 6 February 1879.

79. *Times of Natal*, 5 February 1879; Colenso, *Zulu War*, p. 310.

80. *Natal Advertizer*, 6 February 1879; Colenso, *Zulu War*, p. 310.

81. Colenso, *Zulu War*, p. 310. Marina King describes a panic (*Sunrise to Evening Star*, pp. 139–41), which seems to fit this occasion; however, she places it in time before Isandlwana.

82. Warney Burton, *Oddities of a Zulu Campaign*, London, 1880, pp. 36–7.

83. *Times of Natal*, 5 February 1879.

84. *Natal Witness*, 13 February 1879; *Natal Colonist*, 6, 15, 22 February 1879.

85. *Natal Witness*, 13 February 1879.

86. CSO 653, Minute C39/1879.

87. *Times of Natal*, 17 February 1879. Cf. J.P. Mackinnon and Sydney Shadbolt (comps.), *The South African Campaign, 1879*, London, 1882, pp. 350–1, which suggests that Lieutenant-Colonel Lambert would not have been long there; and p. 342, which states that Major (Brevet Lieutenant-Colonel) W.R.B. Chamberlain, of the 2nd Battalion of the 24th Regiment, 'remained as Commandant of Fort Napier in Pietermaritzburg during the campaign'.

88. The returns are in SNA 1/6/13, no. 34, and SNA 1/6/14, nos. 6 and 30.

89. *Natal Mercury*, 3 March 1879.

90. Buchanan, *Pioneer Days*, p. 115.

91. *Natal Advertizer*, 6 February 1879.

92. Ibid., 1 March 1879.

93. *Times of Natal*, 12 February 1879. Cf. *Natal Colonist*, 1 March 1879.

94. Buchanan, *Pioneer Days*, p. 114.

95. *Natal Colonist*, 30 January 1879.

96. *Natal Witness*, 30 January 1879.

97. GH 1423, Minute 1222/1879.

98. *Natal Colonist*, 1 March 1879.

99. Ibid., 22 February 1879.

100. Ibid., 20 February 1879; *Natal Mercury*, 20 February 1879.

101. *Times of Natal*, 12, 21 February 1879.

102. Ibid., 21 February 1879.

103.   *Natal Colonist*, 1 March 1879.

104.   CSO 653, Minute C39/1879.

105.   Cf. *Times of Natal*, 14, 19, 21 February 1879, and *Natal Mercury*, 20, 22 February 1879. In Durban there were writers who preferred the Maritzburg system.

106.   *Times of Natal*, 28 February 1879; *Natal Mercury*, 3 March 1879.

107.   See *Natal Witness*, 1, 6 February 1879; *Times of Natal*, 3 February 1879; also, the latter, 28 April 1879, for totals up to 19 April.

108.   See the above-mentioned newspapers, as well as the correspondents' reports in the Durban ones, for the several testimonials and functions in honour of Frere, Chelmsford, Wolseley, Wood, as well as the Day of Mourning and Humiliation (12 March).

109.   See *Natal Witness*, 17, 19, 31 July, and 3, 7, 8 August 1879; and *Times of Natal*, 30 July, and 4, 8 August 1879.

110.   Cf. *Times of Natal*, 20 August 1879, and *Natal Advertizer*, 12 July 1879.

111.   *Natal Witness*, 12 July 1879. Cf. CSO 1974: 3349/1879.

112.   *Natal Witness*, 15 July 1879; *Times of Natal*, 16 July 1879; *Natal Mercury*, 21 July 1879.

113.   *Natal Witness*, 19 July 1879.

114.   Ibid., 15 July 1879.

115.   Ibid., 24 July 1879.

116.   Ibid., 31 July 1879.

The Defence of Durban, 1879

P. S. THOMPSON

The Anglo-Zulu War had a pronounced impact on Durban. There was a real fear that the Zulu somehow might attack the town. The protection of it and its people became a major issue. The Town Council was evidently unsuited to this task, and so a Defence Committee was established, dominated by perhaps a dozen men, including the Mayor Richard Vause, Councillors Currie and Ballance, the MLCs Millar and Robinson, and Harry Escombe. These town war leaders collaborated with the military authority in the person of Major Huskisson, the Colonial Commandant for Durban sub-district. His prescription for defence (also Lord Chelmsford's) was typical of contemporary military thought. It afforded safety for the most people. Hence the so-called 'town laager'. The town war leaders took exception to it. Led by Millar, they pressed for a line of earthworks around the town, which would protect property as well as people. Huskisson was willing to adjust his own arrangements, even to a Point stockade, but Millar and some of the others forced the military and the government to a point-blank refusal of their impracticable plan and there was unpleasantness on both sides. The arrival of imperial troops from overseas ended the fear of a Zulu attack, and the Defence Committee fell into abeyance.

The Coming of War

The Base of Operations

By the spring of 1878 it was obvious that a clash would come between the British and Zulu crowns, but the colonial government of Natal, represented by the Lieutenant-Governor, Sir Henry Bulwer, was reluctant to take any steps which would excite alarm among the populace. It was only on 26 November that the government, chiefly at the behest of Lord Chelmsford, the commander of imperial forces, published a notice establishing seven defensive districts. The town of Durban was in Defensive District No. VI, including Durban and Victoria Counties. The first commandant of this district was Major Shapland Graves, 3rd Regiment (the Buffs), the Protector of Immigrants,[1] who in early December was reassigned. Gould A. Lucas, the Resident Magistrate of Alexandra County and formerly a captain in the 73rd Regiment, succeeded him. Lucas dropped in at Durban while passing from his magistracy to the front, on 7–10 December and again on the 28th and 29th, but the organization of a Border Guard along the Thukela soon engrossed his attention.[2]

The port of Natal was too important to be neglected: military headquarters on 14 and 16 December ordered that the garrison of Durban (including its environs) constituted a separate command under an officer responsible to the commanding general; and the colonial government followed suit with an official notice on 21 December, designating Durban a sub-district, no longer under Lucas' control.[3] The officer appointed to be Commandant of Durban and Assistant Quartermaster-General at the base was Major John William Huskisson, of the 56th (West Essex) Regiment of Foot. He had entered the service as an ensign in November 1850 and risen to lieutenant in January 1858. From February to June of 1858 he had served with the Bombay column of the Goa Field Force against the Dessai rebels, which had involved several skirmishes. In October 1865 he became a captain, and in 1868 commanded a company at Duncannon, Ireland. In 1874 he had become adjutant to the West Essex Militia, and in December 1877 been brevetted major, which full rank he attained four months later.[4] He was ordered on special service to Natal, and arrived the week after the local general orders of 14 December announced his appointment to command.[5] The same order also announced that Captain Aylmer Howard Tynte Henry Somerset, of the Rifle Brigade, would serve as his staff officer. He arrived from England about the same time. Somerset had been commissioned in 1855, promoted to lieutenant in 1858 and to captain in 1867. In 1873–1874 he had led a company in the Ashanti expedition.[6]

By the outbreak of the war the new commandant had on his staff, besides Somerset (his officer for general duties), Captain E.J.H. Spratt, 29th Foot, for transport duties; Deputy Commissary S.G. Granville, for the senior commissary office; Assistant Commissary R.S.M. De Ricci as commissary of ordnance; and Dr E. Jennings as senior medical officer.[7] The garrison of the town originally consisted of two companies of the 1/24th,[8] but these were replaced by a company of the 99th (Duke of Edinburgh's) Regiment, which occupied the Durban redoubt.[9]

The importance of Durban in the war cannot be exaggerated. Through the port passed almost all of the men and matériel for the British campaign, and any interruption would have jeopardized the British effort. Huskisson's responsibility was a very great one. In addition he had to deal with the townspeople, some of whom had peculiar ideas about the war and their place in it.

The Town Guard

The population of Durban was officially estimated at 5 312 Europeans and 3 500 Natives in November 1878.[10] A British visitor described it shortly before the war:

> The town consists mainly of three principal streets, parallel with one another, two of which are partially macadamized, while the remainder, with the cross streets, are but mere sandy tracks, over which the traffic is carried with difficulty. The houses and stores are in general only one-storey buildings, and in great part constructed of corrugated iron . . . . In West Street, which is the principal street, however, there are a few buildings of more substantial description, among which are two banks and some general stores of extensive dimensions. The most considerable building in the town, the Court House, in which are united all the offices over which the legislature has direct control, is a fine stone erection, situate at the entrance of a square park, and planted with many beautiful specimens of exotic trees. As a rule, all the private houses in the town lie back from the road, and are all more or less surrounded with a grove of tropical fruit, and aromatic trees, such as oranges, bananas, and amatangula.[11]

The approach of war prompted the civic leaders to act in anticipation. The Mayor, Richard Vause, convened a meeting on 16 September in the Town Office which was attended by himself and six other Town Councillors, the borough's four members of the Legislative Council, and nine other men – twenty in all – to discuss the advisability of establishing a 'Vigilance Committee' or similar organization for defence of the borough. Lieutenant-Colonel A.W. Durnford, Royal Engineers, was also present, apparently to give advice. The meeting was a 'private' one, which conveniently permitted the men without office to participate. It passed 10 to 7 the resolution:

> That the Mayor & Town Council & the members of the Legislative Council resident within the Borough form a Committee, with power to add to their number, to take such steps, in conjunction with the Military Authorities, as they may deem fit, in case of need, to provide for the effective defence of the Borough.[12]

Next day the Mayor sent a copy to the Colonial Secretary, Colonel

C.B.H. Mitchell, in Pietermaritzburg, and also gave details of what the meeting desired. Durnford had told them that 'a complete plan of defence for the town exists', and they wished the government to supply firearms, which, Durnford told them, were available in ample quantity, as well as military instructors in their use, for a Town Guard. Vause finished: 'His Excellency [the Lieutenant-Governor] will understand that not the slightest alarm exists, and that my object is simply to be prepared for any emergency, and to obviate all chance of a "scare".'[13]

The Colonial Secretary replied, thanking the Mayor and instructing him to communicate with Major Graves, whom the Lieutenant-Governor had entrusted with the defence of the coastal district.[14] Vause addressed Graves accordingly on the 21st.[15] It would seem that Graves himself had not been inactive, for the same day that the meeting took the initiative in local defence he circulated an extract from a report of the Defence Committee of the Executive Council of the Colony, dated December 1876, for the information of the officers commanding the Volunteer Corps (the organized militia) in the town. This extract (accompanied by a map) concerned Durban, and recommended the building and manning of detached posts around the town from the ocean to the bay. This was followed on the 20th by a similar plan (also accompanied by a map) which Durnford had drafted.[16] Perhaps these paper projects satisfied the Mayor, for he did not press the matter of defence again until the end of October.[17]

On 31 October, Vause wrote to Graves that he had got the defence programme underway, and awaited his reply. On 5 November he forwarded a preliminary roll of the Town Guard (with 106 signatures) and reported that a supplementary roll was open at the Market House.[18] On 18 November a meeting of the Town Guard was held in the Town Council chamber. Only 150 men had enrolled at that time, but the number was expected to grow, and the objects and organization of the guard were defined in five resolutions. The guard would become active for defence after the imperial military and colonial militia units departed for the front and when a necessity for it arose. The town and suburbs would be divided into blocks, with respective units of the guard under elected leaders. Arms would be obtained from the colonial government and issued by the Superintendent of Police in return for the guardsmen's personal bond.[19] On the 28th another meeting, representing some 204 signatories, elected a number of officers and provided for the election of others for the various units.[20] Meanwhile the *Natal Mercury* explained the guard's purpose on 21 November: 'The movement is simply intended to prevent alarm, and to set our military and volunteers free for other duty, should their services be required elsewhere.' It deprecated panic and reassured readers: 'The Town Guard will simply act as special constables should any unforeseen and at present impossible emergency arise . . . .' It added cryptically: 'We sincerely trust that the townsfolk will be on their guard not to say or do anything which might lead the natives living amongst us to misunderstand the nature of the movement.'[21]

The white settlers' anxiety about the blacks did not seem unfounded, as many fled. (Many of these were Tsonga, abandoning contracts).[22] On 25 November Vause wrote to the Superintendent of Police:

> . . . Please take S[teel?] and Grant round with you to every house in town and [illegible] and quietly inform every Coloured servant that it is desirable that you should know the number of Natives in our midst.
>
> Take down their names, the names of their Chiefs, of their Kraals, and where situated.
>
> This will be some check in case of any disturbance. I would distinguish the Zulus and Amatonga tribes.[23]

By this time the imperial forces were on the way to the front. On 26 November the colonial government called the mounted Volunteer Corps into service, and on the 30th the Durban Mounted Rifles, 66 strong, left for the front.[24] Two days later Harry Escombe, a lawyer and the Town Solicitor,

The Durban Mounted Rifles parading for active service, 1879. Their uniform was dark blue with black facings and scarlet piping.

proceeded to organize the Durban Mounted Reserve, to take their place.[25] The other Volunteer Corps in town – the Royal Durban Rifles and the Durban Volunteer Artillery – were not called up, although a rumour early in the new year said that they, too, were about to be sent to the front.[26] So anxious were some young settlers to go that the remaining units as well as the police momentarily seemed threatened with depletion of their members![27] The Mayor now pressed the organization of the Town Guard, but the colonial government was not forthcoming with arms as expected and then was against letting guardsmen take them home, personal bond or not, although it did relent with regard to those actually living in the town itself. Huskisson seemed sympathetic, but could do little more than send telegrams for the arms to Maritzburg. The feeling gained ground that the colonial government was not treating the Town Guard properly, and the Mayor hinted that the guard might have to disband because of it.[28] The guard's membership seems *not* to have increased despite the imminence of war, and its meetings were not fully attended.[29] Vause and those anxious for the defence movement blamed the government's slowness with arms. Their earnestness was parodied in the anonymous 'War Song for the Town Guard' which appeared in the *Natal Colonist* just before Christmas:

> We don't want to fight,
> But by jingo if we do,
>   Like furies we'll defend the precincts urban;
> No niggers will we shoot,
> Nor we don't want any loot,
>   But we won't let Ketshwayo into Durban.[30]

The war began on 11 January, 1879, by which time rumours were flying, and Huskisson reprimanded the *Colonist* for printing unverified reports about Zulu movements across the Thukela.[31] On the 13th he announced to the Town Guard committee that the colonial government was prepared to hand over 300 Snider rifles to the corporation, and rifles were issued that evening to 83 guardsmen at the drill shed in Field Street. Drill commenced at once – three evenings a week at the Skating Rink on Smith Street, and practice the following Saturday (the 18th) at the butts north of town. The officers met on the 14th to frame rules and regulations with regard to service and arms. A white badge was prescribed, to be worn on the left arm; an officer's badge would bear his unit's number.[32] The officers also approved a plan of measures to be adopted in case of emergency and ordered copies to be printed in readiness for distribution. The single-page notice described the signal alarms, named the buildings to which the people should repair, and specified a few things they should bring with them.[33]

The Isandlwana Panic

The Military Deployment

The British defeat at Isandlwana shocked and frightened the colonists in Natal. They now considered the possibility, if not the probability, that the victorious Zulu might invade the colony. Of course, rumours aggravated doubt and insecurity. The Resident Magistrate, John Francis Kellet Dillon, had assured the officers of the Town Guard that the commanding general had given defence of the town his attention and that in case of an alarm everything would doubtless be found to have properly matured.[34] Now he collapsed, and wrote to the Colonial Secretary for leave of absence. By the time he received permission he was in Port Elizabeth.[35]

Major Huskisson dispatched the troops of the 99th (in company of 50 Engineers) to Stanger on 24 January to secure the line of communication to the Lower Thukela.[36] At the same time he paraded the Royal Durban Rifles (Lieutenant Philip S. Flack), the Durban Volunteer Artillery (Captain A. McNeil) and the Durban Mounted Reserve, whose captain, Harry Escombe, he appointed 'Volunteer Brigade Major' for Durban. The units numbered about 30, 75, and 40, respectively, and the artillery had two guns. At 5.30 p.m. Huskisson and Somerset arrived at the Market Square, where the corps had assembled, and ordered them to march down West Street and back.[37] Apparently this show of force and the appointment of Escombe allayed fears of the townspeople.

Huskisson then ordered the Volunteer Corps to positions between the town and the front. They assembled on Sunday, the 26th. The Durban Mounted Reserve was to be sent to the Mdloti. When they had been recruited, the men had been promised that they would not be obliged to leave the borough; but on the evening of the 24th Escombe had called them to his office and persuaded them to go with him to protect Verulam and incidentally to give warning of any possible Zulu raid to Durban. He called for 30 men, but about 40 assembled on the Market Square at 11.30 a.m., and they went out the north road in fine spirits, accompanied some distance by Huskisson and Somerset. About 1.30 p.m. the Durban Volunteer Artillery and the Royal Durban Rifles assembled on the Market Square, in full marching order. After inspection they moved to the railway station, where a special train waited to take them as far as the Mgeni. There was much adieu, many sweethearts having come for the occasion, and the crowd cheered loudly as the heavily laden train pulled away from the platform. In a short time it arrived at the river, and the two corps disembarked and pitched camp. Meanwhile, the Isipingo Mounted Rifles, about 30 strong, assembled on the square at 2.30, and rode off to Stanger. In addition the Natal Coast Rifle

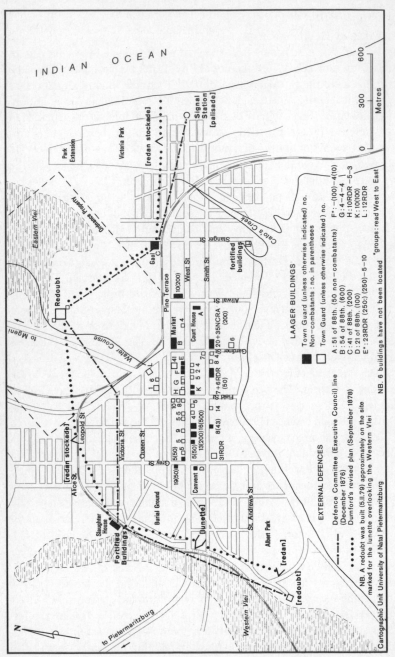

Plans for the defence of Durban, 1879.

Association, apparently blandished by Escombe, came forward as a unit under 'Captain' Rowland Ridgway, and Huskisson assigned it to guard the colonial powder magazine.[38]

Order soon returned in the country to the north, and Huskisson ordered the Durban Volunteer Artillery and the Royal Durban Rifles closer to the town. On the 28th they returned to the outskirts and pitched camp on the Eastern Vlei near the Zingari cricket ground, the artillery just north of the powder magazine and the infantry just south of the railway at the foot of Field Street. Both corps furnished guards to certain public buildings – the artillery to the magazine, the infantry to the Ordnance store and police station. The members of the Natal Coast Rifle Association, who were not really equipped for field duty, dispersed to their homes, leaving two of their 'officers' in charge of the magazine. There was also an accession of regular troops. The company of the 99th had left the redoubt unoccupied when it went to Stanger on the 24th; but on 8 February four companies of the 88th (Connaught Rangers) from Cape Town disembarked at the port and one of these remained to garrison the work.[39]

The Defence Committee

Huskisson's speedy action in disposing forces to secure the line north and to cover the town was only one response to the crisis. The agitated burgesses also responded. The *Mercury* editorialized on 29 January: 'An impression prevails that as this is the richest and most populous town in the country, it is likely to be the subject of a swift and sudden attack by an invading Zulu army.' Defence of the town was the prevailing topic of conversation, remarked the *Colonist* on 1 February. Meanwhile the flight of blacks suggested an exodus. So many Tsonga poured down to the Point that a larger vessel than that chartered was required to carry them off. Many had broken contracts, and by the end of January 126 had either been charged and fined or had warrants out for their detention. The problem of the authorities was probably compounded by the desertion of most of the Native Borough Police. Of course, there were rumours that Cetshwayo had his spies in town, of whom one especially was reported to have been recognized.[40]

About 200 members of the Town Guard turned out for drill at the rink the evening of Friday, 24 January, and some 30 new members were sworn in. Huskisson and Somerset attended, and the commandant expressed great pleasure at their appearance. The guard drilled daily, and every encouragement was given to the men to practice shooting as well. A mounted unit was activated on the Berea, and a unit at Addington received rifles. Three hundred and fourteen rifles were issued to the guard by the 30th, and another hundred were wanted. Further enrollments indicated that the guard might soon number about 500.[41] A programme for first-aid in the field for soldiers, police and volunteers was launched, and a special united prayer meeting was held at the Wesleyan Church.[42] The weather probably discouraged greater activity. The *Advertizer* observed on the 31st:

> . . . The heat of the past week has been really overpowering. Nothing but the proverbial spot of grease will mark the place where each of us last stood, if this sort of thing goes on much longer. The sun so powerfully sends down its rays upon us that cases of sunstroke have been frequent, and only yesterday soldiers were stricken down in the midst of work.[43]

In such circumstances it is not surprising that a public meeting called at the Market Square on 28 January was a failure, with no one prepared to speak or to propose a course of action and those present not sure what the purpose of the meeting was. In contrast the Town Council proceeded with decision. The Mayor had gone to Pietermaritzburg for four days.[44] – perhaps on business, perhaps to meet his son, who had narrowly escaped death at Isandlwana – and the council elected one of their number, Henry William Currie, a 'gentleman' who lived on the Berea, to act as mayor.[45] They convened then as the Vigilance Committee that had met in September, although they now called themselves 'The Committee of Public Safety' – and more often later simply 'The Defence Committee'. The committee, consisting of nine Town Councillors (the tenth was with the Volunteers at the front) and the four members of the Legislative Council resident in the borough, arranged to meet daily (except Sunday) at half past twelve in order to expedite defensive measures that came within their purview. The Town Office was committee headquarters and the Town Clerk was its secretary.[46]

The committee's first business was to ascertain what plans had been and were to be made for the physical defence of the town, to procure accurate intelligence, to obtain removal of loose powder from the magazine and to request that Volunteers in service in town be allowed to return to their normal occupations during the day. It straight away urged Dillon, who had not left yet, to give the black populace as accurate an account of developments as possible in order to forestall further flights. Dillon replied that he had received a minute from the Lieutenant-Governor which should be suitable, but the committee said that it only referred to the defeats up-country, while the fact that there were several imperial columns in Zululand still undefeated should also be communicated. A shot in the dark (literally) prompted the committee to call on the Superintendent of Police for a report

TABLE I

THE DEFENCE COMMITTEE

Public office	Name	Profession	Address	Meetings attended (out of 27 between 28 January and 5 March 1879)
Town Councillor (Mayor)	Richard. V Vause	editor	Berea	21
Town Councillors	Henry William Currie	gentleman	Berea	19
	Robert Jameson	merchant	West Street	9
	*J.S. Steel	veterinary surgeon	Pine Terrace	6
	Alf Millett	merchant	Queen Street	2
	William Cowey	merchant	West Street	7
	John ceX. Ballance	merchant	Montpellier	20
	T. W. Edmonds	storekeeper	Musgrave Road	11
	W. W. Wheeler	merchant	Umgeni	12
Members, Legislative Council	John Robinson	editor	St. Andrew's Street	25
	Benjamin W. Greenacre	merchant	Musgrave Road	12
	George Christopher Cato	gentleman	Smith Street	8
	John Millar	gentleman	St. Andrew's Street	24
Officers, Volunteer Corps				
Durban Volunteer Artillery	Capt. A. McNeil	engineer	Queen Street	0
Royal Durban Rifles	Lt. R[euben] Benningfield	[gentleman]	Smith Street]	0
	1st Lt. Philip Sutton Flack	merchant	Berea	0
	2d Lt. D.J. Nolan	—	—	0
Durban Mounted Reserve	*Capt. Harry Escombe	advocate	Beach Grove	1
	Lt. Morton Green	merchant	Berea	0
	Lt. G. Brunton	—	—	0
Captains. Town Guard (by district)				
1 and 2	John Philip Hoffmann	accountant	—	1
	George Smith	clerk	Prince Alfred Street	0
3	M[eyrick] Bennett	[merchant	Queen Street]	0

TABLE I (cont.)

THE DEFENCE COMMITTEE (cont.)

Public office	Name	Profession	Address	Meetings attended (out of 27 between 28 January and 5 March 1879)
Town Guard (cont.)				
4	W.R. Parker	clerk	Pine Terrace	0
	*J.S. Steel	*	*	*
5	R. Raleigh	—	—	8
6	W.H. Evans	clerk	Berea	0
	R.H.U. Fisher	merchant	Addington	1
7	George Taylor	wagoner	Grey Street	0
8	H.E. Stainbank	—	—	9
	G.E. Robinson	[salesman]	Umgeni]	0
9	*B.W. Greenacre	*	*	*
	*H.W. Currie	*	*	*
10	W[illiam] Shuter	[attorney	Berea]	0
Quartermaster	J.B. Cottam	market master	Pine Terrace	7
	L. Durant	merchant	Berea	1
	J.H. Atkinson	merchant	Berea	0
None (co-opted members)	*Harry Escombe	*	*	11
	R.W. Evans	[merchant	West Street]	15
	Percy Hope	merchant	Berea	14
	Thomas McCubbin	merchant	Berea	7
	W.H. Cullingworth	notary	Gardiner Street	0
	William Grant	merchant	Musgrave Road	5
	William Palmer	accountant	Prince Alfred Street	3

N.B.   The original committee consisted only of the Councillors and MLCs. Information on attendance is from the committee minutes (DCPM), and on professions and addresses as given in the *Natal Almanac, Directory, and Yearly Register. 1879,* Pietermaritzburg, 1878, pp. 318–90, passim. Asterisks indicate double listings, brackets uncertain information.

and any important information which might come to hand, and then to set up an intelligence subcommittee.[47]

The Defence Committee notified its activation to the government and to the Commandant, and the former directed them to take their questions to the latter. Although he was obviously busy otherwise, Huskisson attended the committee's meetings at its invitation. He seemed agreeable enough about letting Volunteers return to their work, so long as a sufficient guard was kept at the magazine. He turned over to the committee the papers with the plans for defence which had been presented in September. The committee seemed to be particularly interested in starting the earthworks, but Huskisson was able to divert this interest to barricades of sand bags which could be thrown up in the streets at relatively short notice. The committee also had a notice to householders about going into 'laager' printed for distribution,[48] while Huskisson drafted a more practical instruction.[49] The Commandant and the committee seemed to be working well together.

Lord Chelmsford's Visit

Lord Chelmsford, who had been reorganizing the defence of the colony in the interior, arrived in Durban and met the Defence Committee on the morning of Wednesday, 6 February. The Mayor (Vause) and three councillors (Edmonds, Jameson and Steel), the market master (Cottam, who was quartermaster of the Town Guard), and three members of the Legislative Council (Cato, Greenacre, and Robinson) were present. The General was accompanied by Major M. W. E. Gossett and possibly Major J. North Crealock, of his staff, as well as Rear Admiral T. V. Sullivan, the commodore at the port. Major Huskisson was also present, perhaps with Captain Somerset. In the afternoon the General, accompanied by the members of the Legislative Council for the borough, inspected various places in town with a view to ascertaining their defensibility. Then another meeting, of the full Defence Committee and the military authorities, took place.[50]

Information concerning these important meetings is remarkably sparse and vague. No detailed minutes seem to have been kept. Apparently members of the Defence Committee suggested the construction of a fortified line on the land side of the town, based on the plans presented in September and given to the committee by Huskisson a few days before. Lord Chelmsford dismissed this scheme as impracticable: the entrenchments would take too long to construct, and there were not enough troops either to construct or to defend them. He favoured an amplification of what Major Huskisson already was undertaking, the fortification of selected buildings

TABLE II

MILITARY AND PARAMILITARY UNITS FOR DEFENCE

Unit	Commander	Strength
GARRISON (imperial)		
until 6 January 1/24th (2nd Warwickshire) Regiment D and F Companies	Maj. R. Upcher	—
6–24 January 99th (Duke of Edinburgh's) Regiment 1 company	—	—
8 February–early April 88th Regiment (Connaught Rangers) 1 company	—	—
early April–early August 58th (Rutlandshire) Regiment 1 company	Capt. H.M. Saunders	—
early August–late October 99th (Duke of Edinburgh's) Regiment 1 company	[Maj. Albert S. Walker]	—
VOLUNTEER CORPS (colonial)		
Royal Durban Rifles	1st Lt. Philip Sutton Flack	96
Durban Volunteer Artillery	Capt. A. McNeil	50; 2 guns
Durban Mounted Reserve	Capt. Harry Escombe	35
Indian Corps	Capts. A.F. Mackintosh and R.P. Beverly-Davies	—
RIFLE ASSOCIATIONS (colonial)		
Natal Coast Rifle Association	Capt. Rowland Ridgeway	35
Lower Umgeni Rifle Association	H.E. Stainbank	—
TOWN GUARD	Richard V. Vause	
(for districts and captains see preceding table)		about 300

which, when linked by barricades, would form a kind of laager. (This was a fairly standard defensive improvisation, and had been implemented in Pietermaritzburg.) The committee apparently acquiesced in the scheme.[51]

Lord Chelmsford's visit was important because his opinion determined the military's plan of defence. It was also important for a disturbing effect: either he stressed or the committee attached undue importance to his warning that a Zulu raid might be directed against the town, in order to hasten on the defensive preparations there. Evidently he said that such a raid was a possibility, not a probability. Whatever the case, his words were not reassuring to the civilians. It is not surprising that the afternoon meeting, which the General apparently did not attend, seems to have been engrossed by arrangements for protection of the townspeople in case of the emergency.[52] The MLC John Robinson recalled much later:

> . . . It must be admitted that his presence did not tend to allay alarm, as both he and his officers frankly recognised the seriousness of the situation and the necessity for action. Said one of the latter to me at a meeting of the Town Committee, 'I never saw such a foe; I never heard of such a foe; I don't think you could meet a worse foe.' After it was over we rode down the streets with his lordship, pointing out such buildings as might be defensible, and generally, in no smothered tones, discussing the possibilities of resistance. Women and children, scared and nervous, gathered by the roadside, wondering what new and alarming danger beset the town. Before nightfall an idea prevailed that the Zulus had crossed the border and were advancing on the town, and hardly any one slept soundly before dawn appeared. What else could the arrival of the Commander of the Forces, and his words of warning while inspecting the town, portend than some sudden and appalling crisis?[53]

Conflicting Plans

The Military's Laager inside the Town

Lord Chelmsford's approval was followed by the elaboration of Huskisson's scheme from a system of a few rendezvous for the guard and civilian refugees and improvised barricades, to one of many fortified and manned buildings, besides designated refuges within a rectangular grid of Smith and West streets between Aliwal and Grey Streets, known as the Durban 'laager'. The manning of the buildings seems to have left none for barricades in between (although Huskisson still mentioned using them), and the popular perception was of individual strongholds, presumably affording mutual support by cross or flanking fires.

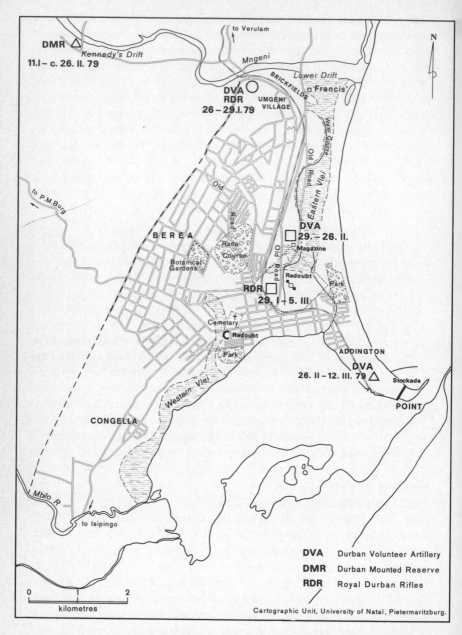

Dispositions of the Volunteer Corps in defence of Durban, 1879.

On 6 February fortification of the selected buildings began. The most remarked-upon fortification was that of the court-house, in which ammunition was also stored and which was barricaded and loopholed. The *Advertizer* mentioned the disfigurement of the building, but the *Colonist* observed after a week that the loopholes had been 'made to look quite natty'. The Market House apparently took about three weeks to be made defensible. Other large buildings were similarly altered.[54] While this work was underway, Huskisson pressed for the removal of all unnecessary explosives and flammables from the windy town, lest defence be complicated by a conflagration, accidental or deliberate.[55] He also turned his attention to the adequacy of the water supply, which was still collected largely in iron tanks, but he seems to have been able to make no improvement on this method of provision.[56]

The existing redoubt (today called the 'Old Fort') looked out across the Eastern Vlei and commanded the northern approach to the town, but there was no similar work on the western approach – the other approaches being by sea, no work was necessary. Huskisson had considered putting some guns on the rising ground overlooking the Western Vlei, and on 5 February a gang of convicts under the personal supervision of Somerset threw up a redoubt there.[57] Huskisson also made a redisposition of the Volunteers. On the 5th the Durban Mounted Reserve returned from the Mdloti and dispersed to their homes. They reassembled on the 11th and rode off to Kennedy's Drift on the Mgeni – engaging in a mock battle with the artillery and infantry on the way out of town. On the 18th he reviewed and inspected the unmounted corps and subsequently ordered the Durban Volunteer Artillery to the Point, where they occupied the Chinese barracks on the 25th. The Royal Durban Rifles remained on the vlei outside town.[58] Huskisson also assumed the responsibility for the defence of Durban County, which Captain Lucas had neglected and which was officially added to his sub-district on 17 February.[59]

The Commandant was also busy working out the details of the laager. After consultation with the Mayor he designated those buildings which would be used for defence and refuge, the number of men which should defend each one and the number of non-combatants for each. In the defence he made use of the Town Guard and the Royal Durban Rifles, as well as the Rifle Association and the company of the 88th Regiment in garrison at the fort.[60] The Mayor was vexed that the number of guardsmen did not increase appreciably, so much so that by 20 February he had published a notice that it was 'totally inadequate' for defence of the borough and urging volunteers to come forward – to no avail. Huskisson did not intervene in the matter. On

18 February his plan of defence was published, and at once there was a popular outcry against it.[61]

The Civilians' Rampart Outside the Town

The Defence Committee met at half past noon on 6 February, with three councillors, the members of the Legislative Council for the borough, the market master, and the Commandant present. Chelmsford's advice probably was fresh in mind. A resolution urging the government to remove all blacks living within eight miles (12,8 km) of the Thukela from the right bank suggests panicky thinking. The committee also decided that the captains of the Town Guard should be co-opted to the committee.[62] Next day Mayor Vause was back in the chair. Councillors Ballance, Jameson, Steel and Wheeler, the MLCs Greenacre, Millar, and Robinson, market master Cottam, and Huskisson were present. A reportedly large number of burgesses were also present 'by invitation',[63] and the *Mercury* commented that 'things went rather awry, as they often do on such occasions.'[64] One J.R. Saunders deplored 'the unnecessary feeling of alarm now being created', and Robinson rejoined, saying the Defence Committee had acted 'in as unobtrusive a way as possible'. Vause asked the meeting to confirm the committee's actions, but a motion of confidence found no seconder. After discussion the unhappy Mayor declared the committee dissolved and left the meeting. Greenacre took the chair, and Millar hastily moved that the Mayor return. The motion was seconded and somewhat mollified, Vause resumed the chair.[65] It was moved and seconded that the Defence Committee be enlarged. The captains of the Town Guard, the officers of the Volunteer Corps, and eight other persons were added, and the committee was authorized to co-opt others.[66]

The enlargement of the Defence Committee suggests that it did not, as initially constituted, enjoy the confidence of certain influential townsmen. (A proposal that would have let the old incumbents co-opt whom they wished failed of a second.)[67]

Huskisson reported to the committee on Thursday, 6 February, on the fortification of the court-house and other buildings, and Vause forwarded at his request on the 7th a list of two-storeyed buildings in the town centre which could be used for defence; but during the next few days Huskisson must have been fully occupied, for he did not reply promptly to the committee when it asked (on the 8th) what his *intentions* were for the defence of the town. The committee inquired again on the 10th, specifically asking after the disposition of residents in defence. Somerset furnished the information.[68] The Colonial Secretary, perhaps anticipating growing mis-

Major John William Huskisson.

givings among the civilians, also wrote that Huskisson was in charge of the defence of Durban. Indeed, one of the new committee members asked what the relative positions were between the civil and the military in this matter, and Vause told him that the military was supreme.[69] Next day the committee *amended* the minutes to read that not all of the members concurred in this view. Just after it did, Huskisson arrived at the meeting, while Somerset was superintending the departure of the Durban Mounted Reserve to Kennedy's Drift. He was questioned about the military's intentions, and replied that he meant to occupy and fortify certain buildings or even blocks, and that he would proceed to select the buildings that afternoon. He added that this plan in principle was the same as that which the officers of the Town Guard themselves had adopted. He stated that he had no intention of defending the outside of the town, partly because it would take a long time to complete a system of forts and trenches, mainly because there would not be enough men to occupy such fortifications: such a line would require 2 000 men, and each fort 100. Since information to hand gave about 1 700 males who could bear arms in the town and the suburbs, the committee could not very well contradict the Major.[70]

The next day, the 12th, Huskisson wrote to Vause, enclosing a list of buildings to be utilized in defence. Most were on three main streets – Smith and West, and Pine Terrace – in the centre of the town. Somerset was already going along the streets conveying instructions to the storekeepers, and the Commandant asked the Defence Committee to appoint subcommittees to assist him with the instruction of the occupants and with the preparation of sacks for barricading and the removal of wood piles as a precaution against fire. The committee promptly did so, and they reported on their progress within the next two days. On the 13th the committee asked after any *further* arrangement for defence of the town and suburbs, and adjourned to await Huskisson's reply before half past three![71] Huskisson wrote to Vause that he also intended to throw up barricades and to place obstacles at selected places to prevent easy access to the town by large numbers of the enemy, and to seek the government railway authorities' assistance in the defence, but these additional arrangements were 'very trifling matters in comparison with the main system of defence which has been explained to you by Lord Chelmsford himself.' He cajoled: 'If the inhabitants of Durban will enter into this system with good will, I anticipate no difficulty.'[72]

The committee assembled at four and Huskisson's letter was read. A long discussion ensued. Finally the committee resolved that the Mayor should wait upon the Commandant with a deputation to inquire after the nature and position of the intended barricades and to express the committee's opinion on defences outside the town. The interview took place, evidently without moving Huskisson. The deputation reported to the committee the next day, and another long discussion ensued. The Mayor was instructed to confer with the Commandant again on the desirability of publishing his scheme of defence for the information of the burgesses.[73] The faction which wanted an external defence were not brooked easily. On the 15th, Millar proposed and Cato seconded a motion that the committee inform the burgesses 'by whom they were appointed' in a public meeting of the military's arrangements for a partial defence of the town and ascertain whether they were satisfied with these or would authorize it 'to carry out such additional mode of Defence as they may deem advisable under the circumstances.'[74]

Vox Populi

The public meeting, on Monday, 17 February, was summoned at short notice. At 11 a.m. a crowd of men duly assembled in the Council Chamber; at least 68 were named in next morning's *Mercury*, which declared that the meeting was both large and representative. The *Advertizer* remarked that the business was calm, earnest and orderly. The *Mercury* also stated that the resolutions were carried unanimously.[75] At Millar's and Cato's urging it resolved that the proceedings were not to be publicized except, of course, the resolutions. Ballance, the secretary, summarized the Defence Committee's activities during the past week, and Millar again addressed the meeting. Then Robinson moved and Superintendent of Police Alexander seconded the following resolution, which was adopted:[76]

That in the opinion of this meeting, the steps taken by the Government for the defence of the seaport of the Colony, are wholly inadequate to the exigencies of the time and place, as represented by the Military Authorities.[77]

All of the speeches were critical of the military plan, because it would secure life but not *property*. If the enemy gained access to the streets and alleys of the town, he could destroy and plunder – and also render concerted defence practically impossible. If possible, he should be kept outside the town. If nothing else, external defence was advisable to inspire confidence and a sense of safety.[78]

Edward Pickering, a Musgrave Road storekeeper, said that in the event of a Zulu advance, a large number of whites, coolies and natives could also be expected to resort to the town, and moved that the Mayor and the corporation be empowered to have entrenchments with bastions thrown up outside town. Cato seconded this, but Millar, seconded by H. E. Stainbank, substituted a motion which added that the Defence Committee take the initiative and costs be covered from the Borough Fund. It was accepted,[79] although the Mayor uttered a 'mild but clear warning against the borough's involvement in what he evidently considered an unnecessary expense.' Similarly, Councillor Steel inquired after the money, and the assemblage agreed that the present rate of three pence in the pound should be doubled, if necessary. The meeting ended,[80] and the Town Council held a special meeting. Some of the councillors were evidently uneasy. Currie asked what funds were available for the outer defences. The Mayor said that a special rate must be passed. Currie estimated that the external defences would cost at least £2 000 and a penny rate would cover it. The Mayor said that the government should pay for them, as it had in Pietermaritzburg. Currie agreed, and proposed that the government be sent a copy of the resolutions passed at the public meeting and that it be asked to provide the funds for the council 'to carry out the defence of the borough.'[81] The council approved,[82] but also resolved that Currie and Vause should inquire after borrowing money from certain property owners said to be ready to make an advance for the purpose of external defence.[83] The Town Council then adjourned and the Defence Committee met at 3.30 p.m. The Mayor reported that he had forwarded the copy of the public resolutions for the colonial government to Huskisson. He mentioned the town's lack of funds for external defences. The committee resolved to suspend action until it received the government's reply to the resolutions.[84]

For the next few days the advocates of external defence must have been on tenterhooks. On the 18th Vause conveyed to Huskisson the Defence Committee's request that he ask the government to telegraph its reply to the resolutions, and the Mayor himself sent a request for an answer by telegram to the Colonial Secretary for good measure. Mitchell promised the Lieutenant-Governor's timely reply.[85] The *Advertizer* fumed in its editorial column at the folly of the military's plan. The *Colonist* and the *Mercury* did not indulge in such unrestrained criticism; however, the *Witness* in Pietermaritzburg reported a considerable popular reaction against the military plan and a feeling that the military had ignored or flouted the popular will for external defence.

Huskisson was not deflected from completion of the 'laager'. On the 18th he had copies of a printed notice, 'Distribution of Women and Children', served out to the various officers. On the 20th he issued a 'Notice to each Householder', informing prospective inmates of the laager what they should do in the event of an emergency; and the newspapers carried descriptions of the buildings to be used for defence and refuge.[86] The same day the government replied to the public resolutions and Vause read the message to the Defence Committee:

> Plan proposed appears on too large a scale to be undertaken in a time of pressure, and would require larger military force, far beyond what could be spared; also, it is not considered a desirable plan by the officer charged with the defence of the town. The expense of any measures that the officer commanding considers advisable for the public defence, will be authorised by the Lieutenant Governor.[87]

The committee was again referred to Huskisson, who had also sent a letter in the same vein. It was read to the committee, which requested the Mayor to call another public meeting and to lay before it the government's reply.[88]

The second public meeting was held on Friday, 21 February, in the Skating Rink on Smith Street. It was scheduled for 11 a.m., but most attending arrived late. Besides the town notables (of whom it named 11), the *Mercury* estimated about 300 present. Huskisson and Somerset were absent.[89] The Town Clerk read the notice convening the meeting, and immediately Pickering challenged its validity from the floor. Mayor Vause, presiding, could not cite an appropriate law, but Town Solicitor Escombe declared the mayoral power ample enough to permit it. Vause said that, law or not, he would have called a meeting in the present emergency. The Town Clerk read the minutes of the Monday meeting and the pertinent resolutions of the Town Council and the Defence Committee. He could scarcely be heard, for the machinery on Mr Milne's premises next door made such noise.

Councillor Ballance asked Milne to have it stopped. 'Who is to pay for it?' retorted Milne, amid much laughter. The Mayor's table and the long benches for the burgesses were drawn closer. Ballance, who was secretary of the Defence Committee, read the telegrams between the Mayor and the Colonial Secretary. Vause then owned that he had no resolutions to present and the corporation had no money for entrenchments: those present must decide what to do and presumably *someone* had proposals. Walter Peace, a Berea merchant, then asked why the Defence Committee had not dealt with all these matters, and in an exchange with Vause and Ballance he cast doubt on the committee's efficiency and ability to work with the military authority. The crowd was becoming unruly; it frequently interrupted the speakers with cheers, laughter, and various calls. Pickering moved to reconstruct the committee with much fewer members but including himself. Millar tried to focus attention on external defence, but failed when he could not recall the Defence Committee's resolution on the subject, while Vause unhelpfully adverted to the matter of funds and then asked for a second to Pickering's motion. One of the benches gave way. Cato quipped that the rear guard was gone. There was laughter and no second.

Millar got the floor. He conceded that a Zulu raid would be unlikely, but said that if there were to be defences outside the town (hear, hear) then the government should bear at least part of the expense (applause) since the imperial government had brought on the war. He moved:

> That this meeting again records the emphatic opinion of the burgesses that the only sure defence for the security of life and property is by bank and ditch outside the town, and that the Government be requested by the Town Council to construct the necessary redoubts upon sound principles, leaving the burgesses to connect them with a bank and ditch at the expense of the borough.

He doubted that anyone would begrudge the halfpenny rate necessary for the connections. The government would help if they showed they were ready to help themselves. He did not doubt the inhabitants would turn out to defend the connections, but he did doubt if members of the Town Guard would defend a couple of houses. (Applause.) He had a rifle and could use it and he would not go into any of those houses, but would take it into the open (hear, hear) – he would not for a moment think of going into the town to be burnt or stewed in one of those houses. (Laughter, applause.) Cato seconded the motion, saying that the government had come forward in all Kafir wars before, but now it had not even sent the Colonial Engineer. (Hear, hear.) They did not even know if they were to get a single cannon or Gatling. Not a popgun even, someone cried. (Laughter.) They are going to try cremation on a very large scale, added another. (More laughter. A councillor imitated a cock crowing!) The meeting approached confusion.

At this juncture Harry Escombe, advocate, Town Solicitor, Brigade Major and Captain of the Durban Mounted Reserve, stood upon the orchestra platform. The *Colonist* next day stated that he delivered 'a long and thoughtful speech'.The *Mercury* called it a 'long and, for him ineffectual speech'. He said he intended to move an amendment to Millar's resolution. He began turgidly, with the usual claque, and eventually protested against the obsessive concern with external defence to the neglect of the hapless non-combatants. Millar, Ballance and Cato interjected that they would be taken care of in a stockade at the Point (of which more will be told presently). Escombe was caught out – he had been absent from the last seven Defence Committee meetings – but tacking quickly he denounced the insufficiency of the arrangements there and rounded on the Defence Committee as 'a cumbrous piece of machinery' which should be divided into efficient subcommittees to get on with the details of defence instead of interfering in properly military affairs. The military men had more experience than they. Look at the disasters of war up-country, Millar retorted. Escombe did not relent. If the corporation needed money then it should get it from the government. He disparaged the Durban merchants as penny-pinchers and wondered if any town in history had had a commercial element which had contributed so little to its own defence. Pickering protested that the merchants would have given if they had been asked and that many indeed had promised handsome sums. Escombe rolled on. What of those with large families and no property? (Hear, hear.) He cared little for the credit of the borough, and property could take care of itself. Why were particular properties selected for defence? There was applause and great cheering. In succession he drubbed the merchants, extolled the Point sanctuary, told the burgesses the best way to fight raiding Zulu (go out to meet them and then fall back slowly on the town), said they would be fools for doing it, and called Millar's scheme of defence 'rash, visionary, chimerical, and impracticable'!

The meeting had essentially to choose between Huskisson's or Millar's plan of defence. Escombe denounced both and suggested a resort to the stockade under construction at the Point as an alternative, which was embodied as an amendment to Millar's resolution. Escombe then apologized to the merchants for going 'further than he should have done' in his remarks. Currie took the floor. Escombe, he said, was in 'utter ignorance' of the Defence Committee's acts. He (Currie) and Fisher had been appointed a committee to confer with Huskisson about securing the women and children at the Point, and had met with Huskisson, who had left the matter to them, giving ample material for a barricade and letting them employ the engineer of harbour works. 'If Mr Escombe had continued speaking a few hours longer, he would have found that the whole barricade had been completed, so quickly was the work being proceeded with.' Old and new speakers wrangled on until finally the Town Clerk read Millar's motion and Escombe's amendment. The Mayor asked for a vote on the amendment. An angry discussion of it ensued. Palmer moved and Pickering seconded that Millar's motion and Escombe's amendment be treated as substantive motions. Vause put Millar's to the vote. 'A forest of arms were held up for it', the *Colonist* reported. Only eight opposed, the *Mercury* noted. Then Escombe's amendment: about a score of hands went up. The Mayor declared Millar's motion carried, and the meeting ended. After the burgesses left the hall, the *Colonist* reporter observed that for some time they formed groups in the streets, eagerly discussing the question 'Where are we now?'

That afternoon Vause sent a copy of the meeting's resolution to Huskisson, with the Town Council's request that he lay it before the proper authority with the request for an early reply. Huskisson did not acknowledge receipt — probably he had enough of meetings — but on the 23rd telegraphed the contents of Vause's letter with the resolution to Pietermaritzburg.[90]

Succeeding Plans

The Point Stockade

Huskisson was not inflexible with regard to defence of the town. He fell in with the Defence Committee's plan for a stockade at the Point. The committee on 6 February had appointed Vause, Escombe and Stainbank to recommend action in anticipation of an influx of Indians into the borough in an emergency. Five days later, Escombe recommended the establishment of a line of defence from the Back Beach past the gaol to the bay, behind which women and children could take refuge, with the hospital reserved especially for the women; however, he added: 'The Major [Huskisson] thought there was the same difficulty of defending a long line.'[91]

The matter remained in abeyance about a week, during which time the Defence Committee concentrated its attention on the matter of external entrenchments. On the 17th the committee received a letter from R.H.U. Fisher, the captain of the Town Guard unit at the Point, containing a plan for defence at the Point. The committee commended it to Huskisson and appointed Fisher and Currie a subcommittee to assist in case he approved the plan. The committee also received an assurance from William Ridley, of the

Natal Government Railways, that railway material, including sleepers; and labour would be forthcoming for defensive work. Huskisson joined the subcommittee at the Point to inspect the site the next day, at which time he authorized the construction of a stockade from the Harbour Works Pier ('James' Jetty') to the bay, beyond the railway line running to the harbour. Work commenced the following day, the 19th, while Vause and five committee members went off to inspect the laager at Pinetown, which was also a stockade.[92]

The Point stockade assumed greater importance on the 20th, when Vause reported to the committee that he had received a letter from the medical authorities, originally addressed to Huskisson, condemning the congregation of women and children in the manner proposed in the laager, for the crowding and excitement and the hot weather would lead to the outbreak of disease. The committee decided that the women and children should be placed behind the stockade at the Point and on board ships, either being preferable to the laager.

The committee believed, of course, that shifting the non-combatants from the laager would considerably affect the military plan and effect a modification of it. Currie put this as a question to Huskisson, who was attending the meeting on the 20th, and the Commandant replied that the shift would enable him to rearrange the forces at his disposal to better advantage – but they would still be insufficient for any line outside the town.

Subsequently the committee adopted a resolution that every assistance should be given to complete the stockade at the Point for the protection of women and children. Vause said that he would be glad for help to push on the work, and Ballance and Raleigh moved that he apply to employers who had offered Indian labour and to the Railways at once. The work at the Point was pressed forward under the superintendence of C.F. Osborne, and on the 21st the Town Clerk reported that the whole of the corporation staff was employed on the Point stockade. Indian labour was provided from several sugar estates. On the 26th Currie reported that 66 whites and 20 more from the artillery, 89 blacks, and 472 Indians were at work there.[93]

The 21st was taken up with the public meeting considering external defence, but on the 22nd the Defence Committee adverted again to the stockade. Huskisson was at the meeting – the last he attended – and undertook to have commissariat stores as well as tents for the women and children and two tanks to supply water placed at the Point. The committee asked Huskisson to have a second line of defence erected which would include the new hospital, and appointed Escombe and Fisher a subcommittee to deal with the matter. Huskisson agreed to the new plan. Escombe reported to the committee on the 24th and Vause was told to get the Town Surveyor to plan the new defence in detail. Ballance interviewed Huskisson and reported on the 25th that he insisted on completing the first line before considering anything else. Escombe recommended that nothing be done until the first line was finished, but now the committee insisted (26th) that the Point stockade did not have space for all the whites and coloureds expected to occupy it and resolved that when extra labour could be obtained a further line of defence should be laid off from the ocean to the bay near the new hospital. This was conveyed to Huskisson, whose reply, if any, has not been found. The original stockade was finished in the first week of March.[94]

Raleigh, captain of the Town Guard 5th District, apparently drafted a plan for removal of women and children to the Point stockade, which the committee regarded so highly that it required all the other captains to make similar arrangements for their districts. Two days later (26th) it instructed Currie and Fisher (the subcommittee) to designate places for the women and children of all races, also bearing in mind that a large male population might fall back to the stockade for refuge.[95]

Naval Guns and Masked Trains

The Defence Committee was also keen for artillery protection. The committee had pressed the government for the dispatch of artillery pieces from the Cape, and Huskisson had told the committee that he had requested them, intending to place guns on the rising ground near the Western Vlei to cover the approach to the town across the flat. A redoubt was built, and the Durban Volunteer Artillery was near enough to occupy it. The notion was that the naval commodore would provide four twelve-pounders and possibly a seven-pounder from H.M.S. *Active* with a detachment of sailors to help the civilians operate the guns. Robinson proposed to the committee that Rear Admiral Sullivan, commodore of the naval flotilla in port, be asked to land all light guns, with or without ammunition, that could be spared for the defence of the town. Vause promptly got off a letter to Sullivan, aboard H.M.S. *Active*, and received a reply the following day: three twelve-pounders on boat carriages, with 150 rounds each, could be supplied, if Huskisson required them. On the 24th Ballance forwarded the Admiral's letter to Huskisson with a request for information about his disposition of the guns. Huskisson told Ballance that the guns would be used to protect the stockade and they were landed, but evidently without the carriages, and lay upon the wharf for some time. Huskisson may have wanted the Durban Volunteer Artillery to handle them, in addition to their two Armstrong guns. He applied to the government to increase the strength of the corps from 50 to

75 on the 22nd, but the application was rejected. On the 25th the Durban Volunteer Artillery moved to the Point, where they occupied the Chinese barracks, overlooking the breakwater. Huskisson said that a gun also might be put on a steamer in the bay to support the defence of the stockade, and probably for more effective fire the trace of the stockade was angled, which required some alteration and delayed completion of the work.[96]

Huskisson also fell in easily with a project to use the railways in the defence of the town. Currie asked Huskisson at the Defence Committee meeting on 11 February what he thought of a scheme which he had proposed earlier, for operating along the line 'masked' engines and cars as moving forts, and the Commandant replied that the idea was an 'excellent one' and apparently indicated that he would take steps with regard to it. On the 12th he said that he would be glad to authorize a subcommittee to negotiate with the Natal Government Railways for the use of line engines, etc., for defensive purposes, and the committee appointed Currie and Robinson for that purpose. Huskisson wrote to the Mayor that he intended to apply to the railway authorities to facilitate certain plans which a burgess had submitted to him. The committee sent him a copy of the subcommittee's report, asking for his authorization to act upon it, but Huskisson abandoned the project for want of drilled, reliable men to man the cars. At length, on the 26th the committee, noting that reinforcements were expected soon, asked Huskisson again to consider the plan for armoured trains. Huskisson replied that he could do nothing until the disposition of the reinforcements was decided, i.e. until Lord Chelmsford made the assignments.[97]

Precedence of the Military

The leaders of the movement for external defences for Durban had shot their bolt at the public meeting of 21 February. The Defence Committee turned to the Point defence scheme, indicating that it accepted that for the other assent might not be forthcoming. Even so the *Colonist* reported, on the 25th, that 75 persons had signed a letter to the Town Council offering to pay up to 1d in additional rates for defence purposes. The committee also busied itself with the revision of instructions to householders, presumably with the view of expediting their retirement to the Point, a matter which Escombe undertook in conjunction with the captains of the Town Guard. The committee also got Huskisson to post a gun at the court-house, for the removal of the Durban Volunteer Artillery to the Point had left no piece to fire a warning signal in case of attack. It also appointed an executive committee consisting of Cato, Millar, Escombe and Grant, to sit in the Town Office through the day and, should the necessity arise, through the night. For a time at least the nightly vigil was kept.[98]

The committee waited impatiently for the government's reply to the resolutions of the public meeting, and expired before one came. On 28 February the Mayor drafted a petition on behalf of the Town Council to the Lieutenant-Governor. This acerbic document conveyed the sense of frustration and pique which certain of them felt.[99] Vause stated that Lord Chelmsford had given the Defence Committee the impression that a large body of Zulu might attack Durban and had prescribed certain modes of defence for the town. Some of these had been carried out by the Commandant, but others had not, since the number of disciplined men were insufficient for him to do so. Durban required a thousand disciplined men, but had only 80 or 90 regulars and the *Active's* three guns, lying on the wharf – yet, Pietermaritzburg had 900 disciplined men and 12 guns. Thus the Commandant 'with every desire to do his best for the protection of this Borough is fettered and thwarted at every point by the evident inadequacy in the number of disciplined men and guns at his command.' Also, no military engineer had been made available to assist the Commandant in erecting defensive works. Nothing had been done to increase the town's water supply in view of the possible influx of refugees into the town. Nor had sufficient firearms been made available to arm the burgesses and others who might come into the town for defence. The Mayor ended on a strong note:

> Your Petitioners without wishing to press their claims for more than a due share of the military protection afforded to the Colony pray that Your Excellency will be pleased, in consideration of the large number of lives, the large value in merchandize, Colonial produce and property with other important interests involved, to provide an adequate number of discipline men to be stationed here, together with a military Engineer to act in conjunction with the Colonial Commander in the execution of such defensive works as may be deemed necessary for the security of life and property within this Borough.[100]

The document did not refer to external defences, but rather complained at the neglect of Durban's defence in general. Of course, with a thousand regulars the town would be much more secure, and possibly Huskisson would relent and get on with some entrenchments which he could man. The *Colonist* blandly assured readers on 1 March that Huskisson was understood to be not unfavourable to outside fortifications, but wished to have the Point barricade finished before giving a definite opinion on them.[101]

Vause transmitted the petition to the Colonial Secretary, who passed it directly to the Lieutenant-Governor on 1 March. There followed an exchange between the officials concerning the claims of the petition. The

Lieutenant-Governor opined that the Town Council's chief purpose was to get a large garrison of regulars for the town and that such a matter was for the military and not the civil authorities; he tartly described as false the invidious comparison between government measures in Durban and Pietermaritzburg.[102]

For his part Huskisson had already written to Mitchell on 24 February that the forces at his disposal were simply insufficient to man the external defences which the burgesses wanted. He continued:

> The agitators for the erection of Forts say that in the event of a Zulu raid on Durban, hundreds of Europeans from the Districts would rush into Durban and that these men on receiving arms at Durban would defend the Forts.
>
> To count on the arrival of these Europeans would be placing reliance on a supposition. Furthermore these strangers coming into the Town would have no cohesion – they would act according to their own wishes and would not obey the orders of the Military Officer in command.
>
> The reply already sent by His Excellency to the Mayor was clear and distinct and it is to be regretted that a small section of the community, which does not represent the feeling of Durban should so influence the Mayor as to cause him to convene Public Meetings.[103]

Mitchell gave this to Bulwer, who remarked that Huskisson's reasons seemed 'unanswerable'.[104] On 6 March, at Bulwer's behest, Mitchell sent the petition and their written remarks to Huskisson for comment. Huskisson duly reported on the 8th, and what he wrote about the leaders of the Defence Committee was blunt and hard. His remarks on the petition were in the same vein. He wrote to Mitchell that Lord Chelmsford had said that it was improbable but not impossible that a Zulu raid could reach Durban; the General had not given the impression that the danger would remain, but referred only to the period while reinforcements were *en route* from England. Huskisson reiterated that the Mayor and Councillors did not represent the feelings of the leading inhabitants of Durban, who indeed protested loudly against surrounding the town with permanent fortifications. He denied flatly that he had been 'fettered and thwarted' by the government. He declared that it was notorious that hundreds of strong and able Europeans living in the town had declined to come forward and to arm themselves with the rifles provided by the government. In view of the reinforcements which would be arriving from England the petition was uncalled for and out of place.[105]

How correct Huskisson was regarding public opinion in Durban is difficult to measure. Certainly the raucous public meeting of 21 February represented a small minority of the white male population. He was correct, however, regarding the burgesses' willingness to come forward to defence. The Town Guard had not increased in strength for all the outcry about defence. On 18 February the Defence Committee instructed the Mayor to call on those able to serve in an emergency but not enrolled to give their names to him.[106] He drafted a notice on the 20th, which subsequently appeared in the press. It stated that the number presently enrolled was totally inadequate for the purpose of defence, and 'earnestly urged' the residents of the town and vicinity 'forthwith to send in their names to me at the Town Office for Registration.'[107] Two days later he told the committee that he had not received a single reply.[108] On the 24th a letter from Somerset reminded the committee that the guard was insufficient for defence. Only Raleigh, captain of the 5th District, reported an increase in enrolment − of ten men![109] There was some hope on the 28th when the Mayor received a letter, from one W. Williams, that 500 railways men had been enrolled as a Durban and Suburban guard. Vause wrote Williams, asking where the roll was kept and to see it.[110] Nothing more appears on record of this large force; probably it was either fictitious, or at best potential.

Relief from Abroad

The air of crisis dissipated at the end of February, as people in Durban realized that imperial forces sent to augment Lord Chelmsford's army would soon arrive in port. It may have been this knowledge which led Huskisson to discount the Defence Committee and the town's more ardent and irritating proponents of defence. Very likely arrangements for the arrival and disposition of the reinforcements engrossed most of his time. Early in March he moved his headquarters next door to Rear Admiral Sullivan's on West Street.[111]

The herald of good tidings was H.M.S. *Shah*. The ship had been returning from the Pacific to England, but at St Helena the captain learned of the British disaster at Isandlwana and set course for Durban, taking on board all the troops that could be spared from the island garrison. These were a company of foot and one battery, which embarked on 12 February. The progress of the *Shah* assumed a symbolic importance. It did not carry sufficient men to affect the fate of Durban or probably any other post in Natal, but it was the first of the ships bringing the reinforcements that would turn the tide of the war and incidentally, of course, secure Durban against any possible Zulu incursion. Captain Bradshaw of the *Shah* became something of a hero. The Admiralty and Parliament duly approved his action.[112] The Defence Committee resolved, on Robinson's motion, that the town record its admiration for his bold and manly action in changing course to give speedy and effective assistance to the imperilled colony, as well as to thank the governor of St Helena for dispatching the bulk if not all of his garrison. The resolution on 25 February was largely anticipatory, for the *Shah* was nowhere near Durban at the time. Vause drafted a letter to Bradshaw, which was sent to Sullivan on 4 March for delivery to him.[113]

On Thursday, 6 March, the *Shah* arrived at the outer anchorage, and next day the naval brigade, under Commander J. Brackenbury, was put ashore. It consisted of sailors as well as men of the Royal Marine Light Infantry and Royal Marine Artillery, in all 394 officers and men. Two nine-pounder guns, two twenty-four-pound rocket tubes, and a Gatling gun were also landed.[114] Lord Chelmsford and Rear Admiral Sullivan were present at the brigade's disembarkation. Presumably Huskisson was, too, for it appears Somerset may have been indisposed by illness.[115] Many civilians were also there, standing at the town end of the wharf. The sailors came ashore in boats, which discharged one at a time since the landing steps were narrow. Then they formed in squads and moved forward to make room for those following. The first squad accordingly tramped along the wharf. 'Alt', shouted the big petty officer in command, again and again, to no avail, and then rushed up to the man in front, punched him in the ribs, and shouted 'Heave to, you—'. The squad stopped, and the spectators laughed. Sullivan turned and remarked to Chelmsford: 'My men may not be very conversant with military tactics but you will find them all right when the fighting begins.'[116] John Robinson later recalled:

> Never were British seamen hailed with truer rejoicing than were those sturdy sailors as they marched with resolute pride up the sandy roadway, gazed at and cheered as tokens of safety and salvation by their anxious and imperilled countrymen.[117]

The force marched on the 10th for the lower Thukela, but their departure did not revive alarm among the people of Durban, for other ships arrived in rapid succession with more reinforcements – the *Tamar*, with the 57th Regiment from Ceylon, on the 11th; the *Pretoria* from Southampton, with the 91st Regiment, on the 17th; the *Dublin Castle* from Gravesend, with six companies of the 3rd Battalion of the 60th on the 20th; and on the 22nd the *Manora* with M Battery, 6th Brigade, and drafts for N Battery, 5th Brigade, and the Ordnance branch of the Army Service Corps, from London. In a fortnight over 2 600 officers and men disembarked, and more were on the way.[118] As the troops passed to camp sites around the town before moving to the front, Durban took on the appearance of a military town.

'The Defence of Durban', remarked the *Colonist* on 11 March, 'now appears to be a thread-bare subject, as a feeling of the most perfect security prevails.'[119] The Defence Committee – the Mayor, Councillors Currie and Wheeler, the MLCs Millar and Robinson, Escombe, Hope and Palmer – met on 5 March. The only item of business was the conversion of the town library to a resort for sailors. Escombe and Robinson proposed that henceforward three members of the committee should constitute a quorum; Millar moved five, but no one seconded him.[120] It was of no consequence. The Town Council could now deal with any defence question in its meetings. The Defence Committee never met again.

There was also no need for the Volunteers to remain in service. Not only were imperial forces abundant, but the government had authorized the organization of Indian corps for defence and fatigue duties in the town.[121] The Durban Mounted Reserve returned from Kennedy's Drift and was dissolved on 3 March. The Royal Durban Rifles disbanded on the 5th. The Durban Volunteer Artillery disbanded on the 12th.[122] The two standing corps, like the Town Guard, remained as reserve units, but were not called up again.

The advocates of external defence of the town found themselves without a cause. In the Town Council it was noted, however, that the government had not replied to the petition. The Town Clerk wrote to Mitchell, who explained that Sir Henry had not had the opportunity to reply because of an absence from the city and other matters and besides, he supposed that the arrival of reinforcements afforded the protection the petitioners wanted. Mitchell also repeated Bulwer's deprecatory remarks. Three days later, on 8 April, Huskisson also wrote, belatedly reporting that he had not forwarded a copy of a minute from the Lieutenant-Governor expressing confidence in himself and in the military's objections to outside defensive works. Thus when the Town Council met, in a special meeting, on Tuesday 22 April, it had the two letters, both attesting the government's rejection of the popular appeals. Vause referred to the Colonial Secretary's communication as 'a warm letter' and Currie called it 'thoroughly heartless'. Currie said that the Lieutenant-Governor's answer was disingenuous, but suggested that no further notice be taken of it. The council agreed.[123] Vause did get the last word. The next day he wrote to Mitchell:

> Having laid your letter before the meeting of the Council yesterday, I am to state in reply that whilst believing themselves to be in a position

to substantiate their Memorial the Council will not trouble His Excellency by prolonging the correspondence.[124]

The End of the War

By April the air of crisis was gone. A British militia officer, who arrived in Durban early in the month and had time on his hands, recorded his impressions:

> The Camp, and that part of the town being used by the military was very busy, but in other parts there was not much life. It was, I suppose, owing to the great heat, that the people remained so much indoors, or the truth may be, as I was informed in answer to my question, as to the reason why there were so few people to be seen, 'Oh, they suffer here a good deal from the Natal fever; very catching I assure you.'
> 'Really,' I said in astonishment, 'and what is this fever?'
> 'Why, laziness that is all, no one will work out here.'[125]

The pace of colonial life might indeed seem too slow to the visitor from home, especially after the crisis. Complacency may have been a contributing factor. The people of Durban doubtless felt well protected by the military, and there was no more talk of local levies and external defences. The war was not altogether remote, of course, for in March there was a Day of Humiliation and Prayer, which the government had fixed to commemorate the reverses in Zululand,[126] and a Zulu War Relief Fund was opened to subscriptions.[127] In April a public meeting declared its confidence in and support for the High Commissioner, Sir Bartle Frere. In June the town honoured the late Prince Imperial and the new High Commissioner for Southeast Africa, Sir Garnet Wolseley. In July and August the Town Council made flattering addresses to the departing Lord Chelmsford, Sir Evelyn Wood, Colonel Redvers Buller and Sir Edward Strickland, for their services during the war.[128]

There was much coming and going in the camps, and if the military presence did something for trade, it also made difficulties. There was some hard feeling owing to the competition for fresh water supplies during the dry months, especially when the town's conduit was damaged owing to military inadvertence.[129] More vexing was the misbehaviour of numbers of troops, even though the town authorities sought to check disreputable houses and police the streets.[130] (The situation apparently became acute when at the return of peace the army from upcountry funnelled through the port.[131]) In early September the *Colonist* wailed:

We barricaded the town against the threatened invasion of the Zulus, but we fear we have even a worse and more savage foe directly in our midst, and if this continued state of alarm and highway robbery go on, it will be necessary to re-erect fortifications, and institute a colonial defence force against the soldiery.[132]

No record of Huskisson's reaction to a Town Council resolution about the soldiers' disturbances in the canteens and streets[133] has been found.

The people of Durban knew that the war was practically over when the Durban Mounted Rifles returned from the front at the end of July,[134] and the improvised fortifications of the town laager were dismantled late in August.[135] The Town Guard returned its arms in late August and early September.[136] At length the imperial troops had passed through and a small garrison was left in the old redoubt.[137] At the end of October Major Huskisson departed. He was brevetted Lieutenant-Colonel in November. The Town Council took no note of his departure or of his services.[138] Perhaps they had learned what he had written to the government, about some of the more prominent agitators for external defence; or the tension evident by the end of February had continued until there was little sympathy left on either side.

[Paper presented at the Conference on the History of Natal and Zululand, University of Natal, Durban, 1985.]

Notes

1. *NGG*, vol. XXX, nos. 1739, 26 November 1878; and 1740, 3 December 1878; CSO 1925, Minute 4144/1878; and CSO 2553, Minute C99/1878; GH 1411, p. 193; Gerald French, *Lord Chelmsford and the Zulu War*, London, 1939, pp. 42–9, passim; Sonia Clarke (ed.), *Invasion of Zululand 1879*, Johannesburg, 1979, pp. 213–14.

2. CSO 674, Minute 4898/1878; and CSO 2479, no. 398; *Natal Colonist* and *Natal Mercury*, 10 December 1878.

3. *Times of Natal*, 18 December 1878; *NGG*, vol. XXX, nos. 1743, 24 December 1878; and 1744, 31 December 1878.

4. This information was supplied by the director of the South African National Museum of Military History, Johannesburg, and by the curator of the Chelmsford and Essex Museum, Chelmsford.

5. *Times of Natal*, 18 December 1878; *Natal Mercury*, 21 December 1878.

6. *Natal Mercury*, 21 December 1878; and information supplied by the curator of the Royal Green Jackets Museum, Winchester.

7. *Narrative of the Field Operations Connected with the Zulu War of 1879*, London, 1881, p. 145.

8. C.T. Atkinson, *The South Wales Borderers 24th Foot 1689–1937*, Cambridge, 1937, pp. 329, 333.

9. J.P. Mackinnon and Sydney Shadbolt (compilers), *The South African Campaign 1879*, London, 1882, p. 357.

10. GH 1412, Minute 4550/1878.

11. R.J. Atcherley, *A Trip to Boërland*, London, 1879, pp. 18–19.

12. DCPM, vol. 236, pp. 48–9.

13. DCPM, vol. 236, p. 60; DCLB, vol. 705, pp. 291–2, 734–5; CSO 659, Minute 3463/1878.

14. CSO 659, Minute 3463/1878.

15. DCLB, vol. 705, p. 364.

16. CSO 689, Minute 1192/1879.

17. See DCLB, vol. 705, p. 496.

18. DCLB, vol. 705, pp. 496 and 507–8; *Natal Mercury*, 6 November 1878; *Natal Colonist*, 7 November 1878.

19. *Natal Colonist* and *Natal Mercury*, 21 November 1878.

20. DCPM, vol. 236, pp. 53, 55–7; *Natal Mercury*, 30 November 1878.

21. *Natal Mercury*, 21 November 1878.

22. See *Natal Advertiser*, 27 November 1878; *Natal Colonist*, 28 November 1878; *Natal Mercury*, 28 and 29 November and 2 December 1878; II, vol. I/5, Minutes 1481, 1560 and 1561 of 1878, and cf. 98 of 1879.

23. DCLB, vol. 705, p. 634.

24. DCPM, vol. 236, pp. 51–2; DCLB, vol. 705, pp. 641, 649, 656, 663–8; *NGG*, vol. XXX, no. 1739, 26 November 1878; *Natal Colonist*, 28 and 30 November and 3 December 1878; Eric Goetzsche, '*Rough but Ready*': *An Official History of the Natal Mounted Rifles* . . . , Durban, n.d., pp. 41–2.

25. *Natal Colonist*, 3 December 1878; *Natal Mercury*, 3, 12 and 28 December 1878. The unit was nicknamed the 'Stinking Fifty', from the malodorous corduroy of their uniform (G. T. Hurst, *Short History of the Volunteer Regiments of Natal and East Griqualand*, Durban, 1945, p. 71).

26. *Natal Mercury*, 4 December 1878; *Natal Witness*, 7 December 1878.

27. DCLB, vol. 705, pp. 639 and 716; CSO 675, Minute 5033/1878; *Natal Colonist*, 23 January 1879. Cf. Atcherley, *A Trip to Boërland*, pp. 261–2.

28. See DCLB, vol. 705, pp. 603–4, 633, 646, 657, 734–5, 778–9, and vol. 706, p. 23; DCPM, vol. 236, pp. 57, 58, 60–2, 65, 69; DTCM, vol. 10, p. 479; *Natal Colonist*, 7 November 1878, and 9 January 1879; *Natal Mercury*, 4 and 9 January 1879; and *Natal Advertizer*, 9 January 1879.

29. A 'large muster' was reported (*Natal Mercury*, 30 November 1878) for the meeting of 28 November 1878. Only about 70 attended the meeting on 11 January 1879 (DCPM, vol. 236, p. 64), and 83 received firearms at the meeting on 30 January (ibid., p. 67).

30. *Natal Colonist*, 21 December 1879.

31. *Natal Mercury*, 6 and 16 January 1879; *Natal Advertizer*, 16 and 18 January 1879.

32. DCPM, vol. 236, pp. 66–71; *Natal Mercury*, 13, 15, 16 and 21 January 1879. A photocopy of the 'Notice to each householder', January 1879, was furnished by the curator of the Local History Museum, Durban. The government's dispensation came too late for one suburban unit – on the 14th the Umgeni contingent disbanded for want of arms, and subsequently formed a rifle association. (See DCLB, vol. 706, pp. 34–6, 38; DTCM, vol. 9, p. 9; CSO 681, Minute 315/1879; CSO 684, Minutes 698 and 880/1879, and 1972, Minute 1045/1879; *Natal Mercury*, 16 January 1879).

33. DCPM, vol. 236 p. 71. For a departing Volunteer's personal instructions on defence to his wife, see Daphne Child (ed.), *Portrait of a Pioneer*, Johannesburg, 1980, p. 94.

34. See DCPM, vol. 236, p. 58.

35. CSO 683, Minute 596/1879.

36. *Natal Mercury*, 25 January 1879. Cf. *Narrative of the Field Operations*, p. 60.

37. *Natal Colonist* and *Natal Mercury*, 25 January 1978.

38. *Natal Mercury*, 25, 27 and 28 January 1879.

39. Ibid., 27, 28 and 29 January 1879; *Natal Advertizer*, 28 and 29 January 1879; *Natal Colonist*, 30 January 1879; *Narrative of the Field Operations*, p. 60.

40. *Natal Advertizer*, 28 January 1879; *Natal Mercury*, 29 January 1879; *Natal Colonist*, 30 January and 1 and 4 February 1879.

41. *Natal Mercury*, 25, 29 and 31 January 1879; *Natal Advertizer*, 28 and 29 January 1879; *Natal Colonist*, 30 January and 1 February 1879.

42. *Natal Mercury*, 25 January 1879; *Natal Advertizer*, 29 January 1879.

43. *Natal Advertizer*, 31 January 1879.

44. See ibid., 29 January 1879; and DCLB, vol.706, p.98.

45. *Natal Advertizer*, 29 January 1879.

46. DCLB, vol.706, p.96; DCPM, vol.236, pp.73–84, passim.

47. DCLB, vol.706, pp.102, 109, 111–13; DCPM, vol.236, pp.73–84, passim.

48. DCLB, vol.706, pp.103–5, 123; DCPM, vol.236, pp.72–82, passim; CSO 684, Minute 602/1879. Cf. Jameson's draft directions, reproduced as 'A contemporary document. Durban, February 1879', in *Natalia*, no.8, December 1978, p.71.

49. CSO 699, Minute 2195/1879.

50. Cf. DCPM, vol.236, p.85, and *Natal Mercury*, 6 February 1879.

51. DCLB, vol.706, p.295; DCPM, vol.236, p.85; *Natal Colonist* and *Natal Mercury*, 22 February 1879.

52. Cf. DCLB, vol.706, pp.294–5 and DCPM, vol.236, p.85; CSO 691, Minute 1301/1879; *Natal Mercury*, 10 February and 6 March 1879; and *Natal Colonist*, 6 March 1879.

53. John Robinson, *A Life Time in South Africa*, London, 1900, pp.133–4. It has been suggested that Lord Chelmsford experienced feelings of great distress in the aftermath of Isandlwana (see Sonia Clarke, *Zululand at War 1879: The conduct of the Anglo-Zulu War*, Houghton, 1984, pp.88 and 94) which may have been reflected in his communication with the councillors.

54. DCLB, vol.706, p.193; DTCM, vol.11, pp.21 and 31; *Natal Advertizer*, 7 (and cf. 24) February 1879; *Natal Colonist*, 8 and 15 February 1879; *Natal Mercury*, 14 February and 6 and 21 March 1879.

55. See DCLB, vols.705, pp.81, 258, 279–80, 562–4, and 706, pp.119, 176, 227, 254–5, 358, 613; CSO 1972, Minute 491/1879; and *Natal Colonist*, 5 December 1878, and 18 February 1879.

56. See DCLB, vol.706, pp.151–2, 296; CSO 685, Minutes 717 and 846/1879; *Natal Mercury*, 15 February 1879; and a letter from Huskisson to Vause, 12 February 1879, in the Local History Museum, Durban.

57. DCPM, vol.236, p.80; *Natal Advertizer* and *Natal Mercury*, 6 February 1879; *Natal Colonist*, 8 February 1879.

58. CSO 691, Minute 1301/1879; *Natal Colonist*, 8, 11, 27 February and 11 March 1879; *Natal Mercury*, 12, 18, 19, 22, 27 February and 6 March 1879.

59. CSO 685, Minute 722/1879; *NGG*, vol.XXXI, no.1752, 18 February 1879.

60. Letters from Huskisson to Vause, 12 and 13 February 1879, in the Local History Museum, Durban; Flyer entitled 'Distribution of Women and Children', 17 February 1879, in the Killie Campbell Africana Library; CSO 699, Minute 2195/1879; DCLB, vol.706, pp.153–4; *Natal Mercury*, 18 February 1879; *Natal Colonist*, 20 February 1879.

61. See *Natal Advertizer*, 19 and 20 February 1879; and *Natal Witness* 20 and 22 February 1879.

62. DCPM, vol.236, pp.86–8. The terms 'native', 'kafir' or 'kaffir', 'coolie' and the like are not used in a pejorative sense, but in paraphrases of contemporary documents.

63. DCPM, vol.236, pp.87–8.

64. *Natal Mercury*, 8 February 1879.

65. DCPM, vol.236, pp.87–8. Curiously, the notice convening the meeting was read *after* Vause resumed the chair.

66. *Natal Mercury*, 8 February 1879; DCPM, vol.236, p.88.

67. See DCPM, pp.89–137, passim; also the *Natal Colonist* and *Natal Mercury*, 18 and 22 February 1879; and the *Natal Almanac, Directory, & Yearly Register 1879* Pietermaritzburg, 1878, pp.318–90, passim.

68. DCPM, vol.236, pp.86, 90, 93–4; DCLB, vol.706, pp.150–2.

69. DCPM, vol.236, pp.92–94; *Natal Mercury*, 12 February 1879.

70. DCPM, vol.236, pp.94–7.

71. DCPM, vol.236, pp.98–101, 104; DCLB, vol.706, p.197; Huskisson's letter to Vause, 12 February 1879; *Natal Mercury*, 14 February 1879; *Natal Advertizer*, 15 February 1879.

72. Huskisson's letter to Vause, 13 February 1879.

73. DCPM, vol.236, pp.102–4.

74. DCPM, vol.236, p.104.

75. DCPM, vol.236, p.106; DCLB, vol.706, p.210; *Natal Advertizer, Natal Colonist* and *Natal Mercury*, 18 February 1879.

76. Cf. *Natal Colonist* and *Natal Mercury*, 18 February 1879; and DCPM, vol.236, pp.106–7.

77. Cf. DCLB, vol.706, pp.213–15; DCPM, vol.236, p.107; and *Natal Mercury*, 18 February 1879.

78. DCPM, vol.236, p.107; *Natal Advertizer*, 18 February 1879.

79. DCPM, vol.236, p.107; *Natal Mercury*, 18 February 1879. Apropos of use of 'native' and 'coolie' see note 62.

80. Cf. DCLB, vol.706, pp.213–15; DCPM, vol.236, pp.107–8; and *Natal Mercury*, 18 February 1879.

81. DTCM, vol.9, p.22; *Natal Mercury*, 18 February 1879.

82. *Natal Mercury*, 18 February 1879.

83. DTCM, vol.9, p.22.

84. DCLB, vol.706, pp.213–15; DCPM, vol.236, pp.109–10; *Natal Mercury*, 18 February 1879.

85. DCLB, vol.706, pp.221 and 236; DCPM, vol.236, p.111; *Natal Colonist* and *Natal Mercury*, 22 February 1879. Huskisson may have misplaced the Mayor's first communication and then had to ask for a copy (see DCLB, vol.706, p.238).

86. DCLB, vol.706, p.238; *Natal Advertizer*, 19 and 20 February 1879; *Natal Colonist*, 20 February 1879; *Natal Witness*, 20 and 21 February 1879.

87. *Natal Colonist* and *Natal Mercury*, 22 February 1879. Cf. DCPM, vol. 236, p. 112.

88. DCPM, vol. 236, pp. 112 and 114.

89. *Natal Mercury*, 22 February 1879. The abridged account of the meeting which follows is based on the two detailed accounts in the *Natal Colonist* and *Natal Mercury*, 22 February 1879. The accounts in the *Natal Advertizer*, 22 February 1879, and DCPM, vol. 236, pp. 116–19 are really summaries and add little to the detailed ones.

90. CSO 689, Minute 1192/1879; DCLB, vol. 706, p. 238; cf. DCPM, vol. 236, p. 120. DTCM, vol. 9, pp. 33 and 57.

91. DCPM, vol. 236, pp. 86 and 95.

92. DCPM, vol. 236, pp. 110 and 127; DCLB, vol. 706, pp. 216–17, 220, and 228; *Natal Mercury*, 19 and 20 February 1879; *Natal Colonist*, 20 and 25 February 1879.

93. DCLB, vol. 706, p. 243; DCPM, vol. 236, pp. 112–15, passim, 129.

94. DCLB, vol. 706, pp. 249–50, 275–6; DCPM, vol. 236, pp. 121, 124, 125, 126 and 131; *Natal Colonist*, 22 February and 1 March 1879; *Natal Mercury*, 22 February and 7 March 1879; *Natal Witness*, 4 March 1879.

95. DCPM, vol. 236, pp. 124–5 and 131.

96. DCPM, vol. 236, pp. 70–80, 115, 118–19, 121, 126–7; DCLB, vol. 706, pp. 241, 258, 260 and 295; *Natal Advertizer*, 6 February 1879; *Natal Mercury*, 6, 22, 26 February and 6 March 1879.

97. DCLB, vol. 706, pp. 203, 278 and 280; DCPM, vol. 236, pp. 95–6, 99–100, 130 and 133; Huskisson's letter to Vause, 13 February 1879.

98. DCLB, vol. 706, p. 248; DCPM, vol. 236, pp. 122, 130, 132–5.

99. See DCLB, vol. 706, pp. 294–9 and DCPM, vol. 236, pp. 120–37, passim. Vause may have acted irregularly, despatching the petition before the Town Council formally approved it, but the council *did* approve, apparently without demur, on 4 March. (Cf. DTCM, vol. 11, p. 33, and the *Natal Colonist* and *Natal Mercury*, 6 March 1879.)

100. DCLB, vol. 706, pp. 294–7.

101. *Natal Colonist*, 1 March 1879.

102. CSO 691, Minute 1301/1879.

103. CSO 689, Minute 1192/1879.

104. CSO 689, Minute 1192/1879. Major J.N. Crealock, Lord Chelmsford's military secretary, wrote privately (2 March) that 'the Durban folk bicker as to the correct way of defending their town, and only agree in one thing – abusing the military.' (Clarke, *Zululand at War*, p. 98.)

105. CSO 691, Minute 1301/1879.

106. DCPM, vol. 236, p. 110.

107. *Natal Mercury*, 22 February 1879 et seq.

108. DCPM, vol. 236, p. 121.

109. DCPM, vol. 236, p. 124.

110. DCPM, vol. 236, p. 133.

111. *Natal Mercury*, 3 February 1879; *Natal Colonist*, 4 February 1879.

112. *Narrative of the Field Operations*, p. 61; Mackinnon and Shadbolt, *The South African Campaign*, p. 374; C. L. Norris-Newman, *In Zululand with the British Throughout the War of 1879*, London, 1880, pp. 124–5.

113. DCLB, vol. 706, p. 315; DCPM, vol. 236, p. 128.

114. Cf. *Natal Colonist*, 11 March 1879; Norris-Newman, *In Zululand with the British*, pp. 124–5; and Mackinnon and Shadbolt, *The South African Campaign*, p. 374.

115. Norris-Newman, *In Zululand with the British*, p. 125; G. Hamilton-Browne, *A Lost Legionary in South Africa*, London, n.d., p. 215. See also *Natal Colonist*, 6 March 1879; and Clarke, *Zululand at War*, p. 266.

116. Hamilton-Browne, *A Lost Legionary*, pp. 215–16. The anecdote fits the occasion, whereas many others by the author are embellishments to events.

117. Robinson, *A Life Time in South Africa*, p. 137.

118. *Narrative of the Field Operations*, p. 62 and Appendix B. Norris-Newman, *In Zululand with the British*, pp. 125–7.

119. *Natal Colonist*, 11 March 1879.

120. DCPM, vol. 236, p. 137.

121. The material on this corps is very fragmentary. The general order (27 March 1879) concerning its organization appears in the *Natal Colonist* and *Natal Mercury*, 29 March 1879.

122. *Natal Colonist*, 4 and 15 March 1879; *Natal Mercury*, 6, 11 and 13 March 1879; *Natal Advertizer*, 6 March 1879.

123. CSO 691, Minute 1301/1879; DTCM, vol. 11, p. 58; *Natal Mercury*, 24 April 1879.

124. DCLB, vol. 706, p. 581.

125. T. St. Lô Malet, *Extracts from a Diary in Zululand*, Upper Norwood, 1880, p. 5.

126. *Natal Advertizer*, 11 March 1879; and *Natal Mercury*, 12 and 13 March 1879.

127. DCPM, vol. 236, p. 138.

128. Ibid., pp. 141–5; DCLB, vol. 707, pp. 75, 121, 123, 127, 236, 329–31 and 342; DTCM, vol. 11, p. 129.

129. DCLB, vols. 706, pp. 479, 508, 663–4, 676; and 707, pp. 112, 116, 168–9, 187, 369, 463, 466–7, 566, 643.

130. DCLB, vols. 706, pp. 9, 218, 682; and 707, p. 191; DTCM, vols. 10, pp. 486–7; and 11, p. 33. Cf. also Hamilton-Browne, *A Lost Legionary*, pp. 198–9, 231, and *Natal Colonist*, 7 January 1879.

131. DTCM, vol. 11, p. 124; *Natal Colonist*, 9 September 1879; *Natal Advertizer*, 30 September 1879.

132. *Natal Colonist*, 9 September 1879.

133. DTCM, vol. 11, p. 124.

134.   DCLB, vol.707, pp.241, 271, 306–7 and 311.

135.   *Natal Colonist*, 26 August 1879.

136.   DCLB, vol.707, pp.377–8; *Natal Mercury*, 20 August and 1 September 1879.

137.   *Natal Mercury*, 21 and 29 October 1879.

138.   *Natal Witness*, 25 October 1879; Letter from the curator of the Chelmsford and Essex Musem, Chelmsford, to the author.

Bibliography

[Only documents and published works referred to in the text or footnotes are cited.]

MANUSCRIPT SOURCES

PRIVATE PAPERS

Great Britain

(a) Hove Central Library
Wolseley Papers:
Letters from Wolseley to his Family:
1: 163/v (1878–87)
2: Typescript Copies of Letters to his
   Wife

**(b) National Army Museum,
Chelsea**
Chelmsford Papers:
68–386– 7: No. 1 Column, Lower
          Tugela, 1878–9
  – 8: No. 3 Column,
          Isandhlwana
  – 9: No. 2 Column
 –13: Peace proposals, real and
          simulated, by Cetewayo
 –14: Inholbane disaster and
          action at Kambula
 –15: No. 1 Division, Lower
          Tugela, 1879
 –16: Advance of the 2nd Divi-
          sion and Ulundi
 –26: Miscellaneous papers
 –35: Telegrams, 30 May –
          6 June 1879

Fairlie Papers:
6302–48–2: W.F. Fairlie's Diary, Zulu
           War 1879

Slade Papers:
6807–235: Capt. F. Slade's Letters to
          his Mother, 1879

**(c) National Maritime Museum,
Greenwich**
Hamilton Papers:
HTN/103: Sir F.T. Hamilton's Journal,
1 April 1878 – 27 September 1879

(d) Public Record Office, Kew
Buller Papers:
WO 132/1: Letters Despatched (Zulu-
land)

Wolseley Papers:
WO 147/7: Sir Garnet Wolseley's South
African Journal, 8 June 1879 – 25 May
1880

(e) Rhodes House, Oxford
Anti-Slavery Society Papers:
G12: Natal, Zululand, Bishop Colenso,
Cetewayo

(f) Collection of Dr. G. Kemble Woodgate, St Peter's College, Oxford

Woodgate Papers:
Capt. Woodgate's Military Diary, 1 January – 6 May 1879
Capt. Woodgate's Private Diary, 28 January – 30 December 1879

South Africa

(a) The Africana Library, Johannesburg

Norman MacLeod's Letters and Document, 1878–80. TS copies and abstracts by E.C. Tabler

(b) The Brenthurst Library, Parktown

Alison Collection:
Book no. 6399: Zulu War: Collection of A. Ls. S. Addressed to General Sir Archibald Alison

(c) Killie Campbell Africana Library, Durban

Cato Papers:
File no. 1: Correspondence

Lt.-Col. W.J. Clarke:
MS 31185: 'My Career in South Africa', Part I (TS)

Colenso Papers:
File no. 27: Chesson Letters, 1875–82
File no. 28: Chesson Letters, 1877–83

Commeline Letters (Microfilm from Gloucester Record Office):
D1233/45: Lt. C. Commeline's Letters to his Father, 1878–84

H.F. Fynn, Jnr. Papers:
File no. 26031: 'My Recollections of a Famous Campaign and a Great Disaster' (TS)

Capt. H.J. Watson:
KCM 4275: Letters from South Africa, 1879–80 (TS)

(d) Natal Archives Depot, Pietermaritzburg

A204: Colenso Collection:
Box no. 2: Letter Book, 1872–82

A863: Fannin Collection:
2/4: Letters Despatched, 29 December 1878 – 5 March 1879
2/5: Letters Despatched, 5 March 1879 – 18 June 1879
2/6: Letters Despatched, 20 June 1879 – 26 September 1879

A131: Carle Faye Papers:
Box no. 8: Statement on Isandlwana by Lugubu Mbata kaMmangaliso, 4 November 1938

A584: H.C. Lugg, 'Short Account of the Battle of Rorke's Drift' (TS, 1 September 1944)

A66: John Shepstone Papers:
Vol. 9: Miscellaneous; General Historical; 'Reminiscences of the Past', pp. 1–81
Vol. 10: 'Reminiscences of the Past', pp. 82–114

A96: Sir Theophilus Shepstone Papers:
Vol. 25: Letters Received, 23 October 1877 – 12 December 1877
Vol. 33: Letters Received, 11 September 1878 – 22 October 1878
Vol. 35: Letters Received, 20 November 1878 – 31 December 1878
Vol. 37: Letters Received, 28 January 1879 – 11 February 1879
Vol. 38: Letters Received, 12–24 February 1879
Vol. 39: Letters Received, 4 March 1879 – 19 April 1879

A160: G.M. Sutton Diary, 1879

A598: Sir Evelyn Wood Collection:
II/2: Incoming Letters, 1878–80

(e) Natal Museum Library, Pietermaritzburg

Maj. H.G. Mainwaring, 'Isandhlwana January 22nd, 1879' (TS, 1895; foreword, May 1921)

(f) **William Cullen Library,**
University of the Witwatersrand,
Johannesburg

A1755f: Clr.-Sgt. A. Booth, V.C.:
Photocopies of transcripts of papers

UNPUBLISHED OFFICIAL PAPERS

Great Britain
(a) Public Record Office, Kew
War Office, Papers Relating to the Anglo-Zulu War:
WO 32/7712: Journal of Operations, 6 January – 8 February 1879
WO 32/7715: Diary of Operations, 10 February – 7 March 1879
WO 32/7717: Report on General Situation
WO 32/7720: Diary of Operations, 6–27 March 1879
WO 32/7737: Report on Defence of Rorke's Drift
WO 32/7740: King Ketchwayo Sues for Peace
WO 32/7745: Peace Overtures by King Cetywayo
WO 32/7747: Further Reports on Suing for Peace
WO 32/7750: Journals of Operations, 7 April – 18 May, 27 April – 21 May 1879
WO 32/7751: Telegraphic Reports on Situation
WO 32/7756: General Situation
WO 32/7760: Measures to Capture King Ketchwayo
WO 32/7761: Diary of Operations, 23–29 June 1879
WO 32/7766: Report on Movement of Forces to Capture King
WO 32/7768: Report on General Plan of Operations
WO 32/7772: Report of Operations, 18 April – 7 July 1879
WO 32/7773: Disposition of Forces to Capture King
WO 32/7775: Submission of Zulu Chiefs

WO 32/7777: Capture of King and Submission of Chiefs
WO 32/7778: Acceptance of Peace Terms
WO 32/7779: Journals of Operations, 26 July – 17 August 1879
WO 32/7780: Report on Conclusion of Hostilities
WO 32/7781: Progress Report on Settlement of Zululand
WO 32/7782: Diary of Operations, 25 August – 7 September 1879
WO 32/7785: Journal of Operations, 1 – 21 September 1879

South Africa
(a) Natal Archives Depot,
Pietermaritzburg
Attorney-General's Office, Natal:
AGO 1/16/1: Depositions and Miscellaneous Papers, Native High Court, 1876–1883
Colonial Engineer, Natal:
Vol. 1: Public Works Department records
Colonial Office (microfilms):
CO 179: Original Correspondence, Secretary of State
Vol. 131: Offices, 1879
Vol. 132: Offices, 1879
Colonial Secretary's Office, Natal:
CSO 648, 666: Letters received, 1878
CSO 680–683,686, 688, 690, 693, 695, 699, 703, 711, 715, 723: Letters received, 1879
CSO 1035: Letters received, 1885
CSO 1574: Miscellaneous Minute Papers, 1898
CSO 1629: Miscellaneous Minute Papers, 1899

CSO 1709: Miscellaneous Minute Papers, 1902

CSO 1925–1927: Zulu War: Special Border Agent Reports, January 1877 – January 1880

CSO 1971–1974: Registers of Letters, June 1878 – November 1879

CSO 2552–2553: Confidential Minute Papers, 1877–1879

CSO 2610: Confidential Register, 1877–1886

CSO 2621: Confidential Letter Book, 1876–1884

CSO 2629–2631: Circulars, 1876–1883

Government House, Natal:

GH 500–501: General Officer Commanding, South Africa: Despatches, 12 November 1875 – 5 January 1880

GH 569: Zulu Sub-District: Maj.-Gen. District II: Zulu War Despatches, 20 February 1879 – 18 January 1880

GH 601: Received from High Commissioner, 15 October 1878 – 31 March 1879

GH 789: Transvaal. Special Commissioner, letters received, 27 December 1876 – 4 December 1877

GH 1054: Letters received from Private Individuals, 1879–80

GH 1221: Secretary of State for Colonies, Copies of Despatches, 16 April 1879 – 16 May 1881

GH 1326: High Commissioner, South Africa: Copies of Despatches, 18 February 1878 – 30 April 1883

GH 1400: Zululand Native: General Memoranda, 21 December 1878 – 4 July 1879

GH 1411–1413: Defence and Military Affairs, General Memoranda, 30 December 1878 – 28 July 1883

GH 1421–1424: Zulu War: Memoranda, 11 January 1879 – 7 January 1880

Greytown Magistracy:
21/3: Correspondence of Resident Magistrate, 1877–1880

Ladysmith Magistracy:
3/3/4 (formerly 12/1/3): Minute Papers, 1876–1880

Pietermaritzburg Magistracy:
PC 1/1/4: Pietermaritzburg Town Council Minute Book, 7 March 1876 – 8 May 1883

Public Works Department, Natal:
Vol. 1: Records of the Colonial Engineer

Records of the Durban Corporation:
1/1/1/1/1/12–14: Durban Town Council Minutes, vols. 9–11, November 1875–August 1880
1/4/3/1: Durban Corporation Public Meetings, vol. 236, 1871–1903
3/1/1/32–34: Durban Corporation Letter Books, vols. 705–7, December 1877–June 1879

Richmond Magistracy:
2/14/6: Correspondence of Resident Magistrate, 1873–1895

Secretary for Native Affairs, Natal:
SNA 1/1/30–35: Minute Papers, 1878–1879
SNA 1/4/2: Confidential and Semi-Official Correspondence, 1878
SNA 1/6/3: Papers relating to Cetewayo, King of the Zulu Nation, 1862–1878
SNA 1/6/11–16: Papers Relating to the Zulu War of 1879 and the Calling Out of the Natives, 1878–1880
SNA 1/7/12: Reports, October 1878 – January 1880

Weenen Magistracy:
6/1/2: Weenen Letter Book, 1875–1882

Zululand Archives:
ZA 19: Reports and Annexures of the Zululand Boundary Commission, 1880 and 1891
ZA 21: Miscellaneous Correspondence, 1878–1879

(b) Transvaal Archives Depot, Pretoria

Argief Utrecht:
No. 13: Landdros, Brieweboek, February 1877 – May 1879
No. 14: Landdros, Brieweboek, May 1879 – September 1880
No. 25: Korrespondensie en Verklarings re Soeloekwessie, 1876–1879

Argief Wakkerstroom:
No. 4: Landdros, Inkomende Stukke, 1873–1878
Staatsekretaris, Transvaal:
SS 236, 281, 286, 291, 306: Inkomende Stukke, 1878
SS 346, 352: Inkomende Stukke, 1879

OFFICIAL PRINTED SOURCES

(a) Department of History, University of Natal, Durban

Colonial Office (microfilms):
CO 879/14: *African Confidential Print* 164 (Memoranda on the Zulu Question)

(b) Killie Campbell Africana Library, Durban
Fynney, F. *The Zulu Army and Zulu Headmen. Published by Direction of the Lieut.-General Commanding*, Pietermaritzburg, April 1879

(c) Library, University of Natal, Pietermaritzburg
Blue Books for the Colony of Natal, Pietermaritzburg, 1877–1881
British Parliamentary Papers:
LII of 1878–9 (C. 2222), (C. 2242). S.A., Correspondence, 1878–9
LIII of 1878–9 (C. 2252), (C. 2260), (C. 2269), (C. 2308), (C. 2318), (C. 2367). S.A., Correspondence, appointment of Wolseley

LIV of 1878–9 (C. 2374). S.A., Correspondence 1878–9
LIV of 1878–9 (C. 2454). S.A., Correspondence, Ulundi, 1878–9
L of 1880 (C. 2482), (C. 2505). S.A. War. Correspondence, 1879–80
Callwell, Col. C. E. *Small Wars. Their Principles and Practice*, London, 3rd edn., 1906
Intelligence Branch of the War Office, *Narrative of the Field Operations Connected with the Zulu War of 1879*, London, 1881
Intelligence Division of the War Office, *Précis of Information Concerning Zululand*, London, 1895
Natal Government Gazette, XXX, 1878, XXXI, 1879
Statutes of Natal, Pietermaritzburg, 1902, 3 vols.

UNOFFICIAL CONTEMPORARY PRINTED SOURCES

NEWSPAPERS AND PERIODICALS

(a) Killie Campbell Africana Library, Durban
The Graphic, 1879
The Illustrated London News, 1879

(b) Natal Society Library, Pietermaritzburg
The Natal Colonist, 1778–9
The Natal Mercantile Advertizer,

1878–9
The Natal Mercury, 1878–9, 1929
The Natal Witness, 1878–9
The Times of Natal, 1878–9

(c) Library, University of Natal, Pietermaritzburg

Natal Almanac, Directory and Yearly Register 1879

ARTICLES

Brown, Surgeon D. Blair 'Surgical Notes on the Zulu War, *Lancet*, 2, 5 July 1879

Colenso, Bishop J.W. 'Cetywayo's Overtures of Peace', *The Aborigines' Friend. A Journal of the Transactions of the Aborigines' Protection Society*, new series, 5, June 1879

Harness, Lt.-Col. A. 'The Zulu Campaign from a Military Point of View', *Fraser's Magazine*, 101, April 1880

Portlock, Maj.-Gen. & Nugent, Col. Sir C. 'Fortification', *Encyclopaedia Britannica*, 9th edn., Edinburgh, 1879, vol. 9

Schermbrucker, F. 'Zholbane and Kambula', *The South African Catholic Magazine*, III, 30 & 31, 1893

PAMPHLETS

'H' [Heron-Maxwell, W.] *Reminiscences of a Red Coat*, London, 1895

Plé, J. *Les Laagers dans La Guerre des Zoulous*, Paris, 1882

Shepstone, Sir T. *The Native Question: Answer to President Reitz*, reprinted from the *Natal Mercury*, 29 January 1892

BOOKS: GENERAL ACCOUNTS; AUTOBIOGRAPHIES; MEMOIRS; REMINISCENCES

Ashe, Maj. W. & Wyatt Edgell, Capt. the Hon. E.V. *The Story of the Zulu Campaign*, London, 1880

Atcherley, R.J. *A Trip to Boërland*, London, 1879

Aubertin, J.J. *Six Months in Cape Colony and Natal*, London, 1886

Buchanan, B.I. *Pioneer Days in Natal*, Pietermaritzburg, 1934

Burton, W. *Oddities of a Zulu Campaign*, London, 1880

Clairemont, E. *The Africander. A Plain Tale of Colonial Life*, London, 1896

Colenso, F.E., assisted by Durnford, Lt.-Col. E. *History of the Zulu War and its Origin*, London, 1880

Colenso, Bishop J.W. & Colenso, H.E. *Digest of Zulu Affairs Compiled by Bishop Colenso and Continued after his Death by his Daughter Harriette Emily Colenso*, Bishopstowe, 1878–88, series no. 1, parts I & II, December 1878 – April 1881

Durnford, E. (ed.) *A Soldier's Life and Work in South Africa, 1872–1879: A Memory of the Late Colonel A.W. Durnford, Royal Engineers*, London, 1882

Haggard, H. Rider *Cetywayo and his White Neighbours; or, Remarks on Recent Events in Zululand, Natal and the Transvaal*, London, 1888

Hallam Parr, Capt. H. *A Sketch of the Kafir and Zulu Wars*, London, 1880

Hamilton-Browne, Col. G. *A Lost Legionary in South Africa*, London, 19[?]

Holden, W.C. *British Rule in South Africa: Illustrated in the Rule of Kama and his Tribe, and of the War in Zululand*, London, 1879

Holt, H.P. *The Mounted Police of Natal*, London, 1913

Ingram, J.F. *The Story of an African City*, Pietermaritzburg, 1898

Jenkinson, T.B. *Amazulu*, London, 1882

King, Marina. *Sunrise to Evening Star: My Seventy Years in South Africa*, London, 1935

Laurence, W.M. *Selected Writings*, Grahamstown, 1882

Ludlow, Capt. W.R. *Zululand and Cetywayo*, London & Birmingham, 1882

Mackinnon J.P. and Shadbolt, S. (comps.) *The South African Campaign, 1879*, London, 1882

Malet, T. St. Lo. *Extracts from a Diary in Zululand*, Upper Norwood, 1880

McToy, E.D. *A Brief History of the 13th Regiment (P.A.L.I.) in South Africa during the Transvaal and Zulu Difficulties*, Devonport, 1880

Mitford, B. *Through the Zulu Country: Its Battlefields and its People*, London, 1883

Montague, Capt. W.E. *Campaigning in South Africa: Reminiscences of an Officer in 1879*, Edinburgh & London, 1880

Moodie, D.C.F. (ed.) *The History of the Battles and Adventures of the British, the Boers and the Zulus in Southern Africa, from 1495 to 1879, Including Every Particular of the Zulu War of 1879, with a Chronology*, Sidney, Melbourne & Adelaide, 1879

Mossop, G. *Running the Gauntlet*, London, 1937

Norbury, Fleet-Surgeon H.F. *The Naval Brigade in South Africa during the Years 1877–78–79*, London, 1880

Norris-Newman, C.L. *In Zululand with the British throughout the War of 1879*, London, 1880

Paton, Col. G., Glennie, Col. F. & Penn Symons, W. (eds.) *Historical Records of the 24th Regiment from its Formation, in 1689*, London, 1892

Robinson, J. *A Life Time in South Africa*, London, 1900

Statham, F.R. *Blacks, Boers and British*, London, 1881

Vijn, C. (tr. from the Dutch and edited with preface and notes by the Rt. Rev. J.W. Colenso, D.D., Bishop of Natal) *Cetshwayo's Dutchman: Being the Private Journal of a White Trader in Zululand during the British Invasion*, London, 1880

Wood, Field Marshal Sir E. *From Midshipman to Field Marshal*, London, 1906, vol. II

LATER EDITED AND ANNOTATED PRINTED COLLECTIONS OF CONTEMPORARY SOURCES

Child, D. (ed.) *The Zulu War Journal of Colonel Henry Harford, C.B.*, Pietermaritzburg, 1978

Clarke S. (ed.) *Invasion of Zululand 1879: Anglo-Zulu War Experiences of Arthur Harness; John Jervis, 4th*

Viscount St Vincent; and Sir Henry Bulwer, Houghton, 1979

Clarke, S. (ed.) *Zululand at War 1879: The Conduct of the Anglo–Zulu War*, Houghton, 1984

Emery, F. *The Red Soldier: Letters from the Zulu War, 1879*, London, 1977

Emery, F. *Marching over Africa: Letters from Victorian Soldiers*, London, 1986

Fuze, M.M. (tr. Lugg, H.C. & ed. Cope, A.T.) *The Black People and Whence They Came: A Zulu View*, Pietermaritzburg & Durban, 1979

Hattersley, A.F. *Later Annals of Natal*, London, 1938

Holme, N. (comp.) *The Silver Wreath: Being the 24th Regiment at Isandhlwana and Rorke's Drift*, London, 1979

Jones. L.T. (ed.) *Reminiscences of the Zulu War by John Maxwell*, Cape Town, 1979

Laband, J. *Fight Us in the Open: The Anglo-Zulu War through Zulu Eyes*, Pietermaritzburg & Ulundi, 1985

Preston, A. (ed.) *Sir Garnet Wolseley's South African Journal, 1879–1880*, Cape Town, 1973

Webb, C. de B. & Wright, J.B. (eds.) *A Zulu King Speaks: Statements Made by Cetshwayo kaMpande on the History and Customs of his People*, Pietermaritzburg & Durban, 1978

Webb, C. de B. & Wright, J.B. (eds. & trs.) *The James Stuart Archive of Recorded Oral Evidence Relating to the History of the Zulu and Neighbouring Peoples*, Pietermaritzburg & Durban, 1976, 1979, 1982, 1986, vols. 1–4

Webb, C. de B. (ed.) 'A Zulu Boy's Recollections of the Zulu War', *Natalia*, 8, December 1978

LATER PRINTED SOURCES

ARTICLES AND PAMPHLETS

Ballard, C. 'John Dunn and Cetshwayo: The Material Foundations of Political Power in the Zulu Kingdom, 1857–1878', *Journal of African Studies*, 21, 1980

Chadwick, G.A. *The Zulu War in Northern Natal*, Natal Educational Activities Association pamphlet, [n.d.]

Hall, Maj. D.D. 'Artillery in the Zulu War, 1879', *Military History Journal*, 4, 4, January 1979

Harries, P. 'History, Ethnicity and the Ingwavuma Land Deal: The Zulu Northern Frontier in the Nineteenth Century', *Journal of Natal and Zulu History*, VI, 1983

Laband, J.P.C. 'Bulwer, Chelmsford and the Border Levies: The Dispute over the Defence of Natal, 1879, *Theoria*, 57, October 1981

Laband, J.P.C. 'The Cohesion of the Zulu Polity under the Impact of the Anglo-Zulu War: A Reassessment', *Journal of Natal and Zulu History*, VIII, 1985

Laband, J.P.C. 'Humbugging the General? King Cetshwayo's Peace Overtures during the Anglo-Zulu War', *Theoria*, 67, October 1986

Laband, J.P.C. 'The Zulu Army in the War of 1879: Some Cautionary Notes', *Journal of Natal and Zulu History*, II, 1979

Potgieter, F.J. 'Die Verstigting van die Blanke in Transvaal (1837–1886) met Spesiale Verwysing na die Verhouding tussen die Mens en die Omgewing', *Archives Year Book for South African History, 1958 (II)*, Pretoria/Cape Town, 1958

Reynecke, G.J. 'Utrecht in die Geskiedenis van die Transvaal tot 1877', *Archives Year Book for South Africa, 1958 (II)*, Pretoria/Cape Town, 1958

Saunders, C.C. 'The Annexation of the Transkeian Territories', *Archives Year Book for South African History, 1976*, Pretoria, 1978

Thompson, P.S. 'Captain Lucas and the Border Guard: The War on the Lower Tugela, 1879', *Journal of Natal and Zulu History*, III, 1980

Van Rooyen, T.S. 'Die Verhouding tussen die Boere, Engelse en Naturelle in die Geskiedenis van die Oos Transvaal tot 1882', *Archives Year Book, 1951 (I)*, Cape Town, 1951

BOOKS

Acocks, J.P.H. *Veld Types of South Africa*, Pretoria, 1951

Atkinson, C.T. *The South Wales Borderers 24th Foot 1689–1937*, Cambridge, 1937

Benyon, J.A. *Proconsul and Paramountcy in South Africa: The High Commission, British Supremacy and the Sub-Continent, 1806–1910*, Pietermaritzburg, 1980

Bonner, P. *Commoners and Concessionaires: The Evolution and Dissolution of the Nineteenth-Century Swazi State*, Johannesburg, 1983

Brookes, E.H. & Webb, C. de B. *A History of Natal*, Pietermaritzburg, 1965

Bryant, A.T. *Olden Times in Zululand and Natal*, London, 1929

Clammer, D. *The Zulu War*, London, 1973

Duminy, A. & Ballard, C. (eds.) *The Anglo-Zulu War: New Perspectives*, Pietermaritzburg, 1981

Fitzroy, V.M. *Dark Bright Land*, Cape Town, 1955

French, Maj. the Hon. G. *Lord Chelmsford and the Zulu War*, London, 1939

Gibson, J.Y. *The Story of the Zulus*, London, 1911

Gordon, R.E. *The Place of the Elephant: A History of Pietermaritzburg*, Pietermaritzburg, 1981

Goetzsche, E. *'Rough but Ready': An Official History of the Natal Mounted Rifles and its Antecedent and Associated Units 1834–1969*, Durban, [n.d.]

Guy, J. *The Destruction of the Zulu Kingdom: The Civil War in Zululand, 1879–1884*, London, 1979

Hattersley, A.F. *Pietermaritzburg Panorama*, Pietermaritzburg, 1938

Hurst, G.T. *Short History of the Volunteer Regiments of Natal and East Griqualand: Past and Present*, Durban, 1945

Knight, I.J. (ed.) *There will be an Awful Row at Home about This*, Shoreham-by-Sea, 1987

Krige, E. *The Social System of the Zulus*, Pietermaritzburg, 1974

Laband, J.P.C. & Thompson, P.S. *War Comes to Umvoti: The Natal-Zululand Border, 1879*, Durban, 1980

Laband, J.P.C. & Thompson, P.S. with S. Henderson. *The Buffalo Border 1879: The Anglo–Zulu War in Northern Natal*, Durban, 1983

Laband, J.P.C. & Thompson, P.S. *A Field Guide to the War in Zululand 1879*, Pietermaritzburg, 1979.

Laband, J. P. C. & Thompson, P. S. *Field Guide to the War in Zululand and the Defence of Natal 1879*, Pietermaritzburg, 2nd revised edition, 1983; reprinted with minor revisions, 1987

Lamar H. & Thompson, L. *The Frontier in History: North America and Southern Africa Compared*, New Haven & London, 1981

Lugg, H. C. *Historic Natal and Zululand*, Pietermaritzburg, 1949

Lugg, H. C. *A Natal Family Looks Back*, Durban, 1970

Martineau, J. *The Life and Correspondence of the Right Hon. Sir Bartle Frere, Bart., G.C.B., F.R.S., Etc.*, London, 1895, vol. II

Morris, D. R. *The Washing of the Spears: A History of the Rise of the Zulu Nation under Shaka and its Fall in the Zulu War of 1879*, London, 1966

Osborn, R. F. *This Man of Purpose: Pioneer of Natal and Zululand: A Biography of Sir James Liege Hulett*, Umhlali, 1973

Peires, J. B. (ed.) *Before and after Shaka: Papers in Nguni History*, Grahamstown, 1981

Samuelson, R. C. A. *Long, Long Ago*, Durban, 1929

Schnackenberg, Pastor J. (ed.) *Geschichte der Freien ev.-luth. Synode in Südafrika 1892–1932*, Celle, 1933

Stalker, J. (ed.) *The Natal Carbineers*, Pietermaritzburg & Durban, 1912

Stuart, J. *A History of the Zulu Rebellion, 1906 and of Dinuzulu's Arrest, Trial and Expatriation*, London, 1913

Worsfold, W. B. *Sir Bartle Frere*, London, 1923

UNPUBLISHED THESES AND CONFERENCE AND SEMINAR PAPERS

Ballard, C. 'The Role of Trade and Hunter-Traders in the Political Economy of Natal and Zululand, 1824–1880' (Paper presented at the Economic History Conference on Southern Africa, University of Natal, Durban, 1980)

Cope, R. L. 'Shepstone and Cetshwayo 1873–1879' (unpublished M.A. thesis, University of Natal, 1967)

Cope, N. L. G. 'The Defection of Hamu' (unpublished B.A. Hons. thesis, University of Natal, 1980)

Dominy, G. A. 'Routine of Empire. The Use of Force to Maintain Authority and Impose Peace as a Principle of Imperial Administration: The Cases of Waikato 1863 and Zululand 1879' (unpublished M.A. thesis, University College of Cork, 1983)

Leuschke, A. M. H. 'The Hermannsburg Mission Society in Natal and Zululand, 1854–1865' (unpublished B.A. Hons. thesis, University of Natal, 1985)

Mael. R. 'The Problem of Political Integration in the Zulu Empire' (unpublished Ph.D. thesis, University of California, 1974)

Mathews, J. 'Lord Chelmsford and the Problems of Transport and Supply during the Anglo-Zulu War of 1879' (unpublished M.A. thesis, University of Natal, 1979)

Mathews, J. 'Lord Chelmsford: British General in Southern Africa, 1878–1879' (unpublished D. Litt. et Phil. thesis, University of South Africa, 1986)

Monteith, M. A. 'Cetshwayo and Sekhukhune 1875–1879' (unpublished M.A. thesis, University of the Witwatersrand, 1978)

Index

Individual military units have all been entered under **British campaign formations; British units; Colonial units; Imperial units; Zulu military system,** *amabutho*. Arrangement of the British and colonial units is conventional, not alphabetical, and proceeds from cavalry, through artillery, engineers and infantry to support corps.

Forts, laagers, etc., have been entered under **fortified posts, colonial; forts, British; laagers, colonial.**

The indexers have attempted to supply the full names of all individuals mentioned in the text but this has not always been possible.

In accordance with modern practice Zulu words are entered under the stem and not under the prefix. Thus *amabutho* will be found after **Buthelezi people,** and *amakhanda* after **Khambula.**